Kundera and Modernity

Comparative Cultural Studies
Steven Tötösy de Zepetnek, Series Editor

The Purdue University Press monograph series of Books in Comparative Cultural Studies publishes single-authored and thematic collected volumes of new scholarship. Manuscripts are invited for publication in the series in fields of the study of culture, literature, the arts, media studies, communication studies, the history of ideas, etc., and related disciplines of the humanities and social sciences to the series editor via email at <clcweb@purdue.edu>. Comparative cultural studies is a contextual approach in the study of culture in a global and intercultural context and work with a plurality of methods and approaches; the theoretical and methodological framework of comparative cultural studies is built on tenets borrowed from the disciplines of cultural studies and comparative literature and from a range of thought including literary and culture theory, (radical) constructivism, communication theories, and systems theories; in comparative cultural studies focus is on theory and method as well as application. For a detailed description of the aims and scope of the series including the style guide of the series link to <http://docs.lib.purdue.edu/clcweblibrary/seriespurdueccs>. Manuscripts submitted to the series are peer reviewed followed by the usual standards of editing, copy editing, marketing, and distribution. The series is affiliated with *CLCWeb: Comparative Literature and Culture* (ISSN 1481-4374), the peer-reviewed, full-text, and open-access quarterly published by Purdue University Press at <http://docs.lib.purdue.edu/clcweb>.

Volumes in the Purdue series of Books in Comparative Cultural Studies include <http://www.thepress.purdue.edu/series/comparative-cultural-studies>

Liisa Steinby, *Kundera and Modernity*
Text and Image in Modern European Culture, Ed. Natasha Grigorian, Thomas Baldwin, and Margaret Rigaud-Drayton
Sheng-mei Ma, *Asian Diaspora and East-West Modernity*
Irene Marques, *Transnational Discourses on Class, Gender, and Cultural Identity*
Comparative Hungarian Cultural Studies, Ed. Steven Tötösy de Zepetnek and Louise O. Vasvári
Hui Zou, *A Jesuit Garden in Beijing and Early Modern Chinese Culture*
Yi Zheng, *From Burke and Wordsworth to the Modern Sublime in Chinese Literature*
Agata Anna Lisiak, *Urban Cultures in (Post)Colonial Central Europe*
Representing Humanity in an Age of Terror, Ed. Sophia A. McClennen and Henry James Morello
Michael Goddard, *Gombrowicz, Polish Modernism, and the Subversion of Form*
Shakespeare in Hollywood, Asia, and Cyberspace, Ed. Alexander C.Y. Huang and Charles S. Ross
Gustav Shpet's Contribution to Philosophy and Cultural Theory, Ed. Galin Tihanov
Comparative Central European Holocaust Studies, Ed. Louise O. Vasvári and Steven Tötösy de Zepetnek
Marko Juvan, *History and Poetics of Intertextuality*
Thomas O. Beebee, *Nation and Region in Modern American and European Fiction*
Paolo Bartoloni, *On the Cultures of Exile, Translation, and Writing*
Justyna Sempruch, *Fantasies of Gender and the Witch in Feminist Theory and Literature*
Kimberly Chabot Davis, *Postmodern Texts and Emotional Audiences*
Philippe Codde, *The Jewish American Novel*
Deborah Streifford Reisinger, *Crime and Media in Contemporary France*
Imre Kertész and Holocaust Literature, Ed. Louise O. Vasvári and Steven Tötösy de Zepetnek
Camilla Fojas, *Cosmopolitanism in the Americas*
Comparative Cultural Studies and Michael Ondaatje's Writing, Ed. Steven Tötösy de Zepetnek

Kundera and Modernity

Liisa Steinby

Purdue University Press
West Lafayette, Indiana

Printed in the United States of America.

Library of Congress Cataloging-in-Publication Data

Steinby, Liisa.

Kundera and Modernity / Liisa Steinby.

p. cm. -- (Comparative cultural studies)

Includes bibliographical references and index.

ISBN 978-1-55753-637-2 (pbk.) -- ISBN 978-1-61249-247-6 (epdf) -- ISBN 978-1-61249-248-3 (epub) 1. Kundera, Milan--Criticism and interpretation. 2. Europe--Intellectual life--20th century. 3. Modernism (Literature)--Europe. 4. Existentialism in literature. I. Title.

PG5039.21.U6Z88 2013

891.8'685409--dc23

2012029233

Cover image: "Milan Kundera" (2007)
Drawing by Joseph Ciardiello <http://www.joeciardiello.com>
Purdue University Press thanks the artist for the copyright release of the drawing.

To Magnus

Contents

Acknowledgments

Milan Kundera's oeuvre first raised my interest when in the late 1980s I was working on a book about the postmodernist novel, which I interpreted as "postindividualistic." *Postindividualistinen romaani* (The Postindividualistic Novel) was published in 1992, and in 1994 a German translation followed, entitled *Der postindividualistische Roman*, both under my then surname Saariluoma. At the time of my research for the book I intended to include analyses of Kundera's novels, but soon noticed that he does not fit in the framework I developed for the analysis. His novels do not fit because he is not a postmodernist (or "postindividualistic") writer, but a late representative of modernist thinking in the novel. A year as a senior research fellow at the Academy of Finland enabled me to continue my analysis of Kundera's work and *Milan Kundera, viimeinen modernisti* (Milan Kundera, the Last Modernist) was published in 2005, of which *Kundera and Modernity* is a substantially revised and updated version. I thank the publisher, Faros, and its director Hannu Salmi, for the copyright release for the English version of the book.

I thank my colleagues, who encouraged and helped me in preparing *Kundera and Modernity*, above all Kübra Ataman-Outinen, Viola Parente-Čapková, and Edith Ulmer. My special thanks go to the always friendly and helpful staff of Turku University Library, without whose assistance this book would not have been possible. I am grateful to Ellen Valle, who assisted me in the revision of my English translation of the Finnish original. My spouse, Magnus Steinby, encouraged and supported me in every possible way. I thank the anonymous reviewers of the English manuscript for their comments to improve my work. Last but not least I thank the editor of the Purdue University Press monograph series of Books in Comparative Cultural Studies, Steven Tötösy de Zepetnek, not only for accepting the book into his series, but also for his help in revising the book for publication.

Liisa Steinby, Turku 10 July 2012

Chapter One
Kundera, a European Novelist

Milan Kundera (born in 1929) is one of the most prominent and widely read authors in contemporary France and is also acknowledged by an international reading public. This apparently simple statement is not, however, free of paradox: paradoxes are apparently not only a distinctive feature of Kundera's fiction, but also characterize his image as an author and the reception of his works. It is arguable whether Kundera, who in 1975 emigrated from Czechoslovakia to France and who until the early 1990s wrote his novels—which are mostly set in Czechoslovakia or in the circles of Czechoslovak émigré(e)s—in Czech, should be called a French author at all. Calling him a Czech author, however, is no less problematic. From the very beginning, he refused the label of Czech emigrant dissident, which until 1989 was attached to him frequently (see, e.g., Petras 69–70). His irritation stems from the purely political content of the concept of "dissident." Kundera does not position himself as a political thinker, but as a novelist, one whose existence implies independent thought—not, however, primarily in the sense of a critique of a particular political system, but more generally (see, e.g., Finkielkraut 37; McEwan 24; Petro 82). He compared Western journalism—which views an "East European" emigrant author in an exclusively political light—with the falsifications of Stalinism (see, e.g., O'Brien, "Meaning" 7).

There is, however, more to it than that. Kundera does not want to be regarded as a Czech author, since in his opinion the habit of classifying authors according to their nationality is misguided and he argues that in European literature national boundaries are not essential. He claims to represent European culture as a whole; more specifically, he suggests a cultural division of Europe that he considers more valid than that defined by the borders of nation-states and thinks of himself as representing Central Europe. Prague and "Bohemia," as he calls his country of origin, are parts of Central Europe, that is, of the Habsburg Empire—particularly its nineteenth- to the twentieth-century formation, the Austro-Hungarian empire—which Kundera considers one of the most culturally creative parts of Europe (see, e.g., Kundera, *The Art* 124–25; "The Tragedy"; *The Curtain* 45–47; "The Czech Wager"; see also Pichova, "Milan Kundera"). His former home country is important for Kundera insofar as it represents the culture of Europe but at the same time he views his act of moving from Prague to Paris as an escape from the situation in his Europe of culture, that is, a Europe that undergoes dramatic and negative changes. He moved to France because he was convinced that the "Russian night" which had fallen upon Czechoslovakia in 1968 would last forever and that hence his Europe of culture was forfeited in his home country ("An Introduction" 476; Finkielkraut 35–36).

One might presume that Kundera's commitment to a European identity rather than to any particular national one makes it impossible for him to identify even with French culture, although from his youth he had admired French literature, especially surrealism and avant-garde poetry (see Bauer 111; Chvatík, "Milan Kundera als Übersetzer" 149–51; du Plessix Gray 49); subsequently he often expressed his admiration for and indebtedness to the eighteenth-century French novel, especially Diderot's *Jacques the Fatalist* (see, e.g., *An Introduction*; *Testaments* 77; see also Pierce; Raynard). Kundera's self-identification as a European author rather than as a representative of any particular national literature may explain his decision not to return to his native country even after the political shift whereby Czechoslovakia was released from Soviet domination and later divided into the Czech Republic and Slovakia. Yet Kundera says that the reasons to not return were partly "existential and incommunicable"; incommunicable because "too intimate" but also because "too wounding for the others," for "what is worse [than the emigrant's pain of nostalgia] is the pain of estrangement: the process whereby what was intimate becomes foreign" (*Testaments* 93). To the disappointment of many of his former compatriots, he declared himself to be satisfied with his life and work in France.

An author living in translations

Another paradox in Kundera's identity is that regardless of his emphasis on a shared European culture and on the need to overcome national boundaries, the fact is that an author's very instrument, his or her language, represents a fundamental restriction on such unity. During most of his career as a novelist, Kundera has been deprived of his native reading public, and as a consequence of the political changes he was bereft of his audience already before his emigration. During the 1950s and early 1960s Kundera had established himself in his home country as a poet and the author of two successful plays; and the publication of his first novel *Žert* (*The Joke*) in 1967 was an event that provoked considerable discussion. After 1968, when Soviet tanks crushed the "sister nation's" efforts to build a "human-faced socialism," Kundera lost his teaching position at the film academy and the possibility of pursuing his career as a writer. In 1970 all his works were blacklisted and removed from public view (see Kundera, *An Introduction* 469; see also Misurella xiii) and he became persona non grata. He wrote his next two novels, *La Vie est ailleurs* (*Life Is Elsewhere*; *Život je jinde*) and *La Valse aux audieux* (*Farewell Waltz* [also published in English as *The Farewell Party*]; *Valčík na rozloučenou*) not knowing whether they would ever be published (Elgrably 66). Yet, as his first novel had brought him fame—it was received favorably in France and was translated into several languages—Kundera was able to have his next two novels published in France in 1973, where *La Vie est ailleurs* was awarded the publisher Gallimard's Medicis Prize for best foreign novel of the year; other translations in several languages followed. *Život je jinde* (*Life Is Elsewhere*) and *Valčík na rozloučenou* (*Farewell Waltz*) were first published in Czech in 1979 by an emigrant publishing house in Toronto (Sixty-Eight Publishers) run by Joseph Škvorecký and thus it reached only a negligible fraction of the Czech reading public.

Well before Kundera moved to France in 1975, he was an author who established contact with his readers almost exclusively through translations. In France he continued writing his novels in Czech and publishing them in translation, until 1993, with the publication of *L'Immortalité* (1993) (*Nesmrtlnost*; *Immortality*; it has emerged since that Kundera himself, simultaneously with the Czech version, created the French "translation" of the novel allegedly prepared by an "Eva Bloch," see Chvatík, "Milan Kundera als Übersetzer" 154). The essay collection, *L'Art du roman*, published in 1986 (*The Art of the Novel*, 1988), was Kundera's first book written directly in French. Subsequently Kundera published *La Lanteur* (1994) (*Slowness* [1996]), *L'Identité* (1997) (*Identity* [1998]), and *L'Ignorance* (2003) (*Ignorance* [2002]), but these novels in French do not change the fact that the major, and weightier, part of his fiction was originally written in Czech, and hence accessible to most of the reading public only in translation.

Thus, Kundera is literally an author living in translation. He himself acknowledges that for him, translations mean everything (e.g., *The Art of the Novel* 121). His books are read, criticized, judged, accepted, or rejected as translations; consequently, he cannot possibly afford not to be scrupulous about the translations of his texts (see Woods, *Translating* 25). Between 1985 and 1987 Kundera dedicated a great deal of time to the editing of the French translations of his novels written in Czech (see *The Art* 13, 41) and he recognized these as equally authentic with regard to the Czech versions. He also intervened in the translation of his novels into other languages, especially English, and rumors of his fierce disputes with the translators have reached the public (see Crain; Woods, *Translating*; "Traduction"). From Kundera's point of view, the conflict has arisen from his insistence that the translations be absolutely faithful to the original. He considers his own language to be clear and explicit and thus his insistence that the translator find exact equivalents; he also insists that nothing in the repetition of words or in the punctuation is allowed to be altered (see Crain 44; Elgrably 63–64; Woods, "Traduction" 200; see also the chapter on translating Kafka in *Testaments*). His demands are often difficult to meet and conflict frequently with the translator's efforts to produce a translation that is as natural and easy to understand as possible.

The problem with the translations, however, goes deeper than Kundera's interest in accuracy. Michelle Woods, who has studied the Czech originals and the various translations of Kundera's works, argues that the difficulty—in addition to what I discuss above—is caused by the fact that Kundera takes the opportunity of close cooperation with his translators to rewrite parts of his texts with the result that the "translations" actually are new, authorized versions of the original. The changes may be—as in the case of *The Joke*—abridgements Kundera considered necessary, since the omitted passages required background knowledge available only to Czech readers (see Crain; Stanger). Woods also finds differences in wording, sentence structure, as well as other aspects of the text. For example, this process of rewriting is repeated in different versions of the English text and the "original" Czech text is revised for reprinting as well. In the case of *The Joke*, Woods counts four different versions in Czech, three in French, and no fewer than five in English, leading her to speak of Kundera's "pathology of rewriting" (*Translating* 66). According to Woods, "Kundera has rewritten almost all his Czech 'originals' so that the translations have no original text to be faithful to" (42–43). She concludes that in Kundera's oeuvre, the "definitive" (or the "authentic") text "is not necessarily a final one. It represents two things: firstly, Kundera's belief that it is the best version in the language at the given time, and, secondly, the degree of Kundera's own involvement in the translation process" (83).

This textual plurality causes confusion not only among readers but especially among scholars, who are faced with the question of where to find the "real" Kundera. Against his critics, Kundera has defended his right to do whatever he likes with his texts: "Because what an author creates doesn't belong to his papa, his mama, his nation or to mankind; it belongs to no one but himself; he can publish it when he wants and if he wants; he can change is, revise it, lengthen it, shorten it" (*The Curtain* 98). Yet, however important he considers the author's freedom to change his texts, Kundera certainly does not aim at encouraging critics and scholars to focus on comparing the different versions of his texts.

Kundera's alterations demonstrate that he does not conceive of his readership as "an entity so abstract, so vague that I couldn't even try to predict its reaction or taste," as he once stated (qtd. in du Plessix Gray 51; see also Elgrably 67). On the contrary: ever since he began to write "for [his] translators only" ("Comedy" 4), he has sought to ensure that his texts have reached his readers exactly as he has meant them. Since his first book written in France, *Le Livre du rire et d'oubli* (1985) (*The Book of Laughter and Forgetting* [1979]; *Kniha smíchu a zapomnění* [1981]) he has striven to write as clearly and simply as possible and to choose expressions which are semantically accurate and unambiguous (see Biron 3; Chvatik, *Die Fallen* 114; Garfinkle 55; Gautier 53; Richterová 51–52) so as "to minimize the translator's potential interference" (Baranczak 249). He also elaborates upon certain concepts with the help of several other European languages. In *The Book of Laughter and Forgetting*, for instance, Kundera elucidates the Czech word "lítost" by means of several examples, and in *L'Insoutenable légèreté de l'être* (1984) (*The Unbearable Lightness of Being* [1984]; *Nesnesitelná lehkost bytí* [1985]) he discusses the concept of "compassion" in the light of the etymology of the word in different European languages.

The fact that Kundera can reach his readers only through translation may, however, not be the only reason for his struggle to control readers' encounters with his texts. In his work on the development of the Czech literary scene during 1967–68, written shortly after the Soviet invasion, Dušan Hamšik tells us that Kundera was already then well-known for his habit of constantly reformulating and rewriting his texts as well as for his reluctance to give way to the dictates of censorship, often at the cost of being unable to publish his writings at all (83–86, 91). Kundera also introduced considerable changes in new editions of his works, for instance, his early collections of poems. Not merely a personal trait of the author, this process probably also indicates the author's vigilance concerning changes in the political atmosphere. What was allowed to be said, and how, changed considerably over a relatively short period of time, with the general atmosphere becoming more permissive in the 1960s. Kundera's great concern for transmitting the author's meaning to readers as authentically as possible is probably to some extent a legacy of being able to publish his texts for twenty years only under more or less severe censorship (see Hamšík 83; Hybler 79).

Kundera's career as a novelist is characterized by yet other paradoxes. What brought him general public recognition was the 1988 film adaptation of the novel *The Unbearable Lightness of Being*, directed by Philip Kaufman. The paradox here is Kundera's objection to the film versions of novels in general. He values the novel, along with music, more highly than any other art form and relegates the adaptation of a novel to another medium, the screen, as a banal oversimplification of the original work. In *Immortality* the author's alter ego says: "The present era grabs everything that was ever written in order to transform it into films, TV programs, or cartoons. What is essential in a novel is precisely what can only be expressed in a novel, and so every adaptation contains nothing but the non-essential" (266; see also *Testaments* 165). The film version of *The Unbearable Lightness of Being* also fueled the misconception that Kundera's work deals above all with "sex and politics" (see Petro, "Authenticity"). It is true that the topics of sex and politics could easily account for Kundera's popularity; however, he denies that his novels deal with politics. Indeed, in his work human behavior is analyzed in the context of specific historical-political conditions, but his attention is always focused on human beings, on their "anthropological possibilities"; the political system or ideology merely constitutes the framework for the manifestation of particular human possibilities (see, e.g., *The Art* 143; see also O'Brien, "Falling" 95). Moreover, although sexual intercourse is abundantly depicted in Kundera's novels, this is not an end in itself either. The reason for the presentation of the sexual act again and again derives from Kundera's conviction that it is precisely in this act that the individual's deepest concerns and the true nature of the relation between two human beings are acutely revealed (see McEwan 30; Raddatz 100).

All in all, Kundera can be regarded as a paradoxical "product" of the historical tumults of twentieth-century Europe. He is a novelist for whom the novel represents the art of the word and the very essence of European culture, but whose texts are conveyed to his readers in translation only and who is an expatriate representative of Central Europe who for a long time, during which he created his most important works, considered that this Europe no longer existed. Nevertheless, Kundera would disapprove of regarding a novelist as the product of any particular historical circumstances. To the contrary, for him being a novelist means breaking away from the grip of history and residing in the realm of freedom (*Testaments* 15–16). The novel as a genre has a history of its own in which the individual author occupies his place; but this is a history in which, unlike world history, freedom is realized (*Testaments* 15). If the relationship between these two kinds of history seems contradictory or paradoxical, this should come as no surprise from an author according to whom all of Europe, that is, the world to which he himself and the entire tradition of the novel belong, are living in, as he calls it, "the period of *terminal paradoxes*" (*The Art* 13).

Brno, Prague, Paris

Ann Jefferson has made the interesting remark that Kundera's leaving Prague for Paris was in fact already his second "exile" because he had earlier chosen to leave his home town, the Moravian city of Brno, to move to Prague. The fact that his father was an influential figure on the Moravian cultural scene—he was a teacher at the Brno Conservatory, a pianist and a scholar of Moravian folk music and of Leos Janáček—suggests that Kundera's leaving the regional center for the capital of the country is to be understood as a conscious choice of his future circle of influence (see Jefferson 120–21). In arguing that Janáček's remaining in the province definitely obstructed recognition of his true status as a great innovative composer on a European scale (see *Testaments* 132–39, 179–95; *Encounter* 127–42), Kundera is commenting obliquely on his own decision not to remain in the province, which he later extended to the demand that not only he himself but also authors, composers, and artists in general should ignore national borders and take their place on the European scene. Nevertheless, Kundera acknowledges his debt to his native town not only by expressing his great admiration for Janáček but also by regarding himself, as a composer of novels, a follower of Janáček's "aesthetic rule," according to which "only absolutely necessary (semantically necessary) notes have a right to exist" (*Testaments* 187–88). Kundera says that his own "art of ellipsis" is a result of following this "Janáčekian" imperative: "to rid the novel of the automatism of novelistic technique, of novelistic verbalism; to make it dense" (*The Art* 73). Furthermore, in his first novel, *The Joke*, when the protagonist returns to his Moravian hometown after several years of absence, he is once again smitten by the spell of Moravian folk music, whose different historical layers are reflected upon in a digression with score samples. In the novel, this re-encounter has of course other than merely autobiographical relevance: identification with folk culture is presented as an alternative in art and life.

Kundera started out as a student of music, but later chose literature as his main field of art. That musical structures serve as patterns for the construction of his novels suggests how closely related these two fields are in his conception of art. However, on the literary scene of the early 1950s Kundera appeared neither as a novelist nor as a distanced observer, but as an author who was well adapted to the prevailing cultural climate. Of his first three published works, two—*Člověk zahrada širá* (1953) (Man, the Vast Garden) and *Monology* (1957) (Monologues)—are collections of poems, while the third, *Poslední máj* (1955) (The Last May) is a long poem on a single topic. These works secured him a significant place on the Czech literary scene.

Since the nineteenth century, lyrical poetry had been dominant in Czech literature. During the First Republic of 1918–1938, the traditional national romantic current in lyrical poetry competed with that of the the modernists, who found their ideals in Apollinaire and other French surrealist and avant-garde poets (see, e.g., Chvatík, "Milan Kundera als Übersetzer" 149–51). After the communist coup in February 1948, only the former mode of writing was permitted. The young Kundera was a devoted admirer of surrealist and avant-garde poetry and translated a number of Apollinaire's poems into Czech (Chvatík, "Milan Kundera als Übersetzer" 151). He joined the communist party at the age of eighteen, just before the February coup; but only a couple of years later, in 1950, he was expelled from the party because he had written a parody of a poem by the celebrated communist poet Vítězslav Nezval (see Steiner, *The Deserts* 207). He was restored to party membership in 1956, but expelled once again in 1970 during the period of "normalization," that is, the reestablishment of Stalinist rule after the Soviet invasion in August 1968.

Člověk zahrada širá (Man, the Vast Garden) is a Stalinist collection of poems, the kind of poetry allowed to be published at the time. It includes a sequence of six poems entitled "The Grand March" (see Hybler 83), the socialist myth of the people's common battle for a better future; a myth that Kundera later ridicules and criticizes in *The Joke* and especially in *The Unbearable Lightness of Being*. During the Prague Spring—a period that actually started in the early 1960s and culminated in 1967–68, a time of the slackening of Stalinist rule in Czechoslovakia in which the loosening of censorship allowed innovative literature to flourish and critical voices to be heard (see Finkielkraut 34–36; Elgrably 62)—Kundera was asked in an interview with Antonin J. Liehm if it was difficult for him to be a poet in the Stalinist period in the 1950s, as he was not allowed to follow his taste for the avant-garde. He answered that although he saw that the introduction of socialism caused a darkening of the cultural scene, he was in favor of socialism because he saw it as a necessary stage in the process of the liberation of humankind (96). He added, however, that now (in 1966) he was inclined to see in his then willingness to cooperate with Stalinism a gesture of an intellectual's self-negation: an intellectual is an individual who doubts everything, and nothing more than himself, and therefore he can end up acting in contradiction to his dearest convictions (Liehm, "Interview" 96–97). Kundera also commented that although the poems in his first collection were relatively conventional, they were criticized by the censors as overly individualistic and even hostile to the party (Liehm, "Interview" 98).

Poslední máj (The Last May) is a long poem about the communist poet Julius Fučík's heroic resistance against his nazi interrogator. Fučík, who was executed by the nazis, was in the 1950s an icon of communist heroism and it has been suggested that Kundera wrote the poem in order to be restored to party membership (Hruby 5).

The book was reprinted twice, and Woods has examined the revisions that Kundera made for the reprints in keeping with the loosening of the ideological climate: in the 1961 version the most conspicuous communist ideologemes have been removed and in the 1963 version the prisoner's name is not mentioned at all, reflecting a shift from an explicitly communist context to a national one (*Translating* 71). In *The Joke*, written during 1961–65, and again in *Life is Elsewhere*, the Fučík icon is taken up again from a different, critical and ironic perspective.

In contrast to the previous books, *Monology* (Monologues) is a collection of erotic poems. In these poems, eroticism and sexuality are stripped of the veil of sentimentality; non- or even anti-ideological in its attitude, the collection opposes conformism, hypocrisy, grand emotions, and conventional patterns in the realm of eroticism (see Haman 141–43; Steiner, *The Deserts* 207). The book was criticized for its "intellectualism" (Haman 143) and "cynicism" (Liehm, "Interview" 99) and for presenting love "deprived of its social content" (Hruby 5). Subsequent critics remarked that in this collection the author's attitude, as well as some of the themes and motifs, already come close to Kundera as we know him from his prose works (Chvatik, *Die Fallen* 21). In the interview with Liehm, Kundera says that what he himself still likes in the collection are "the analytic poems which demythify the erotic situation strained to the point of rupture," and that he has removed from subsequent editions poems which were not of this kind but rather of the romantic type of "grand demonstrations" of sentiment (99).

Already in the 1950s Kundera was a respected author, not only because of his poetry but also because of his articles in a number of literary magazines (see Čulík 212). In the 1960s, when the cultural atmosphere opened up, Kundera gained further in stature. During this decade he published short stories, two plays, and a novel, *Žert* (1967) (*The Joke*). The first of the plays, *Majitelé klíčů* (The Owners of the Keys [1962]), is set in the period of the nazi occupation. Typical of Kundera is the conflict between the individual's great ideological commitment and his private, intimate relationships, a dilemma for which no good or honorable solution is found. Despite its questioning of heroism, Kundera later disliked the play and considered it clichéd (see Hruby 11). The second play, *Ptákovina* (Nonsense [1968]), a satirical farce of eroticism and the misuse of power, written in just a few weeks (see Porter 31), was even more daring. It remained in the repertoire of several theaters until 1970 and Kundera—as an exception—allowed it to be staged in Prague again in 2008 (see Thirouin, "Le Mystère" 13).

In 1963 Kundera published *Směšné lásky* (*Laughable Loves*) as three booklets, containing in all ten short stories; of these, the volume published under this title in the West—first in France in 1972—contains only seven. In the stories, which in Kundera's opinion have the novelty of combining laughter or ridicule and love, we already meet with some of the most essential themes in Kundera's novels, such as the problem of personal identity and the unpredictable repercussions of one's actions. Undoubtedly the most important work of this period, however, is *The Joke*. As Andreas W. Mytze puts it, in this work Kundera abstains from retroactively mystifying his Stalinist youth, but on the contrary "unveils this youth as what it really was and what it wanted to be but because of an inherent insufficiency could not be" (38). Kundera subjects the shared experience of the politically active youth of his generation to ruthless analysis. Although he was not the first to deal with Stalinist terror, Peter Steiner may have been right in saying that "it was Milan Kundera's novel *The Joke* that in 1967 managed to vent in public the suppressed guilt of the past with unprecedented force" (*The Deserts* 22).

On the whole, when Kundera in an interview from the eighties describes himself as having prior to his emigration been "a relatively unknown Czech writer" (Roth 49), this is misleading; on the contrary, those familiar with the 1950s literary scene and literary-political developments in Czechoslovakia bear witness that Kundera had a high profile in the Czech literary life of the time and even more so in the 1960s (see Jungmann; Liehm, "Interview"; Porter). This is supported by the fact that from the end of the 1950s, as Milan Jungmann contends, "no significant congress or conference of the Czechoslovak Writers Union could do without his speech, and his articles were anticipated for their immense impact on public opinion" and he was known as a critic of all kinds of dogmatism and a spokesman for the need to open up Czech culture to Western and world culture (122).

Kundera's importance is reinforced by the role he played at the legendary June 1967 Congress of the Czechoslovak Writers' Union. It was there that Czech writers for the first time clashed openly with the communist leadership and where Kundera gave the speech which, in Jan Čulík's words, "is regarded a landmark in the history of independent, self-critical Czech thought" (214). In his speech, Kundera demanded that writers have to be independent of politicians and of ideological guardians. Typically of Kundera, however, the speech focused on literature rather than on politics. He commented on the tumultuous nature of Czechoslovak history throughout the twentieth century. The collapse of the Habsburg Empire at the end of World War I was followed by a brief period of democracy, cut short in 1938 by nazi occupation, World War II and after that the turn to Stalinist socialism in 1948, and now (in 1967) a period of reformed socialism. The experience of these turns and catastrophes, he pointed out, offer writers "an inexhaustible mine" of materials which compels them to ask the most essential questions concerning humankind, its being, and its history. In his speech, Kundera exhorted Czechoslovak authors to transcend national limits, that is, to reject provincialism and to strive for significance on the European literary scene. In his opinion, a people legitimizes its existence as an independent nation—its refusal to be assimilated into a greater culture (which meant, for Czechs in the nineteenth and early twentieth century, into German culture)—only by original cultural achievements which signify important innovations at a European level (see Hamšík 169–70).

The government's censors prohibited the printing of Kundera's speech in the Writers' Union's periodical *Literární noviny*, which was one of the most important channels of the reform movement (for a description of the congress and the ensuing difficulties with the censors, see Hamšik). In the following months, however, the influence of the reform movement increased in all areas of society, culminating at the beginning of 1968 in the election of a new, reformist Central Committee headed by Alexander Dubček. Liehm comments on this development, saying that it was literature, or more generally Czechoslovak culture, that overthrew the regime (*Trois* 15). Tanks of the Soviet army brought a violent end to the anti-Stalinist reformist movement in August of that year, but the subsequent process of "normalization," that is, the overturning of all reformist changes, took several more months to complete.

In an article entitled "The Czech Destiny," published in the Christmas 1968 issue of *Literární noviny*, Kundera comments on the situation. He starts out on a general level, repeating the idea that the small European nations have to legitimate their existence by contributing something essential to European culture. According to Kundera, the Czechs have now achieved this through their attempt to create a democratic socialism—an attempt which has altered the history of the twentieth century ("Le Destin" 95). In the developments of the autumn of 1968, he insists on seeing a "battle of retreat," which does not necessarily signify ultimate defeat: there is still the hope that the spirit of the Prague Spring has not been vanquished but may be able to turn the future, "not the distant, but the near future" into something better ("Le Destin" 96; unless indicated otherwise, all translations are mine). Kundera's views were heavily criticized by Václav Havel, then a playwright and a noncommunist, who in an article entitled "The Czech Destiny?" accuses Kundera of glorifying the past—especially the near past of August 1968—at the cost of neglecting the necessities of the present. It is true that everything has not yet been lost—people are not yet imprisoned because of their opinions—but the fundamental civil rights of citizens, such as freedom of speech and assembly, as well as the legalization of political pluralism, are endangered. According to Havel, rather than soothing ideas about a "Czech destiny," what is needed at the moment is taking responsibility for the present by concrete political action (see Havel, "Le Destin"). Kundera responded in an offended and offensive tone and Havel continued in a similar vein (see West). In the light of what actually happened in Czechoslovakia after 1968, it is easy—perhaps too easy—to judge who was wrong in the debate and who was right (see Haman 153–54; West). I suggest that it is relevant to observe that the two writers are arguing from different perspectives: where Havel is arguing from the perspective of the concrete political situation in Czechoslovakia, Kundera even here, after the dramatic political defeat, is looking at the situation from a more general cultural perspective.

In France, Kundera tirelessly emphasizes that he is a novelist, not a political thinker or a philosopher. This view of his might be seen as the reason for his repudiation, after his arrival in France, of his early, politically committed works. However, Kundera himself has commented on this, saying that a writer is entitled to exclude from his oeuvre whatever he considers to be immature or unessential. The oeuvre, Kundera declares, "is what the writer will approve in his own final assessment" (*The Curtain* 96). When Kundera moved to the West, he left his past behind. Except for *Laughable Loves* and *The Joke*, he forbade any reprints, translations, or performances of his works published before 1970. In an essay written for the planned publication of his collected works in Czechoslovakia at the beginning of the 1990s, Kundera lists the works he considers as belonging to his oeuvre, assigning them opus numbers like the ones composers give their works. The list includes *Laughable Loves* and all his novels up to then, as well as the play *Jacques and His Master*, a "free variation on Diderot's novel, *Jacques le fataliste*," and the essay collection *The Art of the Novel* (see Misurella 164). The catalog of his works is based on well-defined principles: it excludes everything he considers immature (such as his poetry) or incomplete (such as his two first plays) and everything incidental resulting from external circumstances, such as most of his essays, almost all interviews, and the numerous articles on Czech literature he published in Western newspapers (Misurella 162–64). Thus, Kundera swept aside most of his literary career in Czechoslovakia, presenting himself to the international public as a "mature" novelist (Crain 47). He took the opportunity offered by his emigration to the West to construct a stylized and simplified public image of himself as an author—an opportunity most authors do not have.

Kundera has been accused by his compatriots, and more recently by others as well, of trying to airbrush his collaboration with the Stalinist regime by "forgetting" his lyrics (Bílek, "The East" 110; Gautier 53; Woods, *Translating* 86). It has even been speculated that because of this he has now definitively lost his chance for the Nobel Prize in Literature, since he is no longer acceptable as a "moral institution." For example, Doris Boden asks whether it is right to assign a writer such a role, independently of his or her willingness to assume it ("Kein" 16).

Kundera definitely rejects the idea of judging a writer according to his or her political or moral merits and faults: a writer is responsible only to his or her art and is to be judged solely by literary criteria. In part 8 of *Testaments Betrayed*, entitled "Paths in the Fog," Kundera discusses—and condemns—the contemporary practice of placing writers and thinkers before a tribunal which judges them according to their iniquitous political commitments. First, it is too easy to condemn someone for his or her political ideas in retrospect when the repercussions of a policy have become evident to everyone; the people living through that situation were walking in a fog where they could see scarcely anything in front of them (see also Palouš 41–42). For example, Mayakovsky is "a tremendous poet, one of the greatest" despite being a Stalinist and Céline, despite his early anti-Semitism, is one of the great novelists of the century and one who was able to transform the horrors of century "into existential wisdom" (*Testaments* 231–32). Kundera does not refer to himself in this context, but it is clear that he is responding to the "tribunal" by which he now feels he is being accused. Moreover, the comment, "Some of these people are undergoing a double trial, first accused of betraying the revolution, then accused for services they had rendered it earlier" applies to him as well (*Testaments* 230).

Kundera is probably powerless with regard to the habit of the Nobel Committee, and of the general public, of judging writers in terms of their moral and political integrity. In France he consistently followed the principle that the writer's task is not to participate in politics, nor to apologize if he or she has once done so—since this would be futile—but to use his or her experience as material in achieving some fundamental knowledge of human beings (see also Woods, *Translating* 103). He has seen this in particular as the task of the novelist. Thus the shift from lyrical poetry to the novel did not mean for him merely a change of literary genre (*Testaments* 156), but a profound transformation in his view of the world, a transformation which he compares to a religious conversion: "I did not leave poetry, I betrayed it. For me, lyrical poetry is not only a literary genre but above all a conception of the world, an attitude vis-à-vis the world. I left this attitude as one leaves a religion" (Biron 17). Renouncing lyrical poetry, or, rather, the lyrical stance, meant for Kundera renouncing an attitude to the world which makes acceptance of a totalitarian ideology possible. In his novels from *The Joke* onward, Kundera describes what he now calls the "lyrical attitude" and in *Life Is Elsewhere*, which tells the story of the young revolutionary and poet Jaromil, this is the main theme.

Kundera's ironical attitude toward lyricism, which in his opinion is typical of young age, does not merely reflect his distance from his own youth; rather, the subject of analysis in his books is the experience of a whole generation (see Liehm, *Trois* 16, 21). In a sense, his own development follows the general development of the cultural climate: he feels that his new "novelistic" attitude accords with the atmosphere of the reform movement of the 1960s, which was opposed to the "lyrical" 1950s. In his view, the reformist movement of the Czech 1960s expressed a certain skepticism based on experience, thus being the direct opposite of the 1948 revolution, which was a manifestation of the lyricism of youth (*Encounter* 117; Finkielkraut 36). For Kundera, skepticism is a sign of maturity and therefore something to strive toward. He describes the culture of the 1960s as open-minded, innovative, and creative; in general, culture then played a leading role in society ("The Tragedy"; see also Finkielkraut 34–35). This was all lost after 1968. To illustrate the experience of this loss, Kundera uses the example of the horror with which the Czech intelligentsia received the news that all cultural periodicals were being banned. This horror remained completely beyond the grasp of Kundera's French acquaintances who long ago had laid cultural periodicals aside and were discussing television programs instead ("The Tragedy" 37).

In Czech literary history, a concurrence and alternation of two modes of writing existed, corresponding to the lyrical 1950s and the skeptical 1960s: "an artistic, poetic tradition" and a "far more intellectual, rationalist, practical, pragmatical" tradition of prose writing (Wellek 30) often characterized precisely by the word "skeptical" (Holy 29). While Kundera suggests that it is only the former which was closely connected to politics, Steiner emphasizes that, starting with the nineteenth-century national revival, Czech literature as a whole was assigned an important role in society. Writers were assigned the status of "pundits expected to proffer authoritative positions on all relevant public matters" (*Deserts* 6; see also Hamšík 161). Peter Petro connects Kundera and his whole generation of writers with the skeptical—but not nonpolitical—atmosphere of the 1960s ("Authenticity" 44). It is true that Kundera's novels and short stories are comparable to the writing of a Bohumil Hrabal or Ludvík Vaculík in their sense of irony, satire, and the absurd and the set of their imagination against both realism and lyrical sentimentalism (see Hattingh; Liehm, "Interview"; Rostinsky) or to the works of Vladislav Vančura, about whom Kundera published the study *Umění románu* (*The Art of the Novel*) in 1961 before starting his own career as a novelist (see Chvatik, *Die Fallen* 38–43). However, when he speaks about the art of the European novel in general or his own novels in particular, he scarcely mentions earlier or contemporary Czech authors, albeit he has published several articles on Czech literature and Czech authors in various periodicals (Misurella 163–64). Just as in his study of Vančura he emphasizes the author's position as part of European literature (Chvatik, *Die Fallen* 38), he does not locate himself in the Czech literary tradition but stresses being part of the European tradition of the novel. This is not inconsistent with his avowed attachment to the Czech tradition of skepticism in that he often names skepticism as the core of the Europe novel as a whole.

To make his point, Kundera in his later writings introduces the Goethean concept of *Weltliteratur*. For him "world literature" does not refer merely to works which are commonly ranked as supreme in terms of all literatures—even if this evaluative aspect sometimes seems to be decisive in Kundera's thought (see Biron 3; on the concept of world literature, see, e.g, Auerbach 301; Birus; D'haen, Damrosch, and Kadir; Tötösy de Zepetnek and Vasvári; Varsava). Even more important is the point that national literatures are no longer seen as self-sufficient entities, coming into contact with each other only in certain special cases; rather, for Kundera there exists a common tradition of world literature, or at least Western literature—or, what is most important for Kundera, of the European novel (*The Curtain* 31–56; see also Garfinkle; Slater; Tachtiris). This is the context within which he places himself as a novelist and within which he wants to be read and evaluated.

In *The Curtain* Kundera defines an intermediary entity between the "large" context of the world and the "small" context of the nation and says that for him this entity is Central Europe (45). Kundera's concept of Central Europe resembles a tendency among Czech intellectuals reaching back to the so-called Revivalism of the nineteenth century to place their nation in the center of Europe (see Macura). Kundera's conception is, however, neither nationalistic nor political but cultural. He emphasizes his attachment to the Central European novel of the twentieth century, whose main representatives for him include Jaroslav Hašek, Franz Kafka, Hermann Broch, Robert Musil, and Witold Gombrowicz. These authors—three of whom wrote in German, one in Czech, and one in Polish—are for him "the Pleiades" that revealed to him the possibilities of the "post-Proustian" European novel. It is their innovations which he takes up and goes on to develop in his own work (see "The Tragedy" 109, *The Art*).

Kundera develops his idea of Central Europe in several connections, but of special importance is the article "The Tragedy of Central Europe," originally published in *The New York Review of Books* in April 1984. In defining Europe, the opposite for him is not the Americas; rather, he sees the cultures of Americas as extensions or—in the case of South America—as a fringe of European culture (*The Curtain* 82). The juxtaposition is thus not one of the "Old" and the "New" World, nor is it the one of Europe and an underdeveloped Third World. Kundera ignores the critique of Eurocentrism common in contemporary political and cultural debates. The postcolonial perspective emphasizes that European history and art, or what in Europe is defined as rationality, cannot be identified with history, art, and rationality as such, as assumed traditionally following the Enlightenment; critics of Eurocentrism see in this generalization an unjustifiable claim to European supremacy. Conversely, according to Kundera, it is precisely Europe—as a cultural entity—which today is threatened and in need of advocates. Rather than acting as colonizer, Europe is in danger of being colonized (on this, see also Finkielkraut 45). The first time Kundera experienced this happening was when the Soviet tanks rolled into Prague and European culture was forced to withdraw.

For Kundera the antithesis of Europe is thus "the East," which for him is practically equivalent to Russia (a name he used to refer to the Soviet Union). The opposition between "Europe" and "the East" he sees as a cultural antagonism, an opposition between (Western) Europe and Byzantium (see also *The Curtain* 43). For him Europe embodies the great adventure that started with the Reformation and the Renaissance, when, after the dethronement of God, man became the measure of everything; "the East" was excluded from all of this ("An Introduction" 476; see also Matejka). In Kundera's view, the spirit of Europe is essentially the same as that of the novel: a spirit of quest, adventure, questioning, and challenging, a spirit of the relativity of truths and even of skepticism. "Russia" signifies for him a preference for emotion over reason, which in his opinion leads to totalitarianism and a prohibition on questioning things and on pluralism (Kundera's view was opposed by Joseph Brodsky, the Russian emigrant poet and Nobel Laureate, who pointed out that Soviet communism was of Western origin; see Brodsky; Cooke; Petro, "Apropos" 80). Kundera argues that the geographical area which in the West is indistinctly and mistakenly labeled as Eastern Europe, that is, those parts of Europe that after World War II belonged to the political sphere of Russia (the Soviet Union), actually consists of two different cultures: on the one hand Russia, the genuine "East," on the other such countries as Poland, Czechoslovakia, and Hungary, which belong to the West and to the cultural Europe. In fact, Kundera considers the territories of the former Austro-Hungarian monarchy the cradle of twentieth-century European culture: not only did they give rise to the creators of the "post-Proustian novel," but also to figures like Husserl, Freud, and Schönberg, who led European culture in new directions.

Kundera's "The Tragedy of Central Europe," soon reprinted in several languages, attracted much attention and had an impact on the ongoing discussion on European identity (see, e.g., Abrams 195; Bílek, "Constructing"; Lützeler, *Die Schriftsteller* 444–46; Waever 178–80). A particularly lively debate was provoked by the German translation of the article, in which "Central Europe" was translated as "Mitteleuropa." The notion of "Mitteleuropa," which refers geographically to approximately the same area as Kundera's "Central Europe," has a political and ideological history of its own (see, e.g., Hagen; Lützeler, *Die Schriftsteller*). It was first introduced in 1915 by the German liberal-nationalist politician and author Friedrich

Naumann as referring to the area east of Germany, indicating that this was an area of German hegemony. During World War I, the Czechoslovak president Tomáš Masaryk suggested the existence between West and East, that is, between Germany and Russia, of a middle zone, which might function as a bridge between the two (see Le Rider; Schulze Wessel). Kundera, however, objects to both uses of the concept, and rejects the notion of "Mitteleuropa" as a whole; this part of Europe is for him not a bridge between East and West but definitely part of the West, even if at present (in 1984) occupied by the East. If anything is specific to this geographical part of Europe, it is its nature as "a condensed version of Europe itself in all its cultural variety, a small arch-European Europe," characterized by "the greatest variety within the smallest space" ("The Tragedy" 33). Thus, the discussion provoked by the article adds another paradox to the Kunderan list of paradoxes: his defense of Czechoslovakia, Poland, and Hungary as essential parts of Europe, or even as a small-scale "arch-Europe," has contributed to the discussion of the specificity of Central and East European culture (on the terminological designations and history of terms and concepts for the name of the region, see, e.g., Ash; Cornis-Pope and Neubauer; Tägil; Tötösy de Zepetnek, "Comparative Cultural").

Kundera, who in socialist Czechoslovakia warned his countrymen of provincialism and advocated an opening up in particular to French literature, thus comes to Paris, the European cultural metropolis, to represent Central Europe, which he claims to be at the center of European culture, or at least to have been so in the first half of the twentieth century. He comes to France believing that the most significant event of twentieth-century history has been the destruction of the essence of Europe in its very heart, in Central Europe. The downfall of Central Europe is the downfall of Europe in miniature (on this, see also Finkielkraut 44). This of course is his judgment at that particular historical moment, when he expected the "Russian night" that had befallen Central Europe to last "forever" ("An Introduction" 476). His concern already at this time, however, was more comprehensive, making it still, after 1989, valid: Europe did not erode merely by an attack from outside. Kundera found it scandalous that West Europeans did not share his insight, that the question of "East[ern] Europe" was considered merely in terms of a power struggle between two different political systems and not as a cultural issue. He claimed that this is because Europeans do not recognize who they really are, that is, they do not realize that the essence of Europe is its culture. As a consequence, the greatest enemy of Europe is Europe itself. In the West, a certain process of self-destruction is taking place: we live in an age of "journalism," the dominance of the superficial and homogenizing media, which has abandoned the spirit of experimentation and questioning ("On Criticism" 14; see also Elgrably; Kramer; McEwan; Weiss). This conviction has remained unshaken by more recent historical turns in Central Europe and in his later works, Kundera's warnings about Europeans forgetting their true identity have in fact grown even louder. Thus, as an emigrant arriving from the "edge" of Europe in one of its metropolises, Kundera speaks up on behalf of European culture to Europeans who do not see what is happening to them.

In saying that "Central Europe" is an essential part of European culture, Kundera is placing his fellow countrymen Janáček and Kafka right at the center of cultural Europe (see also Bílek, "The East" 103). In so doing, he can profess his own commitment to Czech culture without having to renounce his European identity. For Kundera it is essential that all cultural achievements be evaluated from a European perspective. He objects to artists being pasted into a national family portrait, which according to him is often the fate of the artists of "small" nations: thus, for example Gombrowicz, rather than being placed in the "*large context*" of the "international modern novel," is seen as a Polish author and is thus pushed back "into the *small context* of the national" (*Testament* 192). Kundera's protest of course concerns himself as well: he regards a "nation's possessiveness towards its artists' works as a *small-context terrorism*, reducing the whole meaning of a work to the role it plays in its homeland" (*The Curtain* 39) and he insists on being viewed in the "large" context, that is, within the European tradition of the novel. However, just as little as Kundera has been able to convince critics and the reading public that writers should not be judged by their political and moral positions but only by their artistic achievements, no more has he been able to prevent his novels being read in a "small," national context. His Czech readers, who are familiar with his "prehistory," have read his works published in the West—insofar as these have been accessible—as part of his overall career. His image as an author has therefore appeared to them less coherent than it has to his Western public, which knows him only as a novelist (see Crain 47). And it is probably not exaggeration to say that his Czech readership has tended to see his elision of the past in beginning anew in France as an act of dishonesty (see Bílek, "A Journey"; "The East" 110; Boisen, "Le Malentendu"; Thirouin and Boyer-Weinmann). In general, the reception of his work in Czechoslovakia was reserved even in the 1980s, when his fame in the West was at its highest (Petras 71).

In France, Kundera was perceived until 1989 as a dissident writer who was read in the political context of his native country, and that doubtlessly contributed to his high esteem and popularity (Baty-Delalande 237; Petras 69–70). After 1989, as Kundera was not interested in returning "home" and as his novels were no longer written in Czech or set in Czechoslovakia or among Czech emigrants, he began to be viewed as a French author, although of foreign origin (see Tautz). The reception of his works was favorable, but no longer enthusiastic (Gautier 56). Applying French standards to Kundera's works entailed harsh criticism of the language in his first two novels written in French, *La Lenteur* (*Slowness*) and *L'Identité* (*Identity*); at the time nobody guessed that Kundera himself had already written the French "translation" of *Immortality.* Kundera reacted by publishing his next novel, *Ignorance*, first in Catalan and Castilian in 2000 and only in 2003 in French. Moreover, a French author, even one of foreign background, is expected to value French literature above all. Kundera is thus often asked about his relation to French literature, the French connection is emphasized in critiques of his works, and he is censured for intimating that he does not hold Victor Hugo's *Les Miserables* in particularly high esteem (Tautz 80–81). Even more significant are certain misunderstandings, which derive, as I see it, from the inability of the French to distinguish between Kundera's understanding of the term "European" and the French one: for the French, equating "European" with "French" appears natural (see Kundera's analysis of the "provincialism of large nations" in *The Curtain* 40–43; see also Miletric 89, 116–17, 156; Slater 925; Waever 184).

In most cases—enumerated by Marie-Odile Thirouin as traits in Kundera's novels which cause an adverse response in his French readers—it is precisely this or a similar conceptual misunderstanding that is involved. For example, when Kundera says that he follows the principles of musical composition in his novels, the French perceive only a vague metaphor, referring primarily to a kind of emotional effect (see Christoffel; Thirouin, "Le Mystère")—which is opposite to the meaning which Kundera gives to the notion. Moreover, French critics cannot understand his unwillingness to accept the idea of *littérature engagée*, which is supported by well-regarded advocates of French literature (see Thirouin, "Le Mystère"). Coming from a society in which literature was subdued to political control and used as a tool in ideological work, Kundera understands the notion of "engaged writer" in the sense of the writer's being a propagandist, a proponent of a given truth (see Baty-Delalande 236–37; *Encounter* 163). For Kundera, in contrast, absolute intellectual freedom is the first prerequisite to being a novelist. Furthermore, in Thirouin's opinion, the French, who love their lyrical poetry, have difficulties with Kundera's "antilyricism" ("Le Mystère"14–15). In saying this, Thirouin does not pay heed to what "lyrical" for Kundera actually means. Unfortunately, those writers who, like Virginie Sauzon and Stéphane Chaudier, try to understand Kundera's "antilyricism" by connecting it with French rationalism and the Enlightenment do not grasp Kundera's critical approach to the lyrical attitude either, which is "Central European" rather than French. The difference is connected with the fact that Kundera's concept of analysis differs from that of French rationalism. Consequently, Sauzon and Chaudier complain that the Kunderan analysis does not simplify, as the French one does—by reducing a complex thing to its simplest, already known constituents—but on the contrary makes the matter appear even more complex (249). This observation is correct, but it leaves undefined how Kundera's analysis actually functions and to what purpose. Another concept difficult for French critics, as Kundera himself has remarked, is that of "kitsch," an important concept in the Central European discussion of the arts since the Romantic era, but at least earlier fairly unknown in the West (see *The Curtain* 51–56).

Despite the criticism and misunderstandings, Kundera was in June 2012 awarded the prize of the Bibliothèque Nationale de France in recognition of his life work as a writer in the French language and in 2007 he was awarded the Czech State Literature Prize. In addition, he has won the Jerusalem Prize in 1985, the Austrian State Prize for European Literature in 1987, the German Herder Prize in 2000, and the Romanian Ovid Prize in 2011. The reception and the recognition of Kundera's works show that his readers place his oeuvre in several national contexts in addition to a European context. However, this does not imply a common understanding of what a "European" writer would be and thus the identity of "the European novel" represents a more complicated problem than is suggested by Kundera's emphasis on a common European tradition. In turn, this implies that the image Kundera has constructed of himself as a European novelist is not enough for the analysis of his texts. Instead, we need to take into account not only his specific understanding of the word "European," but also other contexts of various extensions in order to grasp the specificity of his work, such as European modernity in literature, philosophy and history—especially the history of twentieth century—the modern "life-world" (*Lebenswelt*) and its changes, and Friedrich Nietzsche's work. In general, I agree with the view that determining an accurate literary and cultural context for the study of an author's work is an important methodological element in the contextual and comparative—that is, nonnational—study of literature (see, e.g., Tötösy de Zepetnek, "From Comparative"; "The New Humanities"; Tötösy de Zepetnek and Vasvári).

Studying Kundera's art of the novel

There are certain circumstances that make the study of Kundera difficult and that may explain why, despite his established standing, he has not been extensively studied. There is, of course, a plethora of reviews of his books and of articles, but larger-scale studies remain few. The first and most obvious reason for this is the traditional requirement for philological research that the works of the author are to be read in the original language. The reading public may read the texts in translation, but for the scholar to rely on translations is problematic, since certain features of the original text may be lost or distorted in the processes of translation. In addition, for those unfamiliar with the Czech language, it is difficult to grasp the original context of his early writings with sufficient accuracy. However, Kundera's own insistence that he should be perceived within the great tradition of the European novel justifies an approach which does not place him in a primarily Czech context. Kundera opposes the habit of "professors of foreign literatures" of demonstrating their expertise by making "a great point of identifying with the *small* (national) *context* of the literature they teach" (*The Curtain* 37). Aware of the scandal of discarding the sacrosanct philological rule, he even writes: "Do I mean by this that to judge a novel one can do without a knowledge of its original language? I do indeed mean exactly that!" (*The Curtain* 36). The statement opens the way for international scholarship on the author's work. Moreover, Kundera has declared the French editions of the novels written in Czech, rather than the Czech versions, to be the definitive ones (Woods, *Translating* ix); along with his interference in the English translations of his novels to the point that they too are as good—at least provisionally—as authorized, this means that the problem of language with regard to the works he counts as belonging to his oeuvre proper practically vanishes. While it is difficult to make a virtue of not knowing Czech in studying Kundera's works (as in my own case), the author himself has made the disadvantage as easy to bear as possible.

Another factor that makes the study of Kundera's works problematic is the manner in which he constructs his novels, namely, his inclination to speak out on things which are traditionally left to be articulated by scholars. He displays the thematic level of his novels conspicuously: the characters and their situations are used to unfold a theme named explicitly and often reflected upon by the narrator-author. In addition, in both his novels and his essays Kundera tells us about his own technique of writing, his concept of the novel, and how he relates to the tradition of the European novel. This means that Kundera speaks directly in the language of abstract reflection typical of literary scholarship; he writes, as it were, in a manner that saves scholars from their usual task of grasping the thematic content and formal features of the work and expressing them in the language of abstract concepts. This "assistance" may turn into a drawback, since it often seems difficult to avoid repeating what has already been said by Kundera himself. When he himself describes the structure of his novels, defines concepts such "the novel in the form of variations" or "polyphony," or explains the most important themes of his works, for instance in the essay "Sixty-three Words" in *The Art of the Novel*, the scholar finds himself or herself in a difficult position in trying to avoid repeating the already known.

Nevertheless, Kundera himself is far from thinking that the author makes the work of the scholar redundant. In his article on the importance of literary scholarship and criticism he professes the view that without contextualizing reflection—"the" task of scholarship—the author would remain invisible and undefined as a literary phenomenon; the objective of scholarship and criticism is to define the place of the author in the continuum of European culture ("On Criticism" 13; see also *Testaments* 23). Kundera emphasizes that although his novels contain essay-like passages, he is foremost a novelist. This implies that his explanations in the essayistic parts of the novels, or in separate essays, are hypothetical and playful, rather than exhaustive, systematic, or striving for incontestable truths (*The Art* 78–80; *The Curtain* 77–78).

The scholar's task does not consist merely of assembling and systematizing an author's thoughts; rather, she or he has to make the author's work more comprehensible by pointing out aspects and connections which might have escaped the attention of the author or which the author might have left unmentioned because he or she considers them self-evident. The process of making the work understood may also urge the scholar to shed light on connections which the author hopes to escape. This does not imply that the scholar should not take into account the author's statements about his or her own work. On the contrary: what the author himself or herself focuses on can serve as a sensible starting point for research, even if his or her comments should not be considered to contain the exhaustive truth about the work. Whether in the case of Kundera or any other author, we can say that while in general the author's comments are not "false," they are often one-sided in that they fail to cover all relevant aspects or to elucidate the matter from a point of view which seems essential to the scholar.

As the starting point of the present study, I take up the question put forward by Kundera himself as to the place of his novels in the history of the novel and in European culture in general. Which literary periods and trends, which questions, which representatives of the novel can his works be seen as associated with, and how is he distinct from these?

Kundera has often been called a postmodernist author, a notion which associates him with the literary avant-garde of his time (see, e.g., Adams; Atkinson; Berlatsky; Bilek, "Journey" 21; Cordle 130–33; Cravens 106; du Plessix Gray 57; Eagleton 28; Gaughan 15; Lafargue 256; Lahtinen; Lodge 143, 149; Makarushka; Morello 142; Richter 58; Rizza 351; Ross 351; Weeks 142). Certain features of his novels, such as the absence of a consistent illusion of reality, metafictional reflections on the structure of the novel, the combination of different text types, or the abandonment of the "grand narratives" of history have been considered as evidence of his postmodernity. Kundera himself, however, does not call himself a postmodernist, nor does he talk about postmodernity or postmodernist literature as a phenomenon of the contemporary world (in fact, in *Encounter*, he mentions the word "postmodern" in a pejorative sense [117]). This, however, does not necessarily imply that he cannot be regarded as a postmodernist—albeit as yet no consensus has been reached as to the criteria of postmodernism. Yet, Kundera himself defines his identity as a novelist in relation to the various meanings of the concept of "modern," some of which are positively valued, others negatively. First, he views European culture as a fundamentally modern phenomenon and in this sense for him being modern is necessarily positive (*The Art* 151–52). He relates himself, however, to a narrower form of modernism and sees himself under the roof of the "post-Proustian" European novel, which he has characterized as "antimodern modernism" (*The Art* 141–42, *The Curtain* 56; see also Oppenheim 9). He also is an admirer of the twentieth-century avant-garde, especially French surrealism, although it did not favor the novel (Elgrably 56; *Testaments* 149, *The Curtain* 81). At the same time, he relates with "deep mistrust" to "fashionable modernism," which he sees as conformist and incapable of creating anything new (Raddatz 107). "Fashionable modernism" is equivalent to the endeavor to be "absolutely modern," which eventually means nothing but keeping up uncritically with the *dernier cri*, whatever it implies (see *The Art* 42). His own concept of modernity takes a stand against this attitude of being fashionably modern.

On the basis of Kundera's novels and with regard to his own comments, I argue that the relevant contexts of his works include European modernity in a broad sociohistorical and cultural sense, as well as the modernism of the European and especially the "Central European" novel, but also his own specific historical experiences during his youth in Czechoslovakia. Modernity in the broad sense thus refers here to modern European sensibility and thought as they are manifest in social thinking and practice, in art and philosophy. This corresponds to Kundera's general understanding of Europe, with the novel at its heart, yet with regard to history it is less broad than in his conception. What Kundera understands by modernity does not begin, as he claims, with the dawn of the modern age in the Renaissance, but with the outgoing eighteenth century which gave birth to modern conceptions of reality and the human being. Kundera stands in this tradition but at the same time, as I endeavor to demonstrate, his views differ from it at certain crucial points, namely, in his understanding of history and individual autonomy. In literary modernism authors of special importance to Kundera are his five Central European "post-Proustian" authors, above all, as we will see, Broch and Musil (see Steinby, "Ein mitteleuropäischer").

Elevating questions of modernity and modernism to a key position in interpreting Kundera is not inconsistent with what he himself has said about his novels; in contrast, tracing his novels to the historical events from which he sought an escape as a novelist contradicts his view. The analysis of his works and the study of their background reveal several other features which are at odds with his statements. Among other things, his thinking shows a much higher degree of thematic and even systemic unity than is implied by his conception of the novel as preoccupied with the exploration of human existence in a problem-oriented and nonsystemic way. This, however, does not mean that each and every work should not be studied as an independent entity. The attempt to study Kundera's oeuvre "as a single text" (Le Grand, "Kundera" 1; see also Ricard 46–47) conflicts with Kundera's basic conviction that the whole of an individual work and its composition are of the highest importance. It is not enough that the work communicates something new, it has to be original in its composition as well (*Testaments* 170). Thus, in Kundera's case the concept of the "work" cannot, as in the view of structuralists or poststructuralists, be replaced with that of the "text," seen as part of a group of texts or of a certain discourse, without losing something essential to its character.

Some of the concepts I employ to define the object of study stem from Kundera himself, but are elaborated; I also introduce new concepts in order to deal with aspects which Kundera has ignored or which he has seen differently. In my analysis of Kundera's works, I do not apply any particular theory in the sense of a preconceived conceptual apparatus. Such a mechanical application of theoretical concepts is, I believe, what Kundera is referring to when he says that contemporary historiography and literary theory are becoming ever more "misomusistic" (*Encounter* 67), that is, less and less sensitive to the specificity of literature as art and more and more prone to reduce it to something—history, philosophy, theory—that preexists the literary work of art. Unlike Kundera ("On Criticism" 13), however, I do not claim that in order to be open to what is new in a literary work of art, the scholar must proceed in an essentially nonmethodical manner. On the contrary, there is a great deal of method in the way a literary scholar encounters a literary work of art by reflecting upon his or her concepts and readjusting them to fit more closely the phenomenon in question, relating different aspects of a work to those of another work in the endeavor to uncover its logic, and building up a coherent picture of the object of study without overlooking its discordances. I hope to grasp the essence of Kundera's art through the application of carefully considered concepts and by placing it within literary history and more generally within the cultural history of Europe.

My study proceeds in a hermeneutic circle in the sense that in each chapter I analyze Kundera's novelistic oeuvre from a different point of view so as to gradually deepen our insight into it. I start out with the essay in which he defines his own place within the "tradition of Cervantes" and identify the most important traits of his conception of the novel. In the following chapter I attempt to grasp the basic tenets underlying Kundera's novelistic creation through an analysis of his first novel, *The Joke*, which already displays most of his later themes and basic questions concerning the structure of the novel. As the next step, I compare Kundera's concept of the novel and his method to that of the authors of the "Pleiades," above all Broch and Musil. Next, I tackle the compositions of his novels and his themes in a synoptic analysis, taking into account Kundera's reflections upon these points. Following that, I discuss his novels separately, from *Life Is Elsewhere* to *Immortality*. Thus, I proceed from a preliminary outline of Kundera's art of the novel toward a deeper understanding based on a detailed analysis of individual works. In the closing chapter I focus on Kundera's most recent short novels and present some final conclusions.

Chapter Two
The Legacy of Cervantes

In the essay on Vladislav Vančura (*Umění románu*), Kundera asks whether the grand epic is still possible in our time. Along with Hegel and Georg [György] Lukács, Kundera believes that the time of the epos is past, since in the era of modernity the unity of the individual and society supported by myth no longer exists. Its place has been taken by the novel, which depicts a human being who has become a stranger in the world (see Chvatik, *Die Fallen* 38, 40). Květoslav Chvatík has stressed the relevance of these ideas in Kundera's novels (39, 42). One might object to this, however, by pointing out that when Kundera wrote the essay he was still in his lyrical period; later, as an established novelist, he no longer bemoans the individual's detachment from society, but sees in it the essence of modernity.

Modernity and the novel

The collection of essays published in his 1986 *The Art of the Novel* opens with the essay "The Depreciated Legacy of Cervantes," in which Kundera elaborates his conception of the European novel. The scope of the essay is both narrower and broader than a history of the novel. On the one hand, Kundera does not propose to deal with the whole history of the novel or even its main periods, as this would not be possible in a brief essay. Rather, he presents "a practitioner's view" or a "confession" (see Oppenheim 11) of what he considers to be essential in the history of the novel; this functions as an introduction to his own poetics of the novel. On the other hand, within the brief scope of the essay Kundera deals with something more than the history of the novel: he believes that through the novel he can elucidate some of the essential and distinctive features of modern human existence.

The essay begins with a reference to Edmund Husserl's lectures on "the crisis of European humanity" given in Wien and Prague in 1935 (3). The lectures were published in 1936 in book form, under the title *Die Krisis der europäischen Wissenschaften und die transzendentale Phänomenologie* (*The Crisis of European Sciences and Transcendental Phenomenology*). Husserl observes that in the modern age European thinking has been dominated by the natural sciences and that this is one-sided. Greek philosophy, the beginning of Western scientific and rational thinking, had approached "the world as a whole" as a question to be solved; thus European culture was born from a "passion for knowledge" which had seized humanity. At the beginning of the modern age, however, the concept of knowledge narrowed significantly:

> The roots of the crisis lay for him [Husserl] at the beginning of the Modern Era, in Galileo and Descartes, in the one-sided nature of the European sciences, which reduced the world to a mere object of technical and mechanical investigation and put the concrete world of life, *die Lebenswelt* as he called it, beyond their horizon. . . . Once elevated by Descartes to "master and proprietor of nature," man has now become a mere thing to the forces (of technology, of politics, of history) that bypass him, surpass him, possess him. (*The Art* 3-4)

This narrowed conception of knowledge, the view of reality as a field of interplay between mechanical forces, and the split of science into "the tunnels of specialized disciplines" have driven the European individual—Kundera resorts here to a Heideggerian notion—into the "oblivion of being," in which one has lost sight of oneself and of one's actual experience of the world. Our concrete existence, our life-world (*Lebenswelt*, in the sense of Husserl and Heidegger) "has neither value nor interest: it is eclipsed, forgotten from the start" (4)

Kundera does not go more deeply into Husserl's critique of scientific thinking. He does not, for example, compare it to Theodor W. Adorno and Max Horkheimer's *Dialectic of Enlightenment,* in which Adorno and Horkheimer show how the pursuit of purely technical rationality ends up with its opposite, that is, irrationality. Adorno and Horkheimer's argument resembles Kundera's conviction that the prevalence of scientific-technical knowledge does not release us from the constraints of nature, but on the contrary leads to our subjection to the machineries we have set into motion, namely, technology, politics, and history. In the contemporary debate on humanity, history, and society, similar questions have been raised, for instance, by Jürgen Habermas, a follower of Adorno and Horkheimer's "dialectic of Enlightenment" and yet a proponent of the "project of modernity," by Michel Foucault in his analyses of the interrelationship between power and knowledge, and by the theoretician of the postmodern, Zygmunt Bauman. Kundera's primary concern, however, is not a critique of scientific rationality, but the other side of European culture, which Husserl does not touch upon: "Indeed, for me, the founder of the Modern Era is not only Descartes [whose philosophical principles were derived from Galileo's mechanical-mathematical explanation of nature] but also Cervantes" (*The Art* 4). For if science and even philosophy "have forgotten about man's being, it emerges all the more plainly that with Cervantes a great European art took shape that is nothing other than the investigation of this forgotten being" (4–5). Thus, where Husserl sets up his philosophy of phenomenology derived from an analysis of human cognition in order to counterbalance the one-sided concept of knowledge in European philosophy, Kundera asserts that such a counterweight has always existed. It is found in the novel.

Drawing an analogy between science and the novel as a form of exploring human existence, Kundera emphasizes the cognitive aspect of the latter:

> Indeed, all the great existential themes Heidegger analyzes in *Being and Time*—considering them to have been neglected by all earlier European philosophy—had been unveiled, displayed, illuminated by four centuries of the European novel. In its own way, through its own logic, the novel discovered the various dimensions of existence one by one: with Cervantes and his contemporaries, it inquires into the nature of adventure; with Richardson, it begins to examine "what happens inside," to unmask the secret life of the feelings; with Balzac, it discovers man's rootedness in history; with Flaubert, it explores the *terra* previously *incognita* of the everyday; with Tolstoy, it focuses on the intrusion of the irrational into human behavior and decisions. It probes time: the elusive past with Proust, the elusive present with Joyce. With Thomas Mann, it examines the role of the myths from the remote past that control our present actions. Et cetera, et cetera. . . . A novel that does not discover a hitherto unknown segment of existence is immoral. Knowledge is the novel's only morality. . . . The *sequence of discoveries* (not the sum of what was written) is what constitutes the history of the European novel. (5-6)

In Kundera's account, the novel "unveils," "displays," "illuminates," "elucidates," "discovers," "inquires," "examines," "unmasks," "explores," and "probes." The object of the exploration is human existence, the human life-world, which the science and philosophy of the Modern Age have condemned to the "oblivion of being." This exploration is the "sole raison d'être" of the novel, its "only morality" (5–6). The exploration characteristic of the novel differs from that typical of modern science and philosophy not only in its object, but also in its methods and its conception of knowledge. Instead of the certainty of truth formulated mathematically, the novel comes up with "a welter of contradictory truths" (7). The novel represents a world where "in the absence of the Supreme Judge, the world suddenly appeared in its fearsome ambiguity; the single divine Truth decomposed into myriad relative truths parceled out by men. Thus was born the world of the Modern Era, and with it the novel, the image and model of that world" (6). In a Hegelian mode, Kundera speaks of Descartes's heroism of setting the solitary thinking individual against the whole universe. As a counterpart to this Cartesian heroism, however, he sets Cervantes's courage and willingness to confront an ambiguous world in which no absolute truth can be discovered. Kundera finds that there are two different conceptions of truth at stake here—for Descartes, truth is universal and incontestable and for Cervantes it is relative and ambiguous—but he does not elaborate on this. He merely adds that these "relative truths" are embodied in the characters of the novels, who are to be conceived of as "*imaginary selves*" (7).

Kundera is not interested in giving a detailed description of the history of the European novel nor in placing the novel in a wider literary-historical context, for example, in searching for its historical roots or comparing it to non-European literatures. In *Testaments Betrayed* he comments that "there are of course other novels, the novel of China, of Japan, the novel of ancient Greece, but they are not bound by any continuous evolutionary line to the historical enterprise that began with Rabelais and Cervantes" (28); what actually interests him is the novel which examines modern human existence. We can therefore say that his perspective in the study of the "legacy of Cervantes" is not actually historical, but phenomenological; Kundera seeks to grasp the essence of the European novel in the modern era.

The concept of "phenomenological approach" has sometimes been used to characterize Kundera's own art of the novel (see *The Art* 32). He finds this characterization of the exploration of human existence in his novels acceptable as long as the use of the term does not obliterate the differences between the novelistic approach and the philosophical one (32). Provided that this distinction is taken into account, the term "phenomenological" also applies to Kundera's method in his "novelistic essays" (*The Art* 71), for instance, to his definition of the legacy of Cervantes. Similarly to Husserl in his phenomenological analyses, Kundera rejects the search for any explanation of a phenomenon in terms of historical contextualization; rather, he endeavors to eliminate all that does not belong to the phenomenon itself. Moreover, in accordance with the phenomenological method, he ignores all that is characteristic merely of some representatives of the phenomenon—that is, of individual novels—and seeks what is common to all of them. He is in search of the essential, definitive traits that make a work a novel.

Kundera's phenomenological method, however, differs from the approach of philosophical phenomenology in that he actually relies to a great extent on particular examples. For example, he defines the Cervantean tradition in universal terms as an exploration of human existence, and further explains it by enumerating discoveries made by individual authors from Cervantes to Thomas Mann; in other contexts, he refers to such writers as Carlos Fuentes, Gabriel García Márquez or Salman Rushdie (see *Testaments* 4, 14, 22, 72; *The Curtain* 81). Similarly, in *The Unbearable Lightness of Being* the notions of "weight" and "lightness" or the antagonism of body and soul are considered abstractly, but they are also dealt with more concretely through the experiences of the protagonists Tomas and Tereza. The explication of a notion thereby becomes more vivid, but less definitive and less closed than in an abstract conceptual definition. The same technique is applied for instance in the essay "Sixty-three Words" in *The Art of the Novel*, where Kundera discusses concepts important in his own works, but, as he believes, in the whole of European culture as well. In addition to "the novel," his key terms include, for example, "transparency," "imagination," and "reflection." The definitions are illuminating and thought provoking rather than comprehensive or exhaustive. "Transparency," for instance, is exemplified by André Breton's metaphor of living in a glass house, in addition to a more general and abstract discussion of the difference between public and private (152–53). "Imagination" is explained by the example of a dreamlike episode from *The Book of Laughter and Forgetting*, where imagination is presented as an alternative to realistic narration (*The Art* 131–32). As a whole, rather than operating with abstract and conceptual definitions, Kundera tends to illuminate a phenomenon in terms of its function in a given context (e.g., in a novel), by means of examples (dreamlike narrative) or through metaphors (glass house). In addition, the concepts to be explained are often themselves metaphorical, such as "weight," "lightness," or "infantocracy." If Kundera's novels are often, as he says, "a long quest for some elusive definitions" (*The Art* 143), we can add that—unlike the purely abstract mode of defining concepts in philosophy and science—his definitions are novelistically concrete, elliptical, and metaphorical.

In Kundera's view, the novel is a modern phenomenon and therefore connected with a particular period in history; nevertheless, he does not consider it as determined by history or as following the course of history in its development. Rather than a product of history, the novel is the very core of European cultural history. According to Kundera, the plurality of truths unveiled by the novel corresponds to human experience of the world in the modern era. His definition of the essence of the novel is thus conceived to be valid for the four hundred years of the modern novel, but he pays no attention to the changes in the function of the novel.

Despite the fact that Kundera's definition of the essence and function of the modern novel is general and in a sense historically nondifferentiating, he does consider the novel to have its own internal history, a history of discoveries of the possibilities of human existence. In the passage quoted above, Kundera refers to certain important novels which allow us to discern the main line in the history of the genre as he understands it. This method could be called elliptical, in that only a few illustrative points are chosen to make the main line visible. The historical line sketched need not remain exactly the same when Kundera returns to the topic. In *Testaments Betrayed*, for example, he places the beginning of the modern novel with Rabelais rather than Cervantes (31–32; see also Phillips 145). This does not imply that he has changed his mind; he merely chooses another novelist from among the most important ones to illustrate what is essential in the historical development of the novel. In what follows, I analyze more closely a few authors in Kundera's sequence whom I consider to be useful in clarifying his conception of the modern novel. Where these authors are concerned, Kundera's omissions are as important as what he actually says about them.

The Enlightenment and Romanticism

In seeking a phenomenological definition of the modern novel, Kundera excludes everything he considers inessential by using a few large strokes, often at the cost of historical accuracy. This is the case when, in an obvious parallel to the young Lukács in his *The Theory of the Novel*, he describes how Don Quixote set out on his adventures "in the absence of the Supreme Judge" and came to experience the "fearsome ambiguity" of the world and the fragmentation of the Truth, once based on God, into innumerable human, relative truths (*The Art* 6). The Nietzschean idea of the death of God is here applied to Cervantes's novel from the beginning of the seventeenth century without giving a thought to the fact that Nietzsche, writing in the late nineteenth century, spoke of this event as a recent one. Actually, in the seventeenth century religion had not yet lost its position. For Descartes in the mid-seventeenth century and the creators of philosophical systems following him, God was still a fundamental element of the system and a warranty of truth, even if the foundation on which the construction of the system of knowledge rested was the individual as the autonomous subject of knowledge. Through the method of systemic doubt, Descartes arrives at the incontrovertible proposition "I think, therefore I am," but goes on to conclude that our ideas, insofar as they are clear and distinct, derive from God and must therefore be true: "For reason does not require us to believe that whatever we see or image is true; it does, however, insist that all our ideas or notions must have some basis of truth. Otherwise it could not be that God, who is altogether perfect and trustworthy, should have placed them in us" (*Discourse* 125).

In contrasting Descartes's search for truth with the ambiguity and "the *wisdom of uncertainty*" of the novel (*The Art* 6–7), Kundera is right with respect to Descartes in that for him, and for the Enlightenment thinkers of the following century, truth is not relative. The subject of the acquisition of knowledge is the individual human being, but in following universally valid principles of perception and reason in the pursuit of knowledge, the individual attains unquestionable truth. Truth is relative only in comparison to God's absolute knowledge, encompassing all that exists. Human knowledge is finite and its advancement an endless process (see Blumenberg, "Wirklichkeitsbegriff"; Kondylis). Kundera, however, claims that in contrast to this, the truths in Cervantes's novel are only relative. He points out that in some interpretations, *Don Quixote* is seen as criticizing the idealistic attitude of its hero, while in others it is regarded as praising this idealism. According to Kundera, both interpretations are wrong in that they assume that the novel proposes one, single truth. It is precisely the ambiguity and "essential relativity of things human" that the novel strives to express (*The Art* 6–7).

However, Kundera's view is anachronistic in that he does not take into consideration the fact that the debate over Don Quixote's alleged idealism emerged only in the era of Romanticism. As pointed out by Anthony Close in his study, *The Romantic Approach to* Don Quixote*: A Critical History of the Romantic Tradition in* Quixote *Criticism*, from the time of its publication until the late eighteenth century, *Don Quixote* was read as a comic novel, entertaining readers with the adventures of the mad knight who had lost his mind from excessive reading of chivalric romances. That he takes the windmills for giants was seen as parodying chivalric romances and not as questioning of the prevailing conception of reality. *Don Quixote* belongs to a metaphysically defined world, in which the individual observer—assuming he is not mad—does not construct his own, individually colored conception of the world. Only toward the end of the eighteenth century did the early German Romantics such as Friedrich and August Wilhelm Schlegel, Novalis, Solger, and Schelling project the conception of the world of their idealistic philosophy onto *Don Quixote* and reinterpret the character's madness as a nonconformist world view. By making the mad knight an idealistic rebel against the reality of the prosaic world, they made him one of their own contemporaries. Even though Kundera refutes both the idealistic and the realistic interpretation of the novel, he nevertheless adopts the Romantic anachronism of seeing the novel as being about different views of the world.

Since the point of my discussion of Kundera's essay on the legacy of Cervantes is not to evaluate it as a study in literary history but to gain insight into Kundera's view of the tradition of the novel with which he affiliates himself (see *The Art* 20), it is irrelevant to point out his "errors," where he illustrates his views with examples from literary history; however, I cannot ignore the differences between his ideas and those of contemporary literary scholarship. The modern idea that truth is relative insofar as its validity depends on the point of view of the interpreter or the individual's experience does not go back either in the novel or in European culture as far as the seventeenth century, but originates from the late eighteenth century. That human existence is embedded in history and that our views of the world therefore vary both historically and individually was an idea elaborated in Johann Gottfried Herder's writings from the 1770s to the 1790s (see, e.g., Herder, *Ideen*, *Vom Geist*; Nisbet; Taylor 368–78; Steinby, "Rehabilitation"). This means a questioning of the Cartesian concept of universal reason and of the anthropological concept of a universal human essence. For Herder, Goethe, and the early German Romantics, the subject of experience is the human being whose individuality determines how the world manifests itself to him or her. With their conception of the individual human being as an autonomous, creative subject of knowledge and action, and their notion of the value of individuality, a new period of modernity was launched questioning the Enlightenment's view of universal reason and the generically defined nature of human existence. The era of individualism continued until the dawn of the postmodern age in the latter part of the twentieth century, when the individual's standing as the autonomous subject of judgment and action began to be questioned (see, e.g., Saariluoma [Steinby], *Der postindividualistische*; Taylor 184–85, 384–400). With regard to the still ongoing debate on individuality and subjectivity, it is necessary to note that the Romantic emphasis on autonomy and individuality is often mistaken for seeing the individual as self-sufficient. In fact, Herder stresses the individual's immersion in contemporary culture, where each culture and era creates its own reality with its own values, meanings, and truths. The individual's actions and works are to a great extent determined by his or her culture and historical era (see, e.g., Herder, *Ideen* 336–45).

Kundera, however, does not distinguish between the Enlightenment view of the individual's autonomy in the acquisition of universally valid knowledge—which actually is usually not called "individualism"—and individualism in the sense of individual differences in worldview and in the interpretation of affairs, which originates from the Romantic era. In his definition of "les Temps modernes" or the "modern era" in "Sixty-three Words," Kundera identifies the vanishing of the religion-based worldview directly with the birth of individualism. The modern era is for him the era in which "God becomes *Deus absconditus* [the hidden God] and man the ground of all things. European individualism is born, and with it a new situation for art, for culture, for science" (*The Art* 151). In the "Jerusalem Address," subtitled "The Novel and Europe," Kundera calls individualism the core and "precious essence of the European spirit" (*The Art* 165); he also praises individualism as the primary characteristic of the "legacy of Cervantes."

In my view, Kundera's misconception is a consequence of the fact that after Romanticism an individual-centered way of thinking became part of the common European heritage. Individualism is often thought to have originated in the Renaissance, a misunderstanding that goes back—as Johan Huizinga and Walter Haug have shown—to Jacob Burckhardt's *The Culture of the Renaissance in Italy* (1928). Haug notes that the spirit of the Renaissance was "highly normative, searching for an eternally valid measure of beauty, politics, virtue or truth" and that Burckhardt's error was that he confused cultural creativity with distinct individuality (293–94). Often, however, the question of the precise historical onset of individualism is not posed at all; actually, not until the "death" of the autonomous individual with poststructuralism and postmodernism did a common awareness emerge of the fact that the individualistic way of thinking is situated historically (see Giddens; Taylor). Thus Kundera is not alone in his confusion concerning the content and historical origin of individualism. It remains to examine in what sense the modern novel in Kundera's view has to do with the individual human being and what individual identity actually means for him.

Although the novel focuses on the individual, it stands, in Kundera's view, in opposition to lyrical subjectivity. To him, lyricism means exposing oneself to the gaze of others, surrendering oneself to the power of real or imaginary emotions, and elevating feelings to the status of highest value. Lyricism longs for infinity: merging with others, a dissolving of the boundaries between the self and everything else, and an enlarging of one's emotions so as to encompass everything there is. Kundera sees lyrical subjectivism as the true legacy of Romanticism. This view is not without historical foundation. The Romantic subject is driven by a longing to escape the isolation of his or her individual existence and to rediscover a lost unity with others. He or she seeks to merge with the human community and an all-embracing feeling of unity, of being absorbed into the Absolute (existence as a whole). This appears in Romantic works of art, from Friedrich Schlegel's *Lucinde* (1799) and Novalis's *Heinrich von Ofterdingen* (1802) to Wagner's *Tristan and Isolde* (1865).

While for Friedrich Schlegel the novel was the definitive Romantic genre (*Fragmente* 186–87, *Athenäums-Fragmente* 114), Kundera sees the novel as the opposite of lyricism and Romanticism. He declares that the novel is not a subjective confession by the author, nor does the novelist aim at securing the reader's sympathy and compassion; rather, the novelist's discoveries concerning the various possibilities of human existence invite the reader to engage in further inquiry and reflection (*The Art* 143–44). The novelist stands for a critical distance against mergence, and for inquiry against emotional identification; as a detached observer of phenomena, he or she assumes an attitude similar to that of the scientist, although the object of study is the human life-world (*Lebenswelt*). Ridiculing and criticizing the sentimental or lyrical over-exalted Romantic subjectivity—a topic in his novels from *Life Is Elsewhere* to *Immortality*—Kundera nevertheless disregards the fact that the idea of the relativity of truth, which he considers to be central to the modern novel, presupposes the Romantic idea of individual subjectivity.

In some respect Kundera's ideas about the methods to be applied by the novelist recall the Enlightenment, especially the French Enlightenment, more than Romanticism. In speaking of his admiration for the literature of the French Enlightenment in *Slowness*, he remarks that what impresses him is not its hedonism as such, but the analytical mode in which it is discussed (8–9). An example occurs, for instance, in Denis Diderot's *Rameau's Nephew* (1774) which—along with another literary work greatly prized and often mentioned by Kundera, Choderlos de Laclos's *Dangerous Liaisons* (1782)—reveals the true motifs, thoughts, and attitudes of the lecherous upper class. In addition to hedonism, the literature of the Enlightenment examined other typical human attitudes: Diderot's *The Nun* (1796), for example, inquires not only into sensuality, but also into sadism, aggression, and superstition within the walls of a cloister. Although the analytical method in Kundera's works derives in the first place from his Central European "Pleiades" (see Steinby, "Ein mitteleuropäischer"), his analytical and critical attitude toward the object is shared by many of the authors of the French Enlightenment.

Kundera paid homage to the Enlightenment and especially to Diderot by adapting the latter's novel, *Jacques and His Master* (1796), for the stage. He rejects the notion of "adaptation" and prefers the musical notion "variation," a variation on Diderot's themes but by the same token an "homage to the principle of variation" applied in Diderot's novel, in which each of its three intertwined stories is actually a variation on the others (Kundera, *Jacques* 15–17; *Testaments* 77). The structure is similar to that of Kundera's novels, a composition which is free from the obligation to follow a single story and in which the author may any time interrupt the narration by reflections. What Kundera praises in Diderot's work is its playfulness, its nonserious, humorous, or ironic tone (*The Art* 24), a feature he also discovers in Cervantes, Rabelais, and Sterne. In addition, he is fascinated by the way in which Diderot depicts the effects of unpredictable events on human life; as in many of Kundera's novels, the title of Diderot's *Jacques le Fataliste et son maître* introduces the main theme through a negation in that the work actually challenges and ridicules fatalism. Among the writers of the French Enlightenment, Kundera also praises Voltaire, although less as a novelist than as a "caustic spirit." It is in this sense that Ludvík in *The Joke* is characterized by his fellows as "Voltairean" (see also *Testaments* 13; *The Book of Laughter* 123).

Kundera rarely speaks of the novel of the Romantic era. He mentions Novalis on a few occasions—in his view it was Novalis who introduced the dream into the novel, an innovation which was realized in its full potential by Kafka and García Márquez (*The Art* 81–82, 16; Biron 5)—and he refers to the novels of Victor Hugo as typical of nineteenth-century kitsch (Raddatz 107; *Testaments* 173). In general, Kundera finds that the German Romantics contributed little to the art of the novel: "turning away from the real world, [their fanciful imagining] was seeking after a different life" (*The Curtain* 73). There is one significant exception, Goethe, who for Kundera alone represents the achievement of the Romantic era in the field of the novel. Goethe, of course, did not consider himself a Romantic; on the contrary, he opposed the Romantics because of what he regarded as their excessive subjectivism. Although Kundera does not analyze any of Goethe's novels, we often encounter Goethe's name in his writings. In *Testaments Betrayed*, where Kundera gives a sweeping historical-geographical sketch of the development of the novel, Goethe occupies a prominent place: "First Italy with Boccaccio, the great precursor; then France with Rabelais, and Spain with Cervantes and the picaresque novel; the English novel in the eighteenth century and then, toward the century's end, the German contribution, with Goethe: the nineteenth century, which belonged almost entirely to France, along with the Russian novel in the last third, and, immediately thereafter, the arrival of the Scandinavian novel. Then the twentieth century and its Central European adventure with Kafka, Musil, Broch, and Gombrowicz" (28). In *The Art of the Novel*, Goethe's *The Sorrows of Young Werther* is presented as following Richardson in focusing on the inner life of the protagonist (24). In *The Book of Laughter and Forgetting*, the grand poet of the Czechs (most likely referring to the Nobel Laureate Jaroslav Seifert) is named "Goethe." Calling him and other Czech poets who take part in a "symposium" by names derived from the history of lyrical poetry is a playful gesture, not devoid of irony. In *Immortality*, the historical Goethe, with Bettina Brentano at his side, is the main character in one of the subplots. Here Bettina—as Kundera refers to her in his text—stands for everything negative that Romanticism signifies to Kundera, and since Goethe is the object of her plotting, the irony aimed at her falls partly upon him as well. Still, Kundera refers to Goethe as "a figure placed precisely in the centre of European history. Goethe: the great centre" (*Immortality* 84). What exactly is meant by this he does not explain.

One possible interpretation is that Kundera uses the figure of Goethe to distinguish between that which is invaluable to him in the literature and culture of the late eighteenth century—forming the very core of modernity—and that which is Romanticism (incarnated in Brentano), that is, modernity in a spurious, distorted form. The distinction is valid in the sense that Goethe was actually one of the first novelists to represent the unique experience of an individual without a moralizing schematism, like that of Richardson and even Fielding, or an interest in classifying individuals according to their characteristic oddities, like Sterne, but also one who rejected the Romantic idea of pursuing the Absolute through an individual's experience. In Goethe's conception, the individual's experience is perspective bound and nonabsolute and is subject to a constant process of reinterpretation (see Saariluoma [Steinby], *Erzählstruktur*). From what Kundera says of Goethe in *Immortality* and his other writings, however, we cannot with certainty conclude that he intends such a distinction.

Despite the fact that Kundera bestows upon Goethe the status of "the great center" of European history and recognizes Goethe's significance in the history of the novel, it is obvious that in his phenomenological understanding of the modern novel, Goethe does not play any important role. This implies that Kundera's novels stand only in a remote relation, if any, to those of Goethe. Goethe's significance is on a more general level: he represents the spirit of the modern era as a whole. This is certainly not an original idea; on the contrary, in the German and Central European cultural sphere Goethe has been commonly venerated as an icon of this kind. Thus, rather than speaking of discoveries which he himself has made in studying Goethe's novels, Kundera follows here the common view. Considering Goethe as a great novelist is probably a result of the reasoning that if Goethe epitomizes modern European culture and if it is the novel that lies at the very heart of European culture, it follows that Goethe must be a great novelist. Nevertheless, Goethe's importance for Kundera is in ideas concerning the modern individual rather than the history of the novel. I add that Kundera never ceases to temper his veneration of Goethe with playful, teasing, even mocking tones.

In addition to individualism, Kundera's Cervantes essay raises two further issues essential to his concept of the novel connected to Goethe and Romanticism, namely, the function of art in a modern world dominated by science and the historical nature of human existence. With regard to the function of art Kundera follows Goethe and the Romantics, while with regard to history he takes a different course.

Husserl and Heidegger were not the first to criticize the one-sidedness of scientific knowledge and the way modern society ignores the human life-world; on the contrary, already at the end of the eighteenth century criticism of this kind was not uncommon. The Romantics deplored the way in which the splitting of the sciences into narrow, specialized fields deprives the individual of a synthetic, all-inclusive view of the world (see Schmidt; Bürger, Bürger, and Schulte-Sasse). Schiller criticized his contemporaries for turning the individual into a small cog in a machine, a being ruled by external forces. Rather than encouraging human beings to develop their personality as a whole and valuing them as such, modern society expects its members to specialize and pursue their goals in a particular, narrowly defined professional field (Schiller 21). The arguments of Schiller and others conform to a great extent with certain recent views on the process of modernization. According to Niklas Luhmann, for instance, in the premodern class society the identity of an individual was determined by the class into which he or she was born, whereas in the modern society which emerged in the course of the eighteenth and early nineteenth century, individuals are identified functionally according to their occupations (both of these are unfavorable for the realization of Schiller's ideal of personality; see Luhmann, *Gesellschaftsstruktur*, e.g., 66, 155). This means that modern society recognizes only one part of the individual's humanity, namely his or her occupation (see, e.g., Luckmann 309). As Siegfried J. Schmidt puts it, "The individual acts in each of his different roles no more as a total subjectivity, but in abstract fragments only; i.e., the wholly differentiated social structure allow nothing more than fragments of individual destiny. . . . A person and his occupation fall apart" (69).

Goethe, Schiller, and the Romantics believed that art and literature could counteract this functionalization of the human being; we might say that they opposed human reification, had the term been used in their time. In accordance with their ideas, recent research on social modernization and the emergence of the modern institution of art has shown that at the turn of the nineteenth century a new role was ascribed to literature. The task of literature was to resist the fragmentation of reality and human beings by offering an all-encompassing view of the world and an opportunity for self-reflection. To quote Schmidt again, "The arts shall now reconcile what is separated and, as a kind of device that creates unity between individual and the world, theory and practice, reflection and morality, nature and liberty and, by doing this, so to say compensate the damages caused by the differentiation" (415). Obviously, literature took over this task in a situation in which religion had lost its position as the keystone of human action and our world view. As Luhmann puts it, religion now becomes merely one among other subsystems, whereas earlier it was a universally penetrating principle in all realms of social life (Luhmann, *Gesellschaftsstruktur* 295–357; see also Taylor 310).

Kundera's description of the task of the novel at the beginning of his Cervantes essay coincides to great extent with this view: the novel after "the death of God" resists the disappearance of a human perspective in experiencing the world, caused by the dominance of the natural scientific thinking. Moreover, in his essay on Broch in *The Art of the Novel*, Kundera explicitly takes up Broch's idea—reaching back to Romanticism (see Schlegel, *Athenäums-Fragmente* 114)—that the novel is a genre which strives toward totality: "In the age of the excessive division of labor, of runaway specialization, the novel is one of the last outposts where man can still maintain connections with life in its entirety" (67).

Nevertheless, Kundera's own novels can scarcely be said to strive toward the totality of life; rather, any such attempt is rejected by Kundera, who associates it with lyricism and ideology. Rather, what he considers vital is the never-ending search for and revelation of new dimensions of human existence. What is common to Kundera's thinking and the approach of the Romantics, however, is the conviction that the epistemological function of art is fulfilled through or along with its aesthetic function. Where the classical concept of literature postulated that art should teach universal, well-known truths in a pleasant form—a principle which goes back as far as Aristotle's *Poetics* and holds until eighteenth-century neoclassicism—for Kundera and the Romantics the role of art is to discern and reveal what has not yet been discovered. Beauty in art can only be achieved through truth: "Whatever aspects of existence the novel discovers, it discovers as the beautiful" (*The Art* 122). The connecting of the aesthetic with the cognitive function in art brings Kundera close to Heidegger, who in his philosophy of art relied on the Romantics, especially Hölderlin (see Heidegger, *The Origin*, *Erläuterungen*).

History and adventure

In one crucial issue, the significance of history, Kundera's concept of modernity and the novel as its core deviates from what has commonly been assumed since the late eighteenth century. In a certain sense, Kundera defines the novel as a negation of historical thinking, which arose at the same time as the modern concept of the individual at the turn of the eighteenth century. The idea of the historical nature of human existence and the optimistic nineteenth-century philosophy of history and nationalist way of thinking constitute the background against which Kundera, in *The Art of the Novel* and in later writings, elaborates his own, divergent views on the novel and its history.

When eighteenth-century thinkers started to envisage the human being as an autonomous subject of cognition and action, they also discovered history as the domain of human actions. The world opened up toward the future, which seemed to be something to be built up by human effort (see, e.g., Koselleck). Beginning with the Enlightenment, philosophers began to think of history as an opportunity given to human beings to harness nature so as to satisfy their needs and to find the best possible ways to organize society and to educate the individual. According to this train of thought, history as a human achievement takes over the function of the eternal, divine order of the universe. From the early nineteenth century onward, historical research and the philosophy of history—whose purpose is to discover the inescapable, inner logic of historical developments—replaced theological and metaphysical truth.

The individual's embeddedness in history is not in conflict with his or her individuality; on the contrary, at the end of the eighteenth century the two were conceived as inherently interconnected. According to Herder and Goethe, human beings, in all their individuality, are part of history. In Herder's view, the mode of our experiences and actions is determined by our particular culture and historical situation. In his autobiography, *Truth and Poetry,* Goethe presents an entire historical period through the life story of a single representative individual (see also Jannidis; Meinecke; Müller). The individual is both shaped by and creates history. From the early nineteenth century onward the idea of human existence as historical and as taking part in history refers mainly to national history. In the wake of the Napoleonic wars, nationalist thinking spread across Europe; history was thought to be realized through nations (see, e.g., Hobsbawm). A commitment to the nation gives life a meaning which transcends the meaning of individual existence. What is more, by working for his or her nation the individual participates in the progress of the history of mankind. Hegel and Marx, the most prominent representatives of the nineteenth-century philosophy of history, conceived of this progress as a gradual realization of human freedom.

In the interview with Liehm in 1966, Kundera's stance on the individual's historical existence follows the main line of European thought. What is more, he explicitly connects this historical view of the individual with the blossoming of the novel since the beginning of the nineteenth century: "When man lacks any eternal substance but is, to say it in a Hegelian way, a product of his own activity in history, the literary genre that is most capable of grasping him as such is the novel" (Liehm, Interview 107). However, in Kundera's later view, as presented in his novels and essays, history is no longer a realm within which we create ourselves or within which human freedom is realized; rather, it is a domain of external compulsions. Now he claims that the novel does not explore our historical existence but the ahistorical, anthropological possibilities which are left to us in spite of history. The events of a narrative plot might be set in a historical context; nevertheless, the novel's purpose is not to elucidate history itself, but to inquire into the universal, ahistorical possibilities of human existence which appear in a particular historical situation. History is a kind of "une situation existential en agrandissement" (*L'Art* 53; "magnified existential situation"). A human possibility which appears in the life of an individual may during a particular historical period be realized on a larger scale, at the level of a whole society or nation (see also Finkielkraut 39). History can, for example, demonstrate that being a killer exists among human possibilities, and it is precisely these human possibilities that interest Kundera: "So the anthropological question—the question of what man is capable of—is always there [in his novels] behind the political [or historical] one" (McEwan 33).

Thus, Kundera has made the move from history to anthropology, to the study of the individual's existential possibilities as revealed but not created by history. Yet Kundera does not deny human freedom: the individual makes choices even under conditions in which history exerts the severest constraints upon him. Here Kundera's thinking exhibits a resemblance to Existentalism. Kundera, however, would not place himself in this context. He has articulated his antipathy, not to existential philosophy as such, but to the manner in which in the novels of Camus and Sartre the philosophy precedes the work, the novel acting merely as an illustration of preconceived philosophical ideas (du Plessix Gray 48; Oppenheim 9). In the existential analysis of his novels, he instead considers himself as a follower of his Central European "Pleiades."

In contrast to history, which imposes constraints upon the individual and restricts our freedom, the history of art represents for Kundera a realm in which human freedom can be truly realized. In *Testaments Betrayed* he writes:

> Here I am making a declaration of involvement in the history of the novel, when all my novels breathe a hatred of history, of that hostile, inhuman force that—uninvited, unwanted—invades our lives from the outside and destroys them. Yet there is nothing inconsistent in this double attitude, because the history of humanity and the history of the novel are two different things. The former is not man's to determine, it takes over like an alien force he cannot control, whereas the history of the novel (or of painting, of music) is born of man's freedom, of his wholly personal creations, of his own choices. (15–16)

For Kundera, History—which he occasionally spells with the capital H to refer to the process of world history or the history of nations—does not actually confer on human beings the mastery of the world, or grant us the ability to change it so as to better meet our needs and wishes. History is not human made, but appears as an external force which intrudes into the life of the individual and the whole nation and subjugates or even destroys them. Freedom, if possible at all, can be realized through the individual's choices and actions not within History, but only outside it. Such realms of freedom include in Kundera's view the novel and art in general.

While History does not determine what we as human beings are, it sets limits on us by reducing our freedom to certain existential possibilities. In addition, where in the mid-1960s Kundera found that at the beginning of the nineteenth century history opened up new possibilities for the individual, he now—twenty years later—sees the matter in exactly the opposite way: the closer we approach our own time, the tighter becomes the grip of History. This idea is propounded in the following passage in the Cervantes essay, where Kundera outlines certain stages of the history of the novel:

> Don Quixote set off into a world that opened wide before him. He could go out freely and come home as he pleased. The early European novels are journeys through an apparently unlimited world. The opening of *Jacques le Fataliste* comes upon the two heroes in mid-journey; we don't know where they've come from or where they're going. They exist in a time without beginning or end, in a space without frontiers, in the midst of a Europe whose future will never end. Half a century after Diderot, in Balzac, the distant horizon has disappeared like a landscape behind those modern structures, the social institutions: the police, the law, the world of money and crime, the army, the State. In Balzac's world, time no longer idles happily by as it does for Cervantes and Diderot. It has set forth on the train called History. The train is easy to board, hard to leave. But it isn't at all fearsome yet, it even has its appeal; it promises adventure to every passenger, and with it fame and fortune. Later still, for Emma Bovary, the horizon shrinks to the point of seeming a barrier. Adventure lies beyond it, and the longing becomes intolerable. Within the monotony of the quotidian, dreams and daydreams take on importance. The lost infinity of the outside world is replaced by the infinity of the soul. The great illusion of the irreplaceable uniqueness of the individual—one of Europe's finest illusions—blossoms forth. (*The Art* 8)

Here Kundera expresses a pessimistic conception of History which is the opposite of the Enlightenment or liberalist belief in historical progress and of Hegel's and Marx's philosophies of history, where his process of history advances not toward greater but lesser freedom. As a genre rooted in freedom, the novel voices the escalating lack of it. Although not entirely independent of History, the novel thus works against its force and attempts to escape it by seeking and exploring the existential possibilities of human life.

What is essential in Kundera's conception of the "legacy of Cervantes" is the setting out for adventure. Kundera's comments on *Don Quixote* in the Cervantes essay lack any reference to the fact that the novel parodies the incredible adventures encountered by the knights of chivalric romances on their wanderings (see, however, *The Curtain* 6). In fact, he never tells us how he understands adventure in the pre-Cervantean novel. However, the fact that he ascribes the "discovery" of adventure to Cervantes indicates that he is using the word in a quite specific sense. We have to ask what Kundera actually means here by "adventure," and why he regards its discovery as the birth of the modern genre of the novel.

Adventure, of course, was an essential constituent in the early novel, from the Greek novels of love and adventure of the first centuries AD to the chivalric, pastoral, and picaresque novels of the Renaissance. Yet adventure in this sense has no connection with the ambiguity of the world discussed by Kundera at the beginning of his Cervantes essay. Rather, one might argue that in its original sense, adventure exemplifies precisely an undisputed and unchallenged metaphysical order to the world. The primary purpose of adventures in the novels of late antiquity and in chivalric romances was to entertain the reader, with the secondary aim, by means of an exemplary story, of teaching a moral lesson. Adventures serve as a trial of the knight's integrity or of the constancy of the prince and princess, who have to overcome a series of hardships in order to be reunited in love. In the comic picaresque novel the hero's adventures confront him with the deceitfulness and baseness of the world, from which at the end he withdraws. Thus, adventures exemplify the already established and accepted truths about the world. The prevailing worldview is not called into question; adventures are unexpected only with regard to the occurrence of particular events but do not open up any new perspectives in the experience of the world (see, e.g., Bakhtin, "Forms of Time").

In speaking of Cervantes's "discovery" of adventure, Kundera is using the term in a specific sense to refer to the characteristic modern mode of human existence. He claims that the modern individual is given no eternal, indubitable truth concerning the essence of the world, but any knowledge about the actual world has to be won piece by piece in the course of experiencing the world. Thus, the adventures of modern individuals do not in their content repeat any eternal, pregiven truth. "Adventure" for Kundera actually means an encounter with the new and unknown, an openness toward something that does not belong to any known order of things. What Cervantes "discovers" is thus not adventure in the conventional sense of the word. Originally used to denote something temporary, transitory, and episodic, an "adventure" in this new sense contributes something to one's view of the world or of human beings. In claiming that adventure has been the grand theme during the "four centuries of the European novel" (*The Art* 5), Kundera uses the term in precisely this sense, to refer to the process-like or open nature of encountering reality.

Kundera claims that by discovering adventure in this specific sense Cervantes established the modern tradition of the novel. He enumerates other novelists who made further significant discoveries; in fact, the history of the novel in Kundera's view consists of a series of successive discoveries (6). Richardson unveils the inner life of the individual; Balzac examines how the individual is determined by history; Flaubert discovers everyday life and depicts "the infinity of the soul," which replaces the lost infinity of the external world—in *The Curtain* (127) we are told that Flaubert discovered stupidity "as an indissociable part of 'human nature'"; and Tolstoy explores the irrational in human action (*The Art* 5–9, 57). Although according to Kundera the horizon of adventure starts to shrink already with Balzac, he still considers all novelists down to Kafka or Fuentes—or himself—as adventurers in the sense of being explorers of new realms of being. Yet, as it was Cervantes who discovered adventure as the exploration of the unknown, his discovery is not just one among others. We could call it the "arch-discovery," although Kundera himself does not use this term, in that it opens up the domain within which the subsequent discoveries of other novelists take place.

Kundera does not look for a historical explanation as to why it was precisely Cervantes who discovered adventure or why, as he thinks, this happened in the early seventeenth century. Cervantes's invention takes place outside History insofar as it cannot be traced back to any historical circumstances. Kundera is inclined to think of Cervantes as one of the creators of the modern era, rather than being himself a product of his time. In a way, the arch-discovery of adventure is an act of resisting and transcending History. The history of the novel takes place outside History, in the realm of the novelist's freedom to explore human existence. In fact, in Kundera's view the history of the novel embodies a "counter-history" of European humankind; or, as he puts it in *Testaments Betrayed*, a "revenge on History itself" (15). It is the history of human freedom, which Kundera considers much more significant than the uncontrollable History that has trampled on Europe, that subdues individuals and nations. The history of the novel is not a product of History, but it has substantially, as culture, contributed to the shaping of human history. In Kundera's view, the novel has profoundly affected the spiritual formation of the European individual (see Raddatz 105), who is unthinkable without the novel that created him or her (Weiss 407). In Kundera's view, History and the history of the novel are contrasting entities corresponding to the opposites of necessity and freedom, of History and adventure.

The contemporary world against the novel and the novel against its history

When Kundera declares that the legacy of Cervantes has long been "depreciated," he means two things. First, he is claiming that a Europe oriented toward science and technology has neglected the novel, which in fact constitutes its cultural core. Since Europe is unaware of its own identity, the significance of the process whereby the world has become incompatible with the novel has remained generally unrecognized. Second, Kundera is suggesting that novelists themselves have left the possibilities of the genre to a large extent unexploited.

According to Kundera, the incompatibility between the world and the novel has constantly increased. Where Cervantes's or Diderot's heroes are free to go wherever they like and return when they wish, in Balzac's novels freedom starts to diminish as social institutions and historical processes begin to limit the horizon. In Kafka's works the world has already turned into a trap. By trap Kundera means a world in which human beings are no longer allowed to live as they wish. To counter the loss of the infinity of the external world, the nineteenth century set up the infinity of the soul, but in a world turned into a trap this is no longer of any use: the protagonist of Kafka's *The Trial* cannot even daydream, as once Flaubert's Emma Bovary did: "No, the situation's trap is too terrible, and like a vacuum cleaner it sucks up all his thoughts and feelings: all he can think of is his trial and his surveying job. The infinity of the soul—if it ever existed—has become a nearly useless appendage" (*The*

Art 9). When History manages to grasp us and deprives us of all our freedom of action, adventure becomes impossible:

> What is *adventure* if a K.'s freedom of action is completely illusory? What is *future* if the intellectuals of *The Man Without Qualities* have not the slightest inkling of the war that will sweep their lives away the next day? What is *crime* if Broch's Huguenau not only does not regret but actually forgets the murder he has committed? And if the only great comic novel of the period, Hašek's *Schweik*, uses war as its setting, then what has happened to the *comic*? Where is the difference between *public* and *private* if K., even in bed with a woman, is never without the two emissaries of the Castle? And in that case, what is *solitude*? A burden, a misery, a curse, as some would have us believe, or on the contrary, a supremely precious value in the process of being crushed by the ubiquitous collectivity? (*The Art* 12-13)

The arc of the history of the novel is thus tilted; and this is closely connected with History's ever tightening grasp, proving that eventually not even the novel will be able to escape the constraints of History. Indeed, this is what the twentieth century witnessed: Kundera calls the age of Kafka, Musil, Broch, Hašek, and Gombrowicz the era of "*terminal paradoxes*" (*The Art* 12). In the last moment before its disappearance, the novel reveals the human condition in which the novel becomes impossible. Kundera includes himself in this final stage of the history of the novel, just before it becomes extinct.

For Kundera, History entered the stage in the nineteenth century. In the beginning, "the train called history" seemed to promise new adventures (*The Art* 8), but the twentieth century changed its appearance. Ever since World War I it has been clear that it is impossible to escape History. The situation became further aggravated during World War II and afterwards, when Central Europe fell under Russian hegemony and "for the first time in its modern history" (11) a great part of Europe was amputated. For Kundera, the death of modern Europe also meant a death sentence for the novel. In the Soviet Union and the communist-ruled Central European countries a great number of works called novels were published, but "these novels add[ed] nothing to the conquest of being" (14) and consequently did not perform the function of the genre. Rather than exploring the unknown, they merely repeat and reinforce that which already exists: "By discovering nothing, they fail to participate in the *sequence of discoveries* that for me constitutes the history of the novel; they place themselves *outside* that history, or, if you like: they are *novels that come after the history of the novel*" (14). The novel as the core of modern Europe is thus shown to be mortal: "And we now know how the novel dies: it's not that it disappears; its history stops: after that comes nothing but a period of repetition in which the novel keeps duplicating its form, emptied of its spirit" (15).

In the Cervantes essay Kundera describes the death of the novel from the perspective of his Czechoslovak experiences. When he wrote the essay he was already in France, which means that moving to the West did not change his views as to the incompatibility between the contemporary world and the novel, or even as to the world turned into a trap. Kundera came to realize that even in the West the intellectual atmosphere is not—or at least, as he believes, is no longer—favorable to the novel. In his view we have been caught in a "*whirlpool of reduction*" (*The Art* 17), driven by the media: "they distribute throughout the world the same simplifications and stereotypes easily acceptable by the greatest number, by everyone, by all mankind" (18). We find ourselves in a world where everybody has "the same view of life, reflected in the same ordering of the table of contents, under the same headings, in the same journalistic phrasing, the same vocabulary, and the same style, in the same artistic tastes, and in the same ranking of things they deem important or insignificant" (18). The simplifying and leveling spirit of the mass media which dominates our contemporary society is in Kundera's opinion contrary to the spirit of the novel: "The novel's spirit is the spirit of complexity. Every novel says to the reader: 'Things are not as simple as you think'" (18). The novel is dead, through failing to continue to discover the yet unknown; it has placed itself outside its own history and turned into what Kundera calls "the endless babble of graphomaniacs" (19). While he criticizes philosophers of history not only for their trust in progress but also for their belief that a pattern or inner logic can be discerned in History, Kundera here draws a line for History—a pessimistic one. The Modern Era, he claims, begins with the individual setting out on a series of adventures and ends up with him or her being entrapped, deprived of freedom. The history of the novel, like an arc spanning through four centuries, preserves "safe as in a treasure chest" (*The Art* 165) the history of the modern European individual and his or her intellectual adventures—a history which is now about to come to an end.

Kundera's pessimistic vision is no less prone to criticism than the optimistic Enlightenment view of history. For instance, one might argue that Balzac does not depict a narrowing down of the space for adventure, but rather a world which promises more freedom and which is opening up to more individual initiative. The new bourgeois, capitalist society portrayed in Balzac's novels allows much greater social mobility than the ancien régime ever did, enabling the individual to make choices and to take control of his or her own life. One explanation for Kundera's perception of the nineteenth century as gradually imposing more and more constraints may be the fact that in the literature of the nineteenth century—above all Balzac's novels—the social mechanisms which force the individual to conform are portrayed more vividly than ever before. As a consequence of fundamental changes in the society, these mechanisms have now become visible, whereas earlier the social structure regulated the life of the individual in an unquestioned, self-evident, and therefore inconspicuous way. In other words, increased understanding of the functioning of society and a more acute analysis of the constraints it imposes on the individual may make those constraints more prominent, even though individual freedom has actually increased. One might also challenge Kundera's view of historical development having taken a course unfavorable to the novel. We may doubt whether there has ever been an era of European history in which plurality, relativity, and complexity of truths was the dominant view. What are, then, the reasons for Kundera's pessimism, and how does it impact upon his novelistic work? And what options, in his view, are available to the individual in a world turned into a trap?

For Kundera, the "depreciation" of the legacy of Cervantes also means that some aspects of the potential of the novel have remained unexploited. He claims that the history of the novel embraces several discoveries which have fallen into oblivion or remained generally unexplored. The title of his second essay collection, *Testaments Betrayed*, echoes this idea and reflects its crucial importance in his thinking. Has not the genre of the novel failed to fulfill its freedom, since its history recalls "a cemetery of missed opportunities, of unheard appeals" (*The Art* 15)? In the Cervantes essay Kundera enumerates four such appeals: the appeals of play, dream, thought, and time, possibilities that are opened up in some remarkable novels from the sixteenth to the eighteenth century: "Afterward, the novel got itself tied to the imperative of verisimilitude, to realistic settings, to chronological order" (15).

In several of his later writings, Kundera contrasts the "first half-time" in the history of the modern novel, the period from Rabelais to Sterne and Laclos, with the "second half-time," which includes nineteenth-century realism, starting with authors such as Walter Scott and Balzac ("On Criticism" 14; *Encounter* 439; "Esch Is Luther" 270; *Testaments Betrayed* 57; see also Gambarota 48–49; Maixent 2; Oppenheim 8–9). He often expresses his enthusiasm for the novels of the first half-time for their nonseriousness, their irony and playfulness, their freedom of composition, and their liberty to interrupt the narrative by the author's reflections. These opportunities were lost under the severe regime of the realist conventions of the nineteenth-century novel. In Kundera's view, the norms of realism imposed great limitations upon the novel. He refers to this established set of norms as "the long tradition of psychological realism" (*The Art* 33). The restrictive conventions, which gained the status of "inviolable standards," were the following: "(1) A writer must give the maximum amount of information about a character: about his physical appearance, his way of speaking and behaving; (2) he must let the reader know a character's past, because that is where all the motives for his present behaviour are located; and (3) the character must have complete independence; that is to say, the author with his own considerations must disappear so as not to disturb the reader, who wants to give himself over to illusion and take fiction for reality" (33–34).

In the modernism which comes after the second half-time, the brief period of the "post-Proustian novel" which Kundera also calls (paradoxically) the "third half-time" in the history of the novel, authors such as Kafka, Broch, Musil, Gombrowicz, García Márquez, and Fuentes take up possibilities offered in the novels of the first half-time (Oppenheim 8–9; *Testaments* 72–75). Kafka restores the dream to the novel (*The Art* 16, 81; *Testaments* 48) and assumes a manner of writing which "breaks the plausibility barriers," as does García Márquez, who names Kafka his predecessor and model (*Testaments* 50–51). Musil and Broch, in turn, restore authorial reflection to the novel, making of it a "supreme intellectual synthesis" (*The Art* 16). In the Cervantes essay Kundera writes that the issue of time is still waiting to be expanded beyond the possibilities of Proustian personal memory to embrace collective time, "the time of Europe," enabling Europe to come to grips with its own history (16). In *Testaments Betrayed* he contends that Fuentes has contributed to the inquiry of collective time and that in *Terra nostra*, Fuentes grasped the essence of the Mexican *terra* "in the form of a dream novel where various historical periods telescope into a kind of poetic and oneiric metahistory" (14).

Kundera's discussion of these neglected but later rediscovered and rehabilitated possibilities of the novel suggests that even in a world turned into a trap the novel might still have some freedom of choice, if it only knew how to make use of it. The "unheard appeals" Kundera describes are possibilities that are exploited again after the period of realism; or, more accurately, in the "post-Proustian" period (suggesting that Proust and Joyce did not actually abandon the "long tradition of psychological realism"). In his own novels Kundera avoids descriptions which serve merely to enhance the illusion of reality. The reader is rarely informed about the characters' pasts, and the narrator feels free to interrupt the narration with his own contemplations and reflections, traits that signify his allegiance to the post-Proustian third half-time of the novel (e.g., *Testaments* 75). In *Testaments Betrayed* he sketches a similar three-stage development in the history of music, and concludes by expressing his attachment to the third phase in the histories of both arts: "I am deeply, passionately fond of that third period, that 'sky ablaze at the end of the day,' fond of that period which I believe I myself am part of, even if I am part of something that is already finished" (75).

If we read Kundera's essay on the legacy of Cervantes as a study in the history of the novel, we have to admit that he enjoys freedoms that befit a novelistic writer of essays. Yet, as noted earlier, it is not my intention to evaluate Kundera's achievement as a literary historian, but to consider the essay, along with his later writings on the same subject, as an attempt to construct a history of the novel that gives credence to his own oeuvre. Highlighting certain important points in the course of the history of the novel, he is aiming at a phenomenology of the novel, that is, at a definition of its essence, which can serve as the basis of his own poetics of the novel. There is nothing unusual about an author refraining from becoming absorbed in the "otherness" of other writers' work and instead choosing his own predecessors so that the course of history leads up to his own work—an idea that was made popular by Borges's essay on Kafka and his precursors. A singular feature in Kundera's conception, however, is his radical dissociation from the historical thinking which is characteristic of the modernity of the last two centuries—except with regard to the internal history of the novel. Before we proceed with our discussion of Kundera's understanding of the novel by comparing it to novelists close to him, let us therefore look at his first novel, *The Joke*, which brings to the surface certain crucial circumstances concerning Kundera's hostility toward history.

Chapter Three
Falling Out of History

Kundera acknowledges in retrospect that the theme of lightness, later developed especially in *The Unbearable Lightness of Being*, appears already in *The Joke*, and he wonders whether it is the case with novelists in general that the same basic themes recur throughout their work (*The Art* 136–37). In fact, most of the recurrent principal themes of Kundera's later works are already present in *The Joke*: the antagonism between body and soul, the opposition between the particular and the universal, the themes of lyricism, sentimentalism, falling and vertigo, lightness, "ultimate beauty," the idea of the individual as the constructor of his or her own image, the ugliness of the modern world, the idea of disengagement of the act from the agent's intentions, history as a playground for the immature, and forgetting as an anthropological constant. Actually, several of his most important themes occur already in the short stories of *Laughable Loves* (see Chvatik, *Die Fallen* 21, 64, 65, 80), such as the combinations of love and ridicule and of laughter and seriousness which can suddenly be reversed. The individual's efforts to control events and the ensuing failure are one of the main themes in "Nobody Will Laugh" as well as in "I, the Sad God," Kundera's first short story, which was omitted from the Western edition of *Laughable Loves* (see Woods, *Translating* 76–77). The problem of personal identity is a central theme in several stories, for instance, "The Hitchhiking Game." The story "Eduard and God" deals with the difficulty of finding significance in one's life and actions under oppressive conditions, which determine how one is allowed to act and think and even decide one's profession. In such circumstances significance is sought in the realm of private life, where free choices are to some extent still possible, but even there finding it is difficult.

A comparison between the short stories of *Laughable Loves* and Kundera's later works is rewarding not only on the thematic level but also with regard to the various narrative techniques which Kundera "rehearses" in the short stories and later utilizes in his novels (see Chvatik, *Die Fallen* 21, 51). The "natural" introduction to Kundera's art of the novel, however, is of course his first novel, *The Joke*. The themes which remain important in his novelistic oeuvre—those which are to be considered as his contribution to the novelistic discoveries of man's existential possibilities—are displayed here in a historical setting, which facilitates their comprehension by the reader. *The Joke* also offers access to Kundera's art of novelistic composition. While the narrative mode and structure of *The Joke* are atypical of Kundera and less original than those of his later works, an analysis of the novel allows us to identify certain Kunderan principles of constructing a novel *in statu nascendi* and to understand where they come from. All this is connected with the main objective of this chapter, which is to elucidate the motives and reasoning which prompted Kundera to assume an "anthropological" way of thinking and a pessimistic view of History (on Kundera and history, see also Ivanova).

From the collective to the private, from History to anthropology

The chain of events which takes place in the present of the novel is condensed so as to cover a single weekend, but in a series of retrospective reminiscences the narrative conveys essential elements in the life of the protagonist and to a lesser extent of three or four other characters. Ludvik's story is told largely through his own narration, but skillfully intertwined with it is the first-person narration of three of his acquaintances, explicating his story from different points of view. On the whole the novel is not elliptic, unlike Kundera's later works, in which everything that is thematically irrelevant is omitted. *The Joke* can be characterized as representative of "realist modernism" or "modern realism" (see, e.g., Cravens 106; Lodge 143; Němcová Banerjee, *Terminal* 11; Porter 39), spanning the period from, say, William Faulkner to Saul Bellow and Heinrich Böll. On the one hand, the narration does not spare concrete realistic details and places events in a specific historical and geographical setting; on the other hand, unlike the typical nineteenth-century realist novel, it does not proceed in chronological order and employs the technique of shifting perspective. The point-of-view technique and the complex temporal structures became distinctive features of the modernist novel that emerged in the first half of the twentieth century. In the modernist novel, events are always experienced by someone, and it makes a difference who that character is. Moreover, events are not automatically integrated into the story, which has to be constructed with events brought together so as to form a significant whole. In other words, the experienced reality is no longer the same for everybody, and the story requires acts of arranging, combining, and interpreting events.

Ludvik Jahn had been a devoted communist who, following the revolution of 1948, participated actively in the building of a socialist Czechoslovakia. His story goes back to the moment when his life was changed by a postcard. He sent the card to his girlfriend, who was spending her summer vacation at a communist summer camp, in Ludvik's view wasting the only time they could have devoted to each other. Tormented by the frustration he felt because of her absence, he expresses his irritation over her letter "that was pure Marketa: full of earnest enthusiasm for everything around her; she liked everything: the early-morning calisthenics, the talks, the discussions, even the songs they sang; she praised the 'healthy atmosphere' that reigned there; and diligently she added a few words to the effect that the revolution in the

West would not be long in coming" (32; unless quoted otherwise, references are to the final edition of 1992). Merely to "hurt, shock and confuse her," he writes on an open postcard: "Optimism is the opium of the people! A healthy atmosphere stinks of stupidity! Long live Trotsky! Ludvik" (32). To Ludvik's misfortune, the card is read in a different discursive code from that in which it was written (see Chvatík, "Milan Kundera and the Crisis" 29, "Milan Kundera als Übersetzer" 153): those who read the card do not see a joke in it. Misunderstanding in communication, which is so typical of all of Kundera's works, has in this case fatal consequences (see, e.g., Draper 72–74; Richterová). The post-1948 period was an age of official optimism and cheerfulness, yet it lacked any sense of humor. Joking or doubting in the Voltairean spirit was foreign to this era "of great collective faith," as Ludvik's friend Kostka puts it (224). Ludvik is stigmatized as an enemy of the working class and expelled from the communist party and the university. He then has to do military service in a penal battalion, followed by several years working in a coalmine. An account of his years in the penal battalion is given in retrospective first-person narration, while the events in the present revolve around Ludvik's plan to take his revenge on his former party comrade Pavel Zemanek, who more than anyone else he considers responsible for the tragic turn his life took fifteen years earlier.

For the reader familiar with the main events of Kundera's past, it is not difficult to discover similarities between his life and the protagonist's, such as their commitment to the cause of socialism after the revolution of 1948 and their casting out from the party owing to the intolerance of mockery. However, Kundera argues that any attempt to interpret the oeuvre of a novelist in terms of his life is preposterous and contrary to the novelist's intentions (*The Art* 145–46). This kind of psychological explanation invalidates the truth claim of the novel: truth meant to be relevant to human beings in general is reduced to truth which concerns a single person only. Nevertheless, is not the assumption of a significant connection between Kundera's experience and the content of his works entirely consistent with his view that truths in a novel are always perspectival? Moreover, if he has arrived at his general conclusions as to History, human beings, and the world on the basis of particular experiences—is not experience necessarily particular?—this is no reason why one should not take them seriously or suspect their validity. In my view, following Kundera's path starting with his experiences and ending with his general statements can help us understand the latter.

According to Kundera, *The Joke* is no more a historical or political novel than any of his other novels. Scholars of Czech literature and history, however, maintain that *The Joke* should be studied in relation to Czech history despite Kundera's insistence that for him contemporary Czech history serves as a mere source of materials through which he explores human existence (*The Art* 35–44; see also Doležel; Jungmann; Matejka; Porter; Steiner, "Ironies," "Justice," *The Deserts*). Since the art of the novel is a realm of freedom apart from History, it is in principle wrong to see in the novel an expression of a historical era (see *Testaments* 15–16). However, I argue that Kundera as a novelist is not as independent of History as he claims in that his views of humanity and history have been shaped by his personal historical experience. To put it in the form of a paradox, his denial of individuals' historical existence has historical reasons. This is to say that he does not escape History even when he chooses to found his views about humanity on anthropology rather than history.

In fact, the very idea that history had revealed unexpected human possibilities was the common experience of Czech intellectuals in the 1960s. In an account of the atmosphere shortly before and after 1968, Václav Havel described the experience of having faced completely different modes of existence within a relatively short period of time. What to Kundera appears the anthropological truth of human existence is described by Havel as experience derived from contemporary history:

> None of us know all the potentialities that slumber in the spirit of the population, or all the ways in which that population can surprise us when there is the right interplay of events, both visible and invisible. Who would have believed—at a time when the Novotný regime was corroding away because the entire nation was behaving like Švejks—that half a year later that same society would display a genuine civic-mindedness, and that a year later this recently apathetic, sceptical, and demoralized society would stand up with such courage and intelligence to a foreign power! And who would have suspected that, after scarcely a year had gone by, this same society would, as swiftly as the wind blows, lapse back into a state of demoralization far deeper than its original one! After all these experiences, one must be very careful about coming to any conclusions about the way we are, or what can be expected of us. (*Disturbing* 109)

Kundera does not hide the fact that his vision of History as a playground for the immature has its origin in his experience of the Czech revolution. Kundera is not alone in considering this as a revolution of youth; on the contrary, it was in fact the older generation's failure to consolidate a democratic society before World War II that opened up the field for an effort by the very young to establish a new kind of society (see Liehm, *Trois générations* 16–21). The generalization that revolutions in general are an undertaking of the young, however, stems from Kundera alone. His conviction that a mature person should comprehend that History is beyond human control derives from his experience as a young revolutionary, one who participated in the building of a communist future and became bitterly disappointed. Havel identifies this disappointment as the key to Kundera's later skepticism: "Complete skepticism [concerning politics and history] is a psychologically understandable consequence of discovering that one's enthusiasms were based on illusion" (*Disturbing* 177). Consequently, after this experience Kundera seeks freedom of action only outside History, in private life and in the realm of art. His conviction that the individual preserves some freedom even under the harshest constraints thus originates from a political context, not from his study of Sartre and existentialism, as is sometimes supposed. The similarities between the existentialism of the 1950s and Kundera's worldview may result from a similar experience of spiritual-cultural depression and the sense of being crushed by the events that followed both World War II and the crumbling of the ideals of revolutionary youth.

A friend from Ludvik's youth, Jaroslav, recalls that after 1948 Ludvik had "the look all Communists had at the time. As if he'd made a secret pact with the future and had thereby acquired the right to act in its name" (*The Joke* 139). His Marxist worldview led Ludvik to believe that he knew what the future would bring and dedicated his actions to serve the fulfillment of History. His expulsion from the party, however, shatters his pact with the future and his life is thrown off the path of History. Yet Ludvik's destiny is not the only thread in *The Joke* through which the loss of History as the individual's home and sphere of action is followed. In *Testaments Betrayed* Kundera remarks that in *The Joke* he depicts in the four characters who function as focalizers in the narration four modes of communist ideology, derived from four European heritages: "Ludvik: the communism that springs from the caustic Voltairean spirit; Jaroslav: communism as the desire to reconstruct the patriarchal past that is preserved in folklore; Kostka: communist utopia grafted onto the Gospel; Helena: communism as the wellspring of enthusiasm in a homo sentimentalis" (*Testaments* 13).

Ludvik represents the intellectual and critical "Enlightenment" line of communist ideology. This intellectual and critical attitude he shares with the implied author of *The Joke*. For the reader this is the attitude of Kundera himself as he appears in all of his books, and he demands the same intellectual and critical attitude of other novelists. Kundera considers the concept of the narrator, as distinguished from the real author, as unnecessary, a "phantom of literary theory," not to mention the concept of the implied author (see Parnell 148); it is he himself who speaks in his novels (Vibert, "Milan Kundera" 111). He sees Marxism as representing the critical and self-critical spirit of the Enlightenment, yet under communist rule all forms of criticism were banned. Instead of pursuing intellectual and critical analysis, the dominant attitude turned out to be an emotional identification with the ideal society as well as with the group that was supposed to fulfill this ideal.

Kostka, the Christian communist, claims that the attitude of young people in 1948 and after was more religious than intellectual and that communist ideology was a sort of collective faith that demanded sacrificing individual interests for common goals: "A man who kept in step with this era experienced feelings that were akin to religious ones: he renounced his ego, his person, his private life in favor of something higher, something suprapersonal" (224). However, Kostka finds that the lack of God at the very core of the movement was a weakness that jeopardized its future: "What a pity that it was incapable of taking its religious self-knowledge through to the ultimate conclusion. It had religious gestures and feelings but remained empty and godless within" (225). The quasi-religious attitude was characteristic of the young Ludvik as well, yet he preserves a certain independence of mind, and it is precisely this that eventually causes his catastrophe. The other types of young communists have succeeded in relinquishing their own selves and merging with the collective ideal more completely than he has.

The tension between intellectualism and emotional collectivism in the communist movement is presented on several occasions. The young Ludvik created a picture of a future collective life, one in which people would be connected with each other "by a host of rituals," both old ones, such as traditional seasonal festivals, and new ones, such as May Day celebrations (141). In the present of the novel, the mature Ludvik observes the ritual of the "*welcoming of new citizens to life*," created to supplant the baptismal ceremony (172). The account of the event is accurate but immersed in a delicate irony. In a discussion with Jaroslav, Ludvik criticizes another case of quasi-religious myth making, namely, the way in which Julius Fučík has been turned into an icon of the communists' heroic struggle (154–56), an icon that, as Peter Steiner remarks, contains Christological parallels (*The Deserts* 20). This means that Kundera, through his protagonist, is now criticizing the myth-making process to which he himself as a young poet, the author of *The Last May*, contributed (see Steiner, *The Deserts* 22; Woods, *Translating* 95). Yet, despite his criticism of this deliberate creation of emotionally powerful myths and rituals, Ludvik is enthralled by some forms of traditional collective culture, especially folk music.

Jaroslav represents in the novel the synthesis of two collectivisms, communism and folk culture. Moravian folklore and especially Moravian folk music offer him the possibility of being absorbed into something greater than the individual life. Jaroslav's experience is a typical experience of Romantic de-individuation (most adequately expressed in a passage not included in the "final" English translation): "We heard the folk songs and we suddenly saw that they were the most essential of essentials. I consecrated my life to them. Through them I merge with the stream which flows deep below. I am a wave of this stream. I am both the wave and the river. And I like it" (*The Joke* [1969] 127). This is the experience of the dissolving of the boundaries of the individual, of a sense of being at one with everyone else and with all existing things. Through his identification with the folk culture, Jaroslav feels that his life is following an ancient pattern and that he himself does not need to search for meaning in the events of his life. The fulfillment of the ancient pattern gives these events a meaning and a beauty otherwise unattainable. He falls in love with his future wife when he recognizes in her the "poor servant girl" of folk songs, and he feels as if he were "reliving a love experienced a thousand times over" (145). He also, to his own surprise, recalls the ancient rite of the bride's losing her virginity, as it was performed at their wedding ceremony, much more vividly than the actual event (148). The pattern, the Platonic model of the event, is more real than the event itself, and the possibility of recognizing traditional meanings in events gives Jaroslav access to a meaningful life. His longing is the longing of modern human beings for a premodern security: he wants to recognize "the inexorable order" of things, an order he accepts and merges with (149). Thus, Jaroslav finds in folk culture what the romantic Pasenow in Broch's *The Sleepwalkers* seeks in religion, a return to the security of a world of traditionally established meanings, a world in which the individual, his life, and his deeds are collectively determined.

In the first years after the revolution, communist ideology supported the revival of folk culture and thus it harmonized with Jaroslav's reveries. However, in the end he has had to face the failure of the undertaking: instead of a majority of people, only a shrinking number of amateurs is any longer interested in Moravian folklore. Jaroslav feels that he is living in a world of dreams, one that has drifted far away from the actual world of the present. However, that more is at stake with the folk music and folk culture in *The Joke* than a reverie of a romantic village musician is indicated by the inclusion in the novel of a long nonfictional section on the various historical layers of Moravian folk music, including illustrations with score samples; the earliest layers are traced back to remote pagan centuries. Kundera has commented on the purpose of this section, saying that it opens up in the story a window onto a thousand years of the history of an art, thus connecting the remote past with the present (Biron 4). Layers from different centuries are discerned in contemporary folk music, although it is noted that their original forms and meanings cannot be identified satisfactorily. This mysterious but still attractive folklore which carries an obscure message from a remote past provides the background for Ludvik's reencounter with his own past. The setting of the events in the present is a small Moravian town at the time of a festivity called the Ride of the Kings. The origins of the ritual and its precise meaning have already sunk into oblivion—paradoxically, as folklore is supposed to have a sense-giving function in the collective. Even Ludvik has a sense of nostalgia, watching the performance of the nearly unintelligible remnants of a folkloristic tradition in a world that has turned hostile to it. For Ludvik and Jaroslav the performance represents an "ultimate beauty" which is at the point of disappearing (132).

For Ludvik, folk music is the form of collectivism to which he feels more attracted than any other, yet, unlike Jaroslav, it has for him, in a definitive sense, lost its validity in the present-day world. He criticizes the efforts of Jaroslav and his companions in the folk music group to revive the traditions of folk music and poetry by applying them to modern topics and sees this as artificial and far from how people nowadays actually feel and think (154–56). Yet at the end of the novel Ludvik resumes his place among the players in the group and finds in the old music consolation for his disappointments: "I felt happy inside these songs (inside the glass cabin of these songs) where sorrow is not lightness, laughter is not grimace, love is not laughable" (315). The songs offer him only momentary escape from reality; their beauty belongs to another world and is preserved only under protective glass.

Kostka recognizes in communism the idea of Christian brotherhood. Under the communist regime he has had to suffer because of his religious convictions, but his faith has protected him from disappointments. When he is forced to resign from his post as a lecturer at the university, the wrong that is inflicted on him is transformed in his mind into God's appeal to him, which he willingly follows: "They thought I would find my freedom restrained, but on the contrary I had just discovered the real meaning of freedom" (213). Kostka thus merges with the will of God, which he recognizes even in the oppressive measures taken against him. In his acceptance of God's will he is safe, whatever happens to him. Yet, thinking back on his life on the occasion of Ludvik's visit, he is astonished to realize that the patterns he thought he discerned in the events of his life may be deceptive. He now understands that his decision to divorce his wife was prompted by his fear of women, just as now is his reluctance to take responsibility for a woman who is in love with him. He begins to suspect that what he has previously seen as God's guidance has in fact been his own doing (245–46). Is the significance he surmises in the events truly God's voice or does it originate in himself, in his own hopes and fears?

In all these cases, what is experienced as the essence of the communist ideology is collectivity, of being part of something greater than the individual, whether the basis for this lies in a rational analysis of the history of class struggle, in folklore, or in the Christian faith. For the fourth type, the sentimental communist exemplified by Helena, intellectual reflections play a minor role only. For her, communism means an emotional merging and identification with the crowd, and political meetings are a chance to experience great, elevating emotions. Helena's identification with ideology and her glorification of her life through it is anti-intellectual and leads to a distortion of the facts. Of the four characters, Helena is the only one who after fifteen years is not aware that ideology has brought her to a dead end. She does of course notice that the crowd around her has shrunk considerably and that her views provoke opposition and criticism, but she does not realize that the ideas she still holds have generally proved untenable. For the reader, the hollowness of her ideological pose is clearly visible; nevertheless, like the other three characters, Helena represents an "honest" communist view of life in that she acts out of the deepest conviction (although in Kundera's opinion, sentimentalists like her cannot help constantly embellishing themselves in their own eyes and in this sense are being dishonest). The only character in *The Joke* who actually abuses communist ideology is Helena's husband, the opportunist Pavel Zemanek, who after 1948 was known as a radical communist and a disciplined comrade, but now, fifteen years later, is fashionably liberal. He still teaches Marxism-Leninism at the university, but he prefers to call himself a lecturer in "*philosophy*" (270).

The fact that the four characters representing the four types of "honest" communists act as different points of view through which the narration alternately occurs suggests that *The Joke* is a political and historical novel aiming at a critical analysis of communist ideology and of the reasons why socialism failed in Czechoslovakia. However, Kundera assures us that this is not the case: *The Joke* is not about Stalinism (see the preface to the 1982 English edition of *The Joke*; *The Joke* [1984] v). Indeed, the novel does not offer any record of the political events in Czechoslovakia or search for any historical reasons for political developments; rather, the political sphere is depicted as it is experienced by a number of individuals and as it plays a role in their lives, decisions, and actions. What interests Kundera is how the characters make use of politics to construct their personal views of the world and to satisfy their personal needs. For the protagonist Ludvik, what is ultimately important is what political events reveal to him about human nature, or, as Kundera puts it, about human possibilities of existence. Ludvik starts with a communist view of the world and consequently a political and historical one and with a view of himself as an active subject participating in History, but he ends by searching for possibilities of existence outside History and by valuing individuality and privacy rather than merging with a community or identifying with an idea that transcends himself.

It is important to note that Ludvik does not gradually distance himself from communist ideology through critical thought. Even at the moment of his expulsion from the party, he still supports communism and collectivism with the same enthusiasm as his colleagues. The following quotation is a part of Jaroslav's stream of consciousness, recalling what Ludvik used to preach fifteen years earlier: "Capitalism had destroyed this old collective life. And so folk art had lost its foundations, its reason for being, its function. It would be useless to try to resurrect it while social conditions were such that man lived cut off from man, everyone for himself. But socialism would liberate people from the yoke of their isolation. They would live in a new collectivity. United by a common interest. Their private and public lives would merge. They would be connected by a host of rituals" (141). The art that the communist Ludvik propagates is anonymous folk art that expresses collective feelings, thus the opposite of what Kundera later comes to define as the essence of the art of the novel. Similarly, Ludvik's original belief in the controllability of History is the opposite of what (the mature) Kundera contends: the young revolutionaries believe that they are steering the "steed of History" toward a desired goal in the future.

Expelled from both the university and the party, Ludvik is compelled to release his hold on the reins of History. Falling away from History, he also falls away from the course of his life. He feels that he has lost the ground from under his feet, and this feeling remains with him. At the end of the novel Ludvik comes to realize that this sense of falling is a constant condition in his life: "I told myself with astonishment that my only home was this descent, this searching, eager fall, and I abandoned myself to it and to my sweet vertigo" (316). "Vertigo" is one of Kundera's recurrent keywords. In *The Unbearable Lightness of Being* he explains that vertigo is the "intoxication of the weak," their longing to fall, to give in to their own weakness (76). The notion is defined without reference to any specific historical context. It is interesting to find the same expression used in Liehm's account of the situation in Czechoslovakia in 1966, in the context of the Czechoslovak politics in the 1950s. Liehm describes a sense of vertigo in thinking about the deeds of the young communists back then (*Trois* 64).

For Kundera, "falling," as well as the related metaphor "vertigo," are "existential metaphors." He introduces this concept in the context of Kafka's work, but it applies to his own novels as well. He differentiates between lyrical metaphors and "*existential* or *phenomenological*" ones (*Testaments* 103). Kafka's metaphorical imagination "was driven exclusively by the wish to decipher, to understand, to grasp the meaning of the characters' actions, the meaning of the situations in which they find themselves" (*Testaments* 104). This is precisely how the metaphor of falling works: it gives metaphoric expression to an existential situation, that of finding oneself suddenly without solid ground for one's whole existence. This metaphor characterizes Ludvik's sense of life: it is his existential metaphor, describing the situation which predominantly characterizes his being-in-the-world. This is how existential human situations are dealt with in Kundera's novels: they are represented as experienced by a certain individual and as characteristic of that individual. Kundera himself points out that he defines these situations by means of a theme word which conveys the life theme of an individual (or one of the themes). In *The Unbearable Lightness of Being*, for example, the theme words belonging to Tomas are "lightness" and "weight." In speaking of these theme words, however, Kundera does not mention that they are mostly metaphorical; only in *Immortality*, his last grand novel, does he—or rather his alter ego in the novel—reason that the deepest foundation or "ground" of an individual, from which his or her actions arise, can be grasped only by a metaphor (*Immortality* 265). Yet, most of the theme words that characterize an existential human situation and consequently the individual who experiences that situation recurrently in his or her life are metaphorical.

Along with "falling," denoting a sense of groundlessness, and "vertigo," the temptation to give in to one's weakness and let oneself fall, yet another experience is presented as characteristic of Ludvik's being-in-the-world, as his existential experience. When he is pushed from the track of his life by his fellow students for a trifling reason—because of a joke—Ludvik loses his faith in solidarity, comradeship, and in humankind in general. He has to witness his fellow students and party comrades, without a single exception, unhesitatingly voting against him, thus ruining his life, and he is convinced that they would just as readily have condemned him to death. After this, he cannot help but see in each and every person this same capacity. For him the human being is a creature that is capable of sentencing his fellows to death without a wince. This is for Ludvik an existential experience that defines his concept of humankind forever.

The endless falling and the human capacity to sentence one's fellow human beings to death serve to exemplify Kundera's use of history. Rather than analyzing historical developments and their specific historical backgrounds, Kundera is in search of suprahistorical, anthropological human possibilities which take shape in the experience of an individual, characterizing his or her being-in-the-world (see Liehm, "Interview" 106). Kundera's idea that history reveals anthropological human possibilities may seem flawless: if individuals in a particular historical situation act in a certain way or have a certain kind of experience, such acting or experiencing belongs to the range of human possibilities. Nevertheless, one might object to Kundera's manner of using abstraction. What Kundera presents as a universal human possibility may actually be something that is bound inseparably to a particular historical situation only and would never be realized under other circumstances. In other words, human beings may be changing historically to a greater extent than Kundera assumes. However, while for Hegel and Marx there exists no suprahistorically and anthropologically essential humanity, but a human being becomes what he or she is through the process of history alone, in Kundera's view human beings are not a product of History, nor is (H)istory a human product. Kundera considers history a power which is hostile toward the individual, who has to stand up against it; thus, he separates human beings "as such" from history. History does not produce human beings; it is productive only in the sense that it spurs the realization of certain existential possibilities (*The Art* 36–37, 115). The possibilities revealed by history are general, supra- or nonhistorical, and are limited in number. The sum of these possibilities constitutes what, from an anthropological point of view, the human being is.

Kundera's thinking represents a reversion from historicism back to early Enlightenment thinking, which sought the truth about humanity not in history but in "human nature." Although late Enlightenment thinking was already more historically oriented (see Blanke and Rüsen), the discipline of anthropology was constructed in parallel with that of history not only in the latter part of the eighteenth century, but also later in the "historical" nineteenth century. In the course of the eighteenth century, anthropology was established as a science which was neither a branch of metaphysics nor theologically based, nor did it follow the methods of the experimental natural sciences. Anthropology found its place in an area which overlapped with philosophy and the newer disciplines of geography, ethnography, and the late eighteenth-century "empirical science of the soul" (see Marquardt). The objective of anthropology in the eighteenth century was to provide a general definition of the physical and moral nature of human beings as well as to map differences between the sexes, nations, races, character types, and so on. In the nineteenth century the anthropological view competed with the historical view of man (Marquardt 368–69). In the course of the nineteenth and twentieth centuries new forms of both anthropological and historical views evolved, redefining the basis of the human and social sciences. Likewise, Kundera's anthropological view of humankind is a "modernized" version of anthropology, in that rather than "human nature," his objects of study are the existential possibilities of human beings. Yet, in spite of his applying the Heideggerian concept of existential possibilities, Kundera stands much closer to an ahistorical, anthropological understanding of the essence of humankind than to Heidegger's philosophy of existence, which claims that no definable essence of man can be found. Kundera's views are closer to those of Wilhelm Dilthey, who gave up the idea of the philosophy of history as the basis for an understanding of humankind and resorted to the idea of a common human nature that provides a key to understanding humanity under different cultural and historical conditions. Dilthey occasionally found support for his anthropology in biology (see Marquardt 369), and a similar view is found especially in Kundera's later works.

According to Kundera the same possibilities of human existence which are unveiled in the public sphere of History may appear in the private sphere as well. One example of this is self-culpabilization, which Kundera points out as an anthropological possibility which can be realized under certain circumstances in private life or commonly in society in certain historical situations (*Testaments* 201). An example of socially induced self-culpabilization occurs in Ludvik, who at first tries to preserve his ideological worldview by searching for the weaknesses and defects in his character and the attitude for which he was condemned. A further example of the universality of human possibilities is that in the penal battalion Ludvik encounters precisely the same anthropological possibilities of human existence as everywhere else.

Living in the penal battalion means for Ludvik a life outside of History and therefore also without a future; the only thing he is left with are the meaningless moments of the present. When the first shock of arriving in the penal battalion is over, he experiences his new existence as the sheer passage of time: "All I had left was time. . . . It was not the time with which I had previously had dealings, a time metamorphosed into work, love, effort of every kind . . . Now it came to me stripped, just as it is, in its true and original form, and it forced me to call it by its true name (for now I was living sheer time, sheer empty time) so as not to forget it for a moment, keep it constantly before me, and feel its weight" (*The Joke* 53). That life feels like the passage of "sheer empty time" derives from the fact that the men in the penal battalion experience their living and doing as senseless. External force keeps them following a certain course every day: "Thus, with remarkable speed, each of us was stripped of his own will and became something externally resembling an object (dumped, disposed, dispatched, consigned) and internally something like a man (suffering, irritated, apprehensive). . . . The depersonalization which had overwhelmed us appeared in those first days to be utterly opaque. The impersonal, prescribed functions we carried out replaced every human activity" (*The Joke* [1969] 46). Ludvik feels that he is no longer the subject of his own life but has become an object whose life is determined by others (117).

This impression of depersonalization and dehumanization, however, turns out to be deceptive. When Ludvik leaves the daylight of History in order to enter the "dark room" of the penal settlement, at first he cannot discern anything (49). But soon he is able to recognize differences in the behavior of his fellow convicts. He understands that even under the heaviest constraints of the settlement the convicts act as subjects. In fact, the extreme conditions of the penal settlement provide him with a chance for "anthropological" studies: on a small scale the circumstances represent a world turned into a trap and thus reveal the alternatives left even then for a human being. Later, Kundera remarks in *Testaments Betrayed* that he has no understanding for people who complain about "the forty lost years" under communist rule, as if they had had no life at all during these years (*Testaments* 223–24). He himself is interested in the existential possibilities of man even under the harshest constraints of History.

Ludvik's attitude toward his fellow convicts undergoes a change: he comes to understand that despite the obvious differences, the dynamic of the labor corps resembles that of the community of his old comrades. The members of the penal battalion are, similarly, bound together by solidarity and this enables them to carry out ventures, for instance, covering for each other so as to be able to leave the barracks without permission. However, Ludvik's apprehension of humans who are able to send their fellow human beings to death is reinforced when a young communist called Alexej arrives in the penal battalion. The newcomer intends to obey orders in an exemplary manner so that he can prove his unshaken loyalty to communist ideals. His behavior provokes antipathy among his fellow convicts and this results in bullying and leads ultimately to Alexej's suicide. The event reinforces Ludvik's earlier "fundamental anthropological experience" (*The Art* 37): "I began to have doubts about the value of our solidarity, which was based solely on the force of circumstance and an urge for self-preservation that compressed us into a densely packed flock. And I began to think that the black insignia group was as capable of bullying a man (making him an outcast, hounding him to death) as the group raising their hands in the university lecture hall that day in the past [when Ludvik was expelled from the university], or perhaps as capable as any group" (*The Joke* 115). This experience confirms in him the belief that no trustworthy community exists; there is no true togetherness among humans.

Ludvik's second, even more profound reason to mistrust any collective is his recognition that the judgment of a collective is no less fallible than that of an individual. Upon his arrival in the penal battalion, Ludvik wants to set himself apart from the rest of the convicts by assuring himself and his superiors that he is not a class enemy and that his sentence was due merely to a misunderstanding. However, he soon comes to realize that he is not the only one who has been wrongly sentenced. Earlier he had not found it problematic to categorize people into "us," that is, the (young) communists, the builders of the future and the "others," the bourgeois, the enemy, those representing the past and thus excluded from the making of History. Now he recognizes that ideological categorizers are indifferent as to what happens to the individual. Not only the convicted but also those who pass judgment relinquish their sovereignty as acting subjects. When they act in the name of ideological truth and History, they do not consider themselves as responsible. Ludvik now realizes that when his fellow students condemned him as a traitor, they did not think of themselves as personally responsible for ruining his life. Now awakening from his "lyrical" dream, Ludvik rejects any collective identification and considers each individual's actions as decisions for which he or she alone is responsible.

Yet another reason for the mistrust of History is the individual's inability to control the effects of his or her actions, which are meant to form History. In the present time of *The Joke*, fifteen years after the protagonist was pronounced guilty by the tribunal of his communist comrades, Ludvik, Kostka, and Jaroslav can only feel irony in looking back at the past, when, as Kostka puts it, "people here thought they were but a few steps from paradise. How proud they were: it was their paradise, they were on their way to it with no need of anyone in heaven above. And suddenly it melted away before their eyes" (209). The point is not only that the three protagonists—each for a different, personal reason—have lost their "faith," but that the communist project in general has failed to fulfill its promises. As described in *The Book of Laughter and Forgetting*, the revolutionary acts broke free from their agents and turned into things they were not meant to become (9). From this experience Ludvik draws the conclusion that History cannot be controlled.

In Kundera's opinion, one should accept the relativity of all truths and the uncontrollability of History. Yet we might ask whether in saying this Kundera is not actually replacing one "truth" about History with another: rather than seeing History as graspable and controllable, he regards it as incomprehensible and uninfluenced by human actions and decisions. Everywhere in Kundera's novels and essays, History appears as a destructive force, turning human life into a trap from which there is no escape. Thus, the optimism of the Marxist worldview is replaced by pessimism. History is reified as a mythical power independent of human beings and incomprehensible to us. In the dispute in 1967–68, Kundera was accused by Havel of historical pessimism and of hypostasizing history as a superhuman realm. Later Havel explained that the difference between them was that Kundera looked at history "from above," from the point of view of those who once believed that they could control History, but who, having experienced a great disappointment, thought that the only choice was to flee from it. However, for Havel it is impossible to retreat from history completely, because even our most ordinary actions are embedded in it. If we look at history "from underneath," from a grassroots level, we recognize that while we cannot guide the course of History, we may participate in it by performing small yet significant actions (*Disturbing* 180). One could say that Kundera, who has switched from an optimistic view of history to a pessimistic one, still adheres to the mythical image of the "steed of History." The steed, however, has been transformed into a beast, a mythical monster that cannot be conquered or tamed (see also Papoušek, "Strategy" 13). He believes that to avoid being crushed by this monster, we have to establish our human existence outside its realm.

The Joke is a key to understanding Kundera's thinking and his oeuvre, because through Ludvik's story we can understand how certain conceptions of community, ideology, humanity, and History result from falling from the saddle of History. The changes in Ludvik's view of History take place in three or four phases. The first is the sense of shock which follows his expulsion from the university and the party. This might be called the experience of being pushed from the saddle of History. The second phase follows his insight into the fact that the judgments and sentences of collectives are not the judgments of an infallible History. In the third phase, through his love for Lucie, a modest working girl, he gains a new understanding of life as it is lived outside History. The fourth phase begins when he draws a lesson from the failure of his attempt to take his revenge on Zemanek, who presided over the meeting which fifteen years earlier had decided the course of his life.

Ludvik gets a chance to take his revenge on Zemanek by seducing his wife, Helena. Yet it turns out that Helena's new boyfriend suits the husband's plans perfectly, since their marriage has long since withered and is now merely a formality. Zemanek himself shows up with a much younger and fashionable woman to whom the ideals of the revolution appear remote and quaint. For Ludvik, the envisaged retaliation is transformed into a joke at his own expense. His encounter with Zemanek eventually turns out differently from what he had expected. Zemanek has no intention of apologizing; in fact, he apparently has no compunctions, as if the past no longer matters; he introduces Ludvik to his girlfriend as a fellow student from university and talks to him just as he would to any other old acquaintance. From this Ludvik draws the conclusion that an action meant to correct a past wrong does not reach the past event. History does not allow us to redress past injustices; rather, History makes past events lose their significance and sink into oblivion. If the injustice suffered by Ludvik is not Zemanek's concern or the concern of anyone else who was present, then who is to blame for the wrongdoing? "The errors were so common and universal that they didn't represent exceptions or faults in the order of things; on the contrary, they constituted that order. What was it, then, that was mistaken? History itself? History the divine, the rational? . . . What if history plays jokes?" (288–89). History does not follow the principles of rationality and justice. Either it is indifferent to human beings or—assuming that there is somewhat more intentionality to History's "doings"—it uses them as its toys.

Ludvik's—and Kundera's—reflections on History are meant in the first place as a refutation of the view of history created in the nineteenth century to replace the earlier view of the unchangeable, metaphysical essence of humanity and of the order of things, the view of History on which the twentieth-century communist movements were founded. Consequently, Kundera looks at the communist revolution in Czechoslovakia as merely one example of the nature of historical processes in general. We might ask, however, whether something essential is not being ignored when Kundera proceeds so quickly to his general conclusions. We may agree that the outcome of the revolutionaries' acts did not correspond to their intentions; in fact, in such situations they probably seldom do. Yet, considering that the first years of communist rule in Czechoslovakia resulted, proportionally, in more victims than in other countries of the region (Steiner, *Deserts* 215, "Justice" 676), this may appear to be evading questions of responsibility and guilt.

Kundera has been criticized for a biased narration of Ludvik, who "is eager to paint himself as a victim of communism, not as one of its promoters" (Steiner, "Justice" 676). Ludvik admits that he belonged to the camp of those who expelled people from the university after the coup in 1948 but he also says that he personally had "never voted for anyone's downfall" (*The Joke* 55) and he adds, "but I am perfectly aware that this is of questionable merit, since I was deprived of the right to raise my hand" (77). His career in the party remained too short to be invited to vote at meetings like the one in which he was condemned. Peter Steiner remarks that being a communist student after 1948, Ludvik must have taken part in the firing of ideologically suspicious professors (*Deserts* 206). However, the criticism is based on the presupposition that Ludvik must in every respect represent the real situation in Czechoslovakia at the time; the novel does not assign him such activities. As I discuss above, Kundera does not analyze in any of his novels actual political events in Czechoslovakia after 1948. His persistent preference for looking at History at a general, anthropological level might be interpreted as an evasion of questions of responsibility and guilt. However, the tables can be turned, as Kundera himself does, by arguing that analyzing a historical situation from a general point of view—what human beings are capable of under certain circumstances—rather than stressing the particularity of events is more apt to counteract too facile a judgment of particular individuals in history as the villains, while the judge himself feels innocent and safe (see *Encounter* 48). In Kundera's view, historical catastrophes should teach humankind to think in a more complex, less black-and-white manner (see *Testaments* 232). Moreover, we must not forget that while Ludvik in *The Joke* is presented as a victim of the regime of terror rather than as its perpetrator, in his next novel, *Life Is Elsewhere*, Kundera offers an analysis of the psyche of a young communist who is guilty of destroying the lives of others. Yet, even here Kundera deals with the issue on a general, typical level rather than as a specific historical case.

In Kundera's view, the most general lesson we learn about History is that we must not place any reliance on it. But what grounds are left to justify the individual's decisions and actions, and what is it that gives meaning to life, now that traditional patterns no longer assign meaning to one's acts and experiences? What can we do, now that we can no longer rely either on History—which is beyond human control, lacks any direction, and does not follow the principles of justice or reason—or on the collective, which can at any time ostracize us? In my view, this is precisely the fundamental question pervading Kundera's entire novelistic oeuvre. The reader, however, does not necessarily perceive it as such, since Kundera directs our attention to other themes or key concepts in his novels; "History" is not even listed among his important themes in "Sixty-three Words" in *The Art of the Novel*. What is more, in his "phenomenological" investigation the themes appear as independent of any historical or other restrictions whatsoever. Yet most of them, such as privacy and the public sphere, the "lyrical" attitude to life, vertigo, falling or the lightness of being, attain their full meaning only in the frame of Kundera's conception of History and the individual's existence in relation to it.

From life story of the protagonist to analysis of existential situations

As the consequence of a joke, not only does Ludvik lose touch with History, but his own life ceases to appear to him as a meaningful whole. This experience teaches him, within the framework of an individual's life, the same lesson he learned from History: the consequences of an action may bear no relation whatsoever to the agent's intentions. The discrepancy between intention and consequences is so unbearable that Ludvik first, like his comrades, tries to discover some revelation of his true character in those casually written words on the postcard. After fifteen years it is still difficult for him to accept that the course of his life was determined by such triviality. Although he regards himself as a rational being, he confesses to being haunted by the strange feeling or superstition "that everything in life that happens to me also has a sense, that it *means* something, that life speaks to us about itself through its story, that it gradually reveals a secret, that it takes the form of a rebus whose message must be deciphered, that the stories we live comprise the mythology of our lives and in that mythology lies the key to truth and mystery. Is it an illusion? Possibly, even probably, but I can't rid myself of the need continually to *decipher* my own life" (*The Joke* 164).

In modernity it is assumed that a person's individuality is most perfectly conveyed by his or her life story. In premodern thinking, the individual was defined in terms of general categories: identity was defined by one's place in the natural and social order as well as by one's moral character. Since in modernity a human being is conceived of as an individual personality, these criteria are no longer sufficient to characterize him or her and individuality is to be sought in one's actions, experiences, and feelings, and ultimately in one's life as a whole. The view that emphasizes the individuality of every human being emerged in the late eighteenth century and was manifested in the novels of that period (see Saariluoma [Steinby], *Erzählstruktur*). Kundera, however, claims that the idea that "it is through action that [man] distinguishes himself from others and becomes an individual" is present already in the work of Dante and Boccaccio (*The Art* 23). He also points out that the conviction that the individual is revealed through his or her actions was questioned already by Diderot in his *Jacques le Fatalist*: Jacques "could never recognize himself in his action. Between the act and himself, a chasm opens. Man hopes to reveal his own image through his act, but that image bears no resemblance to him" (24). Kundera shares this Diderotean conception but he seems to overlook the fact that there is actually a fundamental difference in their views arising from the difference in their historical positions. In asserting the incidental nature of a person's life Diderot is questioning the omnipotence of Providence, whereas for Kundera, "incidental" refers to the uncontrollability of human actions and of History.

Starting with Goethe, the modern novel was based on the assumption that an individual's identity can be discovered in his or her life story (see, e.g., Ehrich-Haefeli; Saariluoma [Steinby], "Narrativisation"); this is why it is an individual life story that generally constitutes the basic structure of the novel. But if one's life is coincidental in relation to oneself, any grounds for choosing the life story as the basic structure of the novel no longer exist. In *The Joke*, the protagonist's life story, or rather the story of his personal disaster, still emerges as an organizing principle of the work as a whole. Its role, however, is definitely weakened by two factors. On the one hand, Ludvik's point of view is not the only one in the story but is supplemented by three others; on the other hand, the existential situations or "anthropological truths" which characterize the protagonist's being-in-the-world are strongly emphasized, rather than the turns of his life as a whole. Just as concrete history in *The Joke* is reduced to certain very general lessons conveying the "truth" of History as such, in the protagonist's life story certain existential situations and themes distill the "essence" of his existence. Several of these themes are repeated in different versions in the lives of the three other characters, such as the utopia of the human community and the quest for meaningfulness in one's life. Underneath the surface of the protagonist's story, the typical mode in which Kundera's later novels are constructed is already emerging. Rather than life stories, the whole is constituted by themes and their variations carried by different characters in various situations. With *The Joke*, in which we can recognize *in statu nascendi*, the structural principle of the "novel in the form of variations" (*The Book of Laughter* 227), or the "polyphonic" novel (see Biron 9; Chvatik, *Die Fallen* 64, 65, 84; Čulík 217, 220), it is apparent that much more is at stake than merely a technique of narration and composition. That the novel is for Kundera a kind of thematic composition ensues from the way he conceives life: containing too many incidental and irrelevant elements the individual's life story is without any inner logic and is therefore inadequate to provide a novel with a basic structure. Therefore, Kundera concentrates exclusively on the situations in a character's life which elucidate his or her being-in-the-world and that by the same token serve as material for the exploration of the possibilities of human existence.

What then remains for us as individuals that would allow us to feel our existence as meaningful, now that we are cut off both from History and from any metaphysical order, and are unable even to shape our own life so as to express our true self? One threatens to sink into a meaninglessness of being or feels the "oppressive lightness of the void" (*The Joke* 250). To be rescued, Ludvik needs the experience of meaningfulness, which he is deprived of in his daily life in the penal battalion. As in the story "Eduard and God," meaningfulness can be found only outside the realm of compulsions. To Ludvik this possibility is offered in his relationship to Lucie, the working girl whom he sees on his rare evening leaves. Ludvik speaks of her entering into his life in religious terms: "Lucie had revealed herself to me the way *religious truth* reveals itself" (66). Through her, he "saw spread before [him], hidden beneath history's soaring wings, a forgotten meadow of everyday life" (71–72). She has never even dreamed of touching the great wheel of History: "She knew nothing of history, she lived *beneath* it; it held no attraction to her, it was alien to her; she knew nothing of the *great* and *contemporary* concerns; she lived for her *small* and *eternal* concerns" (72). Ludvik continues the use of quasi-religious terms in describing his sense of being redeemed from History: "And suddenly I'd been liberated; Lucie had come to take me off to her *gray paradise*, and the step that such a short time before had seemed so formidable, the one I would take in getting out of history, was suddenly a step toward release. Lucie held me shyly by the elbow, and I let myself be led" (72) He looks upon her as "a gift from heaven," and their love brings him "a growing sense of inner peace" (77); in the 1969 edition, even more poetically, "from day to day my skies became bluer and bluer" (75). Life for Ludvik is no longer the sheer meaningless passage of time, but full of meaning which structures his time. Although he can see Lucie only seldom, his experience of time is now structured by meetings with her, recalling past ones and anticipating those to come. The religious vocabulary in which Ludvik expresses his new sense of the meaningfulness of life is significant in that it indicates that this new meaningfulness appears to him as a mysterious, quasi-religious gift.

Kundera's claim that *The Joke* is not a political novel but a love story (Preface [1982] v) sounds like a sarcastic comment, provoked by Western critics' assumption that an "East European" dissident writer is necessarily to be read politically, and the comment has therefore seldom been taken seriously. Another reason why Kundera's statement has not been followed may be the image evoked in all our minds by the term "love story," that is, a story intended to make the reader identify with the lovers, feel with them, and follow the development of their relationship until its happy (or sometimes unhappy) end. Instead, in Kundera's novels—in *The Joke*, but in his later novels as well—love is examined as an existential human possibility. In fact, love is regarded as one of the few possibilities of experiencing meaningfulness in life that are still left for human beings, in a world that has turned into a trap. *The Joke*, however, is a novel about the failure of love. For a long time Ludvik's love for Lucie is brotherly and tender and without sensuality, but when eventually he approaches her sexually she refuses him and soon afterwards disappears from the town. In his memories she appears poetized as "the goddess of escape, the goddess of vain pursuit," who still holds his head in her hands (203). Fifteen years later, when he learns more about her from Kostka, he understands that these poetical metaphors covered the unpoetical truth that their love was ruined by his own immaturity. It allowed him to recognize in her only a mirror of himself, not a creature independent of himself and with a past of her own. He was incapable of seeing "what she was in and to herself" (251), she existed for him only as part of their shared love story. Thus their love was doomed to fail not because of the circumstances, but owing to the "anthropological" possibility embodied in the young man he was then, that is, to the narcissistic egocentrism of a youth. The religious vocabulary in which Ludvik was used to think of his love now appears as an indication of his self-centered, sentimental attitude, which makes of another human being a quasi-religious revelation bestowed upon him so as to make his own life significant and beautiful.

In *The Joke*, the discussion of humankind's anthropological possibilities is embedded more smoothly in the narrative than in Kundera's later novels. However, despite the fact that *The Joke* is richer in description and detail than in his later novels, Kundera does not expect the reader to identify with the characters; to the contrary, he requires an analytical and distanced attitude. This is supported by Ludvik's own analytical description of his experiences. For example, he analyzes his relationship with Marketa as follows: "The psychological and physiological mechanism of love is so complex that at a certain period in his life a young man must concentrate all his energy on coming to grips with it, and in this way he misses the actual content of the love: the woman he loves (in this he is much like a young violinist who cannot concentrate on the emotional content of a piece until the technique required to play it comes automatically). Since I have spoken of my school boyish agitation over Marketa, I should point out that it stemmed not so much from my being in love as from my awkward lack of self-assurance, which weighed on me and came to rule my thoughts and feelings much more than Marketa herself" (33). Ludvik analyzes his "awkward age" of erotic inexperience in general terms, from the distance created by his maturity fifteen years later. Yet he confronts his experiences with *impassibilité* and analyticity not only in looking back, but also in speaking of his present self. For instance, he renders an unembellished and detailed description of his state of mind after the seduction of Zemanek's wife Helena, of the satisfaction he feels at the (apparent) success of his revenge, and of the sudden transformation of his state of mind when she tells him that the marriage has long since practically ceased to exist: "But now I saw her nudity in a new light; it was nudity *denuded*, denuded of the power to excite that until now had eliminated all the faults of age . . . her physical unloveliness lost all its power to excite and it too became only itself: a simple unloveliness" (200). Now he would like to get rid of her as soon as possible: "I longed for her to be gone;

for her body (so hopelessly material) to dematerialize, melt, turn into a stream and flow away, or evaporate and vanish out the window—but the body was here, a body I had stolen from no one, in which I'd vanquished no one, destroyed no one, a body abandoned, deserted by its spouse, a body I had intended to use but which had used me and was now insolently enjoying its triumph, exulting, jumping for joy" (201). The embarrassing scene is presented with analytical precision, resulting in multiple ironies aimed in different ways at both Ludvik and Helena, who is—or sentimentally fancies herself to be—in love with him.

Readers might take an ironical attitude even when the narrator is not capable of this. A good example is the section where Helena ponders the criticism she has recently faced within the party. Following her fierce attacks on other party members' extramarital affairs, she is accused of hypocrisy, since the failure of her own marriage has long been common knowledge: "[They] called me a hypocrite, trying to pillory others for breaking up marriages, trying to expel, dismiss, destroy, when I myself was unfaithful to my husband at every opportunity, that was how they put it at the meeting, but behind my back they were even more vicious, they said I was a nun in public and a whore in private, as if they couldn't see that the only reason I was so hard on others was that I knew what an unhappy marriage meant, it wasn't hate that made me do what I did, it was love, love of love, love of their house and home, love of their children, I wanted to help them, I too have a child, a home, and I tremble for them!" (21). The accuracy of this account, the close rendering of her feelings and thoughts, does not cause the reader to identify with the narrator, but calls for a critical and ironic distance.

Analytical, distanced, and ironical attitudes toward the represented object or event are typical of Kundera's art of the novel. In his later novels, however, Kundera uses a narrator who is detached from the fictional world of the novel—or, rather, it is he himself who speaks (see Vibert, "Milan Kundera" 111). The question of how a character like Helena, who lacks any capacity for analytical thought, can possibly articulate her thoughts and emotions so clearly then disappears. The narrator still follows closely what occurs in the mind of the character, but the conceptual accuracy of the account, often transcending that character's capacity, comes from the narrator, that is, from the author himself. In *The Art of the Novel* Kundera gives examples to illustrate his technique: "Even if I'm the one speaking, my reflections are connected to a character. I want to think his attitudes, his way of seeing things, in his stead and more deeply than he could do it himself. Part 2 of *The Unbearable Lightness of Being* begins with a long meditation on the interrelations between the body and the soul. "Yes, it is the author speaking, but everything he says is valid only within the magnetic field of a character: Tereza. It is Tereza's way of seeing things (though never formulated by her)" (79–80); "You see, I don't show you what happens inside Jaromil's head [in *Life Is Elsewhere*]; rather, I show what happens inside my own: I observe my Jaromil for a long while, and I try, step by step, to get to the heart of his attitude, in order to understand it, name it, grasp it" (31). The tradition of this narrative strategy, whereby the experience itself and the ability to articulate the experience through language are kept distinct and are bestowed on different agents, goes back to Kundera's predecessors, Broch und Musil. In the next chapter I focus on Kundera's conception of the novel in relation to the heritage of the Central European "Pleiades."

Chapter Four
Unmasking, Thought, and Analysis in the Post-Proustian Novel

Kundera considers himself to belong "under the same roof" with what he calls "the Pleiades of great Central European novelists": Franz Kafka, Jaroslav Hašek, Robert Musil, Hermann Broch, and Witold Gombrowicz (*The Art* 124; Oppenheim 9). This affinity means not only a shared view of the function of the novel in general and similarities in its construction, but also a parallel perspective on human existence in today's late modern world. In *The Art of the Novel*, Kundera explains his conception of the construction of his novels as making use of possibilities originally expounded by Broch, and several of the essays in *Testaments Betrayed* deal with Kafka. All five writers are for Kundera great novelists who in their work have captured new aspects of existence for human knowledge. In this chapter, I examine these authors primarily in terms of how the "inquiry into human existence" in their novels relates to Kundera's objectives and how Kundera's interpretation of his predecessors brings them into concurrence with his own views on humanity, history, and the novel.

Kafka, Hašek, Gombrowicz

The term "Kafkan" describes for Kundera the experience of living in a trap. Kundera formulates the crucial and radically new question raised by Kafka as follows: "What possibilities remain for man in a world where the external determinants have become so overpowering that internal impulses no longer carry weight?" (*The Art* 26). For Kafka, being crushed by external determinants does not follow from specific historical circumstances. For Kundera, Kafka is neither a prophet who foretold the advent of political totalitarianism—although his works were banned in Czechoslovakia after 1948 (see Thomas 13, 102)—nor a sociologist who depicted capitalism critically. Instead, Kafka described in the individual's experience a general, "anthropological" human possibility, which a few decades later in a particular historical situation became the collective experience of a society (*The Art* 111; Finkielkraut 39). Likewise, the themes of culpabilization and the violation of privacy, associated with the experience of being entrapped, appear in Kafka's works at a familial level, whereas—as Kundera remarks—in totalitarianism they reappear on the large scale of History (*The Art* 103–12). We may note that in seeing these major Kafkan themes exclusively in the context of the author's family background (on the power of the family as a trap, see *The Art* 109–10) and in ignoring any historical or social contextualization, Kundera acknowledges the relevance of biography in the interpretation of an author's work.

According to Kundera, Kafka has discovered the possibility in human existence of being in a trap formed by circumstances (see, e.g., McEwan 36). Kundera, however, never mentions that the metaphor itself derives from Kafka. Among Kafka's short stories is a tale entitled "A Little Fable," in which the metaphor of the trap is presented very much in the Kunderan sense. Because of the brevity of the tale, I give it here in its entirety: "'Alas,' said the mouse, 'the whole world is growing smaller every day. At the beginning it was so big that I was afraid, I kept running and running, and I was glad when I saw walls far away to the right and left, but these long walls have narrowed so quickly that I am in the last chamber already, and there in the corner stands the trap I must run into.' 'You need only to change your direction,' said the cat, and ate it up" (445). The individual's experience of the world, which originally appeared infinitely vast, is described as growing increasingly confined. Kundera does not mention this tale as a source of his "trap" metaphor. In *Testaments Betrayed*, however, he praises Kafka's metaphorical imagination, which he characterizes as existential or phenomenological rather than lyrical, noting that Kafka's metaphors reveal the meaning of the situations in which his characters find themselves. Kundera gives the example of Kafka's description of a sexual encounter between K. and Frieda in *The Castle,* in which the lovers, desperately seeking something from each other, are described metaphorically as dogs pawing the ground (*Testaments* 104–05). The words, Kundera says, do not express "a visual image of what is happening but rather express an ineffable existential situation" (105). This is even more obviously the case in "Small Fable," where the running mouse represents humanity in a world which has become a trap. Kundera also finds existential or phenomenological metaphors in Broch and Musil (see *Testaments* 104, *The Curtain* 70; on Kafka, see, e.g., Corngold; Corngold and Gross; Petrović; Stach; Strelka).

Kundera expresses his admiration for Kafka's ability to depict even "life-denying" situations of "tragic entrapment" with astonishing beauty and poetry (*The Art* 121; *Testaments* 220–24). What makes this beauty possible is that human freedom is not completely extinguished even under the most severe conditions. As an example, Kundera refers to the end of *The Trial*, where Joseph K. is on his way to be executed. Despite being absorbed in the situation, in a fleeting glimpse he looks at the world as Tolstoy sees it, "a world where, even at the harshest moments, characters retain a freedom of decision which gives life the happy incalculability that is the source of poetry" (*Testaments* 224).

Certain themes, attitudes, and techniques in Kafka's work are central to Kundera's practice of constructing the novel. One striking similarity is that neither author endows his characters with complete names. The characters are either anonymous or are identified by a single name rather than a first name and surname. This practice—which we find in other works of the "Pleiades" as well—contradicts the aim, characteristic of literary realism, of creating an illusion of reality. In general, Kafka is for Kundera a great antirealist writer who showed twentieth-century authors such as García Márquez "that it's possible to write *another way*" (*Testaments* 50). It was, likewise, Kafka who introduced dreamlike narration in the modern novel (*The Art* 16; *Testaments* 48–49). In so doing he actually renewed the novel in a manner that, according to the surrealists, was accomplished in poetry only (*Testaments* 48).

The roots of what Kundera calls Kafka's "profound antiromanticism" may in his opinion lie in Kafka's view of sexuality (*Testaments* 44), and Kafka is for Kundera one of the first analysts of sexuality. He is also the first to represent sexuality from the viewpoint of its inherently comical character. An example is the description of the "unfortunate sexual mishap with a housemaid," because of which the sixteen-year-old protagonist of *Amerika* was cast out of the parental home and sent to the US. The realization that the "utterly trivial" event of what Kundera characterizes as a "minor copulation" is the cause of everything that later happens to the hero is depressing, but, as he further remarks, the triviality of the cause makes the matter appear in a comical light as well (*Testaments* 44–45). This specific kind of the comical is another feature which fascinates Kundera in Kafka's work. He contends that in Kafka's world "the comic is not a counterpoint to the tragic (the tragicomic) as in Shakespeare; it's not there to make the tragic more bearable by lightening the tone; it doesn't *accompany* the tragic, not at all, it *nips it in the bud* and thus deprives the victims of the only consolation they could hope for: the consolation to be found in the (real or supposed) grandeur of tragedy" (*The Art* 104–05).

Another example analyzed by Kundera in *Testaments Betrayed* is the passage in *The Trial* where K. is first summoned to appear before the tribunal. He literally runs across the city to arrive in time. Kundera wonders why K. does not take the tram and underlines Kafka's irony: "The reason: he refuses to take the streetcar because 'he had no desire to humble himself before the committee of inquiry by a too-scrupulous punctuality.' He runs to the tribunal, but he runs as a proud man who will not be humiliated" (208). The effect of the comical arises from the unmasking of something ridiculous in characters which they themselves are not aware of or which they want to conceal unconsciously from themselves. Laughter deprives a person of his or her dignity, yet it does not make the matter appear amusing. This mode of laughter comes close to the comic which we encounter in Kundera's own novels. The importance of laughter is indicated by the fact that the words "laughable," "joke," or "laughter" occur in the titles of several of his works: *Laughable Loves*, *The Joke*, *The Book of Laughter and Forgetting*. Kunderan laughter is neither cheerful nor benevolent nor innocent; on the contrary, it is cold, taunting and mocking, denying the dignity of the person or the value of the matter we are laughing at. As Calvin Bedient notes, Kundera's laughter is more an expression of pain than of happiness or joy (96). It is ironic and strips subjects of their dignity by making them seem ridiculous. As Kundera himself puts it in his definition of the word "comic" in "Sixty-three

Words," "by providing us with the lovely illusion of human greatness, the tragic brings us consolation. The comic is crueler: it brutally reveals the meaninglessness of everything" (*The Art* 125).

In addition to Kafka, the other great Prague novelist praised by Kundera as a classic writer of the comic is Jaroslav Hašek (in another context, Kundera refers to Vančura as the Czech writer he loves most [*Testaments* 229]), but he does not include him in his "Pleiades" of the great Central European novelists). While Kafka's characters are not only entrapped but also the victims of ridicule, Hašek's protagonist, the good soldier Schweik, invites readers to laugh together with him at the very machinery by which he is gripped. The comical does not originate in the denial of someone's dignity but is a form of resistance, thus offering the possibility of freedom under the coercive machinery. By obeying the most senseless orders with extreme accuracy, Schweik makes the system itself ridiculous. Yet, surprisingly, Kundera does not emphasize the critique of the military and administrative system in Hašek's laughter; rather, he interprets the laughter as an expression of the experience of the absurd. The mere fact that war has become the subject of a comic novel proves that the comic has arrived at its paradoxical end (*The Art* 10). Schweik "adapts so easily (and with such delight!) to the reigning order not because he sees some sense in it but because he sees it has none at all. He amuses himself, he amuses other people, and by his extravagant conformism, he turns the world into one enormous joke" (*The Art* 49). Kundera's interpretation follows to a certain point the Czech reading of Schweik, who to his fellow countrymen represents the tradition of skepticism and laughter in which any lofty idealism is ridiculed (see Steiner, *The Deserts* 16). According to Kundera's understanding, however, Schweik's laughter signifies a universal denial of meaningfulness, "the non-acceptance of power through the refusal to take seriously anything at all" (*The Art* 49). Expanding the target of laughter until it is all inclusive dulls its edge as a tool of criticism of a certain system. In Kundera's interpretation, Hašek's laughter is in fact—contrary to what Kundera says about Schweik's amusing himself and others—fundamentally joyless, an expression of the existential experience of senselessness. This interpretation of Hašek tells us much about Kundera's own view of the comic (on Hašek see, e.g., Beall; Fábry; Němcová Banerjee; Petrović; Steiner, "Cynic Hero"; Thirouin, *De Hašek*; Winner).

On several occasions, Kundera refers with admiration to Gombrowicz, in particular his first novel *Ferdydurke* (1938). He considers *Ferdydurke* to be one of the most significant novels of the twentieth century, one which would have greatly influenced the history of the genre had it not been written in the language of a "small" nation and had not the outbreak of World War II blocked it from reaching an international audience (*Testaments* 248–50). The novel became known in the West only after 1959 (see Anonymous, "The History" 8; on Gombrowicz, see, e.g., Goddard; Ziarek Płonowska). Kundera considers Gombrowicz, along with Musil and Broch, an "anti-ideological" writer who believed neither in progress nor in revolution and an example of how an author can speak in his own voice in his work (*The Art* 34). In "Sixty-three Words," Kundera illustrates the concept of "absolutely modern" with a passage from *Ferdydurke* where the hostess displays her modernity by openly signifying her intention to go to the toilet (142). While such brief comments make it difficult to establish what Gombrowicz actually means to Kundera, by looking at the novel itself, however, it becomes possible to unearth some of the reasons why he praises *Ferdydurke* and considers it close to his own work.

Ferdydurke corresponds to Kundera's definition of the modern novel, in that in its own way it strives to solve "the secret of the self." As Gombrowicz puts it in the afterword to the English translation, the novel shows how in other people's eyes we appear civilized and mature, while to ourselves we are immature, incoherent, and lacking a unified, stable identity (288). The protagonist Johnnie Kowalski is searching for the "inner truth" within himself, but cannot find it. In fact, an individual consists of "a conglomeration of physical and mental parts" (*Ferdydurke* 74), yet not even these are his own: "We shall soon begin to be afraid of ourselves and our personalities, because we shall discover that they do not completely belong to us. And instead of bellowing and shouting: I believe this, I feel that, I am this, I stand for that, we shall say more humbly: In me there is a belief, a feeling, a thought, I am the vehicle for such-and-such an action, production, or whatever it may be" (86). Thus the individual's identity is deeply problematic.

Closely connected with the problem of identity is that of immaturity, which is an equally important theme in Kundera's work. In the beginning of *Ferdydurke*, the thirty-year-old hero, who is accused of immaturity on the basis of his "Diary from the Time of Maturation," written during his search for his identity—Gombrowicz wrote a text with this title before *Ferdydurke*—is forced to go back to school and tolerate being treated like a sixteen-year-old. The improbable and absurd situation, which immediately manifests the author's distance from the realist mode of narration, leads to the revelation of further absurdities. The main character has to witness a "moue competition" between two schoolboys who represent the parties of "innocent youth" and "lewdness." When the leader of "the lewd" loses, he cannot bear his defeat and forces his victorious rival to listen to the filth he whispers into his ears, which the other cannot endure but falls ill and eventually dies. However, "immaturity" manifests itself not only in the schoolboys' actions, but in the similar behavior provoked by Johnnie among the members of the family who provide him with accommodation. The parents and their teenage daughter have constructed their self-identity on allegedly being "absolutely modern," but the protagonist brings about the collapse of the form on which they have based their identity. He escapes his hosts' house in a scene where family members attack two men who have intruded into the daughter's room with amorous intentions—one of them is the professor who has forced Johnnie back to school—and start biting, beating, and kicking them. When Johnnie decides to flee with a school comrade to the estate of one of his aristocratic relatives, the outcome is once again a breakdown of civilized forms of behavior and Johnnie has to run away again.

Kundera is indebted to Gombrowicz for two of his recurrent concepts: "immaturity" and the "absolutely modern." By the latter, both understand an acquired attitude, a strategy whereby the individual constructs himself or herself by professing to be what counts as the most avant-garde. It is important to observe that "avant-garde" here means the same as the *dernier cri* or the fashionably modern, not the creation of something new and innovative. An even more important concept is "immaturity," which, however, the two authors understand in a significantly different way. In Kundera's conception, "immaturity" is closely associated with such concepts as "sentimentality," "lyricism," "ideology," and "youth." Although he does not define the opposite of "immaturity" in terms of any single concept, it is for him clearly a maturity or adulthood associated with such concepts as "skepticism" and "insight into the relativity of truths," or, in some connections, with "epic" or "novelistic." His characters are divisible into mature and immature ones. In *Ferdydurke*, immaturity is connected with youth or with being "green," yet its counter-concept is not "maturity" but "form." "Form" is what people want to accomplish in the eyes of others and in their own, but the form assumed actually hides their incoherence, their nonrational, chaotic immaturity, which nevertheless is also the source of creativity. Both "form" and "immaturity" are thus to be found in every individual. Johnnie's immaturity has the effect of a catalyst in the unmasking of that of other, apparently well-behaved and respectable people; all three catastrophes in *Ferdydurke* unveil disintegrating immaturity.

For Kundera, the Gombrowiczian unveiling of immaturity is related to Kafka's unsentimental, analytical representation of sexuality and Hašek's laughter at the irrationality of the machinery of war. Along with the discoveries of the other members of the Pleiades, they offer him a model for penetrating the possibilities of human existence. Gombrowicz is especially important, because he dares to lay bare what one tries to conceal not only from others but even from oneself. There is something shameful and gruesome hiding in human beings—the acts and omissions of the characters in *Ferdydurke* are determined partly by shame—something primitive and ignoble whose physical counterpart would more appropriately be the claws of animals and the barking of dogs than human hands and speech. Passing by a village on their way to his relatives' estate, Johnnie and his school comrade are puzzled by the absence of the locals and the high number of dogs. They are told that the peasants have all turned into barking, snarling, biting, howling, and quarrelling dogs in order to evade the influence of the expanding urban culture (202–04). Gombrowicz's view of man can justifiably be called pessimistic, as Czesław Miłosz does in his introduction to *Ferdydurke* (xv), but we might actually go a step further and describe it as misanthropic. It holds true for Kundera as well that his study of human nature often involves the revelation of things one does not want to be faced with because they contradict one's adopted, idealized image of oneself. However, for Kundera this is not equally valid for everyone; while for Gombrowicz everyone is at least to some extent "immature," for Kundera, "mature" men and women do exist.

Furthermore, the influence of Gombrowicz's narrative technique and the architecture of his works on Kundera's art of the novel is beyond doubt. The main storyline in *Ferdydurke* is interrupted by two digressions, both of which begin with

Gombrowicz's abstract reflections and continue by narrating the imaginative, nonrealistic stories of various characters and events that have no connection whatsoever with either the main storyline or each other. In the first digression, in fact, the author tells us that his work consists of unconnected, disjointed fragments, exactly like human beings are in reality (74). Kundera is fascinated by the absurdly comic in Gombrowicz's work and by the manner in which *Ferdydurke* is constructed from a mixture of fantastic, dreamlike, and grotesque-realistic elements, representing—just like Kafka's novels—a novelistic counterpart to the surrealism of lyrical poetry. Gombrowicz's way of building up a whole out of narrative passages and abstract reflections corresponds to that which Kundera praises in Broch's *The Sleepwalkers* and that he wants to develop further in his own novels.

Analysis, irony, and the question of authenticity in Musil's *The Man Without Qualities*

Kundera claims that Musil and Broch introduced "thought" as a structural element and principle into the novel. He talks about the "appeal of thought" as a possibility of the novel which so far has remained underused by other novelists: "Musil and Broch brought a sovereign and radiant intelligence to bear on the novel. Not to transform the novel into philosophy, but to marshal around the story all the means—rational and irrational, narrative and contemplative—that could illuminate man's being; could make of the novel the supreme intellectual synthesis" (*The Art* 16). However, the description leaves unclear what a novel that follows the "appeal of thought" is actually like. Following the appeal of thought, according to Kundera, does not mean that a novel is constructed out of abstract philosophical ideas, but that "rational and irrational, narrative and contemplative" means are used. It is thus difficult to see what exactly differentiates these novels from other kinds of novels, except possibly a higher level of intellectual achievement. In fact, I believe that what is special in Musil's and Broch's novels—as well as in Kundera's—might be more adequately grasped through the term "analysis" than "thinking" or "thought." "Analysis" means that the contents, ingredients, and concatenations of experiences are described with far more accuracy than the characters themselves are able to do. The purpose is to let the invisible become visible and accessible to judgment. Analysis thus does not appeal to the reader's empathy but to our reason (on Musil, see, e.g., Corino; Freed; McBride; Payne, Bartram, and Tihanov; Pike; Thiher).

Musil's colossal unfinished novel, *Der Mann ohne Eigenschaften* (1930–52, *The Man Without Qualities*), is pervaded by irony. The setting is Vienna in the years prior to World War I and the events of the novel are focused on a so-called "Collateral Campaign" planned by the upper circles of Austrian society. To eclipse the celebrations of the thirtieth anniversary of the German emperor's ascent to the throne, prominent circles in Austria are planning to launch a "Year of Austria" in 1918 in honor of the seventieth anniversary of the coronation of emperor Franz Joseph. The intention is thus highly patriotic, but the celebration still lacks a deeper foundation in a leading idea: what is the grand idea that Franz Joseph and Austria might represent that would have universal relevance? The idea must be "grand," but no one knows what it actually is.

Just as the Collateral Campaign is obscure, the participants in the great plan are equally opaque to themselves; in general, the individuals' actions and experiences are far less unified and rational than they imagine and contain much that escapes their own notice. Musil identifies this as the condition of modernity: unlike in Kundera's work, in Musil's work we do not find an exploration of human existence outside History. His characters stand outside History only insofar as they do not apprehend the historical moment in which they exist, but their confusion as such ensues from the fragmentation of the modern world. This fragmentation is demonstrated already in the first chapter, starting with the description of a beautiful August day in Vienna. A day that in an old-fashioned form of speech would be described by the phrase "the weather was fine" is depicted in terms borrowed from meteorology, in a discourse characteristic of the natural sciences. The irony continues in the following passages: upon witnessing an accident, a passer-by is comforted only when she is given a statistical account of the frequency of traffic accidents and is assured that the event does not exceed the limits of the normal. The chapter is about the alarming pluralism of different discourses and reveals that the reassuring effect exerted on us by the discourse of the exact sciences may not be rationally founded.

Musil's method of unmasking consists of a detailed depiction of a character's state of mind—emotions, perceptions, thoughts, and expectations—and of relationships among the characters. The following quotation, which describes how Count Leinsdorf originally came up with the idea of a great patriotic action, is a good example:

> For Count Leinsdorf there lay in this allegory of the aged sovereign the thought both of his country, which he loved, and of the world, to which it was to be an example. Great and agonising hopes stirred in Count Leinsdorf. He could not have said whether what moved him was more pain at not seeing his country occupying the place of honour due to it "in the family of nations," or whether it was jealousy of Prussia, which had thrust Austria down from the place (in 1866, by trickery and cunning!), or whether he was simply filled with pride in the nobility of an old state and the desire to show the world that it was exemplary; for in his view the nations of Europe were all whirling along in the vortex of a materialistic democracy, and he envisaged a lofty symbol that would be to them at once an admonition and a signal for a change of heart. It was clear to him that something must be done that would put Austria at the head of all, so that this "magnificent demonstration of the spirit of Austria" should be a "landmark" for the whole world, so helping it to find the way back to its own true nature, and that all this was bound up with the possession of an eighty-eight-year-old Emperor of Peace. (100)

The count's emotions and thoughts are hazy and their interconnections vague. Some details may be accurate, for instance the idea that the events of 1866 represented a turning point, but his comprehension of these events and their causes is nonrational and emotional (the Prussians thrust Austria out of its place "by trickery and cunning"). The nebulous idea of "the Year of Austria" grows out of the Count's conservative, patriotic emotions—his love of his fatherland, his conviction of the exemplariness of his country for the world—his aristocratic pride and his abhorrence of democracy, his emotionally colored interpretation of a historic turn (the events of 1866), his gratuitous wishes (Austria as an elevated symbol which admonishes the world to self-scrutiny), and a number of clichéd phrases lacking content such as "a magnificent demonstration of the spirit of Austria," "the family of nations," "a landmark for the whole world." This conglomeration of emotions and thoughts is depicted with great precision, but the analytical accuracy of the depiction does not mean that the thoughts lose their vagueness; on the contrary, the analytical accuracy lies in the great precision with which Musil grasps the vagueness that is characteristic of a person's thinking.

In Musil's narrative, what is in a person's mind but remains unrecognized is identified and made visible. The description follows the feelings and thoughts of a person closely, but in its analytical definition of the various elements the representation differs from how the person sees himself or herself. The difference is in the degree of awareness. Characters certainly have all these feelings and thoughts, but are not able to analyze and name them; they are usually content with an approximate, often strongly idealizing picture of their own self and actions. Consequently, the sheer precision of the description gives the narration an ironic tone.

Musil's art of depicting the processes in the human mind is an example of what Kundera means by his claim that a novel should study the human condition but avoid psychological realism. In a psychologically realistic description a character's actions have to be psychologically motivated, while Musil's narration of unmasking does not strive to reveal the characters as they understand themselves. Musil instead endeavors to surpass the limits of characters' self-understanding and to reveal the disparate elements that constitute their emotions, thoughts, and actions. Where psychological realism sought to construct an unbroken chain of causation, Musil focuses on particular phenomena; no rationality holding the whole of events together is to be found. The irony in Musil's novel derives from the characters' inability to realize the lack of rational connections in their thinking or in their experience of the world.

In Kundera's view, "the novel is, by definition, the ironic art" (*The Art* 133). The main tool of irony in his works, as in Musil's, is the analytical precision of description. The following example from *Life Is Elsewhere* describes the feelings of the poet's mother upon reading her son's poems for the first time:

> She read them and she cried. Maybe she didn't know why she was crying, but it's not difficult to guess; flowing from her eyes were four kinds of tears: first of all, she was struck by the resemblance between Jaromil's poems and the poems the painter had lent her, and the tears poured forth, tears for a lost love; then she felt a vague sadness emanating from her son's lines, recalling that her husband had been absent from the house for two days without having said a word, she shed tears of offended humiliation; but soon there were tears of consolation flowing from her eyes, for her son, rushing to her

> with so much confidence and emotion to show her his poems, had spread a balm on all her wounds; and finally, after reading the poems several times, she shed tears of admiration, because Jaromil's lines seemed unintelligible to her, and she therefore told herself that his poems contained much that she couldn't understand and that, as a consequence, she was the mother of a child prodigy. (*Life* 51)

The narrator's ironic distance from the mother's outburst of feelings is underlined through the orderly listing of the different kinds of tears she shed, the entries separated by semicolons. Of course she is actually incapable of making such an analysis of the mixture of different feelings behind the tears, she merely feels moved; and for Jaromil, Mama's (as she is called in the novel) tears serve as convincing proof of the efficacy of his poems. She is incapable of commenting on his poems, but in her husky voice and her damp eyes he discovers "a sacred guarantee of his poems' power; of their real, physical power" (51). These quotations from Musil and Kundera show why an exact analysis of a person's experiences, thoughts, and emotions is needed: human beings live in "the oblivion of being" in the sense that we are not transparent to ourselves. A false self-image, a lack of clarity concerning the motives of our actions, clichéd attitudes, self-palliation, or even self-deception are not the exception but the rule.

The ironic tone in Musil's novel is sometimes reinforced by a poetic device I call the "antilyrical simile," a device Kundera has picked up from Musil to exploit in his own work but which he does not mention, speaking only of existential or phenomenological metaphors in Kafka, Broch, and Musil. For instance, Count Leinsdorf is characterized as a person who acts aptly when it comes to practicing his governmental duties. He manages to make objective decisions without succumbing to the influence of his religious feelings. Yet every now and then, during official meetings of the Upper House, he cannot help voicing his hope that "life would return to the simplicity, naturalness, supernaturalness, soundness and inevitability of Christian principles," and during these moments "it was as though a contact-pin had been pulled out, and he flowed in a different circuit" (113). A servant girl's excitement in the presence of an attractive young guest is expressed by saying that "her heart was thudding like sugar being pounded in a mortar" (212). When the spiritually refined Arnheim falls in love with the equally spiritually refined "Lady Diotima," it is said that the "magic spell" often leads to "propping up one's devotions with a solid scaffolding of thoughts and convictions" (218). The concepts of "religion," "heart," or "love," which people tend to incorporate into the realm of idealities, are dragged away from this sphere by the use of terms from technical or everyday discourse: "contact-pin," "electric circuit," "mortar," "scaffolding." While lyrical similes or metaphors elevate the ordinary to a higher sphere—when for instance the beloved is compared to the goddess of beauty—Musil's antilyrical similes and metaphors have the opposite effect: they bring overheated feelings and effusive attitudes down to the level of everyday life by approaching them from a cool, technical perspective.

In *The Art of the Novel*, Kundera speaks of the "rational and demystifying lucidity" of the Pleiades of the great Central European novelists (124). In an interview, he has commented that his early experience in Czechoslovakia brought about for him a demystification of the great symbols that determined the twentieth century (Finkielkraut 37); later, demystification becomes a central aspiration in his oeuvre (see Donahue 67; Scarpetta xii). His shift from lyrical poetry to the novel actually signifies for him questioning everything that he considers lyrical, in other words everything sentimental, ideological, elevated, or collectively respected as a symbol. One of the means for this demystification is the antilyrical simile and metaphor borrowed from Musil. Where the existential or phenomenological metaphor is used to convey the contents of existential situations, the antilyrical metaphor creates an ironic distance from the object. In *Immortality*, for example, the narrator says of the young man called Rubens, who was preoccupied with his search for a great love, that he was "ready to put the hot pot of his feelings on the fire and wait for the boiling point at which feeling would turn into passion" (315). When in *Life Is Elsewhere* the young poet Jaromil is tormented by jealousy, his girlfriend's tears are capable of dissipating his anger, for "tears are excellent stain removers" (172). The narrator comments on Jaromil's self-suggestion of great feelings as follows: "We can laugh at the poet's immaturity, but we must also marvel at it: in his words there is a droplet that has come from the heart and gives his verse the radiance of beauty. But this droplet has no need for a real experience to draw it out of the poet's heart, and it seems to me rather that the poet himself sometimes squeezes his heart like a cook squeezing a lemon over the salad" (180).

In *The Man Without Qualities* Musil shows that the modern world has become overwhelmingly complex for the individual: we are no longer even able to construct a coherent self from the complex material offered to us by the world. Whether the Goethean dream of the individual who can synthesize all his/her dispositions and experiences into a harmonious personality has ever been realizable or not, it certainly is no longer applicable as an ideal today. This is manifested in Arnheim, the man who enjoys the reputation of uniting in his person "capital and culture," that is, possessions and spirit. Musil makes him appear in an ironic light by ridiculing his intellectual achievements. For example, when Arnheim praises the Collateral Campaign for being in concordance with the spirit of the times and "profoundly necessary," since for him, "the mere fact that a meeting like today's was possible anywhere proved its profound necessity" (203), this is a parody of the Hegelian idea that what is real is also rational and necessary.

One impediment in the construction of a coherent self is that one cannot distinguish between that which is one's "own" and that which is imposed upon one by the environment (in Gombrowicz's opinion, in fact, these cannot be distinguished at all [see *Ferdydurke*]). In Musil's novel the marriage of the Jew Leo Fischel and his non-Jewish wife deteriorates as the general atmosphere turns more and more anti-Semitic. The narrator comments, "The destiny of these two spouses to a great extent depended on a dreary, tough, under-ordered stratification of thoughts that were not even their own but were part of public opinion and had changed with it, without their being able to protect themselves against the process. Compared with this dependence, their personal dependence on each other was only a tiny fraction, a madly over-estimated residue" (244). Public opinion—Heidegger's "das Man" ("the they," see *Being and Time*)—intrudes into the realm of the private and overwhelms it, while individuals do not apprehend what is happening to them. In this case, too, Musil articulates with great accuracy something that as an experience is dim and scarcely graspable for those who undergo it.

In Musil's novel, the characters who live in the "oblivion of being" and whose acts are grounded in a beautified, stupid, or poorly reflected construction of the self are contrasted with the central character, Ulrich, the "man without qualities," a contrast that has no parallel in Gombrowicz, for whom everyone is "immature." In the fictional world of the novel Ulrich personifies Musil's point of view, insofar as he is aware of the problems in the existence of modern humanity. If the self is not born "naturally," so to say, by itself, how does it actually come into existence? How do we choose our qualities? What remains of the self after the layers of imposed attitudes and clichés are peeled off? His inclination for reflection prevents Ulrich from identifying himself not only with the fashionable views and attitudes of the day, but also with any particular actions and qualities whatsoever. This is why his friend Walter calls him the "man without qualities": in his eyes Ulrich never seems to be completely present in anything he does. He never totally identifies with his own feelings or actions, but his self-reflection always offers him a position from which he can perceive other viewpoints, alternative modes of being or acting. Thus he is always at a distance, observing his own actions and experiences, and can always imagine himself acting differently.

The difference between Ulrich and the rest of the characters is one between two opposing types of personalities, the reflective and the nonreflective, the latter of whom are not transparent to themselves. Musil speaks of individuals with "a sense of reality," and of others with "a sense of possibilities" (11–14). The former take the world and themselves self-evidently to be as they know them from experience, and identify with their own actions as well as with the personal qualities manifested in these actions, whereas the latter always reflect upon the numerous alternatives beyond the directly perceptible and accessible. Musil's categorization resembles Heidegger's division of human beings into those who are occupied by "das Man" and constantly act in an inauthentic manner without being conscious of it and those who strive for authenticity, who question their own actions and weigh different alternatives to these actions. Human existence is equally problematic for both types, but only the latter are aware of it. This is why the latter type is spared from Musil's irony, although in Ulrich's case its place is taken by the character's self-irony.

A contrast comparable to that of Musil's "man of the real" and "man of the possible" appears in Kundera's novels as well. The two types can be called the "inauthentic," or "sentimental," and the "authentic," the individual who strives for authenticity. The division, however, does not entirely correspond to Musil's. Kundera's lyrical or sentimental individual and Musil's "man of the real" are both actually "men of the unreal," who identify with an embellished and falsely coherent image of themselves. However, the opposite for Kundera is not the "man of the possible," to whom no qualities "adhere"; rather, it is the individual who endeavors to distinguish between the inauthentic and the authentic and to choose the latter, even if this means giving up any idealization of himself or herself. Whether or not it is possible for a human being to possess an authentic core is a recurring issue in Kundera's fiction.

Similarities in Musil's and Kundera's works can also be seen at the level of particular themes and motives. The motorcycle, for example, is for both writers a symbol of the ugliness of the modern way of life, of thoughtless rush and of a desire to be noticed: "A motor-cyclist came shooting along the empty street, thundering up the perspective, bow-armed and bow-legged, on his face all the solemn, monstrous self-importance of a yelling baby" (*The Man* 64). This could be a quotation from any of Kundera's novels (see *The Joke* 286; *Immortality* 23; *Slowness* 3–4). Moreover, as a narrator Kundera follows the line of Musil in that in his novels he reflects in his own voice on the issues which surface through the experiences of the fictional characters. In *The Man Without Qualities*—as in Kundera's novels—these reflections may take up entire chapters, such as the chapter entitled "The ideal of the three treatises, or the Utopian idea of exact living." However, in Musil's novel these reflective digressions are always connected with a particular character. The reflection does not form a distinct line parallel to the fiction, as is the case in the third part of Hermann Broch's *The Sleepwalkers*. This is why Kundera praises Broch as the inventor of the "polyphonic" novel (*The Art* 73).

Art as knowledge and beauty in Broch's work

In Broch's novel Kundera discovered ways of exploring human existence similar to those in Musil's work (on Broch see, e.g., Cohn; Harrington; Lützeler, *Hermann Broch*; Pérez Gay; Sera). Indeed, along with the great impact of Broch's novelistic technique on his own, which he emphasizes in two of the essays in *The Art of the Novel*, Kundera was also influenced by Broch's views as to the cognitive function of the novel.

For Broch, art in general is essentially knowledge: "Scientific and artistic knowledge are two branches of one and the same trunk and this trunk is knowledge itself," he states categorically ("Denkerische" 48). Broch differentiates between the kinds of knowledge typical of the natural sciences and of the arts, as Kundera does in his Cervantes essay (see *The Art*). For Broch, the function of art in modernity is to overcome the fragmentation of our experience of the world brought about by the breakup of scientific knowledge into separate specialisms. What is essential in art is its striving for a totality and its stress on the value aspect of human existence. Science, which is positivistically limited to what is directly accessible ("Denkerische" 46), cannot possibly provide "an ethical-metaphysical world *organon* such as Christian-Platonic scholasticism" (43). Where science consists of an innumerable amount of tiny bits of knowledge, aiming at grasping a totality but never attaining it, the arts represent the "impatience of knowledge," since "every work of art is a prefiguring symbol of the prefigured totality" (48–49). Broch traces the roots of this conception of art back to Goethe, who, in emphasizing the autonomy of art, was not denying its cognitive function; to the contrary, he was assigning art the task of grasping totality in an intuitive, anticipatory, and symbolic way beyond the limitations of science (45–46). Broch thought of himself as a follower of Goethe's "polyhistorical novel" (see Gambarota 65). Like Goethe, he sees Romanticism in an explicitly negative light, although the Romantics similarly prescribed art, and especially the novel, the task of imaginatively reaching the totality of existence. Broch accuses Romanticism of beautifying reality spuriously and sentimentally, of elevating the common to the sphere of the absolute. Romanticism, as he sees it, turns art into kitsch or pseudo-art, which uses the means of art but aims merely to please and avoids the demanding path of the search for truth (Broch, "Kitsch" 162–63). This view corresponds to how Kundera thinks of Romanticism.

Broch's interest in the cognitive function of the novel is shared by Kundera; however, there are several essential points on which their conceptions of the novel differ greatly, although Kundera himself does not pay any particular attention to these differences. As pointed out by Paola Gambarota, Kundera's view of the novel as a genre is characterized by playfulness and skepticism, as well as by an awareness of the relativity of all truths, which is far from Broch's thinking. In *The Sleepwalkers*, truths are relative only insofar as they belong to the different value systems represented by the characters in the novel, yet it is precisely this kind of relativization of values that troubles Broch. In Kundera's fiction, it is only in *The Joke* that the relativity of truth is bound to the different ideologies represented by the four types of communists (Gambarota 54). In Kundera's later works the relativity of truths is roughly equal to hypotheticality or skepticism: to the doubtfulness of all truths and the inexorable uncertainty of any meaning attached to human existence. For Broch, the idea of truth as necessarily hypothetical is completely alien, and skepticism, as also noted by Gambarota, is for him a negative concept (55). Moreover, for Kundera, the novel as a whole does not symbolically anticipate the attainment of the totality of existence; rather, it is a thematic composition which uncovers particular aspects of human existence. But he again agrees with Broch—without relying explicitly on Goethe—that knowledge and beauty are in art intertwined inseparably: "Whatever aspects of existence the novel discovers, it discovers as the beautiful" (*The Art* 122).

Actually, more resolutely than Goethe—who was a practitioner rather than a theoretician of literature—it was the early German Romantics, Friedrich Schlegel and Novalis, who were among the first to claim that art reveals truth not discovered anywhere else; thus they oppose the classical view of literature as an illustration of truth that in abstract form is known in philosophy. For Schlegel and Novalis, literature is something that essentially transcends everyday experience. Novalis's "magical idealism" was aimed at revealing the presence of the Absolute, that is, the totality of existence in the particular (on this, see, e.g., Frank, "Die Philosophie"; Heinrich; Uerlings), while Schlegel's "transcendental novel" *Lucinde* concerns the subjective conditions of knowledge in creating a meaningful order of the world (see Engel 381–443). It is true that neither Broch's nor Kundera's work suggests that the novel can reveal the absolute or even transcendental truth about the creation of knowledge; rather, the "truths" of the novel concern important phenomena in the modern world. With respect to the cognitive function of the novel, however, there exists a continuity from the early Romantics' concept of the novel to Broch and Kundera, which both of them overlook in their criticism of Romanticism.

Despite fundamental differences between Schlegel and Kundera, there are conspicuous similarities in their conceptions of truth and aesthetic value in the novel. Kundera argues that the unveiling of truths in a novel "causes surprise and the surprise aesthetic pleasure or, in other words, a sensation of beauty" (Elgrably 6). In another context, Kundera writes that a "work of art is a crossroads; the number of paths that meet in it seems to be closely related to the work's aesthetic value" ("Umbrella" 44). He quotes with approval Lautréamont's formula, "as beautiful as when a sewing machine meets an umbrella" (44) and suggests a variation of it to characterize the art of the Martinican author René Depestre (45). Beauty and knowledge, then, are created in art by the unexpected encounter of things which are usually not thought of together. This closely resembles Friedrich Schlegel's concept of "Witz" (wit), that is, the ability to gain unexpected insight into things by combining what is usually thought of as separate (see Engel 391, 400, 440; Frank, *Das Problem* 29, 32–35). This conception of how (new) truths appear in a novel and are perceived as beauty "explains" in a sense Kundera's liking of paradoxes. Obviously, Broch does not show any such sense of paradox in his conception of art.

The main thesis in *The Sleepwalkers* is the disappearance of a comprehensive, tenable system of values in the contemporary world. The trilogy describes the final phase of the process of modernization, in which the traditional Christian-Platonic system of values—which used to serve as the general basis for all human judgment and action—loses its validity without being superseded by a new one. Broch distinguishes three different phases of this process of disintegration, corresponding to the three parts of the trilogy. The first, *Pasenow, or Romanticism* (1931), takes place in the year 1888. Its protagonist, Lieutenant Pasenow, perceives the disintegration of the values of the traditional world, but reacts to this by holding on to the old world order, above all to Christianity—and to the army uniform, without which he feels naked. *Esch, or Anarchy* (1931) takes place fifteen years later, in 1903. The central character, Esch, an accountant, feels that he is living in a state of anarchy, since he cannot find any values that would constitute a sound basis for his actions. The third part, *Huguenau, or Realism* (1932), is again set fifteen years later. Through its central character Huguenau, a businessman, it describes the ultimate disintegration of values. In his professional life, Huguenau acts according to the principles of business life, which are in a sense rational, but their rationality is limited to the business sphere only and does not cover any other aspects of life. Accordingly, in other spheres Huguenau completely lacks any valid guiding principles, which is why he can succumb to the impulse of the moment and even kill a person—who happens to be Esch—without being subsequently concerned by his act. Thus, the last phase of the disintegration occurs when the absence of values is no longer even perceived.

Broch's representation of the differentiation of various types of rationality in modern society—the rationalities of religion, private life, and business life—resembles the analysis of Max Weber and the sociologists who followed him. It is not difficult to recognize a similarity between Broch's critique of technical rationality, as represented in Huguenau, and Horkheimer's and Adorno's critique of scientific rationality (Horkheimer and Adorno; Weber). Comparing the disintegration of values as represented by Broch with the problems of modern man's being in the world in Musil and Kundera, we see that the difference is not so much in their interpretations of the modern condition as in the perspectives from which they approach the issue. While the ongoing decay of the traditional, universally shared system of values fills Broch with anxiety and with the wish that the process could yet be reversed ("Evil in the Value-System of Art" 38–39; Gambarota 54; Steinecke), for Musil and Kundera, this state of affairs is nothing to regret, but is a given fact and the starting point of the analysis. Accordingly, while Broch focuses on the disintegration process itself, Musil and Kundera study the individual's condition after the completion of the process of modernization. They inquire on what foundation the modern individual can base his or her existence. While Broch denies that values can be founded in the individual, Kundera, like Musil, analyzes precisely the existential situation in which the individual has to rely on himself alone. In Kundera's view, this autonomy is actually the source of modern man's dignity.

Like Musil, Broch analyzes what goes on within the characters but which they themselves do not comprehend clearly. The purpose of the description is not to make the reader identify with the characters but to make visible what is occurring within their minds and to expose it for reflection. For Broch, values are not primarily scrutinized by the characters themselves—which is often the case in Kundera's fiction—but rather are treated as an aspect inherent in all human action, thought, and emotion. Let us take as an example the description of the sexual act, which Broch, like Kundera later, found an interesting object of study. He considers the mystification of sexuality to be a characteristic feature of Western culture, which he accounts for as arising out of the hostility of the bourgeois-puritan spirit toward sexuality. According to Broch, puritan bourgeoisie could not tolerate sexuality without embellishing it, disguising erotic desire as a super-terrestrial passion: "Every ordinary and incidental copulation is elevated to the celestial sphere, built up into an absolute or rather a pseudo-absolute, transformed into an unchangeably eternal Tristan-and-Isolde scene" ("Kitsch" 164; Broch's and Kundera's perspectives on sexuality in literature are with reference to German-language literature). For Broch, this is an example of an approach of kitsch. In contrast, his depiction of sexuality in *The Sleepwalkers* is matter-of-fact, unembellished, and analytically accurate. The casual sexual encounter between Huguenau and Mrs. Esch takes place in the restless atmosphere of World War I when Mrs. Esch's husband has left for the city and she is worried about him.

> Why . . . did the woman have such a lamenting voice? why did she have the wrong reaction? He wanted her to comfort him, and instead of that he must keep her here and comfort her, and all on account of Esch too! She was still beseeching him: "Where is he?" and she was still clutching him by the shoulder. Both embarrassed and furious he stroked her thick arm as if she were a weeping child, he could even haven gladly shown her some kindness, he ran his hand up and down her arm, but his mouth spoke unkind words: "What are you sniveling about Esch for? haven't we all had enough of the schoolmaster? . . . after all, you've got me . . ." and only while he was saying this did he himself become aware that he was making a more brutal demand on her . . . as a sort of substitute for what she had failed to give him. Now she guessed what he was after: "Herr Huguenau, for God's sake, Herr Huguenau. . . ." And already almost bereft of will power, she made scarcely any further resistance to his panting urgency. Like a criminal trying to save the hangman trouble she undid her underclothes, and without even a kiss he fell with her on the sofa. . . . Afterwards her first words were: "Save my man!" Huguenau felt indifferent about that. (609-10)

The sexual act is without any emotion or significance and it is just as incidental and inconsequential as any other trivial everyday event. Shortly afterward, Huguenau runs into Esch in the street and kills on the impulse of the moment, for no obvious reason.

The need to depict human experiences in an analytical manner arises in Broch, too, from the fact that human beings are not transparent to themselves. They are "sleepwalkers," lacking an awareness of what is going on inside them and why they act as they do. In the fictional world of *The Sleepwalkers*, there is no character who comes close to the narrator's ability to reflect upon matters, like Ulrich in *The Man without Qualities*. The character who approaches most closely this condition is Pasenow's friend Bertrand, yet his perspective never appears independently, but only filtered through Pasenow's point of view. Abstract reflections on various questions raised by the experiences of the characters are more self-standing in Broch's writing than in Musil's; in the last part of the trilogy, the issue of the disintegration of values is elaborated upon in a series of no less than ten essays.

Kundera claims that in the "post-Proustian" novel, History is regarded as a destructive external force that imposes itself upon human beings and the novel represents the individual's escape from the grip of History, allowing us to establish an independent existence outside its realm. However, this does not hold true for Broch (see Gambarota 58; Saariluoma [Steinby], "Kundera, Broch"). The development of human existence depicted by Broch is a process that takes place within History. What he describes as the disintegration of values is for him the most significant historical process of the contemporary era. The course of History does not lead to a morally superior world, but to the disintegration of value systems. This process of historical disintegration, however, takes place within individuals and is manifested through their concrete and everyday actions. In Kundera's "Grand Narrative," it is not morality that is at stake as it is in Broch, but primarily the individual's autonomy, discovered in one phase of European history but then forfeited. A novelist of the age of "terminal paradoxes" such as Kundera looks back on the era of European adventure with a deep longing, but what remains for him or her is only to explore human possibilities in a world turned into a trap.

The ten essays devoted to the disintegration of values in the third part of *The Sleepwalkers* form a continuous line, running in parallel with the different subordinate storylines and the main thread of Huguenau and the Esches. The term used by Kundera to refer to such a structure, borrowed from Broch (see "Das Weltbild" 117), is "polyphonic," and he regards himself as Broch's successor in developing the polyphonic architecture of the novel.

Chapter Five
The Thematic Structure of Kundera's Novels

Kundera has commented extensively on the structure and technique of his novels. Nevertheless, his comments in the novels themselves and in his novelistic essays call not only for text-based examination and systematization but also for supplementation, in order to grasp the essence of the Kunderan art of constructing a novel. In speaking of his own art of the novel, Kundera overlooks, for instance, the point that ellipsis and polyphony are more than mere techniques: they represent specific modes of thinking and thus contribute to the cognitive function of the novel. What is more, Kundera's analysis of the thematic composition of his novels is far from comprehensive. He ignores, for example, the pattern of polarity in his thinking and the organizing role of the "architheme" of sense giving.

Ellipsis as a technique and a mode of thinking

In an interview, "Dialogue on the Art of Composition," in *The Art of the Novel*, Kundera speaks about the structural principles of his novels. What inspired him in *The Sleepwalkers*, he says, were the innovations Broch had introduced but not carried out. What is not achieved in his work shows the need for "1) a new art of *radical divestment* (which can encompass the complexity of existence in the modern world without losing architectonic clarity); 2) a new art of *novelistic counterpoint* (which can blend philosophy, narrative, and dream into one music); 3) a new art of the *specifically novelistic essay* (which does not claim to bear an apodictic message but remains hypothetical, playful, or ironic)" (*The Art* 71). As noted by the interviewer, Christian Salmon, these three points seem to delineate Kundera's own artistic project (71). "Radical divestment" describes the manner in which things are discussed in the novel. The second point concerns the relations of the different lines of the novel. Narratives are only one of the components of the novel; the second is "philosophy," which in the novel appears in the form of a novelistic essay, and the third is dream or dreamlike narrative. The interplay between these different components, or lines, takes place in a "musical" manner, following the principle of a "novelistic counterpoint." The third point deals with the question of what a specifically novelistic essay should be like. I start by examining Kundera's idea of radical divestment and then analyze the dreamlike and essayistic discourses in his novels; finally, I ask how he understands the intertwinement of the different lines.

Radical divestment, as Kundera understands it, is not in the first place a matter of style, but comes close to what he calls the art of ellipsis. The rendering of the complexity of the contemporary world in a novel necessitates a technique of condensation: "There are anthropological limits—the limits of memory, for instance—that ought not to be exceeded. When you reach the end of a book you should still find it possible to remember the beginning. Otherwise the novel loses shape, its 'architectonic clarity' is clouded" (*The Art* 71–72). Kundera refers in this connection to *The Man Without Qualities*, but he also claims that excessive and superfluous length is a general feature of the novel as a genre. Like a sonata, in which musical themes are developed following particular rules so that the composition of the work involves a great amount of purely technical elaboration, the novel "is weighed down by 'technique,' by the conventions that do the author's work for him: present a character, describe a milieu, bring the action into a historical situation, fill time in the characters' lives with superfluous episodes; each shift of scene calls for new exposition, description, explanation" (73). Kundera found a model for the construction of his own novels in the music of Janáček, in which everything superfluous is omitted so as to keep only the essential: "My own imperative is 'Janacekian': to rid the novel of the automatism of novelistic technique, of novelistic verbalism; to make it dense" (73).

So what is actually "superfluous" for Kundera? In the novels following *The Joke*, Kundera leaves out everything that is thematically insignificant. This method can be contrasted on the one hand with the traditional novel, above all the realist one, and on the other hand with the art of the novel as practiced by Musil and Broch. Kundera himself does not in this connection distinguish between these two; however, when speaking of the traditional verbosity of the novel, he is thinking about the realist novel. Its "superfluous" lengthiness follows from detailed descriptions of the milieu and the historical context, from the depiction of the characters' appearance and background, and from the construction of the plot in the form of a gapless chain of causes and effects (*The Art* 34, 56–59). Without inquiring into the different functions of these conventions, Kundera speaks of the automatism of constructing a novel, as though the conventions were without any justification at all. If, like Roland Barthes, we consider the detailed, rich description typical of the realist novel as a means of creating an illusion of verisimilitude and enhancing the credibility of the story (see Barthes), it certainly is true that these goals do not accord with Kundera's conception of the task of the novel. To him, a novelist should not strive to make the reader identify with the fictional characters; rather, the fictional events should incite the reader to ponder over questions of human existence. He also objects to the assumption that a human being can be "explained" by his or her life or living conditions. An individual's life story is incidental and arbitrary to such an extent that for Kundera it seems completely futile to search in it for the individual himself or herself. For these reasons, anything that is not relevant to the themes of the novel is ignored, including the major part of what the characters experience.

In rejecting the goal of causal explanation or striving for the reader's identification with the characters, Kundera is following the model set by Broch and Musil; however, neither of them is an "elliptical" writer. The bulkiness of their narratives results from the fact that, in their view, the analysis of human existence requires a detailed description of scenes and especially of what happens in the minds of the characters, comprising all the heterogeneous materials that one's experience actually contains. By choosing a different method, Kundera assumes for himself, and assigns to his readers, a different cognitive task. I postulate the difference as follows: while Musil and Broch depict the chaotic and heterogeneous elements of the human experience in which the significant can be distinguished from the insignificant only by great effort if at all, Kundera focuses exclusively on what is existentially and thematically essential to his characters. In contrast to Musil and Broch, Kundera does not confront readers with the problem of distinguishing between the meaningful and the insignificant; in his novels all that is insignificant has been eliminated. Thus, his elliptical narration is not merely a matter of narrative technique, but it also redefines the cognitive task of the novel by confining the analysis to the existential themes in the novel.

An example of how ellipsis functions in Kundera's narration is as follows. In *The Book of Laughter and Forgetting,* the main character of the part entitled "The Border" is named Jan, but we are given no information about his age, his appearance, his profession, or even his most important human relationships, nor are we given an outline of his life story or his experiences as a whole. He simply appears, along with other characters, in a series of concrete situations. One of these characters is Edwige, with whom Jan often meets up for long and enthusiastic conversations. We are not told what the topics of these conversations are, and as a rule these evenings end with their lovemaking. Jan is not sure what the sexual act means for Edwige and he is astonished when on one occasion she reveals her opinion to him: "In the ensuing silence Edwige's face took on the blissful smile that indicated it was getting late, that the time was coming for Jan to unwind the empty film reel on her body. After an instant's reflection, she added: 'Ultimately, making love isn't that important.' Jan's ears pricked up: 'You don't think making love is that important?' She smiled at him tenderly: 'No, making love is not that important.' In a moment, he completely forgot what they had been discussing, because he had just learned something that mattered much more: for Edwige, physical love was merely a sign, merely a symbolic act that confirms friendship" (*The Book of Laughter* 289–90). We are not told anything more about Edwige. The significance of the scene lies in the fact that it makes Jan comprehend a completely new possibility within the thematic complex of love-friendship-sexuality, namely, that physical love can function as a sign of friendship. Thus, Jan infers from Edwige's remark a general "truth," which has nothing to do with her personality or the particular relationship between them. From a particular scene he abstracts a universal human possibility, thus acting as the reader, too, is supposed to.

Kundera's novels have often been criticized for not representing the characters as real men and women with rich personalities, but rendering them as the carriers of abstract ideas (see, e.g., Škvorecký; Woods, *Translating* 171). For Kundera, what is essential in a human being is his or her life theme representing one universal human possibility. In any situation, by identifying the existential theme we can tell what is essential to this human being and we do not need to take a detour through the individual's whole life or the traits of their character to understand them or what exactly this particular situation means to them. In his article, "Esch is Luther," Kundera has further sharpened the universal aspect of characters in novels in general, suggesting that characters should not be understood as individuals but rather as incarnations of certain typical attitudes of being-in-the-world: the character of Esch in Broch's *The Sleepwalkers* is the twentieth-century counterpart of Luther (270–71; see also *The Art* 54–56). This is certainly an exaggeration with regard to the modern novel as a whole, but the comment is relevant when we want to understand Kundera's own art of the novel.

The following quotation from *Life Is Elsewhere* exemplifies Kundera's art of presenting what is essential in a character. Here the narrator analyzes Jaromil's actions after joining the communist party when he follows the example of many of his fellow students in reporting on his professors' political opinions:

> Now that Jaromil has become a rigorous militant whose reports affect the destiny of adults, can I still maintain that he is on the run [from the skirts of maternal love that a lyricist sticks to]? Doesn't it seem instead that he has reached his goal? Not at all. When he was six years old, Mama had put him in the position of being a year younger than his classmates; he is still a year younger. When he is reporting on a professor who has bourgeois opinions, it is not the professor he is thinking about but rather the young people whose eyes he is anxiously watching to see his own image in them; just as he checks his smile and hair in the mirror at home, so he checks in their eyes the firmness, manliness, and harshness of his words. He is always surrounded by a wall of mirrors, and he cannot see beyond it. (139)

Here the narrator does not give an account of any particular event; instead, a recurrent situation typical of the period after 1948 is depicted, in which Jaromil informs the Political Council as to the ideological orientation of his professors. The narrator describes the situation from a point of view that extends beyond Jaromil's insight into his own position: he does not realize that by constantly searching for his own image in the eyes of others he is avoiding any real encounter with the world. From the recurring scenes, the narrator abstracts the essential; thus, what is presented to the reader is an explicit analysis of a universal phenomenon which manifests itself in the particular scenes. The author is not in search of the uniqueness of a person or a situation, but of the universally human as it appears in a person and a situation. In "Dialogue on the Art of Composition," Kundera says that in his novels he aims at "encompassing the complexity of existence in the modern world" (*The Art* 71). Actually, he is not interested in the world's complexity in its entirety or even in the complexity of an individual's experiences as a whole, but in the complexity of particular aspects of being.

In each of his novels Kundera explores a number of themes whose complexity is demonstrated through different variations. In one of the self-reflective passages of *The Book of Laughter and Forgetting*, Kundera defines his novel as "a novel in the form of variations" (227). Through variations on a number of themes, he endeavors to penetrate the bottomless depth of the themes. He compares such variations in a novel to Beethoven's later musical variations, which to him represent an invitation to undertake a journey into the infinity of a theme (226; see also *The Art* 92). According to Kundera, we can accept the fact that we will never be able to grasp the infinity of the universe, but we cannot bear the sense of having missed the opportunity to exhaust the infinity of something within our reach, like the infinity of a beloved person such as our father (*The Book of Laughter* 226). The parallel Kundera draws between Beethoven's variations on a theme and his own feelings of remorse at his father's deathbed is strange and is actually somewhat misleading. While he urges his readers to explore the infinity of their loved ones, in his novels he does not inquire into the infinite richness of his characters' personalities and their actions. Instead, just like Beethoven, he delves into the infinite possibilities of variations on a number of themes. Kundera's directing his attention to certain aspects of human existence which he explores as themes is exactly what he means by his technique of ellipsis.

That a Kunderan novel is a composition of themes means that the central subjectivity in the novel is not that of any of the characters but of the author. For Kundera, it is he himself who is the creator of the work present in it as well as the one who narrates the events and comments on them, not the implied author or the narrator as separated from the real author: Kundera considers these to be unnecessary theoretical constructions, at least in his own case (see O'Brien, "Meaning"; Vibert, "Milan Kundera," "En finir"). The author does not in his works simply mediate the world as experienced by the characters. He is free to make use of experiences selectively for his own purposes, that is, to explore the universal possibilities of human existence. Instead of giving his readers the sense that they have direct access to the experienced world of his characters, the author makes his own presence constantly felt, both as the originator of the characters and their situations and as the most important reflector of what is generally relevant in their experiences. Kundera believes that every great writer in the history of the novel discovered some possibility of human existence and examined this possibility as a theme. In Kundera's view, the only significant difference between his own novels and the main tradition of the novel is his method of eliminating from his works all that is thematically dispensable.

The themes are in Kundera's novels examined in connection with the characters: "Even if I'm the one speaking, my reflections are connected to a character. I want to think his attitudes, his way of seeing things, in his stead and more deeply than he could do it himself. Part 2 of *The Unbearable Lightness of Being* begins with a long meditation on the interrelations between the body and the soul. Yes, it is the author speaking, but everything he says is valid only within the magnetic field of a character. It is Tereza's way of seeing things (though never formulated by her)" (*The Art* 79–80). Kundera's reflections are intellectual and distanced and he strives for clarity, even when the character's experience is a mixture of various, not easily discernible ingredients; however, his reflections are more focused on a specific theme than those of Broch and Musil. Kundera often names the "life theme" of a character directly. For example, in *The Unbearable Lightness of Being,* Tomas' life theme is expressed by the words "lightness" and "weight" and in the sentence "Einmal ist keinmal," while Tereza's existential problem is the irreconcilability of body and soul. These examples show that a character's existential problem does not originate in any ideology determining his or her ways of thinking. While in *The Joke* Kundera explores four different variants of communist ideology through the four focalizers of the novel, in his later novels the different possibilities of existence are not ideological. These possibilities are personal in the sense that they provide a key to understanding the character's way of experiencing life; yet only in some cases is it explained why or how a certain existential question has become a particular character's "fate." For instance, what lies behind Tereza's experience of the painful irreconcilability of the body and the soul is her mother; and betrayal as Sabina's life theme in *The Unbearable Lightness of Being* derives from her father and her socialist education, but we are never told why "weight" and "weightlessness" are the central themes in Tomas's life.

In fact, it is the themes and not the individuals that "bear" them that interests Kundera. Unlike the way in which individuality has been understood in modernity, that is, as the singularity of one's personality and of one's way of experiencing the world, in Kundera's fiction it refers to the actualization or revelation of a universal possibility in a particular human being. Thus, the universal or general has priority over the particular. A particular case appears as an instantiation of the theme or of some of its numerous variations—but not as an individual variation on it. It is because of this presentation of his characters as carriers of general themes, along with his elimination of all nonthematic material, that Kundera's depiction of his characters is highly abstract. Kundera himself seems to be aware of the fact that his elliptic mode of presenting characters is removed from the way we perceive human beings in everyday life. Asked in an interview about the central themes or existential questions of his own life, he replied that they are countless: "In my life, in everyone's life, there are hundreds of motives, hundreds of themes, and I don't know which is the important one" (Kramer 46). A real human being thus cannot be identified with any given set of life-themes. This, however, is exactly what Kundera does with his fictional characters. We might say that Kundera subordinates the verisimilitude of his fictional characters to the thematic elaboration and composition of his works.

In a sense, the reduction of his characters to their existential problems reflects Kundera's pessimistic view of history. That the world has become a trap implies that people cannot be identified with their own experiences, which are externally and incidentally attached to them, nor with their deeds, whose consequences are beyond their control. Consequently, an individual is nothing but his or her existential problems. This view, paradoxically, includes an element of freedom with respect to History. Individuals are sought in what they themselves, standing outside of History, experience as the most important thing in their existence. The idea that individuals are "found" in the existential questions peculiar to themselves resembles Nietzsche's idea that their character is equivalent to the recurring, typical experience in their life (Nietzsche, *Beyond* 59). In Kundera's view, what characterizes an existential experience, in addition to its recurrence, is the significance ascribed to it by the person in question and its generally human validity.

Essay and dream

As quoted earlier in this chapter, in Kundera's opinion the novel should blend elliptic narration, philosophy, and dream. In emphasizing that the post-Proustian novelists conquered territories which earlier had belonged to philosophy, he is not claiming that it is only starting with these writers that the novel has explored human existence in competition with and as supplement to philosophy. In his view, the whole Cervantean tradition of the novel has been such an exploration. What is new in the post-Proustian novel in this respect is that philosophy appears in the novel in the form of nonfictional, essayistic sections dealing with the themes of the novel.

Since in Kundera's novels the reader's attention is constantly diverted from the concrete events of the fictional world to the themes of the novel upon which both the characters themselves and the narrator-author reflect, the remaining step, bringing the author to the inclusion in the novel of a speculative essay, is not a great leap. The difference is further diminished by Kundera's imperative that the essayistic sections must be "novelistic" as well. The themes are to be dealt with in the same experimental, hypothetical, playful manner as in the story (*The Art* 65, 78–79), resisting any tendency to present apodictic truths, to systematize, or to take a didactic tone. We can conclude that Kundera's ideal of the specifically novelistic essay is more akin to the essayistic parts of Musil's novel than to those of Broch's trilogy. Despite his admiration of *The Sleepwalkers*, Kundera does not hesitate to maintain that the essay on the disintegration of values included in it appears more like the author's independent study on the topic and thus lacks the relativity which is indispensable for the spirit of the novel (65, 73; on Broch and Musil see also Goltschnigg).

The demand for the creation of a novelistic essay concordant with the spirit of the novel is thus not only a matter of style but also of the concept of knowledge. For Kundera, all comprehensive theories and systems of knowledge are suspect and he regards them as connected with immaturity, lyricism, and totalitarianism. In *Testaments Betrayed*, Kundera praises the philosophical discourse of Nietzsche as an appropriate model for introducing ideas into the novel. Nietzsche does not strive for a system of thought, but insists that we "neither conceal nor corrupt the actual way our thoughts come to us," namely, as sudden insights or revelations; no deductions or explanations are used to bring coherence to them (148; with regard to

Nietzsche's experimental thought, see aphorisms 7, 51, 110, 289, 319, 324 in *The Gay Science*; see also Kaufmann 63–67). Nietzsche's "experimental thought" corresponds to Kundera's conception of the phenomenological exploration of themes in novels (*Testaments* 172–73). A further similarity between Nietzsche's experimental and hypothetical method and Kundera's quest for truth is that neither of them tries to grasp even a single theme in its entirety and define it once and for all, but both of them explore it in new variations over and over again.

Kundera's "skepticism" should thus not be understood as deconstruction (see O'Brien, *Milan Kundera* 68; Pelikan Straus). In sharp contrast with phenomenology, deconstruction denies the possibility that the object of knowledge can be grasped directly through experience in which it presents itself to our consciousness independently of all preconceptions. Instead, deconstruction argues that an object of knowledge, or a sign, cannot be determined directly per se, but only through an endlessly regressive series of other (linguistic) signs on which it depends and which remain equally undefined (see, e.g., Derrida, *On Grammatology*; *Writing*; "I Have a Taste"). Kundera does not deconstruct experience by tracing it back to something absent or hidden, but like the phenomenologists aspires to grasp content present in experience. Kundera is of course no true phenomenologist in the strictly philosophical, Husserlian sense of the word, since he does not distinguish between the factual existence of things and their constitution in consciousness, which for Husserl is a basic tenet of phenomenology. In Kundera's phenomenology, it is not the "natural" attitude that is being opposed, namely, the assumption that things exist independently of human consciousness. The main target of his criticism is psychologically oriented literary realism. What makes Kundera's approach "phenomenological" is his focus on the essential and universal as it manifests itself in a given situation. His thinking can be labeled as skeptical only insofar as each discovered truth represents merely a partial truth about the phenomenon in question. Within the context of Kundera's novelistic essays, "playfulness" does not refer to the free interplay of linguistic signs, but rather to the open-endedness of the exploration of existence.

Yet the novelistic essay contains another important aspect which Kundera hints at in saying that the essayistic meditation of themes takes place in connection with his characters, for example, in Tereza's "magnetic field" (*The Art* 79–80). This indicates an intimate connection between storytelling and a meditation on themes. "Novelistic thought," as he remarks in connection with Musil's essayistic work, is thought that feeds on concrete situations and characters (in his opinion, Musil is a great thinker only in his novels; see *Testaments* 235). Kundera believes his essays are always novelistic. As Bertrand Vibert puts it, while the storyteller Kundera constantly feels the essayistic temptation of meditation, the essayist Kundera constantly takes recourse in storytelling ("Milan Kundera" 121–25). For example, Kundera's essay dealing with "great" and "small" national cultures illustrates the difference by referring to the historic treaty between Hitler and the Western powers in 1938, which sealed the fate of Czechoslovakia. He quotes the words by which Chamberlain, the

British prime minister, sought to justify the sacrifice of Czechoslovakia: "A faraway country of which we know little" (*The Curtain* 32–33). In *Testaments Betrayed*, Kundera begins his essay on the comic in the novel with an example from Rabelais: "The pregnant Madame Grandgousier ate too much tripe, and they had to give her a purgative" (3). Even the Cervantes essay starts in narrative form by telling about Husserl giving his "celebrated lectures in Vienna and Prague on the crisis of European humanity" (*The Art* 3) and his outline of the history of the modern novel starts by telling what happened when God had left his throne and Don Quixote "set forth from his house into a world he could no longer recognize" (6). Kundera thinks concretely through examples and stories and that is why the essay and storytelling are for him not two separate matters, but are interconnected. The difference between a novel and an essay is not categorical but only relative. Where in a novel the existential themes of the characters are the subject of authorial meditation, in a novelistic essay the story is a means for dealing with the abstract theme of the essay.

The third constituent in the "musical" composition of the novel, in addition to elliptical narration and "philosophy" (in the form of the novelistic essay), is the dream. On several occasions Kundera praises the beauty of dreams or the poetry and imagination they contain (see, e.g., *Unbearable* 17, 55; *The Art* 80–81, 130–31; see also Ceska). Jaromil's daydreams about his alter ego, Xavier, in *Life Is Elsewhere*, Tereza's nightmares in *The Unbearable Lightness of Being*, and the final part of Tamina's story in *The Book of Laughter and Forgetting* are all told in a dreamlike narrative. In the Cervantes essay he declares that it was Kafka, with his fusion of dream and reality, who awoke the "slumbering imagination" of the novel (*The Art* 16; in a later essay in *The Art of the Novel* [81] he mentions Novalis as the first writer to have integrated the dream into the novel). It remains unclear why Kundera considers Kafka's innovation just as crucial as Cervantes's "discovery" of the adventure, which signified the beginning of the modern novel, or Broch's and Musil's introduction of "thought" into the novel, which initiated a new era in the history of the novel. Are beauty and imagination not generally present in the novel? What makes dreamlike narration so important that it becomes one of the three main components of the novel, along with elliptical narration and the novelistic essay?

Kundera's enthusiasm for the dream as imagination, which "freed from the control of reason and from concern for verisimilitude, ventures into landscapes inaccessible to rational thought" (*The Art* 81) can easily be related to his high regard of surrealism. His views are reminiscent of the surrealists' conception that dreamlike imagination opens up the way to "surreality," to a "truer" and "more real" reality than the rationally accessible everyday reality (see, e.g., Breton). Yet Kundera views dreams primarily from the aspect of individual existence: it is precisely in dreams that a character's existential problems come most clearly to the fore. Jaromil's daydreaming about Xavier reveals his immaturity, Tereza's recurring nightmare shows how Tomas's infidelity executes her metaphorically, and the dreamlike closing of Tamina's story brings with it "the forgetting of forgetting" which she had both feared and longed for. Thus, dreamlike narration does not manifest the novelist's imagination alone but also that of the fictional characters. The images and events occurring in our dreams are rooted in our deepest desires and fears. In Kundera's view, the significance of a dream lies precisely in the fact that it represents a realm of free subjectivity. An individual's existential problems are exhibited more clearly in dreams than in real life, since dreams escape the pressure of incidental external circumstances. They arise exclusively from the individual's inner world. Through this mechanism, dreams in their own language reveal the individual much more accurately and completely than his or her actions and experiences in the "real" world.

The idea that dreams are a form of subjective creativity rooted in the individual's subconscious is the basis for Freud's theory of dreams. What is less widely known is that the idea actually goes back to Herder and the early Romantics. Peter Bürger summarizes Herder's conception of dreams as follows: "dreams do not come from a superior world, but from the one who dreams; it is his hopes, desires and intuitions that gain shape in the dream. Dreaming is the spiritual-sensual activity in which the individual encounters himself, a locus where he gives shape to himself and his life" (182–83). In Kunderan terms, it is Herder who "discovered" the dream as a form of creative imagination akin to poetry. This is part of Herder's idea that individuals naturally form their experiences into meaningful images and linguistic expressions (see *Über den Ursprung*, *Vom Geist*, "Über Bild"). Later, Freud demonstrated that meaning emerges in dreams following the same symbolic, metaphorical, and metonymic means of sense giving as in poetry (Freud; see also Jakobson). As we can see, Kundera's concept of the dream and its origins, tightly intertwined with his concepts of beauty, poetry and imagination, has its place in an established tradition originating in Herder's work and the early Romantics through Freud and Kafka to the surrealists, although he himself places its beginning somewhat later.

Kundera claims that the dream was incorporated into the novel in an era when the world around human beings started becoming darker and darker. He locates this moment in the time between Goethe and Beethoven: "Beethoven's work begins where Goethe's centre ends. It is located in the moment when the world starts gradually losing its transparency, darkens, becomes more and more incomprehensible, rushes into the unknown, while man, betrayed by the world, escapes into his self, into his nostalgia, his dreams, his revolt, and lets himself be deafened by the voices inside him so that he no longer hears the voices outside" (*Immortality* 85). Listening to inner voices clearly refers to Romanticism, while the outside world's loss of transparency applies to nineteenth-century developments leading to a disappointment with History. With the individual alienated both from History and from his or her own actions, the only remaining realm of unlimited freedom is that of dreams, that is, the realm of pure subjectivity. Naturally, dreams as the realm of pure subjectivity represent as well a domain of unreality. Appropriately for the literature of an era of terminal paradoxes, it is only in the unreality of dreams that the individual free of all external constraints is found.

In *The Birth of Tragedy*, where Nietzsche's idea of human cultural creativity actually comes close to that of Herder, he uses the word "dream" as a metaphorical-metonymical name for man's Apollonian, figure-creating activity. Myths, according to Nietzsche, are indispensable for the construction of a meaningful, shared life-world for a society: "Only a horizon defined by myths completes and unifies a whole cultural movement. Myth alone saves all the powers of the imagination and of the Apollinian [*sic*] dream from their aimless wanderings" (*The Birth* 135). This is to say that in order to become culturally significant, dreams—the products of individual creativity—have to be accepted by society as part of its sensemaking practice of collective mythology. By this means the subjective "idiocy" of the dream is overcome and the figure-forming creativity of the individual is made beneficial to the whole of society. In contrast, Kundera does not see myths as a genuine source of meaning at all. Kundera suspects or even repudiates all forms of collective sense giving, such as indisputable religious truths, ideologies, or collective symbols. Where for Nietzsche the imaginative figures created by a dreaming individual are dubious until they have been accepted as meaningful by a collective, without which they remain useless or are even regarded as madness, for Kundera it is precisely the ineradicable subjectivity of a dream that makes it an authentic and reliable expression of human existence.

The polyphonic novel as a contrapuntal thematic composition

Although Kundera lists elliptical narrative, the novelistic essay, and dreamlike narration as the main components of his novels, he employs other types of discourse in them. In *The Book of Laughter and Forgetting*, for instance, he uses historical anecdotes and autobiographical narrative. Following the principle of "novelistic counterpoint" (*The Art* 65), Kundera composes out of the different ingredients a whole, which—using another musical metaphor, borrowed from Broch—he calls a "polyphonic" novel.

For Kundera, the unity of a novel is traditionally based on unity of action, yet this need not be the case: the "novel in the form of variations" is one where unity no longer depends on the story, but where different stories are connected on the thematic level alone. We can understand this form of the novel as a further development of Kundera's idea of the interconnection between novelistic and essayistic writing. The novel in the form of variations is, in a sense, an intermediate form between a novelistic and an essayistic structure. The themes, reflected upon in essayistic passages, are developed through multiple narratives. The concept of polyphony is a further development of this idea.

In the polyphonic novel, the different lines, not all of which need to be narrative, stand with each other in a relation which he calls "contrapuntal," together forming the polyphonic whole of the novel. Kundera refers to the third volume of *The Sleepwalkers* as an example. The book comprises several heterogeneous narrative lines: the novelistic narrative, the intimate short story, reportage, and poetic narrative. These lines tell completely different stories, which means that their characters never meet each other within the same fictional world; they also represent different types of discourse. In addition, the work also contains the line of a series of philosophical essays. The different lines deal with the same or similar themes in different variations, with the effect that the appearance of a theme in one line stands in a contrapuntal relation to its appearance in another (*The Art* 73, 75). The other musical metaphor used, polyphony, or a plurality of "voices," refers to the same phenomenon from a slightly different perspective: the themes in different lines (voices) sound together contrapuntally, and in combination the lines form a polyphonic composition. Of course, the different voices of the novel cannot be truly simultaneous, in the way they are in a polyphonic piece of music. What Kundera (following Broch) means is that in a polyphonic novelistic composition, the voice of a particular part persists in the background while the reader is engaged with the following parts (this resembles Husserl's description of retention in listening to music; see Husserl, *Zeitbewusstsein* 390–96.) The impression of the simultaneity of voices is enhanced by dividing a line (voice) into several parts, thereby ensuring that the first voice remains audible across the gap when another voice is heard.

As the popularity of Mikhail Bakhtin's theoretical thinking has made the concept of polyphony a metaphor frequently applied to the novel, it may be necessary to point out that Kundera's concept of polyphony is not derived from Bakhtin (see, e.g., Morello, "Questions" 146–47) and that he actually assigns to the term a different meaning (see Le Grand, "L'Esthétique" 57). Bakhtin developed his concept of polyphony within the context of Dostoyevsky's novels to refer to the plurality of the fictional characters' "voices," or rather their perspectives (see Bakhtin, *Problems*). According to Bakhtin, in Dostoyevsky's narration the different voices are given as such, without being filtered through the superior point of view of an author-narrator from which the perspectives of the characters are "objectively" evaluated and ranked. For Bakhtin, polyphony actually means poly-subjectivity, the equality of the charachers' different points of view. In Kundera's oeuvre, the only work where something comparable to Bakhtinian polyphony appears is *The Joke*, in which the four main characters give an account of (more or less) the same events; therefore, Jocelyn Maixent's term "plurivocalisme," which she uses to describe the "Symposium" section in *Laughable Loves*, is applicable to *The Joke* as well (234; see also Howell 203). Kundera's own concept of polyphony, however, has a different meaning: it refers, as noted above, to the parallel treatment of the same themes in different variations in several lines of a novel, with the effect that the whole takes shape as the simultaneity of the various thematic elaborations. It is thus undoubtedly a fallacy, arising from the use of the same term for different phenomena, to consider Bakhtin as a precursor of Kundera (see, e.g., Benson 293, 301). Kundera's conception of the novel as a polyphonic thematic composition is more akin to Thomas Mann's novelistic polyphony in his *Doctor Faustus* (see Mann, "Genesis" 41, 64), where "polyphony" is used to refer to the several layers of meaning—realist-biographical, mythical, historical, "musical"-thematic—which resonate simultaneously throughout the work (see Saariluoma [Steinby], *Nietzsche*). However, albeit Kundera in some connections expresses his admiration of Thomas Mann (e.g., *Testaments* 9–13), he denies that Mann's novels are thematic compositions in the same sense as Musil's or his own (*Testaments* 161–63). Clearly, he does not place himself "under the same roof" (Oppenheim 9) with Mann. Nor does Kundera refer to the Romantic origin of the idea of a novel as a musical composition; we find this idea, for instance, in Schlegel's enthusiastic comments on Goethe's *Wilhelm Meister's Apprenticeship* ("Über Goethes" 159). Those who think that Kundera's idea of a musical composition of the novel is of Romantic origin are, however, right (see Papoušek, "Ne Vous" 211), but this does not mean that this idea has anything nebulous or sentimental to it (see Christoffel).

While in the third book of *The Sleepwalkers* the narrative dealing with Huguenau and the Esches has superior status as the main story in relation to the other narrative and essay lines in the novel, Kundera demands that all the different voices in a polyphonic novel be equal and indispensable parts of the composition (*The Art* 75–76). He does not explain why this equality of voices is so important; he may consider the use of the musical metaphor as a sufficient argument, since music is truly polyphonic only when the voices are at all times both simultaneous and mutually independent. Such true equality of voices, however, can be questioned even in Kundera's own novels. *Life Is Elsewhere*, for instance, tells the story of Jaromil, despite the fact that the author compares the character and fate of the young poet to those of known poets of literary history, and although the sixth section, which in Kundera's words "opens a secret window through the novel's wall" is about another person, a "man in his forties" (85). *The Unbearable Lightness of Being* is primarily the story of Tomas and Tereza; that of Franz and Sabina is an important parallel sideline in which the same themes are partly repeated and varied, while the other lines, like the story of Stalin's son or the author's digressions, constitute smaller units completing the composition. *Immortality* focuses more on Agnes and her close relatives than on Goethe and Bettina Brentano, and even in *The Book of Laughter and Forgetting*, which more than any other of Kundera's novels follows the polyphonic principles of distinctness and simultaneity of voices, Tamina's figure rises above the other characters simply because she appears in two of the seven parts, whereas the others each appear in just one.

In addition to polyphony, Kundera stresses alternations in tempo and in the mathematical proportions of the length of different sections as significant factors in the composition of a novel (*The Art* 85–93). In these respects, too, a novel is comparable to a musical composition. Kundera points out that his own novels emerge mostly as seven-part compositions, obeying an inescapable "deep, unconscious, incomprehensible drive, an archetype of form" (86). In an interview with Norman Biron, however, he offers an explanation for this "inner imperative," as a means of creating formal unity in a novel: "Had a novel two, four or eight parts, it would tend to be split up into two halves. It is not sufficiently bound up, unified, compact. To ensure genuine unity of construction, this construction must be indivisible. That is the meaning of uneven numbers" (Biron 9).

The analogy of a musical composition should be seen as Kundera's answer to the question, "what are the constitutive principles of the whole of a novel?" While the idea of the "musical composition of a literary work of art," according to David Christoffel, is often taken by French scholars as a vague idea inspired by German Romanticism and a "poor metaphor" (Christoffel 287–88), for Kundera the concept has a well-defined meaning. It means that a novel is an artistic whole, consisting primarily of its themes in relation to each other, and secondarily of the mathematical relations of its parts. With this understanding of the construction of the novel as a whole, Kundera is definitely distancing himself from the realist tradition of the novel, which suggests that the work as a whole emerges seemingly without any overt act of construction by the author. The latter is merely following nature; in other words, events in the fictional world follow the inevitable course of events in the real world. In rejecting the idea of the "natural" coming into being of the form of the novel, Kundera agrees with modernist authors who doubted authorial insight into the order of things in either the natural or the human world. Yet Kundera does not follow those modernists who find that the author has to focus on a person's subjective, incoherent, inner experience only. The thematic composition of a novel, as Kundera understands it, is not derived from any object of presentation itself, but is a product of the creative imagination of the author. Assigning the novelist a role, as composer of the novel, similar to that of the musician as creator of musical compositions means ascribing to him the part of omnipotent, omnipresent organizer of the whole. Kundera stresses that the composition is an important part of the author's individual creation, "an invention that engages all the author's originality" (*Testaments* 170). However, just as in a musical composition, nothing hinders the writer from developing a theme—one of his or her own or one borrowed from someone else—in new works in ever newer variations.

In a contrapuntal composition of themes, the whole is not equal to the sum of all the themes, or of "ideas and witticisms simply stand[ing] by themselves" (Welfing 110), nor is it their synthesis (see Le Grand, "L'Esthétique" 57, 63). Thinking of the work as a synthesis of themes would imply that each and every individual theme is mediated through the others as a whole. In contrast, in Kundera's "phenomenological" thinking, each particular theme is grasped through the concrete situation in which it appears; as such it does not presuppose any mediation through the others. A contrapuntal composition maintains precisely this mutual independence of themes: they are separate and appear only in a contrapuntal or oppositional relationship to one another. The partial truths unveiled in the themes remain distinct and are not synthesized in a higher truth (in the Hegelian sense). This corresponds to what Kundera says about Nietzsche's aphoristic philosophizing as a model of his own novelistic compositions: the thematic materials are dealt with nonsystematically, building up a composition in which the themes appear bare and clearly articulated (*Testaments* 165–68). In addition, in Kundera's novels themes tend to challenge rather than support one another.

The thematic composition, in addition to being a manner of dealing with truth, is an aesthetic composition as well (see, e.g., *The Art* 64, 79, 154). Beauty, for Kundera, is at least in part a concept that is related to form or structure. As noted, beauty arises when two things that we are not used to think together suddenly meet ("Umbrella"): "it is the surprise I experience before something which hasn't already been said, demonstrated, seen" (Elgrably 4). It is in the aesthetic principle followed in a contrapuntal composition where Kundera's affinity to the Romantic idea of wit (*Witz*)—the ability to create meaning and beauty through surprising connections—appears most clearly. The example Kundera gives is, however, not from his own works: When Anna Karenina at the end of Tolstoy's novel commits suicide by throwing herself under a train, recalling the crushed man she had seen at the station the day she first met Vronsky, this gives "her love story a finished, beautiful shape" (*The Curtain* 25). Thus, an event which appeared incidental takes on additional significance when connected to another. Poetry, the beauty in a literary work of art, a concept which Kundera contrasts with lyricism (see *The Curtain* 51, 82), is the opposite of the "prose" of everyday life, in which things preserve their separateness and concreteness (see *The Curtain* 8).

As thematic compositions not all of Kundera's novels are equally elaborated. The polyphonic principle is realized most consistently in *The Book of Laughter and Forgetting* and to a somewhat lesser extent in *The Unbearable Lightness of Being* and *Immortality*, whereas in his earlier novels, and the three late short novels, only few polyphonic features are present. On the basis of these compositional differences, Kundera's fictional oeuvre can be divided into three periods (see also Boden, *Irritation* 42). The first group consists of *The Joke* (1967), *Life Is Elsewhere* (1973), and *Farewell Waltz* (1973). These novels were written in Czechoslovakia and they reflect Kundera's experiences in his native culture; however, they are not autobiographical but deal with issues on a general, thematic level. Each novel is set in a single fictive world and tells a single story, which, especially in the case of the first two novels, coincides with the life story of the main character. The second group of texts encompasses the polyphonic novels *The Book of Laughter and Forgetting* (1979), *The Unbearable Lightness of Being* (1984), and *Immortality* (1990), all created after his emigration to France but still written in Czech (or, as in the case of *Immortality*, in both languages simultaneously). The third group consists of Kundera's late, short novels, *Slowness* (1994), *Identity* (1998), and *Ignorance* (2000), which originally appeared as "French" novels, and which, I argue, are less significant than the works in the other two groups. Moreover, as noted, the composition of the final version of *Laughable Loves*, comprising seven short stories in which love and ridicule are combined, already heralds the polyphonic structure of the novels and may therefore be viewed as a bridge between the early works and the polyphonic novels (see Carroll). Kundera has partly objected to such a division but partly supported it. On the one hand he stresses the continuity of his oeuvre, in which he has always explored the possibilities of human existence, of which socialism and the Western world merely offer different variations ("La 'Parole'" 24). On the other hand, he has acknowledged two breaks in his novelistic work, the first after *Farewell Waltz*, the second after *Immortality*. He says that after *Immortality* he knew that he had completed a cycle of novels and that if he were to start something new this would be a completely different thing (Morello, "Questions" 145).

The architecture of the one-story novels

The story told in *The Joke* has an inner coherence, although the narration is chronologically nonlinear and the perspectives of the four first-person narrators vary: the different perspectives in *The Joke* are perspectives on the same reality. As I mention previously, the composition intertwining the voices of four characters results in a polyphony that stands closer to the Bakhtinian idea of polyphony than to Kundera's later conception of the novel as a thematic composition. Most of Kundera's pivotal themes, although enfolded in the story, are already present in this early novel. Such themes are those of laughter, lightness turning into heaviness, the relationship between the private and the public, the idyllic and the circle dance, the lyrical age, the hardly bearable lightness of life without ties, disharmony between body and soul, fidelity, forgetting, and escape and falling. The themes do not draw the reader's attention away from the fictive world, because they are elaborated solely by the characters themselves, above all by Ludvik.

Life Is Elsewhere, like *The Joke*, covers the most important events in the life of its main character, this time from the moment of conception until death. The reason for this is not Kundera's trust in biography as the natural grounding structure of the novel, but rather his conviction that a lyrical poet is the product of a special kind of mother-son relationship, a relationship that is in control of the poet's life until the very end. Kundera confesses that he originally intended to entitle the novel *The Lyrical Age*, but was persuaded by his friends to change it at the last moment (*The Art* 31–32). He admits that in hindsight he regrets having accepted their advice. The original title corresponds much more closely to his wish to reveal the "main category" of the novel already in its title, as in the case, for instance, of *The Joke* and *The Unbearable Lightness of Being* (*The Art* 32). We should note, however, that while many of the titles of Kundera's novels do indeed articulate a main theme, it would be misleading to identify these keywords with the main categories of the work, for the keywords in the title usually represent merely one aspect of the thematic core of the novel. The title of *The Joke*, for instance, masks the point that the novel is not only about joking, but about how a joke suddenly turns into a serious matter. In his naming the novel *The Joke* we can actually discern a typically Kunderan sort of irony, an intimation that an enunciated truth is always just one part of a larger truth. The title *Life Is Elsewhere* is an ironic quotation of a piece of graffiti from the 1968 Parisian student revolts, itself a quotation from Arthur Rimbaud, the same with which André Breton ends his 1924 *Manifesto of Surrealism*. The title evokes the modernist lyrical tradition, as well as alluding to the parallel Kundera draws between the Czech revolution of 1948 and the Paris riots in 1968. The slogan expresses the young poet

Jaromil's attitude toward life, toward which Kundera takes an ironical stand. His own conviction is closer to the opposite view, namely, that life is here and now (as represented in the novel by the man in his forties). The titles in Kundera's novels do not simply display the main theme but are highly ambiguous; they mostly manifest only one aspect of a matter, and conceal its opposite, which is equally important.

Jaromil's character is meant to represent the "anthropological" truth that being a poet, a revolutionary, and a denouncer essentially belong together and are all associated with youth and immaturity. Kundera depicts a piece of Czech history—and in Jaromil's story also a great part of his own "lyrical" youth—but elevates the perspective to what he considers universally relevant. Characteristic of the lyrical attitude is egocentrism: the individual's inclination to regard one's fellow human beings as mirrors of oneself and to prop up one's weak ego by borrowed or fancied grand ideas and feelings. For Kundera it is important that his readers take Jaromil seriously as a poet. If he is regarded merely as a daydreamer, the story loses its point (*Testaments* 231).

Kundera also speaks about polyphony in connection with *Life Is Elsewhere* (*The Art* 85–89), although it consists almost solely of the story of Jaromil the poet. Kundera's reason is that the various parts of the novel make use of different modes of narration and different angles on the events narrated. First, in the midst of realistic narration, the novel contains two sections of dreamlike narrative that relate Jaromil's daydreams about Xavier, his idealized, imaginary alter ego. Second, part 6, entitled "The Man in His Forties," is set outside Jaromil's story. It takes place three years after the poet's death and depicts an encounter between the forty-year-old and Jaromil's former beloved, after her release from prison. In Kundera's words, the purpose of this part is to serve as an "observatory," looking at Jaromil's life from a different perspective, and it should be regarded as an essential part of the composition (*Life* 229–30; *The Art* 85). The novel, however, is not polyphonic in the strict sense, in that the individual stories are held together solely by means of their thematic unity. Instead, all chapters are either part of Jaromil's story or are closely connected to it. Kundera fails to mention in this connection that the novel also includes short digressions, such as passages about Rimbaud, Lermontov, and Shelley—figures parallel to the poet Jaromil—or references to the 1968 demonstrations in Paris which are presented as a parallel to Czechoslovakia in 1948. Sometimes Kundera brings together incidents in Jaromil's and other poets' lives in a single sentence, for instance, "a shot rings out, Lermontov clutches his chest, and Jaromil falls to the icy concrete floor of the balcony" (*Life* 254; see also Chvatík, *Die Fallen* 82–83). This transparency between Jaromil and other poets, making present and past meet, as Kundera himself remarks (Biron 4), has the effect of emphasizing the general and thematic aspects of events. The digressions into other poets' lives and other political events do not, however, form independent and distinct lines of a polyphonic composition.

The original title of *Farewell Waltz—Epilogue*—shows that Kundera thought of it as the last in a series of three novels intended to conclude his career as a novelist when he was barred from publishing (*Testaments* 165). The three novels form a thematically unified whole, giving an account of the author's past experiences viewed at the level of existential themes. *The Joke* is a story about falling outside History as a consequence of being expelled from the communist party. In *Life Is Elsewhere* Kundera looks back at the young communist and lyrical poet, and in *Farewell Waltz* one of the main characters is a middle-aged cynical intellectual who has suffered his punishment for a political "crime" and is about to emigrate. In *The Art of the Novel*, Kundera characterizes *Farewell Waltz* as vaudeville (in English translation "farce" likely changed because for the English reading public "vaudeville" has a somewhat different meaning). In vaudeville—in the French sense of the word—a light and amusing theatrical piece, often interspersed with songs and dances, Kundera is attracted by "a form that puts enormous stress on plot, with its whole machinery of unforeseen and exaggerated coincidences" (*The Art* 93). By borrowing the form of vaudeville, Kundera suggests that the action of a novel need not follow verisimilitude, which dominated literature from nineteenth-century realism onward (*The Art* 93–94). The construction of a realistic plot is merely a convention which can be replaced with another. Kundera believes that the vaudeville form enables him "to bring together the extreme gravity of the question and the extreme lightness of the form," which has always been his ambition (*The Art* 95).

The events in *Farewell Waltz* take place during a period of five days in a small Czech spa town. While *The Joke* and *Life Is Elsewhere* tell the story of a single character, *Farewell Waltz* intertwines fragments from the lives of several characters within a spatially and temporally limited framework. The narration is more elliptical; the characters are pictured rather sketchily as they are portrayed through their life themes which come to the fore over the five days. In the main story, the famous trumpeter Klima tries to persuade Ruzena, a bath attendant from the spa, to abort her baby. The novel begins with Ruzena calling Klima to let him know that she is carrying his child and ends with Ruzena's death owing to an oversight just after she has obtained the committee's permission to have the abortion. Another storyline follows an intellectual called Jakub, who just before his emigration pays a farewell visit to his friend, Dr. Skreta, as well as to his protégé Olga, who is staying for a treatment in the same spa. The two story lines intersect when the deadly pill that Jakub, who is the ethical focus of the novel, has carried with him all these years accidentally gets into Ruzena's hands and eventually causes her death. Thus, the novel not only is Kundera's farewell to his audience, but also deals both with Jakub's farewell to his home country and Ruzena's farewell to life; nevertheless, the gravity of parting for good is wrapped up in the light form of a "waltz" or vaudeville. The main storyline also includes the development of the relationship between Klima and his wife Kamila, and Olga, Dr. Skreta, and a patient of his, the (US) American millionaire Bertlef, appear in several scenes.

What brings the whimsical turns of the plot and the diversity of action to simple, mechanical order is the tight chronological frame of events. The novel is divided into five parts, entitled "First Day," "Second Day," and so on, according to the five days covered by the events of the story. The division is not entailed by the inner logic of the plot, but by the external course of time. Unity of time and space is of course a characteristic feature of classical tragedy, as is the division into five parts or acts. Thus, a playful vaudeville hides in its structure an allusion to tragedy. The further division of the parts of *Farewell Waltz* is content based. Each of the short chapters presents a scene or a phase of a conversation. For example, the encounter between Klima and Bertlef takes up several short chapters. In the first an account of how they first meet is provided, in the second Klima speaks about his problem with Ruzena, in the third he gains Bertlef's approval for the idea of abortion, in the fourth Bertlef talks about his similar experiences in the past, and so on. The division of the action into such elementary scenes endows the narration with a quick, light rhythm. *Farewell Waltz* is a good example of how the chapter functions as a unit in Kundera's novels. The typical Kunderan chapter, as François Ricard remarks, is characterized by a tendency toward brevity, extreme condensation, and maximal expression (163). A chapter always means a moment in the exploration of a theme. Consequently, it is closely comparable to the aphorism—called "chapter" by Kundera—in Nietzsche's writings. It is the basic unit of the book and as such the basic medium of the enquiry into the thematic complex of the work (see *Testaments* 167–68).

Farewell Waltz bears a resemblance to the vaudeville—more generally the drama of the prerealist age—in terms of its content as well insofar as deception and pretense play an important role in it. Ruzena pretends to be absolutely sure that Klima is the father of her child, Klima pretends love to persuade Ruzena to have the abortion, Jakub pretends to be a colleague of Dr. Skreta in the presence of the doctor's patients, and Dr. Skreta cheats childless women in his clinic by injecting his own sperm into them in the name of treatment. The novel appears as a carnivalistic comedy, but in spite of its playful form it deals with the most serious matters. The fifth act begins with the death of the "heroine," when Ruzena accidentally swallows a poison pill and dies. Shortly before, Jakub discovered the hidden murderer in himself; he has not done everything in his power to prevent the death of the nurse. Yet the end scene of the novel gives us a hilarious family reunion of Dr. Skreta and his financée, Bertlef, his wife, and their young son where everyone seems to have forgotten the death of the nurse which took place only a few hours earlier. One might ask whether Kundera has achieved the intended balance between extreme lightness of form and extreme seriousness of content. In Kundera's opinion, it is a characteristic of kitsch to hide the fact of death behind an artificial screen, so my question is whether *Farewell Waltz*, then, ends in kitsch.

The architecture of the polyphonic novels, polarity, and the "architheme" of sense giving

The definition of the novel as a thematic composition raises a question: what distinguishes a novel from a collection short stories linked thematically? In the "Dialogue on the Art of Composition," the interviewer Christian Salmon asks whether, by Kundera's criteria, Boccaccio's *Decameron* should not be defined as a novel. Its stories, after all, are connected by the common theme of love and are narrated by the fictional characters of the frame story (*The Art* 83). Kundera is reluctant to be so "provocative" as to call Boccaccio's work a novel, but he acknowledges that *The Decameron* is one of the first "large-scale composition[s] in narrative prose" which deserves "a place in the history of the novel *at least* as its source and forerunner" (83). As we can see, Kundera's thematic concept of the structure of the novel blurs the borderline differentiating a collection of short stories from a novel. In this respect his own collection of short stories is a good example. The seven short stories of *Laughable Loves* are linked by the same or similar themes; in each of them, love or lovemaking is connected one way or another with laughter. The theme is provocative. In the modern view, originating from the time of Romanticism, love is conceived of as something sublime and irreconcilable with laughter. Indeed, in this link between love and laughter we recognize one of Kundera's "discoveries" in the same sense as, according to him, the separation of love from sexuality and the triviality of the sexual act were "discovered" by Kafka and Broch.

The themes of ridiculousness and love appear in the short stories intertwined in many different ways with each other and with several other themes. In the first story of the collection, "Nobody Will Laugh," a young man finds that it is an illusion that we are able to "saddle events and control their course" (40) and that we "pass through the present with our eyes blindfolded" and only later discover the actual meaning of a past experience (5). In the story, "The Golden Apple of Eternal Desire," the first-person narrator introduces a middle-aged friend of his, whose main preoccupation is seducing women. Seduction has become for him a pastime in which physical love in itself is of little importance. The mere idea or possibility of sexual intercourse is enough for him; he only needs to make the first moves of his well-planned seduction scheme to maintain his image of a womanizer. The protagonist of the last short story, "Eduard and God," is a young teacher who "always tried hard to distinguish between the serious and the unserious" (244–45), regarding everything he was compelled to do, such as his education and profession, as not serious, and searching for the serious in that which is a matter of free choice. In his girlfriend he supposes her religious commitment to be serious, that is, an authentic and ineradicable part of her very essence. The girl considers sexual abstinence as God's commandment; nevertheless, she eventually gives up her principles and is willing to become Eduard's lover. At that moment, however, Eduard realizes that he no longer has any interest in her. In giving up her principles without any remorse, she has lost her integrity and authenticity in his eyes. Eduard reaches the conclusion that human beings are conglomerations of heterogeneous, incidentally acquired features and that they lack an authentic self. He longs for God, who is "essence," but is too honest to believe in him or to find anything essential in his own life.

In *Laughable Loves,* it is the individual short stories rather than the individual themes that parallel one another. Connected to the main themes are several other typical themes of Kundera, including the impossibility of controlling the course of events, the problem of the self, the great variety of intellectual and spiritual content potentially bound up with the sexual act (in contrast to the uniformity of the bodily movements), and young people's need to see themselves mirrored in the eyes of others. Yet here the themes are not elaborated as abstract keywords or reflected upon in digressions, but are built into the stories. The repetition of the combination of love and laughter, however, makes the text more unified than a traditional collection of short stories. In addition, Dr. Havel—the main character of the sixth short story, "Dr. Havel After Twenty Years"—makes his appearance already in the fourth one. In this way the structure of the work as a whole resembles that of *The Book of Laughter and Forgetting,* where Tamina is the main character in two of the seven parts. Furthermore, Kundera's remark that the collection (published in the West) follows his "unconscious imperative" of a seven-part composition shows that he sees the work as a novel-like whole rather than as a collection of separate stories (*The Art* 85–86). Although his criteria for the novel—thematic unity and variation, along with a composition consisting of individual parts that are indispensable for the whole—are fulfilled in the case of *Laughable Loves*, Kundera nevertheless does not consider the text to be a novel (qtd. in Misurella 189). One possible reason for this is that the short stories were originally written independently of each other and published in various combinations. Only when Kundera arranged them in their final form did they emerge as a coherent whole, approaching the form of a (polyphonic) novel.

The Book of Laughter and Forgetting opens a new phase in Kundera's oeuvre. The novels are now more elliptical than the earlier ones, meaning that the narration focuses increasingly on thematically important scenes alone. They are also more abstract in the sense that the themes are even more clearly than before examined from an existential and anthropological point of view, rather than being considered part of a particular historical setting. The narrator comments amply on both the themes and the structure of the novel. It is in these novels—*The Book of Laughter and Forgetting*, *The Unbearable Lightness of Being*, and *Immortality*—that the polyphonic architecture is developed to its highest point.

The Book of Laughter and Forgetting is Kundera's most expressly and programmatically polyphonic novel. Unlike in the case of *Life Is Elsewhere*, here we can no longer talk about any main story and digressions from it, since the story lines—highly elliptical, focusing on the thematically essential—are equal and independent of one another. Tamina's story acquires special significance only insofar as it is rendered in two of the seven parts of the novel. The thematic approach is foregrounded not only in the title of the novel—which names two of the central themes of the work: "laughter" and "forgetting"—but also in the titles of the individual parts, which refer to further themes. Two titles appear twice in the work. Both the first part, about Mirek, and the fourth, about Tamina, bear the title "Lost Letters," while both part 3 and part 6, the latter in which Tamina's story is taken up again, are entitled "The Angels." This doubling up stresses the thematic coherence of the otherwise independent parts.

The parts may further consist of components of different kinds. The first chapter, for example, opens with a report of a historical event, the Czech revolution of February 1948 and how this historical event was subsequently retouched. In a photograph taken at the historic moment, a politician who had fallen from grace was later airbrushed out of the image. This opens up a perspective on the story of Mirek, who preserves documents of political significance risking his own and his companions' safety. At the same time, however, he strives to revise his own past by destroying some love letters, which in hindsight he finds compromising. This demonstrates that the same willingness to retouch the past occurs in both public and private history writing. Part 3, "The Angels," consists of four kinds of material: the story of two (US) American girls interpreting Ionesco's *Rhinoceros* (the story starts realistically but ends with a surrealistic ascension to the heavens), essay-like reflections on laughter, the author-narrator's recollections from soon after 1968 when he earned his living by writing an astrology column for a popular Prague weekly, and the description of a circle dance of young communists in 1948, which again ends with the surrealistic ascension of the dancers. The passages, which differ entirely in their contents, are united by the theme of laughter. The essay-like passages on laughter serve as a commentary on the girls' interpretation of Ionesco's play as a comedy in the sense of an innocent amusement. The narrator's laughter at the party functionary who believes in horoscopes is "devilish," ironic in nature, whereas the laughter that accompanies the ring dance of both the young communists and the girls and their teacher represents an affirmative rejoicing in existence, which Kundera calls the "laughter of the angels." All four lines focus on laughter in one or both of its two opposite variants: the ironic, mocking laughter of the Devil and the rejoicing, jubilant laughter of the angels.

Part 2 of *The Book of Laughter and Forgetting*, entitled "Mama," has a single story line dealing with a young couple, their friend, and the husband's mother. Similarly, part 4, "Lost Letters," is set in a single fictional world. Its central character is Tamina, a Czech emigrant, who attempts with great effort to get hold of her own diary and letters, dating from the time of her marriage, in order to preserve the memory of that time. Part 5, "Litost," gives an account of a night of the love affair, laughable but gilded by poetry, between a student and a butcher's wife. Part 6, "Angels," describing Tamina's death, consists of several kinds of material. It begins with examples from contemporary Czechoslovakia or from recent or more remote events in Czech history showing how a nation is forced to let its own past sink into oblivion. Parallel to these events, the author-narrator describes his father's death and how before his death he lost the faculty of speech. The narration then returns to Tamina, who finds herself on the "children's island." Here the narration, as Kundera says himself, is dreamlike (*The Art* 76). In the seventh and last part of the novel, "The Border," the central character is a 45-year-old Czech emigrant called Jan, but the events narrated are only loosely interconnected. This lack of unity of events directs the reader's attention to the thematic level.

In the first, fourth, and sixth parts of the novel the themes of forgetting and remembering take various forms. While in the first part the tendency toward deliberate forgetting or the retouching of the past is depicted as a characteristic of both the community and the individual, in Tamina's story involuntary forgetting is presented as an inexorable constant of human existence. In the first part of her story (in part 4), Tamina does her best to save the past from falling into oblivion, because all that is significant for her was her marriage, yet in the second part of her story (told in part 6) such forgetting has taken place. Some of the contrapuntal passages of this part deal with exhortations by the political leaders of a totalitarian regime to its citizens to forget the past, while others depict the process of forgetting that takes place when human life comes to an end, in the story of the last phase of the author's father's life. Part 2, "Mama," reveals the connection between remembering past events and experiencing the present as meaningful, thus supplementing the exploration of this theme in Tamina's story. The part concerning the student and the butcher's wife, "Litost," deals with the "lyrical" view of the world and how this generates an experience of meaningfulness. The seventh and last part focuses on the experience of the "border," exploring how a meaning suddenly turns into its opposite. A serious thing, for instance, becomes comical, an important matter unimportant, and vice versa. Looking back at the previous parts from the perspective of the last one, we now realize that the theme of the border is present throughout the whole novel. "Mama," for example, deals with the changes that occur in the meaning of the sexual act; in the part describing the student's love affair with the butcher's wife, the pathetic turns into the comic and the comic by the force of poetry back into the pathetic; in the section about the girls interpreting Ionesco, the mocking laughter of the audience turns into the angelic laughter of delight by the girls and their teacher.

An analysis of the structure of *The Book of Laughter and Forgetting* shows that the term "novel in the form of variations" applies to it well. As noted, writing a novel "in the form of variations" is not merely a matter of the technical construction of the work, but also assumes a specific manner of dealing with "truths" in the novel. A theme appears within different contexts in a number of variations, each of which represents a partial truth about it. However, another important aspect of the thematic composition of Kundera's novels, namely, his tendency to think about themes as pairs of opposites, is not encompassed by the concept of the "novel in the form of variations," nor does he ever refer to this, although it is present in *The Book of Laughter and Forgetting*, as well as in both earlier and later novels. He often speaks of his intention to explore particular themes in different variations, but what actually interests him is the ambiguity of things, the intimate relationship between something and its opposite, and the sudden shifts and reversals which take place between the two extremes. His analysis of remembering is intertwined with that of forgetting, the joke is weighed against and contrasted with seriousness, the "lyrical" attitude with maturity, weight with weightlessness, mortality with immortality, haste with slowness. Both opposites are studied in several variations. What fascinates Kundera is the experience of the boundary at which a matter is suddenly transformed into its opposite or where its value suddenly changes. For instance, forgetting, which is generally thought of as negative, may under certain circumstances seem beneficial; the act of love-making, which has felt like hard work performed out of a sense of duty, may suddenly turn into a supreme feeling of floating in an ocean of human love only to lose this meaning once more within a second. The most solemn and serious thing can all of a sudden appear ridiculous and vice versa whereby the ridiculous and insignificant can turn into something serious. Laughter in itself has two meanings. The malicious laughter of the devil can at any moment be transformed into the joyous laughter of angels praising the perfection of creation. What is crucial here is precisely the experience that a given phenomenon may at any moment reach the border, where it completely changes in meaning. In the experience of the border, we can perhaps discern an important further dimension of what Kundera calls the skepticism of the genre of the novel. His skepticism does not derive merely from his recognition of the infinite number of (partial) truths, but also from his conviction that it is impossible to determine a phenomenon definitively, because it may undergo an abrupt and total change of meaning.

The oppositions in Kundera's thinking are polar. In other words, they are opposite ends on one and the same scale: weight and weightlessness, maturity and immaturity, forgetting and remembering. In one case only Kundera's opposites cannot be thought of as polar, but as a metaphysical, dualistic antagonism between two entities which exist independent of each other and are in constant struggle. Such a dualistic antagonism is that of the body and the soul (and their derivatives). It is characteristic of his thinking in polarities that a phenomenon cannot be permanently fixed at either pole of the scale, but keeps fluctuating between them. What appears weightless (for example a joke) may at any moment become heavy. Similarly, the values of the poles resist being permanently fixed and may change from positive to negative or vice versa; for instance, weight and weightlessness, and remembering and forgetting, may both be perceived either negatively or positively.

Kundera's thinking has occasionally been labeled as based on binary oppositions (see, e.g., Jefferson). Yet the structuralist concept of binary oppositions refers to the definition of linguistic signs through their opposites, whereas in Kundera's fiction the characters experience the phenomena directly and independently of each other in a given situation, in a word, "phenomenologically," without the mediation of their opposites. Rather than considering two opposite meanings as mutually interdependent, what attracts Kundera are the fluctuations of a phenomenon between the two poles, which is a temporal phenomenon. Examples of this kind of thinking are found, for instance, in Goethe and Nietzsche (see Degner; Schmitt). Of these two, Kundera's thinking in polarities resembles more closely that of Nietzsche. For Goethe, polarity as a mode of thinking does not exclude progress or the struggle for a synthesis, whereas Nietzsche conceives changes in phenomena as a constant oscillation between the poles, excluding any idea of (historical) progress or the possibility of an all-encompassing synthesis. In Kundera's work, it is precisely the border where this oscillation alters the content or value of a phenomenon that forms the hidden, "inverted" center of his non- or antisystematic thinking; "inverted," because the oscillation of phenomena at the border makes it impossible to fix them through definitions and consequently to construct a theoretical system of knowledge based on these definitions. As the point at which a phenomenon changes its meaning, border is a concept that does not have a thematic opposite. One can talk only about a shorter or greater distance from the border or from the point where the meaning changes. The modern individual's existence is essentially being close to this border, which implies an uncertainty in his or her sense giving.

Kundera's thinking is rooted in the mode of human existence typical of modernity in which the individual is caught up in an endless search of the meaning of events and his or her own actions with no guarantee that the meanings discovered will be true or definitive. It is not an exaggeration to say that sense giving, in this modern sense, is the cornerstone of Kundera's entire novelistic thinking. It is, I argue, the "architheme" underpinning all his explorations of the different themes of human existence in his novels. Moreover, it is the architheme which he follows in his sketches of the history of the novel. The modern novel was born when the all-inclusive theological-metaphysical system of truth had lost its credibility. With the Enlightenment, universal reason was assigned the task of defining the content and meanings of different phenomena; and after the beginning of the nineteenth century it was the prevailing view that such content and meanings develop within the historical process within which we produce our own reality. Sensemaking, as the central problem in Kundera's work, has to be seen within this frame. On what grounds, he asks, do we experience something as significant? Is any significance now possible, once man has fallen outside of History, or now that History has been transformed from the realm of the realization of human ideals into a trap? Unlike Broch, Kundera refuses to take for granted that the state of the modern individual who has to determine the value of things by himself or herself is unbearable. In the last essay in *The Sleepwalkers*, Broch writes that "the final indivisible unit in the disintegration of values is the human individual. And the less that individual partakes in some authoritative system, and the more he is left to his own empirical autonomy . . . the narrower and more modest does his 'private theology' become, the more incapable is it of comprehending any values beyond its immediate and most personal environment" (628). Kundera's object of scrutiny, in contrast, is precisely the individual's construction of meanings, changes in them, and the preconditions of meaningfulness outside of History.

It is from this perspective of sense giving that remembering and forgetting, as well as the two different kinds of laughter, are examined in *The Book of Laughter and Forgetting*. Remembering is the precondition for experiencing life as meaningful, while forgetting deprives things of their meanings. The matter is made more complicated, however, by retouching, a kind of retroactive improving of the meanings of past things, and by the fact that beneficial kinds of forgetting also exist. The ironic laughter of the devil questions given meanings, while angelic laughter expresses absolute trust in the highest meaningfulness of everything. The latter is actually a kind of utmost seriousness, as illustrated in the following quotation from *The Joke*: "It was the first year after February 1948; a new life had begun, a genuinely new and different life, and its features, as I remember them, were rigidly serious. The odd thing was that the seriousness took the form not of a frown but of a smile, yes, what those years said of themselves was that they were the most joyous years, and anyone who failed to rejoice was immediately suspected of lamenting the victory of the working class or (what was equally sinful) giving way *individualistically* to inner sorrows" (31). The absolute approval of existence can again turn into the experience of complete meaninglessness, as Tamina realizes on the children's island. Likewise, the themes of "weight" and "weightlessness" fall under the architheme of sense giving, insofar as they refer metaphorically to the experience of meaningfulness and meaninglessness, respectively.

In Kundera's novels, the architheme of sense giving is implicit or invisible in the sense that it is never named as a theme. It does not appear in any of the titles of the novels or their individual parts, nor among the sixty-three keywords listed in *The Art of the Novel*, by means of which Kundera defines some of the important themes of his novels. Why Kundera does not recognize this architheme as a theme at all may be owing to the fact that he sees the novel in general as a genre dealing with the existence of the modern individual who is occupied with the problem of determining the content and meaning of things. Thus he does not regard the architheme as characteristic of his own novels alone, in contrast to those themes which he considers as his own discoveries. Unearthing the architheme of sense giving, as well as Kundera's typical thinking in terms of polarities, shows that his own comments on the thematic composition of his novels are far from exhaustive. He speaks of polyphony and of the novel in the form of variations from a primarily technical perspective, and in so doing overlooks the extent to which the thematic structuring of his works is rooted in modern existence, in problems of sense giving and of changing meanings.

The title of *The Book of Laughter and Forgetting* is only ostensibly of the same type of title as *Romeo and Juliet* or *Sense and Sensibility*, titles referring to two things which either go together or are opposites. The title actually conceals as much as it reveals, the second half in each of the two pairs of themes "laughter" and "seriousness," that is, "forgetting" and "remembering." Similarly, the title of *The Unbearable Lightness of Being* refers to only one of the two central themes, while the opposite of lightness, namely, weight or weightiness, remains concealed. "Lightness" and "weight" refer, as in *The Joke* or in Tamina's story in *The Book of Laughter and Forgetting*, to the experiences of meaninglessness and meaningfulness, respectively: life is light when it lacks the weight of important, meaningful matters. In *The Unbearable Lightness of Being*, lightness and its opposite are examined as threats and as possibilities in the individual's life. Most parts of *The Unbearable Lightness of Being* bear thematic titles as well, once again underlining the thematic composition of the novel. The first and fifth parts both bear the title of "Lightness and Weight," while the title of both part 2 and part 4 is "Soul and Body," again emphasizing the variation of the themes and the structure of the whole as a novel in variation form. The remaining parts are entitled "Words Misunderstood," "The Grand March" and "Karenin's Smile." The pair, "lightness" and "weight," articulates the existential problem of the male protagonist, Tomas: what makes a certain experience or issue, or one's life, "weighty"?

"Soul" and "body" are the keywords of his wife Tereza. The question is how they are interconnected with each other, separated from each other, in opposition to each other. In both of the parts entitled "Soul and Body," as well as in the last one, "Karenin's Smile," the story is narrated alternately from Tomas's and Tereza's perspective. The narration proceeds in a single line, even though the events are not chronologically ordered. The novel contains some dreamlike passages which convey Tereza's nightmares, yet these passages are not separate from the narrative concerning the couple's life. The parts entitled "Words Misunderstood" and "The Grand March" deal with the other couple of the novel, Franz and Sabina, who belong to the same fictional world as Tomas and Tereza, Sabina being one of Tomas's lovers. The fictional world of the novel is thus more unified than that of *The Book of Laughter and Forgetting*, in which, following the principle of polyphony, different fictional and nonfictional worlds exist separately from one another. In *The Unbearable Lightness of Being,* the characters are linked both through concrete events and theme. Sabina experiences the same problem of lightness as Tomas; the expression "the unbearable lightness of being" is actually used in reference to her.

Part 3 of *The Unbearable Lightness of Being* contains "A Short Dictionary of Misunderstood Words," a list of words and concepts—including, for example, "fidelity," "betrayal," "woman," "cemetery," and "Grand March"—which Sabina and Franz conceive of differently and which thus stand in the way of their mutual understanding. The motif of the Grand March is taken up again in the eponymous part 6. The "Grand March," as a demonstration of the common will to fight for a better world, is for Kundera a synecdoche-like representation of "leftist kitsch." The main theme of part 6 is in fact kitsch, defined by Kundera—just like the angels' laughter, but from a different viewpoint—as the absolute approval of existence. Throughout the chapter, the concept of kitsch is elaborated on the abstract level, but it is also elucidated through a brief story about the death of Stalin's son in which the opposite of kitsch is introduced, namely "shit," a word by which Kundera refers to whatever is in principle unacceptable in the world order. The title of part 7, "Karenin's Smile," is again a synecdoche or metaphor, which by way of Tereza's dog refers to the part's main theme, the "idyllic."

Another important theme that appears at the story level in all of Kundera's novels, but is usually not reflected upon at the thematic level, is death. Many of Kundera's protagonists die: in *Life Is Elsewhere* the poet Jaromil, in *Farewell Waltz* Ruzena, in *The Book of Laughter and Forgetting* Tamina, in *The Unbearable Lightness of Being* Tomas, Tereza, and Franz, and in *Immortality* Agnes. In addition to these protagonists, several minor characters die. Kundera mitigates the strikingness of the ubiquitous presence of death by way of, for instance, foreshadowing, announcing the death long before it actually occurs and thus removing the suspense or not placing a death at the end of the novel. For example, in *The Unbearable Lightness of Being,* readers learn about the fatal accident that will cause Tomas's and Tereza's death around the middle of the novel and several of the following parts deal with their problems and the development of their relationship. Consequently, their death does not constitute the final point of the narrative and death does not present itself as the final "truth" about their story; rather, it is the perspective from which we look back at their lives. This is a necessary perspective, because concealing the inescapability of death means kitsch, as is said in *The Unbearable Lightness of Being,* following Broch ("Evil" 36–37).

Immortality is another example of the way in which the thematic titles of Kundera's novels both reveal and conceal simultaneously. In this novel, the main theme is not the one announced by the title but its opposite, death or mortality, which is an inescapable part of human existence. The novel deals with the reality that, despite our mortality, we "cannot" die. While Heidegger declares that humanity's existence is "being towards death" (*Being* 46–53), Kundera claims that the individual does not take his or her mortality into account. This manifests itself on the one hand in a longing for immortality, on the other in the attitude of kitsch which denies or veils the fact of death. The novel consists of four lines, two of which are intertwined. The main line, taking up four of the seven parts, tells about Agnes and her family members, her husband, her daughter, her sister, and the sister's lover. Except for part 3, "Fighting," which describes Agnes's relationship with her sister Laura in twenty-one chapters with titles of their own, the chapters of the parts are merely numbered. In part 2, "Immortality," and 4 "*Homo sentimentalis,*" the main characters are Goethe and Bettina Brentano. In these parts, death and the longing for immortality are widely reflected upon. Similarly to the sixth part of *Life Is Elsewhere*, here too part 6, "The Dial," functions as a window opening up onto the world outside. It tells about the erotic life of a man called Rubens, connected loosely to Agnes's story. The part deals with the temporality of human existence and with remembering and sense giving, which are connected to it. With the vanishing of meaningfulness, death is looming. The fourth line, intertwined with all the others, deals with the author himself, as he is writing the novel. He describes how the idea of the heroine was born in his head, originating in the gesture of a sixty-year-old woman. A car accident, just like the one in which Agnes will die, is reported in the news he is listening to on the radio. In the last part of the novel its author makes an appearance as a character and meets with Professor Avenarius, a character in Agnes's story, and at the end he becomes acquainted with Paul, Agnes's husband, who after her death has married her younger sister Laura, who makes a brief appearance. The alter ego of Kundera points out that the characters are his own creations; nevertheless, he discovers some features in them he had not expected them to possess. Thus, the creative process of writing the novel is presented within the work itself with capricious playfulness, which makes it metafictional in a different manner than Kundera's earlier novels, resembling the metafictionality typical of postmodern literature.

Besides death, mortality, and the longing for immortality, further themes elaborated in *Immortality* are body and soul, beauty and ugliness, the temporal dimension of human life, and the individual construction of the self by either subtracting or adding attributes, as well as *homo sentimentalis* and "imagology." The themes reflect Kundera's thinking in polarities: for the opposite of *homo sentimentalis* no name is given, but in the story an opposition emerges between on the one hand Bettina and Laura, depicted as sentimentalists, and on the other Agnes, who, like Tomas and Sabina in *The Unbearable Lightness of Being*, can be seen as an individual striving for authenticity and autonomy. This opposition is similar to that between a "lyrical" or immature view of life and an adult or mature one. While the former are determined from the outside, using other people as mirrors, the latter endeavor to determine their identity independently of others. Kundera's concept of imagology, however, raises the question of whether an individual is even in principle able to construct an identity independently of the public image ascribed to him or her. The author-narrator and several of his characters reflect upon a contemporary world dominated by the visual and the image.

In comparison with *The Unbearable Lightness of Being*, *Immortality* is more clearly a thematic composition or a novel in the form of variations. With regard to the degree of the independence and distinctness of the narrative lines, *Immortality* occupies a place somewhere between *The Book of Laughter and Forgetting* and *The Unbearable Lightness of Being*. What distinguishes it from the earlier novels is that in *Immortality*, the author-narrator as a person penetrates into the fictional world of his protagonists. The intersection and entwinement of the different narrative lines violate one of the basic criteria of the polyphonic novel, that of the independence of the voices.

The architecture of the short novels

The blending of different narrative lines or different types of discourse is also characteristic of Kundera's three late short novels, *Slowness*, *Identity*, and *Ignorance*. *Slowness* is set in a French château which has been transformed into a hotel. In the frame story of the novel, Kundera and his wife arrive at the château, which in the fictional story is also hosting a conference on entomology. It is during this conference that the first encounter takes place between Vincent and Julie, and the young man makes it clear early in their conversation that he intends to sleep with her. According to the author-narrator, the château had once been the setting of another love affair, between its lady and a young knight, as told in Vivant Denon's novella *Point de lendemain*. The different narrative lines are not kept separate. The entomological conference, a fictional event invented by the author, appears in the author's wife's dreams as well. As Vincent is leaving, he meets the Chevalier of the eighteenth-century story and the author and his wife see Vincent mount his motorcycle and leave the château. The three different story lines—and three different realities—thus cross and are at odds with one another. The main theme in the novel is hedonism, the possibility of which is scrutinized through the opposition between the rapid pace of the contemporary world and the slowness of the eighteenth century. This pair of themes is connected with the themes of beauty and meaning or of their absence. Further themes of the novel are the construction of the self by performing in front of others—characteristic of particular individuals, whom the author now calls "dancers" (17–20)—and the instability of individual identity in the modern world.

The title of the novel *Identity* calls attention to one of Kundera's main themes. Its themes—how the individual self is distinguished from others, how a man's gaze selects a woman as an individual in a crowd, questions of self and remembering, soul and body—are familiar from Kundera's other novels, but are here developed in new variations. The themes are embedded in a single narrative line about Chantal and Jean-Marc, keeping the structure of the novel simpler than those of Kundera's other novels. The only point where *Identity* differs from a plain, chronologically told narrative with flashbacks is its ending, where Chantal gets locked up in an odd house in London and Jean-Marc wakes her up. It turns out that some of the events have taken place only in a dream. Unlike the part describing Tamina's sojourn on the children's island in *The Book of Laughter and Forgetting*, the Xavier passages of *Life Is Elsewhere,* or Goethe's and Hemingway's celestial conversations in *Immortality*, here the dreamlike narrative is not a distinct line separate from the realistic narration. The dream in *Identity*—unlike Tereza's dreams in *The Unbearable Lightness of Being*—does not appear as an integral part of the realistic narration either. The transition between realistic narration and dream is blurred, and the author-narrator asks "Where is the border?" (153). Here the concept of border has a new meaning. Where earlier it referred to the point where the meanings of things suddenly change, it now represents the point of transition from reality to dream, and this point cannot be grasped or defined. The structure of the novel is not polyphonic in the sense of mixing different story lines; yet *Identity* is a composition of themes rather than an account of the protagonists' lives, although the chronology of events is followed more closely than in many others of Kundera's texts. By dissolving the border between dream and reality, which in Kundera's earlier novels are kept distinct, the novel comes closer, in a sense, to the "ontological uncertainty" that is often regarded as characteristic of the postmodern novel (see McHale 10; Saariluoma [Steinby], *Der postindividualistische* [40–41] where I argue that rather than the shift from epistemological to ontological questions, it is the weakness of the epistemological subject that should be seen as the cause of ontological uncertainty).

Ignorance does not contribute anything essentially new to Kundera's way of composing novels, but it resumes some of his themes and develops them in a partly new way, especially the theme of the temporality of human existence. Where in *Slowness* and *Identity* the events are set in France, *Ignorance* is set among Czech emigrants shortly after the turning point of 1989. The novel is about Irena, a Czech émigrée living in France who is confronted with the fact that after the events of 1989 both her French friends and her old Czech acquaintances expect her to return to her native country. To her, this expectation is equal to a demand to deny or forget that she has spent the most important years of her life in France. Irena's dilemma—whether or not to return—is compared with the experiences of the mythic traveler Ulysses returning to his home in Ithaca. Another Czech émigré, called Josef, who is visiting his relatives in Bohemia, has similar feelings. When the two of them meet by chance, Irena recognizes in him someone to whom she had once been attracted, but picking up their thread from that point proves problematic. When Josef decides to return to Denmark to cherish the memory of his deceased wife, Irena comes to realize that nothing remains for her for the rest of her life (as she thinks) but solitude. The story is simple and the themes are familiar, although the variations are new: the immaturity of youth, the sense of duty toward the deceased and therefore endlessly weak spouse (Tamina was guided by a similar feeling toward her late husband), repetitiveness leading to the transformation of physical love into something insignificant, and forgetting—even of the most important things connected to one's love—as human destiny. In *Ignorance,* the themes appear in the form of individual motifs or ideas rather than as elements of a complex thematic structure. The prevailing sense is the feeling of having reached the last phase of life and of looking back retrospectively, whereupon melancholy supersedes the ironic playfulness to which we are accustomed in Kundera's novels.

Chapter Six
The Sentimental and the Authentic Self

Kundera emphasizes the idea that being open to facing the new is a virtue in a novelist, but where he is concerned with the possibilities of human existence, his oeuvre is in fact unified thematically. This recurrence of themes makes it difficult to avoid repetition in the analysis of his novels. To divorce the themes from the works, however, contradicts Kundera's conviction that a novel has to be conceived as a whole and as a unified thematic composition created by its author. In this and the next three chapters, I therefore analyze each of Kundera's most important novels, from *Life Is Elsewhere* to *Immortality*, in terms of one or more themes that are pivotal in Kundera's oeuvre as a whole but are dealt with most thoroughly in each specific novel. The same themes in other novels are referred to less extensively in order to provide additional insight. The purpose of such an analysis is to achieve a comprehensive overview of Kundera's novelistic work, emphasizing both its thematic continuity and the uniqueness of each individual work.

Kundera in his art of the novel aspires to examine some of the possibilities of human existence in the era of "terminal paradoxes," where trust not only in a metaphysical order but also in History is lacking. In a previous chapter I discuss *The Joke,* which depicts the basic situation of a man who has fallen out of History. Here I discuss *Life Is Elsewhere* and *Farewell Waltz* from the point of view of the two contrasting existential strategies of modern individuals: the sentimental and the authentic mode of existence. The problematic of these two novels still arises out of Kundera's historical experiences in Czechoslovakia, but in contrasting the sentimental and the authentic mode of existence he examines universal "anthropological" possibilities. In chapter 7 I discuss *The Book of Laughter and Forgetting* from the point of view of the effect of ridicule, remembering, and forgetting on the individual's sense of leading a meaningful life. In *The Unbearable Lightness of Being*, Kundera explores the three principal modes of sense-making practices available to the nonsentimental individual as Kundera sees them, namely, hedonism, aestheticism, and love. Finally, in the analysis of *Immortality*, I look at the relevance of the fact of death, or rather of mortality, for efforts by the modern individual to discover meaning in life itself without any underpinning of religion, ideology, or History.

Kundera asks: how does sense giving take place in the contemporary world which the individual cannot hope to change? In other words, in a world where History is no longer an open space of opportunities but a trap? There are two kinds of answers. On the one hand, there are those who do dare to face what they really experience and orient their action accordingly. These individuals have given up on all ideologies and have turned their back on History in searching for the meaningful solely in private life. For Kundera it is only these individuals who represent the autonomous modern individual in search of authenticity and who relies upon himself or herself alone in defining his or her own existence. On the other hand, there are those who identify themselves with ideologies or "grand" ideas and feelings. These individuals might be called inauthentic; the notions Kundera uses are "sentimental" and "lyrical"—in *Immortality* (218-19), *homo sentimentalis* and *homo hystericus*—but "immaturity" and "youth" are for him also close in meaning to the former. Characteristic of this attitude is the adoration of the individual's own feelings. *Homo sentimentalis* or *homo hystericus* is not a human being who has feelings, which we all have, but one "who has raised feelings to a category of value" (*Immortality* 218). This leads to propping up his or her identity with assumed great feelings. In his criticism of artificially nourished feelings, Kundera actually comes close to Kant and other Enlightenment writers who criticized the (first) sentimental current in literature in the mid-eighteenth century (see Kant 509; see also Jäger; Sauder). Kundera deepens the analysis of the sentimental attitude by connecting it with immaturity, the propensity to give up personal autonomy and let others decide what things actually mean and even what one actually is in oneself. Since other persons function for such an individual as mirrors, he or she is incapable of perceiving others as they in themselves really are.

For the opposite of the sentimental or lyrical Kundera has no name. He sometimes refers to the "epic" attitude as opposed to the "lyrical," meaning by the former an attitude of acceptance of the plurality and the relativity of matters as opposed to lyrical subjectivity and egocentrism. Accordingly, in *The Unbearable Lightness of Being,* "epic womanizers" are distinguished from lyrical ones (194–95). In *Life Is Elsewhere*, the opposite of the young poet Jaromil is the anonymous "man in his forties." The appellation here indicates that the attitude which a person in a mature age may have adopted is the opposite of lyricism and sentimentality, typical of youth. However, not everyone achieves this attitude simply by aging; on the contrary, most people reveal at least some propensity to sentimentality. This is why it would be more accurate to speak of a person's sentimental or authentic attitude toward a certain matter or in a given situation, rather than of a sentimental or an authentic individual in general. Yet often one of these two attitudes prevails in a person to the extent that speaking of either a sentimental individual or an individual striving for authenticity is justified.

The opposition between the sentimental and the authentic types of personality or attitude exists within the framework of modernity. Neither alternative means a return to the premodern order of things in which meanings are determined independently of individuals. It is true that the sentimental individual relinquishes his or her autonomy because of a great truth or a beautiful feeling, but this too is regarded as an individual choice, because the individual could have chosen differently. In all of Kundera's novels there appear different versions of sentimental individuals and of those striving for authenticity, facing the uncertainty of existence. The author shows a constant interest in unveiling and analyzing inauthentic attitudes, sentiments, and decisions he regards with irony, but the question that bothers him more than anything else is whether it is possible for the individual who strives for authenticity and who searches for meaning without recourse to ideologies, myths, or History to succeed in this endeavor and avoid ending up with the unbearable lightness of being.

Life Is Elsewhere as an analysis of the lyrical attitude

In his second and the third novels, *Life is Elsewhere* and *Farewell Waltz*, Kundera continues the analysis of "anthropological findings" in the same political and historical situation which is the basis of the explorations of human possibilities in *The Joke*. Where Ludvik in *The Joke* appears first and foremost as a victim of communist rule, Jaromil, the young poet and informer in *Life Is Elsewhere*, is a perpetrator of terror and ultimately a victim of his own attitude. The novel is not autobiographical, but the reader is aware that Kundera himself, as a young poet and revolutionary, took part in the communist movement after 1948 and that the type analyzed by Kundera therefore includes himself. I agree with Andreas W. Mytze in that few writers have been so recklessly critical about themselves and their country as Kundera is in *Life Is Elsewhere* (50). In Kundera's analysis, the fact that the young revolutionary is a poet and therefore unworldly is not offered as an excuse purifying him of all guilt. The new insight that Kundera insists on having discovered is that it is precisely the "lyrical" attitude that makes the poet a revolutionary, an informer, and a perpetrator of terror. Kundera himself contends in *Testaments Betrayed* that "more than the Terror, the lyricization of the Terror was a trauma for me" (155). It is this complex of lyricism and terror that is his topic in *Life Is Elsewhere*. Again, he does not analyze historical events as such, but focuses on what the historical situation reveals about human beings, what it demonstrates to be possible for the individual.

The lyrical or sentimental attitude was depicted already in *The Joke*, although not with the same poignancy as in *Life Is Elsewhere*. In *Testaments Betrayed*, Kundera calls Helena of *The Joke* a *homo sentimentalis* for whom communism serves as "the wellspring of enthusiasm" (13). Actually, any ideological attitude is in Kundera's view sentimental. In *The Joke*, this is depicted not only by Helena's "enthusiastic" communism, but also by Kostka's Christian communism, Jaroslav's folkloristic romanticism, and Ludvik's pact with History. Of the four characters, Ludvik is the one who later distances himself most determinedly from any ideology; as already noted, however, this change does not take place as a gradual process of inner maturation but is precipitated by a sudden blow from the outside. None of Kundera's novels actually depicts the gradual maturation process whereby a person overcomes sentimentalism, the attitude characteristic of youth. Depicting the psychological development of a human being is of no interest to Kundera, because any search for causal psychological explanations for a person's behavior—an objective typical of the novels of the age of realism—diverts attention away from what he sees as crucial, namely, the possibilities of existence in a given situation and the choices made by the individual in that situation. Each of Kundera's first three novels, however, portrays an intellectual at a certain stage of his development, so that they allow us to envisage a certain continuity between the different phases. *The Joke* is about the disillusionment of a young intellectual, *Life Is Elsewhere* takes a step back in depicting as its hero a young revolutionary and poet, and in *Farewell Waltz* one of the main figures, Jakub, is about to emigrate after experiencing deep disillusionment with politics. It is characteristic of Kundera that rather than depicting these as stages in the development of a single character, he splits up the material between three separate novels with three different protagonists and three different settings and scrutinizes each one as a distinct human situation.

The narration in *Life Is Elsewhere* is bitingly ironic. The novel tells the story of Jaromil and his mother, Mama. According to Kundera, a poet is born from an unusually close relationship between mother and son. The son remains bound to his mother and "will walk in the world like a dog on a long leash" (*Life* 102). The story opens with Mama convincing herself that her son was conceived on the seashore in a romantic landscape, although a less romantic alternative is actually the more probable. Concomitantly, she embellishes her love for Jaromil's father into an unfettered elemental force; however, as her husband does not display a sentimental embellishment of his feelings toward her, she starts imagining an alabaster statuette of Apollo, standing on the bedside table, to be the father of her child. From the beginning she thus appears as a sentimental person who adores great emotions and for their sake is willing to retouch reality to suit herself. Disappointed in her husband, whom she vainly expects "to invest an equal amount of feeling in their joint account" (4), she turns to Jaromil for compensation. The joy of suckling her baby gives her the feeling of an "*Edenic* state": "the body could be fully body and had no need to hide itself with a fig leaf; they were plunged into the limitless space of a calm time; they lived together like Adam and Eve before they bit into the apple of the tree of knowledge" (9). Paradise represents a state prior to any differentiation. Body and soul, good and evil, self and other are not yet separate. This paradise is a state in the remote, mythic past, a time when the fundamental problems of existence had not yet emerged and the symbiosis between mother and infant represents a temporary return to it. In the case of the poet, this symbiosis does not end with early childhood. The relationship undergoes some changes, but the unity between mother and son essentially preserves its nature: "Their mothers' skirts spread over them [the poets] like the sky" (*The Book of Laughter* 185), preventing the sons from growing up into the real world of uncertainty and plurality (typical of Kundera is that his "explanation" ignores the existence of women poets). Jaromil's mother does everything to preserve the special relationship with her son, to exclude any possible rivals and to protect her son from an encounter with the real world, thus effectively obstructing him from reaching adulthood.

For Kundera adulthood means accepting the expulsion from paradise, the necessity of living separately from others, and the obligation of dealing with the problems of the world. A tendency to regress toward a symbiotic unity is nevertheless common at both the individual and the community level. In the case of revolutionaries, this is manifested as a longing for universal brotherhood, as a desire to be absorbed in the human community and as a dream of returning to the state of unity that prevailed before the emergence of any controversies. In *The Book of Laughter and Forgetting*, Kundera says that the revolutionaries wanted to create an idyll for all, because "all human beings have always aspired to an idyll, to that garden where nightingales sing, to that realm of harmony where the world does not rise up as a stranger against man and man against other men, but rather where the world and all men are shaped from one and the same matter" (11). Those who were unwilling to take part in the common idyll were imprisoned or sent to death. Instead of a political analysis, Kundera thus offers an analysis of the attitude which predominated in the political situation in question.

In this desire to return to a state of unity, we can recognize the romantic aspiration for de-individuation, which we encountered already in *The Joke*. While Romanticism as a historical movement contributed fundamentally to the birth of the modern understanding of the individual, at the same time individuality was experienced as a burden. The separation of the individual from the collective, the individual's responsibility, and the uncertainty brought about by autonomy resulted in a longing for a merging with something greater. For the Romantics, this escape from the separateness of the individual was attained by uniting with the beloved, by a religious-mystical experience, by the revival of mythical modes of thinking, or, as the ultimate and most perfect deliverance from individuality, by death; all of these appear, for instance, in Wagner's operas (see, e.g., Cicora; Williams). In the nineteenth and twentieth century the emergence of nationalism brought about a new realm within which the individual could identify with something greater than his or her own self, namely the nation, and through its participation in History, one could identify with this as well (see, e.g., Hobsbawm). Kundera looks upon all of these aspirations to transcend the individual as sentimental tendencies. In *The Joke*, Kostka and Jaroslav personify religious-mystical and mythical thinking, respectively; the theme of identification with the nation and with History appears both in *The Joke* and in *Life Is Elsewhere*; and the theme of sentimental love occurs in *Life Is Elsewhere*, *The Unbearable Lightness of Being*, and *Immortality*. To these forms of sentimental merging originating in Romanticism Kundera adds political ideology and the dream of an earthly paradise.

The young Jaromil is in constant need to prop up his ego with appropriated great emotions and thoughts. His mother has incited this habit by praising the richness of his "inner world" as displayed in his childish scribbles: "'Inner world!' Those were grand words, and Jaromil heard them with extreme satisfaction" (25). The inner world is supposed to be the source of a poet's greatness, yet whenever Jaromil "bent over that self in order to peer into it . . . all he could find was the reflection of himself bending over himself to peer into that self" (27). Lacking an "inner world" as a source of true poetry, Jaromil "wrote poems about the artificial childhood of tenderness, he wrote poems about an unreal death, he wrote poems about an unreal old age" (116–17), all in imitation of the surrealist poems he found in books borrowed from his mother's lover, the painter. The author discovers behind this artificiality the young man's anguish arising out of his lack of experience of physical love: "he moved toward the undressed body of a young woman as if he were treading on thorns; he desired this body and he was afraid of it; that is why, in his poems of tenderness, he fled from the tangibility of the body to take refuge in the world of childish imagination" (116).

Jaromil's lyrical poetry originates in the absence of coition, an idea later repeated in *The Book of Laughter and Forgetting* in the part dealing with the student and the butcher's wife and the poets' symposium. "Coition" stands here for maturity; Jaromil's feeling of inadequacy, of lacking manhood, is epitomized by its absence. The weakness deriving from his immaturity drives him to identify with great ideas and to take a radical stand. He joins the communist party to defy his uncle and take revenge on him for having humiliated him. Later he denounces avant-garde poetry in the name of the revolution, because he feels that he has been treated like a child in the circle of those who cultivate this poetry. However, when he raises his voice in opposition to the painter who until then had been his mentor in the world of arts, the unpleasant feeling overcomes him that he is still imitating the painter's gestures and his manner of speech: "In a fury of humiliation, he expressed his ideas, as he himself was aware, precisely and spitefully. Only one thing unsettled him from his very first words on: once again he was hearing the painter's distinctive, authoritative tone in his own voice, and he was unable to prevent his right hand from describing in the air the painter's characteristic gestures" (125). While speaking, he realizes that he is actually denouncing the whole of his own poetry, which he had until then considered as the most precious of his possessions, but "there was something more precious than his poems; something far away he didn't yet possess and longed for—manliness" (126).

In *Life Is Elsewhere*, for Kundera what lurks behind poetry, revolution, and the politics of art is the poet's immaturity. The actions of a lyrical or sentimental individual are always determined by small, private motives that concern his or her ego. Kundera denies the idea that ideologies can ever be the true motive behind our deeds. The display of great ideas and emotions is nothing but a folding screen, used to conceal the smallness of one's ego. The conviction that the world can be grasped in a single idea, however great, testifies as such, in Kundera's view, to immaturity. Such a conviction derives from a fear of "the relativized adult world" (186) and "that is why young people are passionate monists, emissaries of the absolute . . . that is why the young revolutionary demands a radically new world forged from a single clear idea" (186–87).

Kundera's contention that any great ideal or ideology functions merely as a disguise and as a means of self-aggrandizement of a small ego manifests, I argue, more profoundly than anything else his skepticism, or rather his cynicism, about politics and public affairs. When Kundera denounced the ideology he had been committed to as a young man, he was actually not only rejecting a particular ideology—Marxism, its faith in History, its conception of the relationship between individual and community—but also the belief that individuals can ever devote themselves to a "grand idea" simply because they are convinced of its truthfulness and value. This attitude is displayed in the polemic of the 1970s with Václav Havel over a petition for the liberation of political prisoners in which Havel criticized Kundera's view that the signing of the petition was good for nothing but the manifestation of one's own moral superiority (Havel, *Disturbing* 173–77). According to Kundera, the actual, hidden motive is always to be found at a completely different level—one that is petty, private, egocentric—than the arguments offered in support of the idea in question. From this it follows that Kundera's unveiling and analysis of sentimental or ideological attitudes is less variable than Musil's or Broch's rendering. The manner in which Musil's characters think of themselves is inaccurate, embellishing, and abounding in clichés, but their motives need not be limited to insignificant, personal interests alone. This is even less the case with Broch, who thinks that our actions must necessarily be based on general conceptions of morality in order to avoid the individual's complete disintegration. In *The Sleepwalkers*, Broch approves of Esch in his search for an ideology or a system of values, while he condemns Huguenau as a monster precisely for not feeling the same need. Kundera's skepticism toward any putatively universal ideology or system of values implies that for him only what is "small," personal, and nonideological can be authentic.

In the dreamlike passages of *Life Is Elsewhere*, Jaromil's imaginary alter ego Xavier does whatever Jaromil himself wishes to do: he seduces and leaves women, leads a revolutionary group on its dangerous journey on the rooftops, and keeps a notebook with a "list of all the enemies of the people, who were to be executed on the first day of the revolution" (75). Especially striking and alarming is Jaromil's flirtation with death. Jaromil's alter ego wants death, the greatest and most relentless matter of all, to give weight to his deeds: "He wished each of his acts, indeed each day, each hour, each second of his life to be measured against the supreme criterion, which is death" (70). He derives satisfaction from the idea that he has caused the death of the blond girl who was in love with him, as well as from the conviction that "she had not stopped loving him and that love lasts beyond the grave" (73). Jaromil's story shows how dangerous the desire to be measured in one's actions by the greatest ideas only might be.

In real life, Jaromil needs the alliance with political power and History to conceal his lack of maturity and he becomes a member of the communist party, one who is unwilling to accept any compromise and who checks "the firmness, manliness and harshness of his words" (139) in the eyes of his comrades. Yet this does not alter anything about the fact that "every mirror presented him with the grinning ugliness of his immaturity" (120). Finally, he comes to experience physical love with a salesgirl, but not even this love affair with "the redhead" brings him maturity. Although his original advances were meant for a fellow worker of hers, he now makes his love swell up into immensity. The redhead is not beautiful and when an acquaintance of his once makes an ironic remark about her appearance, Jaromil denies any more intimate relationship with her. Yet a better strategy for denying the significance of the girl's ugliness is to let it dissolve in the infinity of his love: "Yes, he was ready to make all her faults vanish in the all-forgiving solvent of his love, but only under one condition: that she obediently immerse herself in that solvent, that she never be anywhere else but in that bathtub of love, that she never try, not even in a single thought, to leave that tub" (178). Instead of the girl he perceives only his own passion, aggrandized into an absolute (depicted here with a Musil-like antilyric metaphor, a solvent). The girl has no other right but to be the object of his passion.

Yet the state of being the mere object of the other's amplified sentiments is dangerous, since one aggrandized emotion can be replaced by another. Jaromil eventually ruins the life of both the girl and her brother by reporting to the police that the brother is about to defect. The girl is immediately arrested and Jaromil never sees her again. The motif of sending a fellow human being to death without the slightest remorse reappears once again, this time with the victim as a lover. Since for Jaromil only his own feelings and not the girl herself are important, he does not lose anything. On the contrary, after the arrest he is overwhelmed by a feeling even greater than love, namely, the sense of having fulfilled his duty: "Of course, it was terrible to sacrifice an actual woman (redheaded, nice, delicate, talkative) for the sake of the future world, but it was probably the only tragedy of our time that was worthy of beautiful verse, worthy of a great poem!" (*Life* 225).

In the end, Jaromil himself becomes the victim of his own sentimental immaturity. After being ridiculed by a young man in the company of some young intellectuals with whom he aspires to feel equal, to conceal his shame he sits for a long time in the freezing cold on the balcony. As a consequence he catches a cold, develops pneumonia, and finally dies under his mother's nursing. Kundera draws a parallel with the death of the poet Lermontov in a duel. I add that in *The Sleepwalkers* the brother of the romantic Pasenow is likewise killed in a duel "for the sake of honor." Laughter and the sentimental are archenemies which cannot be reconciled. For the sentimentalist, ironic laughter is a matter of deadly seriousness in the most literal sense of the word. In a radio interview, Kundera has said that in the character of Jaromil, he intended to demystify the myth that "a poet can never be a spy and stoolpigeon together" (qtd. in Liehm, "Kundera" 32). Using Kundera's own expression, we can say that the new aspect of human existence which he has uncovered in *Life Is Elsewhere* is the fact that being a poet and being a perpetrator are two sides of the same coin. Yet we may add that he has also shown that a poet is as dangerous to himself or herself as to others.

The sixth, penultimate part of the novel takes place after Jaromil's death and deals with the encounter between the redhead who has just been released after three years in prison and her ex-lover, the man in his forties. As noted, according to the author, this part functions as an "observatory," opening up a new perspective into Jaromil's world. Jaromil himself "never knew anything about anyone" but himself (*Life* 229). While in other parts of the novel the criticism of Jaromil (and his mother) is articulated through the heavy irony of the description, in the sixth part the narration is nonironic and the criticism of Jaromil ensues from the presence of a contrasting, mature attitude. The man, who is presented sympathetically, is himself a victim of the constructors of a paradise. At the beginning of the war he had left the country to fight the Germans with the British Air Force, but when he returned after the war "the authorities determined that he had been too closely tied to capitalist England" to be reliable enough for the socialist army, and he had to earn his living working in a factory (238). Although ever since his wife's death he has led a "colourful erotic life," he is "basically an idyllist and saw to it that his adventures were calm and orderly" (235). His attitude toward life is hedonistic and skeptical. He enjoys reading books, taking warm baths, and spending time with his mistresses, none of which demands too much commitment from him. The expression "calm and orderliness in his adventures" suggests that he is no longer devoted to the passionate exploration of existence, but looks for minor love affairs which do not disturb his peace. His hedonistic and skeptical attitude, however, does not exclude being considerate toward his fellow creatures. He is now overwhelmed by feelings of compassion toward the girl and offers her a temporary resting place: "The physical desire had vanished, but his great and steady warmth for her was still there, and he felt a need for light; the man in his forties turned on the small bedside lamp and gazed at the girl" (242). The light of "the lamp of kindness" (243) lit by the man is the exact opposite of Jaromil's grandiose but imaginary devotion to her. The poet promised the girl never-ending love, while the man does not promise her anything more than he can really give her, some pleasant moments, and she feels that the moments with the man are the most beautiful in her entire life.

The man in his forties is the figure who in *Life Is Elsewhere* represents maturity and for whom life is here and now. In Kundera's other novels, other mature characters are depicted, several of them more thoroughly than the man in his forties. Kundera claims in *The Art of the Novel* that the forty-year-old is of all his characters closest to himself (127; after writing *Immortality*, however, he has said that he loves professor Avenarius in that novel the most of all of his characters; see "La 'Parole'" 24). One can imagine the "relief" the author feels when for a moment he abandons his mortifying analysis of immaturity in which he recognizes his own past. Moreover, it is perhaps precisely the brevity of the man's appearance that allows Kundera to bring him and his hedonistic-skeptical views on stage in a positive light. In his later works, when—through such figures as Jakub in *Farewell Waltz*, Tamina in *The Book of Laughter and Forgetting*, Tomas in *The Unbearable Lightness of Being*, and Agnes in *Immortality*—Kundera penetrates more deeply into the existence of the nonsentimental, autonomous individual striving for authenticity, this existence turns out to be problematic indeed.

While the figure of the man in his forties, outlined in a few strokes, appears as Jaromil's strict opposite, there are actually fundamental similarities between them as well, making the discerning of the "mature" alternative difficult. For the man, what is essential is the passing moment—enjoying it and making it as beautiful as possible—whereas Jaromil seeks beauty in matters greater than life; nevertheless, what is common to both is the search for beauty. Kundera states that the Czech revolution produced beautiful poetry—because in poetry "anything backed by the power of experienced emotion" may appear true, important, and beautiful (*Life* 230). The difficulty then remains not only to distinguish between beauty and kitsch, the latter being beauty worn out because used too many times and unable to reveal any new truth, but also to distinguish between the beauty produced by the coloring of the object by sentimental emotions and that found or produced without such embellishments. An example of the former occurs when Mama, after renouncing her lover—because of her exhaustion, caused by his fancies, but telling him that she is giving up her great but guilty love because of her maternal love for her son—feels a "beautiful sadness" (45); she herself believes her noble motives to be true. For Jaromil, it is not only the freedom of movement in his dreams of Xavier that is beautiful (35, 73). Death, too, has for the young Jaromil the beauty of a dream (88), Xavier's betraying of a beloved woman is beautiful (75), and the feeling that the redhead's life is in his hands incites in him a beautiful feeling of power that intoxicates him (170). He even admires the "cruel beauty (or beautiful cruelty) of *real life* in the police's work" (185) and after denouncing the girl to the police considers the policeman's face as beautiful: "it was furrowed with deep wrinkles testifying to a hard, manly life" (222). The same word, "beautiful," is used in the sixth part, when the girl thinks that the most beautiful parts of her life were the moments she spent with the forty-year-old man (238), when the man lit "the lamp of kindness" for her. The task remains to discern between true moments of beauty and beauty produced by sentimental, false embellishment.

Kundera's interest in moments in which the presence of beauty is immediately sensed resembles Husserl's idea of phenomenology as the study of what is immediately presented to our consciousness but is still organized by the sense giving activity of the mind. Husserl's concept for this is the "living present" (*lebendige Gegenwart*), in which something is immediately experienced as having a certain meaning or sense (*Sinn*) (see Husserl, *Ideen*). However, while the question of meaning in our apperception leads Husserl to a philosophical reflection on intentionality, Kundera is in search of the different ways that it is possible for the modern individual to experience life as meaningful.

Farewell Waltz, a "comedy of errors" about life and death

The same catastrophic history of Czechoslovakia which sets the scene both in Jaromil's story and in Ludvik's story in *The Joke* serves as the background to events in *Farewell Waltz*, but the focus differs. *Farewell Waltz* is an ironic novel, but the irony is no longer the all-pervasive mode of narration of *Life Is Elsewhere*. It now has multiple facets and it functions at the level of events rather than in the mode of presentation. In terms of style and plot structure, *Farewell Waltz* might be called a comedy of errors, for it is full of amusing details, irony, and vaudeville-like coincidences, turns, and revelations. The outcome of these events, however, is not comical. While in a classic comedy or vaudeville (in the French sense, see above), misunderstandings and intrigues are eventually resolved and the status quo is reestablished—with the difference that some marriages are usually arranged and some lost children may be reunited with their parents—in *Farewell Waltz*, the end shows nothing restored. The accidents and misunderstandings are far from harmless. In fact, just as in *The Joke* or *Laughable Loves*, they change the characters' lives fundamentally and irreversibly and may even lead to their death.

The trumpeter Klima and the intellectual Jakub, who are the protagonists in the two intertwined story lines, have little in common. Klima, a typical Kunderan man, is a womanizer who nevertheless loves his wife. He finds himself in serious difficulties when the bath attendant Ruzena informs him of her pregnancy. Jakub, just like Ludvik in *The Joke*, has during the worst years of communist rule become aware of the "anthropological truth" that individuals are capable of sending their fellows to death without a wince, but until now he has considered himself exempt from this truth. In the course of the events taking place in the spa town, he is now forced to change this view. Back in the years when Jakub was politically active he had asked his friend, Dr. Skreta, for a poison pill, allowing him to put an end to his life should he find himself in a hopeless situation. During his stay at the spa resort, when the pill accidentally ends up in Ruzena's hands, Jakub makes only weak efforts to prevent her from unintentionally swallowing it. The reason for his passivity is his antipathy toward her. Seeing her take the part of the old men who are chasing free-running dogs (while he himself saves a dog from being taken away and possibly killed), he concludes that she belongs to the unpleasant company of "the hangman's assistants" so well-known to him, those who identify with the persecutor rather than the victim (109, 160). Paradoxically, his conviction as to Ruzena being one of the hangman's assistants turns Jakub himself into her executioner. Jakub leaves the resort believing that the pill was actually not poisonous, since Ruzena—as he assumes—does not die after swallowing it and he never learns the truth that she has in fact died. Nevertheless, he is forced to face this newly discovered aspect of his own character. Until now he has felt superior to those who were prepared without scruple to send their comrades to their death, but he must realize that he is no exception.

Jakub may not appear in every respect sympathetic—in fact, the negative traits in his character are emphasized—but he is definitely someone to be taken seriously. This is because he is a mature and nonsentimental person who wants to see himself as he really is, even if the truth may be unpleasant to face. He plays his role in the "comedy of errors," yet he is not a comic figure. The weight of the "anthropological conclusions," drawn from terrible historical experience, is placed above all on his shoulders. In contrast, Klima, whose concerns are of a purely personal character, is from the outset a comic figure. We may ask why this is so, unlike the case of Tomas in *The Unbearable Lightness of Being*, although his situation closely resembles Klima's. Both men indulge in countless love affairs in spite of their deep love for their wives, both wives are tormented by jealousy and neither of the men understands why, since they believe that their affairs do not imperil their love. Tomas's reflections and questions concerning his life are nevertheless dealt with seriously, whereas Klima's sympathetic figure is presented in an unmistakably comic light. The difference in the presentation of the two characters arises, I suggest, from the classical Aristotelian concept of the comic, wherein characters that are suitable for comedy are those inferior to us, the spectators (*Poetics* 1448b). Tomas does not do anything which in Kundera's view would be inappropriate for a mature person. Klima, on the other hand, discredits himself and becomes ridiculous from the outset, asking his colleagues for advice on how to persuade Ruzena to have an abortion. In Kundera's eyes, the fact that he discusses his private life in public deprives him of dignity. After Ruzena's call, Klima has the feeling that an old fear of his has come true. What exactly this fear consists of is not said, but he is of course afraid of his wife Kamila's reaction; nevertheless, he seems to be less concerned about the pain he is about to cause her than about the fate of their marriage. Accordingly, both men do their best to conceal their affairs from their wives. The difference between them is that while Tomas acts out of compassion toward his wife, Klima is worried about his own future. In addition, Klima's helplessness about the emotions that overwhelm him brings a comic overtone or a touch of irony to his depiction.

Ruzena, too, appears in an ironic light right from the start. Instead of keeping the memory of the amorous night spent with the famous trumpeter to herself, she shares the experience with a whole group of colleagues, who are now eager to advise her as to how to take advantage of her pregnancy. The question which preoccupies Ruzena is not whether or not she should keep the baby, but how the pregnancy might offer her a chance to break free from the depressing environment of her home town. This is why she "decides" that Klima, rather than her boyfriend, is the child's father, although the latter is actually more probable. Nevertheless, Kundera assures us that this is not a malicious design on Ruzena's part; soon she herself is convinced of the truth of her words (162). The comic distance between Ruzena and the reader is provoked by her inability to think consistently and honestly. For example, she no longer has any clear recollection of the night spent with Klima, yet she claims to be in love with him. Further, she does not perceive the existence of a chasm between her alleged love and her intention to take advantage of her condition. Her attitude is not sentimental in the sense of overemphasizing grand ideas and puffed-up feelings; rather, she is an "ordinary," somewhat sordid human being incapable of reflection, who in a critical situation chooses instinctively the alternative which appears to be the most advantageous for her. Through the figures of Ruzena and Klima, the character of the mature and skeptical Jakub is thus contrasted not with sentimental, lyrical types, but with ordinary human beings who never ponder the questions that preoccupy Jakub. They do not engage with the great questions of life at the level of reflection, even when these actually come up in their own lives. For them abortion is an exclusively practical issue and not a decision over someone's life and death.

Jakub reveals his cynical views on humankind in a discussion with his protégée Olga, the daughter of an old comrade, the man who sent him to prison right before he was himself jailed and executed. Olga, an intelligent young woman who only now has been permitted to study at the university, asks Jakub about her father. She finds it difficult to believe that her father was purely the victim of terror and not also its perpetrator, as he was politically active at a time when "a hundred thousand people were put in prison" without trial, "often without any grounds," and of whom "thousands never came back" (88). She regards as a scandal the fact that "not a single one of those responsible was ever punished" (88). Although Jakub denies that her father took part in these crimes, he acknowledges that those who were imprisoned were in principle the same as those who sent others to jail. He comments on this by saying that "to come to the conclusion that there's no difference between the guilty and the victims is to *abandon all hope*. And that, my girl, is what is called *hell*" (89). This is the mental background to Jakub's behavior when Ruzena's life is threatened and to a great extent also to the reactions of others to her death.

In a conversation with Bertlef, the worth of humankind is discussed at a more general, "anthropological" level. Jakub says that the creation of mankind was a mistake on God's part, which he must regret. When king Herod ordered that all male babies be killed, he made a decision for the whole of mankind: the human race would no longer be propagated (121). Jakub himself does not want to become a father, because he thinks that having a child equals the absolute approval of humanity: "'Having a child is to show an absolute accord with mankind. If I have a child, it's as though I'm saying: I was born and have tasted life and declare it so good that it merits being duplicated.' 'And you have not found life to be good?' asked Bertlef. Jakub tried to be precise, and said cautiously: 'All I know is that I could never say with complete conviction: Man is a wonderful being and I want to reproduce him'" (118). His disgust with mankind derives from his love of what could be precious in a human being, scrupulousness and high-mindedness, but "he was persuaded that these were not human qualities. Jakub knew human beings well, and that is why he did not love them" (257).

When Jakub discovers the "inner murderer" in himself, he ponders his motives: "Why then had he given the poison to the nurse? Was it simply by chance? Raskolnikov had actually spent a long time plotting and preparing for his crime, while Jakub had acted on the impulse of a moment. But Jakub realized that he, too, had unknowingly for many years been preparing for his act of murder, and that the instant he gave the poison to Ruzena was a fissure into which had been shoveled all of his past life, all of his disgust with mankind" (256). Trying to imagine that Ruzena might already be dead, killed by the pill he has handed her, he observes that he does not feel a shattering sense of guilt: "Jakub was amazed that his act was so light, so weightless, amazed that it did not overwhelm him. And he wondered if this lightness was not more terrifying than the Russian character's hysterical feelings" (257). The horror felt in the lightness of killing is a theme familiar from Broch's description of Huguenau at the end of *The Sleepwalkers*. However, while in *The Sleepwalkers* it is not the killer himself but the author who is repelled by the casualness of the deed, Jakub, who recognizes his resentment toward mankind as the cause of his act, nevertheless wonders at the lightness of his act. Moreover, Jakub makes other unflattering observations concerning himself. He now realizes that the poison he has been carrying in his pocket for years "had given his every step a theatrical solemnity and allowed him to turn his life into a grandiose myth!" (225). He also becomes aware of the fact that his taking care of Olga, the daughter of a comrade turned into his enemy, has always furnished him with a sense of being high-minded. That is to say, in hindsight he discovers in himself a certain tendency toward sentimental self-flattery, and he now feels laid bare and ridiculous.

Jakub's opponent in the conversation concerning the value of human life and the dignity of man is the (US) American millionaire Bertlef. In the figure of Bertlef, a comic saint, Kundera's mixing of parody and seriousness reaches its climax. Bertlef is a paradoxical and laughable combination of Kostka's religiosity in *The Joke* and the hedonism of the man in his forties in *Life Is Elsewhere*. Nevertheless, his thoughts and actions, in offering a challenge to Jakub's misanthropy, are not devoid of seriousness. Bertlef, a connoisseur of food, drink, and erotic pleasure and an amateur painter, expresses his respect and admiration for God's creation through his love for women: "Saint Paul would condemn me because I love women. But Jesus would not. I don't see anything bad about loving women, many women, and about being loved by women, many women" (130). That his love pleases God is proven by the blue halo that surrounds him during meditation: according to him, "people who become attached to God with a particularly powerful love are rewarded by experiencing a sacred joy that flows through their entire being and radiates out from there. The light of this divine joy is soft and peaceful, and its color is the celestial azure" (113).

Bertlef is a curious mixture of sentimental and mature attitudes. He is a hedonist not despite his religiosity but because of it and for him hedonism is a form of devotion. Behind the halo we discern in him personality traits belonging to a mature individual, similar to those of the forty-year-old of *Life Is Elsewhere,* such as being able to enjoy the good things at hand, and yet—or maybe precisely for this reason—also able to be considerate toward others and to contribute to their welfare. Bertlef declares that we should respond to the challenge of human unworthiness with love for our neighbors. Even when a person is not lovable, treating him or her lovingly improves life. Bertlef demonstrates how this works by spending a wonderful night of love with Ruzena and making the bath attendant feel like a queen for the first time in her life, charming, good, and beautiful. The experience opens up her eyes toward new perspectives in her life and she realizes that she need not cling to Klima, since the future might hold further opportunities for her. Thus Bertlef, who is in principle against the idea of abortion, actually causes Ruzena to decide upon an abortion. When she dies and her death is declared a suicide, Bertlef refuses to believe this. Ruzena had thought positively about life and therefore could not have committed the worst kind of crime, which is to "throw one's life down contemptuously at God's feet. To commit suicide is to spit in the Creator's face" (264).

While Bertlef's character carnivalizes the Christian ideal of love for one's neighbor by realizing it in a literal sense in making love to many women, Dr. Skreta carnivalizes the grand ideas of national unity and human brotherhood by producing brothers in the most concrete sense of the word. By injecting in his clinic his own semen into childless women he creates a nation where one truly is "among one's own" (*Farewell Waltz* 137). The great ideas, treated in *The Joke* with earnestness and even nostalgia, and in *Life Is Elsewhere* with irony and a recognition of their dangerousness, now return in carnivalist, farcical, and satirical form. Jakub thinks of the Holy Family and the Immaculate Conception as he looks at the innkeeper couple with their big-nosed toddler, unquestionably a result of Dr. Skreta's fertility treatment. Universal brotherhood, patriotism, love of one's neighbor, the Holy Family—all these important ideas or ideologemes of European culture are turned into objects of ridicule.

While Bertlef is a comic saint, Dr. Skreta is no less a comic version of God himself, the lord of life and death. With his insemination program he has taken over the task of the Creator (who now practices eugenics, as he chooses only beautiful women for his treatment), and in preparing the poison for Jakub he does not hesitate to take the decision over death into his hands as well, passing it on to his friend. This is carnivalization of humankind attempting to fill the vacancy after God's death; it also can be seen as a carnivalization of Nietzsche's prophecy of man transformed into an *Übermensch* who takes the place of God. Replacing God as the ruler of all things was exactly what the makers of History wanted to do. The goals pursued by Bertlef and Dr. Skreta are in fact essentially the same as those that the builders of paradise had aimed at through political action. The Christian commandment to love one's neighbor is related to the spirit of nineteenth-century nationalism and to the ideal of the universal brotherhood of humanity, as expressed in both the French and the Russian revolution. Dr. Skreta accuses Jakub of remaining stuck in politics, while as a medical practitioner he considers himself able to actually change the world. It seems as if Kundera, having abandoned the idea of reigning History, is seeking opportunities to realize the ideals of the revolution outside politics and History, but he is doing so unseriously, carnivalizing the effort to create an earthly paradise. Nevertheless, while Dr. Skreta and Bertlef appear throughout the novel as comic and eccentric figures, this does not diminish the gravity of their deeds as evinced by the existence of a number of big-nosed children, Ruzena's consent to abortion, and, finally, her death.

The significance of the moment

Along with the carnivalization of efforts to follow grand ideas, in *Farewell Waltz* something "serious" is also being said about the possibilities of human existence in the present historical situation. This happens especially through Jakub's experiences. The novel offers little information as to Jakub's past or the development of his thinking. Nevertheless, in the course of the five days covered by the plot he becomes aware of certain sentimental tendencies in himself. Now that he has been stripped of the last remaining means to construct an embellished image of himself, what remains for him to live for, outside of History or any ideologies?

Since Jakub believes neither in afterlife nor in History, he has no choice but to look for meaningfulness in his own experiences. While his mind is preoccupied with what will happen to Ruzena, he begins to read hidden messages in concrete situations. After some half-hearted attempts at getting in touch with Ruzena to save her, at the afternoon concert he notices that she is sitting only two seats away from him, which would make it easy to warn her:

> And all of a sudden he understood clearly why the young woman was sitting in the same row as he: the unexpected encounter in the brasserie [where he had given the poison pill to Ruzena] a while ago had been a temptation, a test. It had occurred only so that he might see his own image in the mirror: the image of a man who gives his neighbor poison. But the One who is testing him (God, in whom he does not believe) demands no bloody sacrifice, no blood of innocents. The test might end not in a death but only in Jakub's self-revelation, which might confiscate his inappropriate moral pride. The nurse is now sitting in the same row to enable him, at the last moment, to save her life. (195)

Jakub interprets the incident as a message addressed to him, despite knowing that no sender exists and that consequently there can be no message. God is still preserved as a function, as a gap, an empty space, in the process whereby we try to make sense of the world—even if that space is not occupied by anyone and the individual realizes that identifying messages within events is pure imagination. This coincides with Ludvik's pondering in *The Joke* about how we continue interpreting events so as to find in them some meaning related to ourselves, although in reality no such meaning exists.

In a similar manner Ruzena interprets the night spent with Bertlef as a meaningful sign intended for her. That evening, Bertlef had saved her from being humiliated by a convivial company mocking her because of her apparently inconsequent behavior when one of the men makes indecent advances to her. They agree that Bertlef had turned up just at the right moment and with this thought Ruzena is overcome by "a confused but delightful feeling of relief: Bertlef's appearing precisely today meant that everything that happened had been ordained elsewhere, and she could relax and put herself in the hands of that higher power" (199). The irony in the situation is biting and the reader is aware of the danger Ruzena is in, and in fact she will die the next morning.

Thus *Farewell Waltz* is a "comedy of errors" on a deeper, more "philosophical" level than its plot alone: it shows that every assumption of benevolent (or for that matter, malevolent) guidance in what happens is erroneous and that life is actually intolerably fortuitous. Jakub's assumption—that in spite of everything there is a higher power which makes sure that no human life is wasted—proves to be wrong. In fact, the most insignificant and incidental things, the slightest misunderstandings, may have the most serious and even fatal consequences. The case of Jakub and Ruzena indicates this power of misunderstandings and erroneous interpretations. At the brasserie, Jakub observes Ruzena and Klima engaged in a conversation about, as it appears to him, deadly serious matters. Since he has already formed his opinion of Ruzena in the dog-chasing scene, he now assumes automatically that in the dispute at the restaurant, too, she is the one arguing for death and the man for life, although in dealing with the question of abortion the exact opposite is true. Jakub's negative judgment of her, based partly on this misunderstanding, later restrains him from doing his best to save her. Another false conclusion Jakub reaches is that the pill Dr. Skreta had given him was not poisonous at all, a misjudgment which further contributes to Ruzena's death as he then gives up efforts to inform her about the pill. As Jakub's behavior is affected by his loathing of humankind, derived in turn from his experience of the terror, it would be exaggerated to say that Ruzena's death is a matter of mere chance, but it is certainly true that chance plays an intolerably large part in her fate.

The misunderstanding concerning the pill also changes Jakub's relationship with Skreta. Until then he had thought that when Skreta originally prepared the deadly pill for him he trusted that Jakub would not misuse it. The two friends, possessing power over life and death but confident that they would not abuse that power, felt "like two gods forced to live among humans—and that was beautiful" (226). Now, if the pill was not poisonous, Skreta had saved his friend from being a murderer—and had taken from him the possibility of committing suicide by swallowing the pill—but at the same time had reduced him back to an ordinary mortal. Jakub's misconception about his friend will probably never be rectified, because the information about Ruzena's death does not reach him. She dies at the moment he is leaving the spa, whence he heads right to the border to leave the country for good.

If Providence originating in an unknown source is an unconvincing substitute for God, humankind does not succeed much better when they themselves take the place of God. An individual does not need to be a murderer from conviction, like the perpetrators of terror, to effect catastrophes; rather, in acting he or she is constantly in danger of committing errors which might have the most serious consequences. Accordingly, *Farewell Waltz* only seems to be a "comedy of errors" in that it lacks the solid basis necessary for laughter available to traditional comedy, namely, the certainty that at the end all the misunderstandings will be clarified and the order of things restored. It is only this confidence that makes errors harmless and comic. The confidence in the harmlessness of errors lacking, is there any escape from the human condition that humankind when left to follow their own faculty of judgment alone is not only ridiculous but eventually also disastrous to themselves and others?

Kundera seems to be suggesting that we ought to abandon the efforts to command the course of events and seek meaning in the experience of the present moment only. The possibilities of meaningful existence found in the momentary experience are analyzed in Kundera's later novels; yet already in a few of Jakub's experiences—and even of Ruzena's—some of these possibilities flash by. During his last day in his home country, Jakub experiences two such moments which open his eyes to new possibilities of existence. At the hotel he runs across Klima's wife Kamila and her exceptional beauty affects him like a revelation. He wonders what the "message" of this encounter may be even as he is aware of being himself the "sender" of the message. He realizes that it is the timing—his being about to leave his native country for good—that endows every incident with special significance, turning each one "into a symbolic message" (228). The woman represents everything that is desirable but that he can no longer obtain. He feels, however, that the encounter opens his eyes not only to the beauty of this woman, but to "beauty itself" (229). The experience suggests to him, now that he has no time left, "that one could live here in a different way and for something different, that beauty is more than justice, that beauty is more than truth, that it is more real, more indisputable, and also more accessible, that beauty is superior to everything else and that it was now permanently lost to him" (229–30). In this revelation of beauty, Jakub experiences the vivid presence of meaningfulness in a moment (a phenomenon which Husserl describes in similar words) and he now thinks that one could perhaps live outside the realm of politics and History, in search of beauty.

Ruzena, a simple bath attendant who is neither exceptionally intelligent nor exceptionally amiable, undergoes a similar experience of sudden revelation. During the night spent with Bertlef, she asks the man: "'You love me?' 'Yes, I love you.' Frantisek [her boyfriend] and Klima had already said the word to her, but only now did she see it as it really is when it comes unasked for, unexpected, naked. The word entered the room like a miracle. It was totally inexplicable, but to Ruzena it seemed all the more real, for the most basic things in this world exist without explanation and without motive, drawing from within themselves their reason for being" (200). For Kundera, an experience is real when we do not derive it from anything else by way of reason or sentiment, but have a sense of its immediate presence. Just as the possibility of beauty was revealed in a flash to Jakub, the possibility of love is revealed to Ruzena. For Kundera, both are genuine, nonsentimental possibilities of a meaningful existence, yet in *Farewell Waltz* these are not developed any further. New possibilities are revealed to both Jakub and Ruzena, but how Jakub will use them is not said—and Ruzena will die before benefiting from this new insight.

On his way to the border, Jakub experiences one more revelation. Again, an event occurring during his last day in his native country takes on a symbolic or metaphoric meaning. Jakub drives past a house where in a window he catches sight of a boy wearing thick eyeglasses. The boy becomes for him a symbol of all those who have to accommodate themselves to live their lives with an inborn impediment, like all of us: "And he reflected further that what he had held against others was something given, something they came into the world with and carried with them like a heavy wire fence. He reflected that he had no privileged right to high-mindedness and that the highest degree of high-mindedness is to love people even though they are murderers" (271). Paradoxically, he discovers this feeling of brotherhood only when he has become aware of being a murderer himself. It is a brotherhood following from humans' inborn impediment of being a potential murderer of their fellow beings. This is the biggest step toward love of one's neighbor, of compassion with them, of which the misanthropic Jakub is capable.

Farewell Waltz offers only a few flashes of the possibilities of existence outside of ideology and History, since the author's primary intention in this novel is to ridicule humankind's *hubris* in thinking that the course of events is controllable. That the course taken by an individual's life is accidental and fortuitous, based on errors and misunderstandings, applies not only to the main characters but also to several of the minor ones. Jakub's protégée Olga, for example, is irritated by the "museum" or "monument" that Jakub has erected to his own humanity by taking care of her. It is this museum that she intends to demolish in seducing Jakub; by the same token, she tries by this act to reinforce her weak self-confidence as a woman. Jakub gives in to the seduction only out of sympathy toward Olga, but she does not realize this and her feeling of the triumph of her femininity over her protector is thus based on misjudgment. A further example of how human lives are shaped by incident and error is the case of Frantisek, Ruzena's boyfriend, who is convinced of his paternity and presses her not to let their child be aborted. Ruzena reproaches Frantisek saying that his persistent and aggressive behavior is going to kill her. After the session with the abortion committee, Ruzena meets the furious Frantisek and she swallows the poison, taking it for a tranquillizer, and dies in front of Frantisek's eyes. As Kundera remarks, Frantisek will throughout his life bear the false—but no less crushing—consciousness of having driven his beloved to her death.

In sum, having taken over God's role as ruler of the world, humankind is not particularly successful. Having in his earlier novels criticized politicians' vain and disastrous efforts to create a paradise, in *Farewell Waltz* Kundera ridicules individuals' ambition to command the course of events. Although this is impossible to achieve, an individual's actions may have a tremendous impact both on one's own life and the lives of others. A human being's profound insufficiency as successor to God might be a reason to consider humanity a tragic character, were a human being playing God not so utterly comical.

In the carnivalistic end, Ruzena's death seems to be forgotten by everyone. Bertlef's young wife and his young son—another big-nosed toddler—arrive at the resort town and so does Skreta's girlfriend, who has just managed to wring a marriage proposal from him. Blended with the happy end of a marriage is another kind of happy ending, equally typical of classic comedy, when "father" and "son" likewise find each other. Dr. Skreta is accepted as an adopted son in the Bertlef family, guaranteeing him the freedom to travel abroad, even if the "son" is fifteen years junior to his "mother" and in addition the father of his "brother." Despite this carnivalistic-comedic ending, however, readers do not quit the novel with cordial laughter; in fact, our laughter sticks in our throat. As Chvatík remarks, *Farewell Waltz* remains a tragicomedy without catharsis (*Die Fallen* 108). The question posed earlier, whether the carnivalistic end is intended, kitsch-like, to cover the fact of the nurse's death from the sight of the reader, must be answered in the negative. An attentive reader perceives that in the "forgetting" of the death by everyone present the author depicts an act of repression caused by the fact that the characters are living in a world where people tend to "disappear" suddenly. The forced "forgetting" or repression also applies to the connection between a person's sudden death and the unpleasant lesson taught by recent history, that every one of us is a potential murderer of our neighbor.

Chapter Seven
The Dangers of Forgetting and Laughter

Kundera wrote that at the beginning of the 1970s he thought he ended his career as a novelist with *Farewell Waltz* (*Testaments* 165). After emigrating to France he took up writing again with the intention of creating a continuation to *Laughable Loves*. Instead of a collection of short stories, with *The Book of Laughter and Forgetting* something "entirely different" (*Testaments* 165) was born: a "polyphonic" novel. Yet there is a thematic continuity, in that the theme of laughable love is tackled once again in *The Book of Laughter and Forgetting*. Love is an issue in all the story lines and in several of them it appears in a ridiculous light. The themes of love and laughter, however, appear in this novel in a new manner, intertwined in a complex thematic web.

In a thematic synopsis of *The Book of Laughter and Forgetting* in *Testaments Betrayed*, Kundera makes the novel appear as a successor to *The Joke* in having history as its main theme. According to his account, part 1 "introduces the theme of man and history in its basic version: man collides with history and it crushes him"; part 2, "Mama," contrasts historic events with small, perennial, quotidian ones; part 6 deals with the death of the heroine, thereby seemingly forming "the tragic conclusion of the novel"; and the last, part 7, touches upon the experience of the loss of meaning of the greatest events in history (166–67). Added to this theme of history, as a commentary on it, is the theme of two kinds of laughter (167). Yet this synopsis is a one-sided account of the thematic content of the novel. As a whole, *The Book of Laughter and Forgetting* is neither in its composition nor in its themes a new version of either *Laughable Loves* or *The Joke*. There is compositional as well as thematic continuity, but there are also important differences. Not only does *The Book of Laughter and Forgetting* represent a decisive step toward a new kind of thematic composition, but the enrichment of the themes is considerable as well, and in dealing with these themes the universal existential aspect is even more pronounced than in previous works.

Where in *Farewell Waltz* Kundera suggests that authentic meanings can only be discovered in the present moment of experience, *The Book of Laughter and Forgetting* can be read as an elaboration of this thesis, making it appear a more complex matter. *The Book of Laughter and Forgetting* shows that what is experienced as meaningful in the present moment is, despite its apparent immediateness, closely connected with remembering. However, remembering can also falsify the experience; this occurs especially in sentimental recollection. Laughter is similarly ambivalent in that it can either deny or corroborate the meaningfulness of what is present. *The Book of Laughter and Forgetting* is not merely a thematic composition of the themes named in the title or even of the two themes and their opposite poles, seriousness and remembering. Variations on remembering and forgetting, on laughter and seriousness are regarded as parts of the process of sense giving in either a sentimental or an authentic form, this process being mostly connected with the theme of love. The novel in its entirety can then be conceived of as a study of the "architheme" of sense giving.

The first part of the novel, "Lost Letters," deals with the question of selective memory—that is, deliberate forgetting—in three different variations. The novel begins with a recollection of a historic scene which was later retouched by those in power. Kundera writes that when the proclamation of the Socialist Republic of Czechoslovakia by the communist leader Klement Gottwald took place in February 1948 on the balcony of a Baroque palace in Prague, Gottwald stood side by side with foreign secretary Vladimir Clementis, who had lent him his fur cap. Some years later, Clementis was accused of treason and hanged and was airbrushed from the historic photograph of the memorable moment on the balcony. According to Kundera, all that remained of Clementis in the photo was his fur cap on Gottwald's head. The anecdote exemplifies the sensitivity to the past of those holding political power. Functioning as a legitimization of the present, the past—in this case the crucial moment of the founding of the new order of the state—is allowed to contain only elements which are acceptable from the perspective of the present. For Kundera, this does not only hold true in the case of an autocratic party's dealing with history but is common to all societies and individuals (*The Book of Laughter* 30; see also McEwan 32–33).

According to Hana Píchová, Kundera has fabricated the airbrushing of the historic photograph (102). In addition, the building where the event took place was not a Baroque palace (such palaces are characteristic of Prague), but "a typical rococo style building of the eighteenth century" (Bílek, "The East" 111). Why does Kundera alter historical facts? Is it a joke, a playful, self-reflective gesture to demonstrate the truth of his claim that each of us is constantly rewriting history? One difficulty with this hypothesis is that Kundera, who is now writing for a non-Czech readership, cannot expect his readers to detect such "falsifications." On the first pages of *The Book of Laughter* we encounter an instance of another kind of "falsification" of historical facts. When the protagonist of part 1 meets his former lover, who is in tears because of the death of the Soviet statesman Masturbov, any reader understands that this is not the actual surname. Readers also realize that the "falsification" does not change anything in the truthfulness of the kind of incident told here. Kundera probably considers his freedom to alter historical facts as the authorial privilege of the novelist who is searching for truth in terms of the essence of things and not of historical details.

Mirek, the protagonist of part 1, resists the political system by refusing to obey the order to "forget" given by those in power. His opposition manifests itself in the act of preserving a bundle of political notes in his home, which may at any time cause him trouble. As he is "in love with his destiny" (14)—that is, he wants to be recognized as an opponent of the system—he refuses to destroy the notes to save himself. Mirek's choice is a sentimental one. With no political significance, his sole aim is to create a certain image of himself in the eyes of others. Moreover, as is typical of a sentimentalist, Mirek disregards the consequences his action might have on the lives of his friends and family. At the end of part 1, the narrator mentions laconically how many years of imprisonment he, his son, and his friends were sentenced to.

Yet, shortly before his "destiny" is fulfilled, Mirek makes an effort to recover his letters to Zdena, his love in early youth. The main reason he wants to destroy the letters, thereby erasing her from his life, is that with her very big nose she is uncommonly ugly. The passionate love letters he wrote to her would reveal him to everyone as a wretch who thought of himself as being worthy only of an ugly woman's love. This "wretchedness" now appears as a blemish on his otherwise beautiful "destiny." Mirek is driven by the same desire as those in power, to revise and embellish the past. The paradox is twofold in that his love letters were themselves the product of a sentimental act of embellishing himself. He tried to convince himself—and his imaginary audience—of his passionate love, because only then, he thought, could his affair with an ugly woman be excusable.

An individual who chooses beauty instead of truth is following the principle of kitsch in his or her search for meaningfulness. Like all sentimentalists, Mirek looks for the image of himself in the eyes of others. He now recognizes that the political radicalism of his youth was actually conceived to "conceal his pimples," that is, his adolescent immaturity (24). For Zdena, on the other hand, faithfulness plays a similar role as deliberate forgetting does for Mirek. She has remained faithful to party ideology because ever since Mirek left her she has valued fidelity higher than anything else—whether to a person or to an ideology. In Kundera's view, fidelity is an ideal of the sentimental. It is a stubborn insistence on something that has already lost its meaning. Since Zdena's faithfulness to the communist party is motivated by her unrequited love, her private life, despite appearances, actually outweighs her public, political activities. The pattern is typical of Kundera in that adherence to grand ideas has private motives related to the individual's sentimental project of self-making.

For the sentimental person or the follower of an ideology, remembering might be embarrassing; for the nonsentimentalist, who is interested in truth alone, what is problematic in terms of human sense giving is not remembering, but forgetting. The "anthropological fact" that a human being forgets even that which once was most significant to him or her is explored especially in part 2 of the novel, "Mama," and in the storyline concerning Tamina. Part 2 begins with Karel's and his wife Marketa's observation that his mother's remarks have lost their former edge. Mama's reproachful words, which earlier were a sufficient reason for the couple to avoid her, no longer have the same effect now that she has grown old. When she visits the couple, she appears small, fragile, and harmless: "Mama had relinquished the marshal's baton of her motherhood and gone into a different world" (41). The "different world" is old age where nothing new or significant ever happens and when recollection alone is important; everything that is significant lies in the past. Rather than trying to interfere in her son's life, the mother only wants to talk to him, his wife, and their friend about her youth. She recalls a school celebration organized on the occasion of the declaration of the country's independence where she recited a patriotic poem. According to the old lady's account, she could not remember the closing lines and the principal of the school himself consoled her. It turns out, however, that her memory has played a trick on her. She had left school before the declaration of independence; the occasion was actually a Christmas celebration, and the poem was a seasonal one. An important personal reminiscence from her early years was by a slip of memory connected to a historic event. There is no reason to assume that she deliberately wanted to heighten the significance of the incident in the eyes of her son and her daughter-in-law. When she recognizes her mistake, however, she is reluctant to correct the story, because she does not want to diminish herself in their eyes. In other words, she is unwilling to take back the unintended retouching of the past. This shows that the mother too speaks to an "audience," even if that audience consists of just two or three persons. The incident has no consequences, since the couple knows that the mother's world has always been limited to petty, personal issues. When the Soviet tanks rolled into Czechoslovakia, she was worried about the pears in her garden not being picked, something that at that time infuriated her son and daughter-in-law.

When the mother is introduced to the young couple's friend, Eva, whom Karel and Marketa invited for an erotic threesome, she discovers immediately some resemblance between Eva and an old-time acquaintance of hers, Nora: "Nora lacked kindness and modesty, and Mama had often been wounded by her behaviour. But she wasn't thinking about that now. What mattered more to her was that she had suddenly found a bit of her youth here, a greeting reaching her from the distance of half a century. She was thrilled by the thought that everything she long ago experienced was still with her, surrounding her in her loneliness and speaking to her. Although she had never liked Nora, she was glad to meet her here, all the more because she was thoroughly tamed and embodied in someone who appeared to be filled with respect for Mama" (58). The mother is happy about Eva's friendly behavior toward her, but the encounter gains further importance from the connection between present and past. What Kundera is saying is that for someone who is living in the "different world" of old age, even the most superficial connection with the past—a resemblance to an unsympathetic acquaintance from decades ago—may give significance to the present.

In a different way, the recollection of Nora makes the experience of the present more meaningful for Karel as well. Through Karel and Marketa Kundera explores questions of love and sexuality, the difficulty of reconciling body and soul and the meaningfulness of sexual encounters. Physical love is a source of pleasure, but Kundera's novels often voice the view that pleasure is of too little significance to confer meaning on the endlessly repeated movements of the physical act of lovemaking. In remembering Mrs. Nora, Karel is able to use physical lovemaking as a way to readdress a piece of the past. Karel recalls vividly how as a child, in the dressing room of a spa, he once caught sight of Mrs. Nora's beautiful naked body, which back then seemed enormous to him. Now, in making love to Eva, in his imagination he takes possession of Mrs. Nora's body and experiences a feeling of great satisfaction: "He had the impression that this leap onto her [Eva's] body was a leap across an immense period of time, the leap of a little boy hurling himself from childhood to manhood. And then, while he was moving back and forth on her, he seemed incessantly to be describing the same movement, from childhood to adulthood and then in reverse, and once again from the little boy miserably gazing at the gigantic body of a woman to the man clasping that body and taming it. That movement, usually measuring fifteen centimetres at most, was as long as three decades" (66). Karel experiences the junction of two ages as beauty: "beauty is an abolition of chronology and a rebellion against time" (73). A coupling of the childhood recollection with the present moment bestows an unexpected significance on the latter.

The theme of forgetting appears in part 2 in connection with that of repetition. Karel, who is a womanizer, has observed that he has forgotten most of "his two or three thousand acts of love . . . no more than two or three are really essential and unforgettable, while the others are merely recurrences, imitations, repetitions, or evocations" (71). Here repetition appears in a new sense. In contrast to the repetition of a theme in different variations, "the same" recurs without any noteworthy differences. The two types of repetition, as Eva Le Grand points, resemble what Gilles Deleuze and J. Hillis Miller call "Platonic" or mimetic repetition, in which "the same" is conceived as a replica of the same archetypal model, and what they call "Nietzschean" or variational repetition in which similarities are detected between different concrete phenomena without recourse to any archetypal model ("Voyage" 91; see also Boisen, *Une fois* 29–30). The resemblance, however, is only a remote one in that in Kundera the relevant difference does not derive from the presence or absence of a Platonic model. His nonsentimental individuals acknowledge no Platonic models. The difference between the two types of repetition is that where in variational recurrence the differences between various cases are important, in "pure repetition" they are not. In Karel's case this means that every act of love is different, but that after having the "same" experience a number of times the differences no longer matter. Instead of an infinity of variations, one faces monotonous repetition (see also *Ignorance* 80). In Kundera's novels, we find a shift taking place from the predominance of an experience of infinite variation to that of a tedious repetition of the same. In addition, we encounter in Kundera's works further variants of the theme of repetition, indicating that repetition in itself is for him a theme with important variations.

During the lovemaking scene between Marketa, Eva, and Karel, it turns out that nonremembering may mean relief as well. Marketa and Karel's marriage is based on a "contract." The husband would, despite the wife's jealousy, be unfaithful, but "Marketa would have the right to be the better of the two and Karel should feel guilty toward her" (51). For both, the contract is heavy to bear. When Marketa now imagines her husband as a headless male body making love to Eva, that is, when she ignores his "soul," she can forget her jealousy and enjoy the erotic pleasures of the threesome. Having switched off the person in the body, Marketa is able to enjoy the "light," purely physical pleasure of sex. In her case, forgetting brings a weightlessness experienced as something positive, even if it means loss of meaningfulness.

The storyline concerning Tamina in parts 4 and 6 deals with making the present significant through remembering the past, as well as with the lack of sense caused by forgetting. While for Marketa forgetting for a moment everything and enjoying purely physical pleasure means relief and is therefore desirable, for Tamina, forgetting threatens to bereave her of everything precious. In her case the turning to the past and the danger of forgetting do not ensue from great age but from the special conditions of her life, which make it impossible for her to preserve the significant moments of the past from sinking into oblivion. If the storyline concerning Tamina is the main story of the novel and the other stories merely variations on it—contradicting the principle of the equality of lines in a polyphonic composition—this means that the main themes of remembering and forgetting are elaborated in the narration already before they are presented in the main storyline.

Part 4, "Lost Letters," introduces readers to the "heroine" of the novel (100), Tamina, who lives as an emigrant in a small West European town where she works as a waitress in a café. She left Czechoslovakia a few years earlier together with her husband, who soon thereafter fell ill and died. Although they loved each other very much and their marriage was happy, to her astonishment she now realizes that she can no longer recall the details of their shared life. According to Kundera, it is an "anthropologic fact" that a human being forgets even what was most important in his or her life. Tamina feels a need to get hold of their love letters and her diaries from the time of the marriage, which she left in Prague, so that she can construct "a house she can live in" out of the important details of the past (119). Otherwise nothing is left for her except the bare present, "that invisible point, that nothingness moving slowly toward death" (119). The question is not one of her insistence on fidelity to her late husband. She simply does not find anything of significance in the present but everything of value to her lies in the past. The narrative does not contain a detailed account of her present life, but it is obvious that the owners of the café and its customers are not the kind who would realize that the quiet waitress has had her important experiences too. Kundera stresses that Tamina's preoccupation with the past is not sentimental: "She does not want to give back to the past its poetry. She wants to give back to it its lost body" (119). Unlike Mirek and Mama, she does not want to embellish her past in order to impress an audience, but she needs the details of the past for herself alone. A mere vague idea of her past happiness and love is insufficient for the construction of a habitable "house" in the present, and that is why she needs concrete details such as what her husband looked like, what endearments he used to call her by, and where they spent their summer holidays.

Tamina's efforts to evoke the past are contrasted with another kind of interest in recollection in Bibi, one of her regular customers who plans to write a book about herself. Kundera calls this kind of desire to write "graphomania" and he regards it as a form of the perpetual "battle to seize the ear of others" (110). People want to have someone who listens to them without their having to listen to anyone in return. Behind this desire, Kundera recognizes people's narcissistic tendency to impose themselves on others, which is "the most grotesque version of the will to power" (*The Art* 130). All those whose scribbling derives from the desire to expose their personal life to others and who do not make it their task to explore universal aspects of human existence are graphomaniacs. In Kundera's view we live in an age of universal graphomania, where "everyone [is] surrounded by his own words as by a wall of mirrors, which allows no voice to filter through from outside" (*The Book of Laughter* 128). The difference between a graphomaniac and Tamina lies in the former's attitude toward publicity. Tamina's notes are not meant for the eyes of anyone else. She feels degraded when it turns out that her mother-in-law has seen her notebooks. Thus the difference is precisely between those who construct meanings for themselves only and those who do it for the gaze of others, which is the difference between the authentic and the sentimental attitude. For Kundera, the individual striving for authenticity wants to keep his or her private realm hidden from the eyes of outsiders.

In part 6, "The Angels," the author-narrator draws a parallel between Tamina's forgetting the past and his own mortally ill father losing the ability to speak, and suggests both cases as the disappearance of previously available distinctions. Tamina cannot evoke the details of her past love and the father is unable to make the distinctions enabled by speech, so that for him things "merged into single, undifferentiated being" (219). What happens to the individual through losing—forgetting—speech or memories is compared to the forgetting that takes place in the public sphere of politics. As the father lies dying, president Gustav Husák gives a speech to young pioneers: "The President of Forgetting" encourages the children to think of the future only and never look back (217, 239). In conformity with this, Prague is presented as the city of forgetting, serving both as the background and as a historical-political parallel to Tamina's story. More than once in the course of history, successive rulers forced Czechs to forget their past, thus crushing the identity of a nation and ushering it to its death. In the replacing of Czech street names in Prague with Russian ones, Kundera saw a step toward Bohemia's becoming a colony of the Soviet Union and toward the obliteration of the Czech nation. Analogously, Tamina is prevented from keeping in touch with her private past. In both cases, constraining circumstances cause the fulfillment of the same anthropological possibility of forgetting. In both cases, forgetting causes the loss of meaningful existence, a condition that foreshadows death. Interestingly, in speaking of the annihilation of a nation the author-narrator's tone becomes tragic. Although Kundera underlines a common European identity, it is evident that the nation too is an indispensable entity for him (see Macura

23). In accordance with a tradition going back to Herder (*Ideen*; see also Irmscher 136–41), Kundera ascribes a singular identity and the claim of autonomy not only to the individual, but also to the nation.

The circumstances in which the past does not endow the present with meaning are elaborated in Kundera's depiction of the "children's island." For him the word "child" is deprived of the positive connotations usually attached to it since the age of Romanticism. In his usage, the word refers to the original state of humankind, to the zero point prior to any development. Childhood is a state of pure existence with no self-reflection and with no relation to either past or future. It precedes even the immaturity of adolescence where questions first arise concerning the individual's own existence (and are answered in the sentimental mode). Kundera refuses to extol children's innocence and genuineness (see Gaughan 19; Webb 357). Children are rarely present in Kundera's novels and loving couples, such as Tamina and her husband or Tomas and Tereza in *The Unbearable Lightness of Being*, do not seem to be longing for children. If children do make an appearance, they are mostly depicted as noisy and disturbing, and adults who prefer children are depicted as poor judges of humanity. For Kundera, childhood has a primarily metaphorical meaning. Humans are proceeding toward "infantocracy," that is, a thoughtless life in the present moment (see *The Art* 132). To this perpetual present Kundera prefers history, which means constant change, history being the "epic" or adult form of experience: "History is a series of ephemeral changes, while eternal values are immutable, perpetuated outside history, and have no need of memory. Husak is president of the eternal, not of the ephemeral. He is on the side of children, and children are life, and living is 'seeing, hearing, touching, drinking, eating, urinating, defecating, diving into the water and gazing at the sky, laughing and crying'" (*The Book of Laughter* 257; Kundera's quotation is from Annie Leclerc's *Parole de femme*, see *The Book of Laughter* 106).

The dreamlike passages describing Tamina's sojourn on the children's island show how unbearable a childlike life is for an adult. Childish "innocence" is a state prior to guilt and responsibility, right and wrong. Being in this state, children may from an adult perspective treat those who do not belong to their world with utter cruelty. Anyone different is excluded, and the children's world is characterized by total uniformity. "Infantocracy" is a state which precedes individuation, separation of body and soul, of private and public, and the coupling of the perspectives of past and future with the present. It is playing hopscotch and plain corporeality, sensuality without shame (shame being for Kundera the beginning of eroticism and indicating the presence of the "soul" in physical love), it is living in the present of physical sensations and the rules of the game. Childhood may be a paradise—children's unquestioned celebration of their world, a kind of angelic laughter, corroborates this—but Kundera cannot esteem a paradise that is actually a state of existence prior to distinctions, which alone create significance. The childish existence in the pure present stands in contrast to Tamina's efforts to preserve the past, which would make the present meaningful. The end of Tamina's story is dreamlike similarly to Kafka's *Amerika*, which ends with the absurd dreamlike scene of the young protagonist joining the enormously big Oklahoma Outdoors Theater (see *Testaments* 79). The dreamlike narration sets the narrator and the reader free from the framework of a realistic story. The fantastic, unrealistic narration reveals something essential in the character, which, in Tamina's case, is the last phase of forgetting, the forgetting of forgetting. The children's island represents this forgetting of forgetting metaphorically, as a return to the primary state preceding all distinctions. By the same token, the fantasy of the children's island symbolizes the future to which the Czech nation will be led by "the President of Forgetting," and which to Kundera all humankind is approaching.

Kundera's analysis of "infantocracy" shows that authentic existence is not equivalent to living in the present in the sense that a child is. For Kundera, a mature, nonsentimental person makes distinctions, and she or he knows that genuinely significant moments are rare. Making distinctions presupposes memory. A significant moment is set off from the flow of all experienced moments only by the help of memory, which makes comparison possible, even if one seems just to be enjoying a spontaneous encounter with something unexpected. Moreover, in order to be able to build the foundation of our existence on moments of the living presence of meaning, we must preserve them in our memory.

Yet remembering the past can also prevent one from experiencing the present moment as meaningful. This phenomenon is explored in the last, seventh part of *The Book of Laughter and Forgetting*, "The Border," which offers a further variation on the relationship between temporality and sense giving. As I have noted, the border refers to the point where the meaning of a thing suddenly changes. The woman with whom Jan was in love had talked to him about the border at which everything loses its meaning: "It takes so little, so infinitely little, for someone to find himself on the other side of the border, where everything—love, convictions, faith, history—no longer has meaning. The whole mystery of human life resides in the fact that it is spent in the immediate proximity of, and even in direct contact with, that border, that it is separated from it not by kilometers but by barely a millimeter" (281). The passage contains the essence of Kundera's view of modern human existence as characterized by an openness to meanings which may reveal themselves at any moment only to vanish in the next. Any attempt to consolidate meanings as permanent transforms them into an ideology, which destroys the individual's openness toward the actual present. Jan discovers the willingness to accept this continuous shift of meanings in his mortally ill friend, Passer. In general, however, he thinks that humankind is marching in the direction of a total disappearance of meanings, of sinking into an existence where no distinctions are made any longer. He regards this as a consequence of repetition, a theme which was introduced in part 2 and is now taken up for more thorough examination.

According to Jan, repetition deprives experience of its meaningfulness: "He tells himself it is because he is getting old: When things are repeated, they lose a fraction of their meaning. Or more exactly, they lose, drop by drop, the vital strength that gives them their illusory meaning. For Jan, therefore, the border is the maximum acceptable dose of repetitions" (295–96). The narrator comments on this by saying that it is not true that repetition creates the border where meaningfulness disappears, it makes the border between the meaningful and meaningless visible (297–98). The idea is illustrated by the story of Jan's failed attempt to seduce a girl on a train. He has recourse to his routine, well-tried gestures, but this time they fail to work. Jan feels that he is standing in front of a "board of examiners, which knew full well that he was repeating himself and informed him that all repetition was mere imitation and all imitation was worthless. Jan suddenly saw himself through the young woman's eyes. He saw the pitiful pantomime of his gaze and gestures, that stereotyped gesticulation emptied of all meaning by years of repetition" (284). A recalled pattern of behavior fails to produce a new, meaningful experience; on the contrary, repetition turns the action into a meaningless imitation of a meaningful action. Here, repetition is connected with the temporality of human experience. Jan is afflicted by the fear that the female body—the erotic dream of his youth—might as a consequence of his increasing experience soon become completely unerotic for him. He longs for the moment just prior to entering the world of eroticism, the time depicted with so much beauty in Longus's *Daphnis and Chloe*. These reflections indicate that for Kundera an erotic encounter is not something unique, resulting—as assumed by the Romantic concept of love—from the meeting of two particular individuals; rather, it is a repeatable act in which the individual encounters a member of the opposite sex, or rather the body of a member of the opposite sex.

In part 7, eroticism is seen from the perspective of human history as well. Jan ponders the fact that our erotic experiences are a repetition of the eternal pattern between man and woman, where the man chases the fleeing woman. Edwige protests against this clichéd way of thinking, but Jan questions whether eroticism is at all imaginable without such clichés (289). Here we once again meet a Kunderan paradox. Some pages earlier, Jan claimed that repetition deprives the erotic experience of its significance, yet now he is saying that the meaning of an erotic experience is based on the repetition of a supra-individual and transhistorical pattern. The contradiction, however, is only seeming. The individual's experience can be fresh and new, even if others have had the same experience countless times in the course of human history. Nevertheless, the closing scene of the novel suggests that eroticism is a historical phenomenon which is vanishing today. Jan visits a nudist beach, which does not present itself to him as a place of erotic liberation, but as one where nakedness has lost its erotic significance. In other words, eroticism as a world-historical phenomenon reaches its end on the nudist beach.

The intertwining of the themes of remembering, forgetting, and meaning in *The Book of Laughter and Forgetting* illustrates not only several of Kundera's crucial ideas about humankind and history, but also his method of composing a novel out of different themes. The reader is expected to approach the novel with the same attentiveness to change that is required of human beings living in the modern world. We have to be able to recognize the precise meaning ascribed to a particular thing in a given context and to accept that the same thing or theme may be repeatedly redefined in new contexts. The whole of the novel which explores and elaborates these themes is more contrapuntal than synthetic.

Kundera, Nietzsche, and the vanishing of heaviness through laughter

In Kundera's novels there is much laughter, yet they are not humorous or even particularly amusing (see my discussion above; see also Galmiche). *The Book of Laughter and Forgetting* is a study of laughter rather than a book that makes the reader laugh, and *The Joke* is far from being a comical or jocular novel. What, then, does laughter actually mean for Kundera?

In Kundera's works, the objects of laughter are mostly people who experience something other than they imagine or expect to, or who act out of different motives from those they are aware of. A falsely beautified self-image and a sentimental attitude are often the object of ridicule and irony. Laughter is likewise provoked by cliché-like attitudes or by a comic clash between incompatible views or when events slip out of the participants' control, with unexpected outcomes. In fact, there is little that Kundera cannot laugh at. The actions of revolutionaries, consequential and dangerous as they might be, are not void of ridiculousness, nor is love or human aspirations to immortality. History, which subjugates individuals and nations, can also poke fun at them; even God—if he existed—would be a joker and even he would be afraid of becoming an object of ridicule: "God can't make Himself ridiculous by constantly changing His decisions" (*Farewell Waltz* 121). Of human beings, the most ridiculous for Kundera are the sentimental, who take themselves with absolute seriousness; but overall, few are completely or nearly safe from being laughed at—of his characters only the "positive" heroes such as Tamina, Agnes, Tomas, and Tereza. In fact, only art is for Kundera exempt from universal ridiculousness; ridicule does not attach to music, painting, or the novel. Artists themselves, on the other hand, do not stand above ridicule; this applies to Hemingway just as much as to Rimbaud or Goethe. While the history of the novel is not ridiculous, laughing and playfulness are of course important characteristics of the novel as a genre and Kundera's attribution of the birth of modern novel to Cervantes or Rabelais makes this clear. Laughter is a possibility which in Kundera's opinion ought to have been exploited in the novel to an even greater extent than has actually been the case.

While all of Kundera's novels contain some matters of ridicule, in *The Book of Laughter and Forgetting* the author-narrator offers an explicit discussion of the different functions of laughter. The two main kinds of laughter are explored in relation to sense giving and remembering. In Kundera's genealogy, the original form of laughter is the malicious laughter of the Devil, which reveals that something is not what it seems to be; it is less valuable, serious, or weighty than it appears. Despite its maliciousness, this mocking laughter also carries a certain "beneficent relief," suggesting that "things are less weighty than they appeared to be, letting us live more freely, no longer oppressing us with their austere seriousness" (*The Book of Laughter*

86). When the angels first heard the devils' malicious laughter, aimed against God and his creation, they did not know how to respond to it except by producing a similar sound—yet in a higher key—which they endowed with the opposite meaning (86–87). Angelic laughter was born, then, to express their rejoicing over God's creation.

Kundera gives several examples of this kind of laughter. The laughter of children running on grass conveys their joy of existence and is an approval of existence in its primordial state. The young communists' ring dance in the street is likewise a form of angelic laughter which proclaims their rejoicing over the revolution and their faith in the paradise that is about to arise. In their self-assured innocence they ignore the evil they themselves commit: "And the dancing young Czechs, knowing that the day before, in the same city, a woman and a surrealist had been swinging from the end of ropes, were dancing all the more frenetically, because their dance was a demonstration of their innocence, in shining contrast to the guilty darkness of the two who were hanged, those betrayers of the people and its hopes" (92–93). In the ring dance, evil is excluded. Those who do not join the circle of the jubilant remain beyond the magical border. If someone doubting the goodness of existence is hanged, this does not disturb the rejoicers in the circle. Kundera reveals that he himself was once a participant in this dance, but was then expelled from the circle and left in a constant state of falling; nonetheless he watches the dancing "with envy and yearning" (93). Tamina encounters the same phenomenon on the children's island. The children do not bully her out of malice, but they treat her without empathy and use her as their toy because she does not belong to their world. They want to hurt anyone beyond the border of their own world only "in order to exalt their own world and its law" (255). The angels' laughter simplifies the world in a naïve way, yet this naïveté is not harmless but indeed dangerous.

The Devil's laughter denies, where the angels' laughter approves. In Kundera's view, the art of human existence involves maintaining an equilibrium between denial and approval. If nothing has inherent value and anything may be the target of mocking laughter, life loses its meaningfulness, while in the opposite case the weight of things turns them into an unbearable burden. Human existence requires an equilibrium between the power of the angels and that of the devils, so that one is neither crushed by the weight of existence under the reign of the angels, nor does life become completely meaningless under that of the devils (86).

A deeper insight into Kundera's view of laughter can be gained, I argue, by comparing it to that of Nietzsche. For Kundera, as for many other authors of the late twentieth century, Nietzsche is the foremost philosopher of modernity (for some Nietzsche is the philosopher of postmodernity before the postmodern era). Kundera's metaphor for the mode of existence of modern humankind—the death of God—is taken from Nietzsche. Human beings are left alone in the midst of existing things and encounter a world without sensible order. As Nietzsche puts it in *The Gay Science*, "The total character of the world . . . is for all eternity chaos, not in the sense of a lack of necessity but of a lack of order, organization, form, beauty, wisdom, and whatever else our aesthetic anthropomorphisms are called" (109). Nietzsche's

Zarathustra teaches that "Uncanny is human existence and still without meaning . . . a buffoon can be fatal to it" (*Thus Spoke Zarathustra* 49), and Kundera entirely agrees with this, as demonstrated, for example, in *The Joke* and *Farewell Waltz*. Humankind poses questions and sets out on a quest, yet the individual has to learn that no absolute truths are available to him or her. The person who believes himself or herself to be in possession of absolute truth is wrong. In Zarathustra's words, "Truth has never yet clung to the arm of an inflexible man" (*Thus Spoke Zarathustra* 79), where "inflexible" (*ein Unbedingter* [*Also sprach Zarathustra* 66]) refers to a person in search of absolute truth. Along with their common conviction concerning the relativity of all knowledge, Kundera speaks, as I have discussed, of Nietzsche's "experimental" method of thinking as a model for his own, where thoughts are expressed directly as they come to mind without being developed as part of a comprehensive system of ideas (*Testaments* 147–48, 172–74). This means, I would add, that thoughts appear in a text like variations on themes in a thematic composition.

A further aspect of Nietzsche's method of thinking to which Kundera is also attracted but which he never mentions is the metaphorical and, more generally, poetic or imaginative. Kundera emphasizes the novelist's metaphorical thinking in connection with his Central European Pleiades, for whom existential or phenomenological metaphors are essential devices in the novelistic exploration of the possibilities of human existence (see *The Art* 140, *Testaments* 103–05, *The Curtain* 70). Yet another important source for his own use of metaphors is, I suggest, Nietzsche, who often tackles philosophical problems with a metaphor, as indicated, for example, by the titles of his works *Daybreak* and *The Twilight of Idols*. The "death of God" is a metaphor on which Kundera has seized with pleasure. Thinking philosophically in metaphors was an innovation of Nietzsche's that brought his works close to poetry. Kundera's novelistic thinking comes close to Nietzsche in that he thinks of the existential problems of his characters in terms of metaphors such as lightness and weight. Moreover, especially in *Thus Spoke Zarathustra*, Nietzsche elucidates abstract ideas not only through metaphors but also through scenes in the life of the protagonist. Philosophizing takes a narrative form, and philosophical content is presented through imagined characters and events, just as in a literary work of art. In short, what has been praised or censured as "poetry" in *Zarathustra*, namely, its metaphorical language and its representation of philosophical thought in the form of persons and scenes, shows a striking resemblance to Kundera's manner of dealing with themes.

What makes Nietzsche still more important for Kundera is that not only does Kundera's method of thinking have a counterpart in Nietzsche, but in several cases the theme words themselves coincide with Nietzsche's metaphors. "Weight" and "lightness," "dance" and "laughter" are important metaphors in Nietzsche's *Thus Spoke Zarathustra* and *The Gay Science*. Weight and lightness are determinants of human existence and are connected with laughter in Nietzsche's philosophy too. Were I to take the risk of interpreting the not always lucid symbolism of *Thus Spoke Zarathustra*, I would claim that the way "weight" is connected to "life" in Kundera's fictional world can be found in Nietzsche's writings. Humankind is compared to a camel bearing the burdens of life: "The weight-bearing spirit takes upon itself all these heaviest things: like a camel hurrying laden into the desert, thus it hurries into its desert" (*Thus Spoke Zarathustra* 54) . . . "But only man is hard to bear! That is because he bears too many foreign things upon his shoulders. Like the camel, he kneels down and lets himself be well laden. Especially the strong, weight-bearing man in whom dwell respect and awe: he has laden too many *foreign* heavy words and values upon himself—now life seems to him a desert!" (*Thus Spoke Zarathustra* 211). The question that preoccupies Zarathustra is not how to dissolve the meaninglessness of human existence by discovering weighty things lending meaning to life, but rather how to learn to live bravely and cheerfully amidst meaninglessness. Humankind should seek to free itself from the burdens of life. By climbing a mountain, dancing, and singing, Zarathustra manifests his ability to confront the weight of living. His mission is to teach human beings how to dance, laugh, and fly (*Thus Spoke Zarathustra* 213). Laughter is a means whereby the burden of life can be eased. "Corrective laughter" turns the tragedy of life into a comedy (*The Gay Science* 29) and defeats the dreadfulness of existence (*Thus Spoke Zarathustra* 156). Zarathustra laughs in the face of the winter that makes his fingers livid with cold and welcomes it to kill the flies (192). Although mankind has always considered it indispensable to rule that certain things absolutely may not be laughed at (*The Gay Science* 29), wisdom is the strength and ability to free oneself of weighty things through laughter. The philosopher's spirit endeavors to be a good dancer (*The Gay Science* 246), and a fool's cap does good to man, who by nature is disposed to place too much weight on his shoulders (104). Zarathustra's archfiend, his "Devil," is "the Spirit of Gravity," whom he defeats with laughter by learning how to fly (*Thus Spoke Zarathustra* 67–68, 210–13) or by dancing "over every Here and There and Over-there" (238). "Does one then straightway have to curse where one does not love? That—seems to me bad taste" (*Thus Spoke Zarathustra* 304), says Zarathustra, who prefers laughing to cursing.

Although Nietzsche's and Kundera's metaphors appear strikingly similar, they are not identical in content. A "dancer" in *Thus Spoke Zarathustra* is a positive figure, while in Kundera's works dancing carries different, mostly negative meanings. The dancers of the ring dance belong to the sphere of "totalitarian kitsch" and are dangerous to those whom they exclude from their circle. In *Farewell Waltz*, the naked, fat elderly women in the pool perform a "necrophiliac ring dance around the transience of youth" (148), where the dance has a mocking character. In the concluding chapter of *The Unbearable Lightness of Being*, in which Tomas and Tereza amuse themselves in the restaurant of the nearby town, the couples' dance bears the conventional meaning of erotic togetherness and content, while in other contexts in the novel dancing seems to attract especially those who desire to merge with music and with their dancing partner. In *Slowness*, a dancer is someone who performs in front of an audience (17–20).

Furthermore, while in *Zarathustra* the Devil is the symbol of weight, for Kundera the Devil symbolizes the denial of heaviness through laughter, and lightness appears in Nietzsche's work not as unbearable but as something desirable. The idea of the heaviness of life and of laughter as easing this weight, however, is common to both Nietzsche and Kundera. Laughter is not a manifestation of exhilaration, but by diminishing the heavy burden of existence it is apt to make life more bearable. Nietzsche's mountain climber "laughs at all tragedies, real or imaginary" (68; the pun in the German original, "der lacht über alle Trauer-Spiele und Trauer-Ernste" [*Also sprach Zarathustra* 49] is not mediated in the translation). Furthermore, unlike Kundera's laughter, Nietzsche's has an undertone of Dionysian rapture and dancing that challenges Schopenhauerian pessimism. Schopenhauer asks, "*Does existence have any meaning at all?*" (*The Gay Science* 219) but his pessimism over a world that has become "stupid, blind, crazed, and questionable" (*The Gay Science* 221) is defied by Zarathustra's Dionysian and rapturous approval of existence. In contrast, Kundera's laughter of the Devil lacks this Dionysian character and is, rather, a laughter of disillusionment. Kundera's devilish laughter is thus closer to Schopenhauer's pessimism, arising from the meaninglessness of life, than to Nietzsche's enthusiastic, Dionysian approval of life. The angels' laughter, as an expression of their rejoicing over existence, is ostensibly more akin to the Dionysian rapture, yet it is based on a false confidence in the goodness of the world order, which of course is alien to Nietzsche's view of the Dionysian. Zarathustra's dancing is an approval of existence despite its dreadfulness. For Nietzsche, this dance is infinitely far from the eulogies of those who celebrate existence without reservation and whom Zarathustra calls "the all-contented" (*The Gay Science* 212). Towards the end of *Thus Spoke Zarathustra* "the Ass Festival" is celebrated, in which people worship the ass as their god. By braying its heehaw (which Nietzsche spells in German as "Ja!" ["Yes!"]), the ass praises the world as its own creation and this appraisal is echoed by its worshippers (321–22). We can draw a parallel between the ass and its worshippers and Kundera's angels and ring dancers, who express their uncritical approval of existence.

Kundera's two kinds of laughter thus represent two contrary attitudes toward existence, which are also of different value. The angels' all-approving laughter is a sign either of an ideological attitude or of childish naïveté, whereas mocking laughter expresses the attitude of a rational human being toward things that "cannot be loved." Life as a whole cannot be loved, maintains Kundera. Zarathustra assures us that we love life not because we are used to life but because we are used to love (68). So many particular things feign to be better than they really are, that is, feign lovability; therefore there is plenty to laugh at. In *The Book of Laughter and Forgetting*, the member of the party committee who secretly orders a horoscope for himself is ridiculous, but so is Mirek's airbrushing of a past love and the big-nosed Zdena's stubborn fidelity. Trying to avoid ridicule can itself appear ridiculous indeed, as does Jaromil's death resulting from his fear of being laughed at. Part 5 in *The Book of Laughter and Forgetting*, "Litost," dealing with the student and the butcher's wife, refers to a character's specific feeling at the sight of his own ridiculousness. According to Kundera, the Czech word *lítost* refers to "a state of torment created by the sudden sight of one's own misery" (*The Book of Laughter* 167; see also *Life Is*

Elsewhere 48–49). For Kundera, this state of mind is typical of youth, when misery derives from youthful immaturity. Lítost is a sense of wretchedness and self-pity and leads neither to relieving laughter nor to beneficent self-reflection. According to Kundera, lítost does not occur in the lives of individuals alone but also in the history of nations. The Spartans, in their belligerent history, made irrational, self-destructive decisions out of lítost and Czech history, too, is full of lítost, crushed as it was by a stronger enemy time and again (206–07).

In the first essayistic passage in part 3, "The Angels," Kundera comments on "Saint Annie Leclerc's" description of the laughter of delight: "Unquestionably, such laughter is 'beyond joking, mockery, ridicule.' The two sisters stretched out on their bed are not laughing about anything in particular, their laughter has no object, it is the expression of being rejoicing in being. Just as someone in pain is linked by his groans to the present moment (and is entirely outside past and future), so someone bursting out in such ecstatic laughter is without memory and without desire, for he is emitting his shout into the world's present moment and wishes to know only that" (80–81). The laughter of unconditional approval, from which everything but the momentary present is excluded, is a praise of nothingness. It is a primordial state of being, prior to the opening of the perspectives of temporality, of past and future, and thus of comparisons and distinctions, which alone create meaningfulness.

Indeed, another important theme in *The Book of Laughter and Forgetting*, although not articulated as a key word, is "beginning." It was not only for the Romantics that childhood was the most poetic age. Nietzsche, too, valued childhood as a new beginning in human existence: "The child is innocence and forgetfulness, a new beginning, a sport, a self-propelling wheel, a first motion, a sacred Yes" (*Thus Spoke Zarathustra* 55). In contrast, for Kundera, the child's "yes" to life is not sacred but equal to the wisdom of the ass. In *The Book of Laughter and Forgetting*, the beginning is not explored only as the primal state of human existence; in the context of music, the primordial state of culture is pondered on as well. On his deathbed, the father—who has almost entirely lost his ability to speak—says something about "the stupidity of music." The author-narrator is puzzled as to what his father, a passionate lover of music, might mean by his words, and comes to the conclusion that he must have been referring to a primordial state of music before the beginning of its history: "That primeval state of music (music without thought) mirrors the human being's inherent stupidity. It required an immense effort of heart and mind for music to rise above that essential stupidity, and it is that splendid arc over centuries of European history which has been extinguished like a skyrocket at the peak of its trajectory" (248).

Kundera, like Nietzsche, sees meaning as a human, cultural product, brought about in the first place through artistic creation. Nietzsche's early work, *The Birth of Tragedy*, is as a whole a testimony to his conviction of the crucial role of the arts in the creation of culture. This is confirmed in the philosopher's unpublished notebooks: "Art and nothing but art! Art is the great enabler of life, she is the great temptress alluring us to live, the great stimulator of life. . . . Art as *the redeemer of the one who has knowledge*—who perceives the appalling and questionable nature of existence, who insists on conceiving—of the one with tragic knowledge" (*Nachgelassene* 521). Here we encounter once again the view that the essence of art is a combination of knowledge and beauty, a view which Kundera shares with Broch and Musil. Moreover, Kundera's conviction that what is essential in human history is not political history but the history of the arts accords with Nietzsche. But Kundera also maintains that in the contemporary world art can no longer fulfill its creative cultural function. The final phase in the history of music—here representing the arts in general—has now been reached and this state is similar to its beginning. This is a state in which Schönberg, as the epitome of where the development of music in the course of its history has led, is forgotten, but popular music conceived of as music preceding its historical development lives on eternally: "Stereotyped harmonies, banal melodies, and rhythms all the more insistent the more monotonous they are—that is what remains of music, that is music's eternity" (*The Book of Laughter* 247). With the throb of the guitar the existence expresses its rejoicing: "'I'm here!' There is no more boisterous, no more unanimous agreement than the agreement with being" (*The Book of Laughter* 247). Again, the similarity to Nietzsche's feast of the ass is striking.

Kundera traces the "stupidity" of music in its primordial state back to "the human being's inherent stupidity" (*The Book of Laughter* 248). Meanings cannot be discovered either in the arts or in a human life in their undifferentiated primordial state; they emerge only through a process of differentiation. The meaningless eternity of existence—the endless repetition of the mere functions of life, "seeing, hearing, eating, drinking, urinating, defecating"—is unbearable. For Kundera, there is no escape from the unbearable state of meaninglessness through a Dionysian ecstasy. With his absolutely negative attitude toward ecstasy—represented for him by rock music, in which the borders of the self, between now and then, and ultimately all distinctions, are obliterated in a state of rapture (see *Testaments* 82–88, 233)—Kundera is the exact opposite of Nietzsche's dancing Zarathustra; he is an advocate of distinctions, of rational analysis and critique.

According to Kundera, the history of music consists of subsequent discoveries revealing unexpected possibilities in the basic material. A corresponding temporal dimension is also present in the individual's search for meaning in his or her life: the individual striving for authenticity tries to grasp the meaning in the present, but that the present is related to the past is a prerequisite of all distinctions. Yet history as a continuous process of differentiation has in Kundera's view now come to an end—however difficult it may be to conceive of the end of history or just of the history of music or that of a particular nation (see *The Book of Laughter* 246). Rather than producing something new, the culture of our age—whether music, painting, or the novel—produces only constantly changing repetitions of the old. This may be laughable, until it is no longer even that, but merely meaningless. Laughter appears here in its final form, as an exhausted, dying laughter. Jan ponders what will happen when things that have undergone endless repetition have lost not only their meaning but at last also their ridiculousness: "Jan imagines that the Greek gods at first passionately participated in the adventures of humans. Then they settled in on Olympus to look down and have a good laugh. And by now they have been asleep for a long time" (295–96). When the constant repetition of the old no longer provokes even mocking laughter, we are in a state beyond all meaningfulness.

Chapter Eight
Hedonism, Aestheticism, and Love as Modes of Authentic Sense Giving

In his later works, Kundera's exploration of the possibilities of human existence focuses on the search for meaningfulness which can be found immanently in the individual's experiences. The possibility of authentic existence is indicated already in *The Joke*, where Ludvik ponders his love for Lucie as a chance to establish his life outside History; in *Life Is Elsewhere*, where it is represented by the middle-aged hedonist; in *Farewell Waltz*, where beauty opens Jakub's eyes to a new possibility; and in *The Book of Laughter and Forgetting*, where the most important characters in search of authentic modes of living are Tamina and Jan, she finding meaningfulness in her past love, he pondering the significance of eroticism. Despite its title, it is *The Unbearable Lightness of Being* that presents Kundera's most profound and most optimistic—or perhaps least pessimistic—inquiry into the possibilities of meaningful authentic being.

The title, *The Unbearable Lightness of Being*, reflects the thematic content of the novel only in part and in fact misleadingly. In this it resembles *The Joke*, where the joke turns into something serious or *Life Is Elsewhere*, which actually proclaims the opposite, that life is here and now, even if a sentimentalist is incapable of understanding this. In *The Unbearable Lightness of Being*, a tolerable balance between lightness and weightiness is reached at least by some of the main characters, at least temporarily. This novel is again about love, even if not in the sentimental sense of the word or in the conventional sense of a love story. Rather, it explores love as an existential possibility, that is, love that does not offer an emotion greater than life, a merging with the beloved, or pure happiness, but that is nevertheless a source of meaningfulness. Most of the themes are familiar from Kundera's earlier texts. The theme of "the oppressive lightness of the void" is present already in *The Joke* (250) and is repeated in the later novels (see *The Art* 136–37). In *The Book of Laughter and Forgetting,* the appropriate weight is pursued in terms of a balance between the angels' and the devils' laughter, while in *Farewell Waltz,* Jakub is perplexed by the fact that his awareness of being a murderer is so light to bear. Some of the paired themes of the earlier works—sentimental and authentic, kitsch and beauty, body and soul—also reappear in *The Unbearable Lightness of Being,* along with questions of the temporality of existence and of human freedom, but the perspectives from which they are seen and the meanings they convey are new.

That the nonsentimental, autonomous person striving for authenticity has to discover what is meaningful in his or her own experience means for Kundera that experience must be private, in contrast to that which is public, collective, and ideological. The requirement that sense giving has to be based on the individual's experience does not conflict with Kundera's search for general human possibilities. Every individual has to carry out this search on his or her own, as meaning is not to be found for everyone in the same things; yet because of the anthropological constants of human existence there are not countless alternatives but only a few. In *The Unbearable Lightness of Being,* there are three basic alternative ways of nonsentimental sense giving, namely, hedonism, aestheticism, and love. In other words, a nonsentimental person may find his or her existence in sensual pleasure, as Jan does in *The Book of Laughter and Forgetting* and the man in his forties in *Life Is Elsewhere*, or he or she can find meaningfulness in love, like Tamina in *The Book of Laughter and Forgetting* and Ludvik in *The Joke*, or he or she can discover the meaningfulness of beauty, as Jakub does at the end of *Farewell Waltz*. Yet while in the earlier novels these possibilities were raised only in passing, in *The Unbearable Lightness of Being* they are painstakingly and meticulously elaborated upon. In addition to alternative forms of authentic sense giving, *The Unbearable Lightness of Being* also deals with the conditions which are prerequisite to authentic sense giving. There are two such conditions, namely, the individual's freedom to choose between alternatives and the possibility that a unique event is meaningful. I start with an analysis of these two prerequisites, which form the framework within which authentic sense giving takes place.

Freedom of choice and the singularity of events as preconditions of authentic sense giving

In *The Unbearable Lightness of Being* the lightness and weight of existence are explored through the main story of Tomas and Tereza and the parallel side story of Sabina and Franz. In neither of the stories does anything extraordinary happen. Tomas and Tereza meet, fall in love, and get married and after 1968, like so many others, they emigrate, but then decide to return to Prague. For political reasons, Tomas has to give up his work as a surgeon and gets a job as a window cleaner. After some time the couple move to the country, where they work on a collective farm until they are killed in a car accident. Sabina, a painter and likewise a Czech emigrée living in Switzerland, is one of Tomas's lovers, but she also has a relationship with Franz, a professor in Geneva. Franz decides to leave his wife for Sabina, but Sabina flees from him and Franz decides not to return home but starts to live with a student who is in love with him. However, he unexpectedly dies from injuries suffered in a street attack during a trip to Thailand. Sabina carries on with her life in the US. Tomas,

Tereza, and Sabina try to establish bearable modes of existence in a world that has turned into a trap. Of the four main characters, Franz is the only one who, despite his intelligence, shows a strong tendency toward sentimentalism. He is also the only sentimental character in Kundera's novels who is depicted with sympathy. Through his figure, we see how difficult it is for anyone to avoid sentimentalism, which in this novel is labeled "kitsch."

In the opening scene of the novel, Tomas is standing at the window of his apartment wondering whether to invite Tereza, a waitress from a provincial town he had met a few weeks earlier, to visit him in Prague. He knows that if he invites her she will come and offer him her whole life, and he hesitates. His hesitation annoys him since he feels that he may be spoiling the most beautiful moment of his life. But how can he know whether his feeling for her is love or a hysterical, sentimental illusion of love? (6–7). Kundera no longer asks what choices one can make in History, but what one's private, small choices are like. To be able to escape History, the individual must retain a realm of freedom outside it, but what is this freedom like? According to Kundera, there are inherent restrictions on this freedom arising from the fact that we live only once and therefore cannot know how our lives would have been affected by a different choice.

Part 1 of the novel, "Lightness and Weight," opens abstractly by asking what Nietzsche might have meant by his notion of the "eternal return." Nietzsche's idea of everything we have once experienced recurring infinitely, exactly as it was, is for Kundera a "mad myth" (3). The idea makes sense to him, however, when he interprets it as a comment on what it actually means that things happen only once. According to him, the myth of eternal return means *per negationem* that "a life which disappears once and for all, which does not return, is like a shadow, without weight, dead in advance, and whether it was horrible, beautiful, or sublime, its horror, sublimity, and beauty meant nothing" (3). A fourteenth-century war in Africa, in which hundreds of thousands were killed, would not much trouble anybody; yet if this war were to recur again and again, it would become "a solid mass, permanently protuberant, its inanity irreparable" (3). Should the French Revolution recur again and again, the beheadings ordered by Robespierre would attain a completely different meaning. Such an eternal return would give all our deeds an immense weight, whereas their transitory and unrepeatable nature makes our actions weightless. Thus weightlessness appears as an unavoidable, constitutive characteristic of human existence. The relationship between meaning and repetition is viewed here from a new perspective. While Jan's ruminations in *The Book of Laughter and Forgetting* suggest that repetition is a threat to an event appearing as significant, now the significance of an event is at risk precisely because it occurs only once. The explanation for this apparent contradiction is that the word "repetition" is used in two different meanings. In *The Book of Laughter and Forgetting* it is a type of action or event that recurs, for instance, the act of lovemaking; the question raised in *The Unbearable Lightness of Being*, in contrast, is how a single event in history or in an individual's life can attain significance at all, if it is only transitory.

The uniqueness of events renders the making of decisions more difficult. Kundera tells us that Tomas's figure originally appeared to his mind's eye in the scene in which Tomas is standing in front of the window trying to make up his mind whether he should live with Tereza or not and recognizing that he lacks reasonable arguments for a well-founded decision. Actually, an individual can never know whether such decisions were right or not, because he or she lives only once: "'*Einmal ist keinmal*' says Tomas to himself. What happened just once, says the German adage, might as well not have happened at all. If we have only one life to live, we might as well not have lived at all" (8). As I understand it, the German saying, *Einmal ist keinmal,* has a slightly different meaning. It refers to actions or situations that occur only once and therefore should not carry great weight in our judgment of someone's character or the event itself. What is at stake in Tomas's—and Kundera's—view is rather the possibility of human sense giving, given that meanings have to be determined immanently, within the one and only life that we have. How can we judge the significance of an action or an experience, when everything that occurs in life occurs only once and cannot be compared to anything else?

Nietzsche was also preoccupied with the question of how we can live immanently, that is, without a transcendent foundation to our existence that would define the true essence and value of things. He claimed that humankind creates categories of thinking to serve the process of living. By means of these categories, we hold up for a moment the flow of existence in which everything is in a continuous state of change. This allows us to grasp it so as to make it serve our needs. With his view of existence as process of continuous change, with no direction or goal, Nietzsche denies the Enlightenment conception of historical progress. Rather than of conceiving of change as progress, he thinks of existence as an eternal return of the same. The following passage in *The Gay Science*, "The Heaviest Weight," connects the idea of the eternal return of the same to that of the weight of life:

> What if some day or night a demon were to steal into your loneliest loneliness and say to you: "This life as you now live it and have lived it you will have to live once again and innumerable times again; and there will be nothing new in it, but every pain and every joy and every thought and sigh and everything unspeakably small or great in your life must return to you, all in the same succession and sequence." Would you not throw yourself down and gnash your teeth and curse the demon who spoke thus? Or have you once experienced a tremendous moment when you would have answered him: "You are a god, and never have I heard anything more divine." If this thought gained power over you, as you are it would transform and possibly crush you; the question in each and every thing, "Do you want this again and innumerable times again?" would lie on your actions as the heaviest weight! (194)

The idea of eternal return is presented here in the form of a thought experiment, just as in Kundera's novel (and unlike in Nietzsche's later works, where this idea represents a metaphysical truth; see Heidegger, *Nietzsche*, vol. 1, part 2). This hypothesis endows the individual with a new perspective on his or her actions, since owing to the process of endless recurrence, each deed attains an enormous weight. Yet, while the thought experiment leads Tomas to reflections on the weightlessness of a life that is lived only once, Nietzsche's aim is different, that is, to accept life exactly as it is. We have to live life facing the fact that it has no transcendence; that is to say, we can rely neither on religion's promises of an afterlife, nor on those of History of a better future which will redeem the present. Life has to be accepted just as it is, entailing our willingness to relive the very same an endless number of times. The idea is put succinctly by Nietzsche's Zarathustra: "'Was that—life?' I will say to death. 'Very well! Once more!'" (*Thus Spoke Zarathustra* 326).

In contrast to Nietzsche, in Tomas's thought experiment what recurs is not exactly the same; rather, what is thought to recur are different variations on a life, so that the individual is able to compare the different versions with one another (*The Unbearable Lightness* 218). If we had a chance to make comparisons, we would know the significance of our choices. Thus, while for Nietzsche the idea of the eternal recurrence of the same aims at acceptance of a life without transcendence, for Kundera it implies that our deeds lack a rational foundation because of our ignorance of the possibilities available to us. Since the ultimate significance of our deeds therefore remains unclear, the only thing left to us is to experience something as significant in the given moment. Tomas experiences his love for Tereza as meaningful, but there is no way to know what the decision to live without her would have meant to him. One can distinguish between the significant and the insignificant exclusively within the frame of the one and only life a person has chosen, without knowing what the alternatives would have been. That Kundera originally intended to call his novel *The Planet of Inexperience* indicates the centrality of this idea to it. He explains the idea as follows: "We are born one time only, we can never start a new life equipped with the experience we've gained from a previous one. We leave childhood without knowing what youth is, we marry without knowing what it is to be married, and even when we enter old age, we don't know what it is we are heading for: the old are innocent children of their old age. In that sense, man's world is the planet of inexperience" (*The Art* 132). Although the individual stages of human life, from childhood to old age, are common to all humankind, nobody really knows beforehand what each stage will be like. This means that even if individuals experience something that has already been experienced by others—such as being married—they still have to live through it before they can know what it is truly like. Listening to others or empathizing with them cannot replace actual experience.

What is true of the individual's life again applies equally to nations and History. The Czechs will never know what course their national history would have taken, had they not initiated the Thirty Years War in 1618 or had they fought against Hitler instead of surrendering to him. That is why we can never decide if a particular historical decision was right or wrong. The sentence expressing Tomas's insight into his life is repeated later in reference to history: "*Einmal ist keinmal*. What happens but once might as well not have happened at all. The history of the Czechs will not be repeated, nor will the history of Europe. The history of the Czechs and of Europe is a pair of sketches from the pen of mankind's fateful inexperience. History is as light as individual human life, unbearably light, light as a feather, as dust swirling into the air, as whatever will no longer exist tomorrow" (217; here Kundera expresses the weightlessness of human history through metaphors which closely resemble those used in the Bible in rendering the transience of human life). Neither the individual's life nor History, contrary to what the revolutionaries believed, is a "work" of man, in the sense that a work of art is; they are mere sketches, outlines, which will never reach completion in a "work" (7–8). Neither History nor the life of an individual is therefore controllable, not only because acts break free from actors, but also because we will never know what the consequences of alternative decisions would have been.

The Unbearable Lightness of Being starts with an ontological reflection on the unavoidable lightness of man's doings and of his whole existence. What does choosing mean, if we do not actually know what the choice is between? And what, then, is the individual's freedom, which constitutes the basis of his or her autonomy? Making free choices is presented, since "Eduard and God," as a prerequisite for meaningful action. What we are forced to do is not truly an act of our own; the authentic and meaningful must be sought only in acts which we have freely chosen (see *Laughable Loves* 244–45). This concurs with the chief surgeon's comment in *The Unbearable Lightness of Being* on statements which the totalitarian regime forces its citizens to make: they cannot be taken seriously, because they are forced (173). Only free action counts. But if we do not know what we are choosing, what weight can our choices have?

In *The Unbearable Lightness of Being,* the figure parallel to Tomas is Sabina, through whom Kundera likewise explores the themes of choice and freedom and their connection to lightness and weight. The recurring choice in Sabina's life is betrayal, that is, acting against the expectations and wishes of authority. As an adolescent, she disappoints her father, later she betrays the party and her teachers at the Academy, and in the end she leaves Franz because she does not want to play a part in the show in which, under the eyes of all of Geneva, she takes the place of his wife "in his large conjugal bed" (111). Sabina's "history of betrayals" is not spared the author's irony. When she was fourteen her father made her break up with her first boyfriend, after which she had a compulsion to act against her father's will. She adored Picasso because her father could not stand him, and she married a drunk until she betrayed her betrayal as well and broke off the marriage. Yet the temptation of betrayal is depicted throughout the novel with sympathetic understanding, in that Sabina wants to preserve her independence, solitude, and freedom. She considers anything aiming at uniformity or sameness as evil: "The image of that evil was a parade of people marching by with raised fists and shouting identical syllables in unison" (96). Through gesture and voice, a demonstrator identifies with the collective. To Sabina's mind, the unity of a marching crowd epitomizes the complete renunciation of individual autonomy. The loss of privacy is an evil to Sabina and this is what her marriage with Franz would mean to her. She observes that a person who loses the privacy of his or her own life loses everything (109), an attitude typical of Kundera's nonsentimental, autonomous characters who strive for authenticity.

To Sabina, freedom means escape from the power of others over oneself, but this does not say anything about the ends for which freedom is used. Freedom does not imply that an individual is free to choose what is best for himself or herself, because this cannot be known. This view is traditionally called the negative concept of freedom. It is important to note that no other concept of freedom actually occurs in Kundera's works (for the concept of freedom, see, e.g., Spaemann). In this negative concept of freedom, the content of freedom remains undetermined. Any determination, even if it ensues from the very essence of the matter, is regarded as a limitation of freedom. This is why Sabina's freedom appears inherently connected with betrayal, understood as an escape from being determined and labeled: "Betrayal means breaking ranks and going off into the unknown. Sabina knew of nothing more magnificent than going off into the unknown" (87). However, it is evident that Sabina does not in fact escape being determined by others, although in reverse: she tends to choose the exact opposite of what others expect of her. Her chain of betrayals equals a series of rebellious gestures, of refusals to obey. The boundless "expanse of freedom," which Sabina feels opening up for her as she follows "the golden horn of betrayal" (113), is not filled with any particular content of her own. There is a moment when Sabina wishes that Franz would use his love for her to put an end to her fleeing. For Franz, however, love means renouncing his strength and consequently he is incapable of cutting her chain of betrayals. The ultimate question remaining is what is left for someone after betraying everything and everybody: "One could betray one's parents, husband, country, love, but when parents, husband, country, and love were gone—what was left to betray? . . . Sabina was unaware of the goal that lay behind her longing to betray. The unbearable lightness of being—was that the goal?" (118–19). Sabina's flight leads to a void. In defending her autonomy and her freedom she achieves the state of the complete weightlessness of existence.

The first and fifth parts of the novel, both entitled "Lightness and Weight," deal with Tomas, whose existential problem is defined by the same themes as Sabina's, lightness and weight, freedom, and the difficulty of making decisions. Like her, he wishes to evade all forms of external compulsion. The paradox in his efforts, as in hers, is that he cannot avoid being determined, in negation, by the demands of others. For instance, after an article of his, dealing with the problem of the guilt of those who committed atrocities in the early years of communist rule, is published in a magazine, he is asked to publicly retract it because the article has been taken as an assault on the regime. Tomas refuses, not because he desires to become a hero in the eyes of others or in his own, but because he realizes that if he complies, everyone will smile at him understandingly, both those who have not yet been forced to denounce their opinions and to proclaim their support of the oppressive regime (smiling with a sense of moral superiority) and those who have already done so (smiling out of a shared sense of guilt). Thinking about this, he is filled with panic, forcing him to give up his career as a surgeon. He has a similar experience when his young son, with whom he has had no contact since his divorce from his first wife, gets in touch with him to ask him to sign a petition demanding the release of political prisoners. When his son says he feels it his father's duty to sign the petition, Tomas refuses to do so.

On what basis can individuals make independent decisions? We cannot rely on what others or the authorities tell us to do, nor can we learn from the experience of others. Lacking sufficient experience of our own—as is almost always the case in the great decisions of life—what in ourselves can guide our freedom so that decisions are not arbitrary and incidental? According to the positive notion of freedom, we may in our free decisions follow our inner needs and inclinations, the "internal necessity," rather than external compulsion. Herder and Goethe, for example, thought that we are free when we follows our individual inclinations or "individual nature" (Herder, "Selbstgespräch," *Journal* 191; see also Jannidis). According to them, following our "individual nature" implies determination without loss of freedom. The idea of internal necessity, of an internal imperative, is present in Kundera's works as well; yet he does not accept it as an answer to these questions, but holds fast to the negative concept of freedom.

The second of the two parts entitled "Lightness and Weight" deals with the idea of the internal imperative and the question of weight raised by this imperative. In contrast to Herder and Goethe, for whom the individual's identity cannot be defined by any classificatory concepts (see Ehrich-Haefeli; Saariluoma [Steinby], *Erzählstruktur*), in Kundera's view a basis for the classification of human beings is formed by the internal imperative: "Insofar as it is possible to divide people into categories, the surest criterion is the deep-seated desires that orient them to one or another lifelong activity" (187). Tomas recognizes an internal imperative in his choice of profession. A surgeon's internal imperative is the readiness and the courage to involve himself or herself with the machinery of the human body. Considering that for Tomas his work as a surgeon is rooted in a personal imperative which he must obey, why is he willing to make a living as a window cleaner? First, he gives up his position as a surgeon and is given a menial position in another clinic. Then the secret police offer him the chance to return to his earlier position as a surgeon on the condition that he cooperates with the authorities. He does not accept the offer and leaves the clinic. On this the author-narrator comments, "The way he rushed into his decision seems rather odd to me. Could it perhaps conceal something else, something deeper that escaped his reasoning?" (188). The author continues his reflections on the nature of the internal imperative: "It is my feeling that Tomas had long been secretly irritated by the stern, aggressive, solemn *Es muss sein!* and that he harboured a deep desire to follow the spirit of Parmenides [or Nietzsche] and make heavy go to light" (189). Tomas wants to know what lies beyond the *Es muss sein!* (It Must Be!); in other words, "what remains of life when a person rejects what he previously considered his mission" (190).

If a person in the name of freedom renounces the internal imperative, he or she faces a paradox, because this freedom is an empty, negative determinant, in that the self will lack any definite content. This means that freedom, which Tomas considers an essential prerequisite of his autonomy, turns out for him to be a form of denial of the self. Freedom thus appears as an absolute value that stands above everything else, including any particular content of life or any reason for action. When Tomas refuses to sign the petition for the release of political prisoners, his feelings are similar to those he had when he gave up his career as a surgeon: "It was the same black intoxication he had felt when he sent off the letter that meant the end of his career in medicine. He was not at all sure he was doing the right thing, but he was sure he was doing what he wanted to do" (214). Tomas's last words in the novel are "I have no mission. No one has. And it's a terrific relief to realize you're free, free of all missions" (305). Although Tomas has recognized his internal imperative, he renounces it in order to make his freedom absolute, just as Sabina did.

Like Marketa in *The Book of Laughter and Forgetting*, who, tormented by jealousy, feels relieved when she imagines her husband making love to another woman as a mere body, or like Tamina who occasionally longs for the lightness of forgetting, Tomas, too, feels a new lightness of being after renouncing his inner imperative. Working as a window cleaner is like being on holiday from his own life: "Now he understood what made people (people he always pitied) happy when they took a job without feeling the compulsion of an internal *Es muss sein!* and forgot it the moment they left for home every evening" (190). Nevertheless, like Tamina, Tomas realizes that lightness soon turns into a burden. The maximum length of a holiday, he thinks, is two years; after that it starts to feel oppressive. Too heavy a weight is crushing, but a long-lasting preoccupation with merely weightless things is no less unbearable.

Eventually Tomas gives up even his erotic adventures when he realizes that these, too, spring from a kind of internal imperative. What he does not give up is his love for Tereza. When he follows Tereza from Switzerland back to Prague, he first thinks that he is obeying the *Es muss sein!* of his life. However, he later acknowledges that there was no necessity in his love for her and that things could have turned out differently. Tereza's arrival at "the riverbank of his bed" (6) was actually the result of a chain of coincidences (six in number, he counts). In a later scene, Tomas wakes up from a dream about a girl who seems familiar to him, but whom he has actually never met. The girl in the dream is obviously the object of his deepest desires, produced by his own imagination, another romantic motif in Kundera. Tomas performs a thought experiment. The girl in the dream might be the *Es muss sein!* of his life or his missing half as described in Plato's *Symposium*. What would he do if he met Tereza while living with the girl?: "And he knows that time and again he will abandon the house of his happiness, time and again abandon his paradise and the woman from his dream and betray the '*Es muss sein!*' of his love to go off with Tereza, the woman born of six laughable fortuities" (233). The relationship between freedom and the internal imperative appears even more complex than before. Love is not rooted in the internal imperative, or at least it does not need to be rooted there, because love is based on freedom. The object of love is not the missing half of the self and it is not the answer to any need which the beloved can satisfy. Despite its absolute freedom and "nonnecessity," by giving life the required weight love can make it bearable to someone who otherwise would be condemned to the lightness of existence.

Hedonism as a mode of authentic sense giving

The three possible sources of authentic sense giving for an individual striving for autonomy—sensual pleasure, love, and beauty—which Kundera explores are, of course, nothing new in European culture. The first theoretical justification of hedonism is found in the writings of the Greek Epicurean school. Love between a man and a woman has been considered one of the most important principles legitimating the identity and existence of the modern individual since the age of Romanticism (see, e.g., Luhmann, *Love as Passion*; Schmidt). Aestheticism in turn was one of the main threads in the "philosophy of life" of the turn of the twentieth century, in a situation where God was dead and morality lacked any absolute foundation.

Kundera calls himself a disappointed hedonist (see du Plessix Gray 47) or a hedonist "trapped in a world politicized in the extreme" ("An Introduction" 471). He pays tribute to hedonism in the characters of the forty-year-old man in *Life Is Elsewhere* and Bertlef in *Farewell Waltz*, both of whom are depicted as masters of the art of living. In *Slowness*, hedonism is the main theme; "slowness" here refers to the ability to enhance pleasure by prolonging the state of erotic arousal. Kundera retells the eighteenth-century story of a young chevalier's night with a lady who introduces him to the art of creating erotic tension and prolonging pleasure. After recounting the story, he poses a series of questions: "Is it possible to live in pleasure and for pleasure and be happy? Can the ideal of hedonism be realized? Does that hope exist? Or at least some feeble gleam of that hope?" (121). The anticlimactic repetition of the question in ever weaker form suggests that Kundera doubts the possibility of living happily in pleasure. From the first pages of *Slowness* he depicts hedonism as conflicting with the obsession with speed typical of our contemporary world, which wants only orgasms but not the whole range of eroticism (4). He draws a parallel with the contemporary habit of recounting history in a highly abbreviated version, noting that this is like performing Beethoven's complete works by playing only the first few bars of each piece (79). Kundera suspects that with this loss of slowness our ability to be happy or to enjoy life is vanishing as well (131–32).

While in Kundera's earlier novels hedonism was presented as a possible, desirable, and admirable attitude toward life—even if, for instance, Bertlef's hedonism is not depicted without irony—his later works seem to suggest that hedonism is no longer a feasible alternative in our contemporary world. Notwithstanding this negative conclusion, Kundera's hedonism deserves to be examined more closely, since erotic hedonism is engaged in not only by the exemplary hedonists, but also by numerous other characters in his novels, in fact, by almost every adult who is not a sentimentalist. Almost all of his "mature" male characters and a great number of his female figures are open to new erotic experiences. Many of them, like Martin and Dr. Havel in *Laughable Loves*, as well as Tomas, are true collectors of such experiences.

Among the rest, too, almost everyone sets great value on erotic experiences and those who resist their lure usually later look back upon this as a loss, like Kamila in *Farewell Waltz*, Chantal in *Identity*, and Franz in *The Unbearable Lightness of Being* (the latter two only transiently). It is worth noting that in Kundera's view, the collecting of erotic experiences is not characteristic of youth; on the contrary, youth is a time when experience in eroticism is typically sparse or lacking. Examples of this are Jaromil in *Life Is Elsewhere* and the young man in *Laughable Loves*, who asks the opinion of the womanizing Dr. Havel about his girlfriend, or in fact any young man in the novels. For Kundera, the collecting of erotic experiences belongs to mature age and has nothing to do with the reinforcement of an individual's weak ego in the eyes of either others or himself or herself. In the life of a mature person erotic affairs are not to be displayed in public nor are they a means of discovering identity. Where, then, does the significance of erotic adventures lie? The cases of Marketa, Tamina, and Jan in *The Book of Laughter and Forgetting* elucidate—each from a different point of view—a problematic aspect of pure sensuality. Their experiences show that under certain circumstances pure sensuality may bring a sense of relief, yet the same feeling may soon turn into a sense of emptiness and meaninglessness. How, then, can erotic pleasure be desirable, if instead of meaningfulness it creates emptiness? The question is complicated, because what is at stake for Kundera in the sexual act need not be sensual pleasure alone. What is at stake here is the relationship between body and soul.

Kundera seems to adopt the Cartesian dualism of soul and body insofar as human beings are for him autonomously perceiving, evaluating, and acting subjects, but ones that also have a material object attached or belonging to them, namely, the body, a kind of machine. The idea of the body as a digestive and reproductive mechanism appears in Kundera's works in several contexts. On a number of occasions, for example, he remarks that the mouth, kissed in moments of erotic arousal with pleasure, is actually the beginning of the digestive tract. In *Farewell Waltz,* Klima notices that "only now, having lost its charm, was the mouth suddenly what it was, a *real* mouth, an industrious orifice thought which the young woman had already taken in cubic meters of dumplings, potatoes, and soups" (60). In *Immortality*, Agnes looks upon her body as "a dirty machine which she was forced to maintain" (178), and in *The Unbearable Lightness of Being,* Tomas thinks that the body functions as a machine of sexual arousal (231). The functions of the body, however, cannot be entirely separated from those of the soul—Kundera uses this old-fashioned word (see Němcová Banerjee, *Terminal* 39)—but are interconnected in ways that often cause problems. For instance, in "The Hitchhiking Game" in *Laughable Loves*, the girl is ashamed of her bodily functions. In *Farewell Waltz,* Olga denies that her face and body are manifestations of her true, inner self, and in *The Unbearable Lightness of Being,* Tereza feels threatened by Tomas's erotic affairs, although he believes that they concern only the body. Kundera's view of "the irreconcilable duality of body and soul" as a "fundamental human experience" (*The Unbearable Lightness* 37) is similar to Tereza's. Yet rather than speaking of duality, one could claim that the problem arises precisely from the fact that body and soul cannot be kept separate from one another. For example, when Tereza turns up at Tomas's door to offer him her life, her stomach growls, making her feel embarrassed. At a decisive moment in her life, when she would like to be pure soul, her body betrays her.

Things might be much simpler if the dualism of body and soul were absolute, that is, if the body were merely a machine in an incidental relationship with the soul dwelling in it. This is a recurrent thought in Kundera's works, fostered in particular by his intelligent women characters such as Tereza, Olga, and Agnes. As individuals we appear to others in our corporeal form, making our identity greatly dependent on our body. As a young girl Tereza would stare at the mirror, alarmed to discover her mother's features in her own face. She was waiting impatiently for the moment when her features would at last reveal her individuality and "her soul would rise to the surface of her body" (39). In order to be revenged for her own disappointment with life, however, Tereza's mother deliberately deprived her daughter of her individuality by refusing to endow her body with any other value than that of any female body, that of a machine subject to the law of decay. Tereza feels that the sentence once passed by her mother is actually carried out by Tomas, who, by making love to countless women, deprives her body of any specific value deriving from her unique individuality.

Tereza feels weak. She cannot hold on to her identity once her beloved deprives her of it. A similar weakness is again found at the macro level of politics and history. A nation incapable of resisting its stronger antagonist, like Czechoslovakia after the first days of the Soviet occupation in August 1968, reveals the same kind of weakness. For Kundera, and for his Tereza, the symbol of the Czechs' weakness is president Dubček, who, having been kidnapped, arrested, and threatened by the Soviets while giving a radio speech, needs to take long pauses to catch his breath. Under pressure exerted upon them by the stronger, the weaker give up their will and their own self. In addition to "body," "soul," and "weakness," Tereza's fourth key word is "vertigo," the desire to surrender to her own weakness, to give up her "fate and soul," and as a mere body mingle with other bodies (56). Tereza's vertigo is a metaphorical concept expressing a temptation to give in that is like Tamina's longing for the forgetting of forgetting (again, we find a similar metaphor in Nietzsche's *Zarathustra*: "It is not the height, it is the abyss that is terrible! The abyss where the glance plunges *downward* and the hand grasps *upward*. There the heart grows giddy through its twofold will" [164]).

Theresa's jealousy turns her love for Tomas into suffering and Tomas's love to her into "com-passion," a suffering with her. For Kundera, the root of the problem lies in Tereza's attitude and not, as one might imagine, in Tomas's, who separates love from sexual arousal. Tomas thinks that while love concerns the soul, lovemaking concerns the body only, that is, the arousal of the body does not mean that the soul is affected. Tomas reasons that it would be preferable if the male body were aroused sexually by, say, a swallow's flight, rather than by the female body. If this were the case, even Tereza could understand that physical arousal and sexual pleasure represent no threat to their mutual love (231). The author-narrator recounts Tomas's thought experiment without irony, indicating that he concurs with Tomas's dualistic thinking. He shows sympathy toward Tereza as well, but he indicates that her difficulties derive from her childhood experiences and her traumatic relationship with her mother. In Tomas's case, no psychological explanations are deemed necessary.

Kundera's manner of depicting sexual encounters or encounters between human beings in general does not, however, support such a dualistic view, one in which the body, as a realm of its own, is completely separate from the soul. Nearly always physical appearance influences—profoundly and often decisively—one person's attitude toward another. In particular, Kundera's depiction of women betrays a strong, unthinking macho and patriarchal attitude (see O'Brien, *Milan Kundera*). Kundera himself gives the word "macho" a nonstandard definition in "Sixty-three Words": a macho man is a sentimentalist who "adores femaleness and wants to dominate what he adores" (*The Art* 139). Here, however, I prefer to use the phrase "macho attitude" to refer to men's claim that women's most important function is to be attractive and that all women enjoy being chased by men. Women in Kundera's works are observed and appraised with respect to their sexual attractiveness, which depends on the beauty of their faces and bodies. All of his "heroines," such as Tamina, Tereza, Sabina, and Agnes are (relatively) young and attractive, which means that they are tall and slim, have long legs, beautiful breasts, and regular features. An ugly, fat, or old woman is automatically excluded from the circle of the sexually attractive, and Kundera does not show any interest in such. Elderly female bodies, depicted as repulsive or at least as pitiable and ridiculous, serve merely as a kind of *memento mori* by demonstrating the destiny of everything that is mortal, including young and interesting female bodies (see the pool scene in *Farewell Waltz* 145–49). But even the wearing of glasses diminishes the attractiveness of a woman and makes her, as an object of erotic desire, somewhat ridiculous. For example, when Franz with Sabina's flight has lost his "unearthly" love, he becomes involved with a bespectacled female student, who represents "earthly" love for him and whom Franz arch-romantically imagines to have been sent for his comfort by his departed, heavenly love (*The Unbearable Lightness* 122; see also Novalis 321, 324–25). The girl's wearing glasses is mentioned several times to underline the decline in the standard of Franz's objects of love. Even having legs slightly too short casts a shadow of ridiculousness on an otherwise attractive woman, such as Mama in *Life Is Elsewhere* or Laura in *Immortality*. Moreover, for a woman, ugliness is absolutely disastrous: Zdena's fate is written in her big-nosed face. For a man, being fat or bald is a precarious but not fatal feature as regards his sexual appeal and not even advanced age is an insurmountable obstacle, as the example of Bertlef shows. Wearing glasses and having a big nose does not hamper Dr. Skreta's erotic life or his manliness in the least. Although Kundera and several of his women characters such as Olga, Tereza, and Agnes claim that the individual should not be identified by his or her body—the machine to which he or she is incidentally but inseparably bound—in fact his fictional characters, the female ones in particular, are constantly being evaluated and classified on the basis of their external, physical characteristics. Being human is corporeal indeed, because having a beautiful body and face is what makes one attractive to the opposite sex and being attractive determines in Kundera's world whether a person can be taken seriously at all. Although it may be the case that our uniqueness is to be sought in our soul alone, our body can definitely condemn us to be among those who cannot by any means be interesting.

Kundera describes Tomas as omnivorous in his erotic adventures, one who as a collector of women is fascinated by the most diverse looking women, although not by "monsters" à la Fellini (195), probably meaning that women who expressly look abnormal do not come into question. However, the main goal of Tomas's pursuit of women is not physical pleasure. We can even ask why he needs to seduce more and more women if he desires only the sensual pleasure produced by identically repeated bodily movements. Tomas's answer is that what he is interested in is the individuality of a woman as revealed in the part that is different in the sexual act with her: "He was not obsessed with women; he was obsessed with what in each of them is unimaginable, obsessed, in other words, with the one-millionth part that makes a woman dissimilar to others of her sex" (193). In his opinion, "the individual 'I' is what differs from the common stock, that is, what cannot be guessed at or calculated, what must be unveiled, uncovered, conquered" (193). At this point the body does not appear as an impersonal machine standing in opposition to the individual soul. Tomas is searching for tiny differences in the woman's physical being or her bodily movements and identifies her individuality with these. The author-narrator completes Tomas's reasoning by remarking that differences exist in other areas as well, yet the dissimilarities revealed in sexuality are especially precious because they are not publicly displayed but access to them must be won in conquest (194). They are especially precious also because in sex one cannot pretend being something other that one really is. For example, as Ludvik in *The Joke* remarks, Helena is "real and exact" only in the erotic "convulsion" (195), whereas in talking about her culinary taste she cannot be taken seriously because she is then trying to exhibit herself through consciously chosen attributes (180).

Tomas's conception of a human being's (or, rather, a woman's) individuality is peculiar indeed, being atomistic, behavioristic, and scientistic. In the modern conception of the personality, individuality is a whole revealed in the totality of our actions and experiences and manifests some aspects of itself in such actions and experiences. In contrast, for Kundera a human being, just like any object of nature, is divisible into basic components which are similar to those of other representatives of the species. "Individuality" is reduced to the tiny differences that distinguish any real object from another. Searching in this manner for dissimilarities in women through his erotic affairs, Tomas registers women's features on the basis of external observations, just as a natural scientist observes an object belonging to a category. This is why in a sense he is certainly right in claiming that in such erotic encounters, the "souls" do not meet; for him the meeting takes place wholly externally.

Tomas has developed a special method for memorizing the observations he has collected. This is demonstrated in his encounter with a woman with long legs and arms, who in his opinion resembles a giraffe and a stork: "He went off in the best of moods, trying to fix her essence in his memory, to reduce that memory to a chemical formula capable of defining her uniqueness (her millionth part dissimilarity). The result was a formula consisting of three givens: (1) clumsiness with ardour, (2) the frightened face of one who has lost her equilibrium and is falling, and (3) legs raised in the air like the arms of a soldier surrendering to a pointed gun. Going over them, he felt the joy of having acquired yet another piece of the world, of having taken his imaginary scalpel and snipped yet another strip off the infinite canvas of the universe" (200). Slitting the tissue open with a scalpel, reducing the encounter to a "chemical formula," conquering a new piece of the world; all this indicates that during love making Tomas observes his partner as a scientist, rather than approaching her with all of his person and seeing her as a whole person. In Kundera's fictional world, however, Tomas's attitude does not cause problems, because apparently his casual partners do not expect sex to involve an encounter between two individual personalities either. Yet it is curious that Kundera presents Tomas's bizarre "memory book" without ridicule or irony, but on the contrary seems to accept his attitude. He describes Tomas as an "epic" womanizer whose fascination with the variety of femaleness stands in sharp contrast to the "lyrical" womanizer's search for an ideal woman—ultimately his own mother—in all women. Thus there is a parallel between Tomas's pursuit of women and the novelist's conquest of the world. In Kundera's vocabulary, "epic" denotes an openness toward the objective plurality of the world. The epic womanizer "projects no subjective ideal on women, and since everything interests him, nothing can disappoint him" (195). In contrast to Jan, who after abundant experience is frightened by the monotonous repetition of the same in lovemaking, for the "epic womanizer" Tomas, this repetition is not "pure repetition" but has significant variations. The value of these minuscule differences is evinced in his efforts to preserve them in his memory.

In Kundera's "epic womanizer" we can see an answer to Nietzsche's search for a "Don Juan of knowledge" (see also Boisen, *Une fois* 108–10). Nietzsche describes this character, "who has not yet been discovered by any philosopher or poet," as follows: "He does not love the things he knows, but has spirit and appetite for and enjoyment of the chase and intrigues of knowledge" (*Daybreak* 161). Similarly, Tomas's pursuit of knowledge of women in sexual situations takes place outside of love; his attitude can therefore easily be perceived as cold, even though the author explicitly rejects this accusation. What makes Tomas a carnivalistic incarnation of Nietzsche's wish to find a "Don Juan of knowledge" is of course the fact that Tomas is such a being in an even more literal sense than Nietzsche intended, since the knowledge of an "epic womanizer" concerns the object of interest of the Don Juan proper.

Thus, Tomas's pursuit of women does not aim at physical pleasure alone, nor does he seek an encounter of souls, nor are sexual experiences for him a means of discovering himself or his own sexuality. The object of investigation is solely the behavior of his partners. It is worth noting that Kundera does not consider sexual pleasure as such to be worthy of study. Similar to Foucault in his *History of Sexuality*, Kundera takes sexual pleasure as something self-evident and constant, with no history (note that despite its title, the topics in *History of Sexuality* are the sources of sexual pleasure and the mechanisms used to control it in European history, not how sexual pleasure in itself has changed in the course of history; on the contrary, sexual pleasure appears as something supra- or ahistorical). Positing the realm of the purely sensual-corporeal, as well as the dualism of body and soul as something beyond history, Kundera rejects the tradition of historicizing human phenomena which reaches as far back as to Herder and Goethe. According to Herder, a human being is "present" in his or her entirety in all his or her actions. Not even human sensuality can be identified with that of animals, because sensuality and the functioning of the senses are different in a thinking and speaking being (see Herder, *Über den Ursprung* 99–100). Since human beings are formed as part of the culture they belong to, sensuality, too, is formed culturally. The young Marx picked up on this line of thought when he wrote that even the way we sense is formed historically: "It is obvious that the *human* eye gratifies itself in a way different from the crude, non-human eye; the human *ear* different from the crude ear, etc. . . . For not only the five senses but also the so-called mental senses—the practical senses (will, love, etc.),—in a word, *human* sense—the humanness of the senses—comes to be by virtue of its object, by virtue of *humanized* nature. The *forming* of the five senses is a labour of the entire history of the world down to the present" (107–08). Foucault and Kundera do not share this view; according to them, historical change affects only the human being's relationship toward erotic pleasure—its sources and its place in life—and the practices belonging to it, not pleasure itself. Yet there is an important difference between the basic tenets in Kundera's exploration of human sexuality and that of Foucault, in that for Kundera the knowledge of sexuality has no connection whatsoever with questions of power and control. According to Foucault, the goal of discourses on sexuality, from the ancient philosophers through the Enlightenment thinkers to their present followers has been to bring this realm of life under rational control. Tomas's thirst for knowledge is devoid of any practical goals; indeed, he is fascinated by the cognitive conquest of the world of sexuality for the sake of knowledge alone.

In Kundera's macho thinking, on the other hand, the erotic situation as such includes an aspect of power, because in its essence it is a matter of conquest: the man wants to conquer and the woman to be conquered. Eroticism is a struggle in which the one subjugates the other. From one point of view, Franz loses Sabina because he does not want to subjugate her: "Not that he lacks sensuality; he simply lacks the strength to give orders. There are things that can be accomplished only by violence. Physical love is unthinkable without violence" (108). Violence, of course, does not refer here to the concrete exertion of physical power, but to the idea that exerting power is an inherent part of the act of conquest. What Kundera adds to the traditional motifs of the erotic conquest is the pursuit of knowledge of individual dissimilarities in the sexual act.

Bertlef and the man in his forties were proclamations and advertisements of the hedonistic attitude toward life. Nevertheless, if we consider Tomas as representing Kundera's study of the possibility of hedonism as an attitude toward life, we have to conclude that hedonism as a mere striving for sensual or sexual pleasure does not after all appear as a real possibility of an authentic life. This is not due merely to the irreconcilability between hedonism and our contemporary world, as elaborated in *Slowness*. It is important to note that Bertlef and the forty-year-old man are not pure embodiments of the hedonistic attitude either. They do not aspire to sensual pleasure alone, but also to the beauty offered by the moment. What is more, they treat their partners with empathy and altruism, bestowing upon them a beautiful moment. Tomas's hedonism is even less pure, in that for him sensual pleasure is of secondary value compared to the goal of the exploration of reality. Moreover, when necessary, he is capable of giving up his erotic liaisons; what he cannot give up, without losing the meaningfulness of life, lies elsewhere.

Authentic sense giving through love

At the same time that human individuality was discovered in the late eighteenth century as a unique way of encountering the world and as an inalienable value, romantic love, in which the individual's world opens up to another individual and is thereby reinforced in its uniqueness, was also discovered, or rather invented. As Siegfried J. Schmidt suggests, until the eighteenth century erotic love was tied in European culture to the idea of the beloved person's perfection. The object of one's affections had to be beautiful, wealthy, and virtuous. At the end of the eighteenth century, love becomes self-contained, which is to say that it is no longer based on the "objectively" laudable characteristics of the beloved, but is a relationship between two individuals, which need not and indeed cannot be explained. Love, which mutually corroborates the individuality of both partners and constitutes the basis of marriage and family life, is itself not based on anything (see Schmidt 121–27; Luhmann, *Love as Passion*). The idea that love lacks a foundation is articulated by Ruzena in *Farewell Waltz*, when suddenly, in the night spent with Bertlef, she encounters love: "The word [love] entered the room like a miracle. It was totally inexplicable, but to Ruzena it seemed all the more real, for the most basic things in this world exist without explanation and without motive, drawing from within themselves their reason for being" (200). That Kundera actually thinks of love as something "absolute," in the sense that no rational ground can be required for one person's love of another, is evident from several of his characters, from Tamina through Tomas and Tereza to Chantal and Jean-Marc. In this sense, Kundera's conception of love derives from the era of Romanticism. The significance of love is expressed most emphatically in *Immortality*: "Life's value is conditional and justified only by the fact that it enables you to live your love. The one you love means more to you than God's creation, more than life itself" (286). What this means and how such love differs from sentimental love is the subject of constant search in Kundera's novels, but especially in *The Unbearable Lightness of Being*.

For the sentimental lover, the feeling of love is more important than its object; an example of this is Jaromil in *Life Is Elsewhere*. In Lucie's love in *The Joke,* the possibility of a meaningful life outside of History presents itself for Ludvik, but his youthful narcissism prevents him from rewarding this love. In *The Book of Laughter and Forgetting,* Tamina's love of her husband is a real, nonsentimental love. Love is defined here through Tamina's husband as constantly asking questions. The lover wants to grasp the infinity of the beloved by listening to her and continuously asking her about how she thinks and feels about various matters (223). Here, Kundera's concept corresponds to the modern view of love, according to which love means the partners' mutual willingness to learn to know each other's individuality and thereby to reinforce it (see, e.g., Luhmann, *Love as Passion*).

The Unbearable Lightness of Being is a love story more clearly than any other of Kundera's novels, with the reservation that here, too, Kundera's interest lies more in the exploration of love as an existential possibility than in telling a love story. The story of the love between Tomas and Tereza starts where a conventional love story ends, that is, with the lovers' decision that they will lead their lives together. It is the story of their mutual love in the everyday life of their marriage. For both, love is linked with their respective existential problems. For Tomas this is the question of the meaningfulness of events that occur only once and the roles of internal necessity and the incidental in his life; for Tereza it is the relationship between body and soul. Kundera has planned the thematic composition of the novel carefully. He says that when writing about love one has to be exceptionally mistrustful, because it is easy for the author to be misled by emotions (see Kramer). To avoid this, an author should not write a love story without embedding into it some criticism of sentimentality. For this reason, Kundera originally intended to incorporate into the novel a storyline about Goethe and Bettina Brentano, which eventually came to be part of *Immortality* (see Kramer). Bettina's love for Goethe is here depicted as a sentimental love for the emotion of love and she herself appears as a personification of the dishonest attitudes of Romanticism. In *Immortality*, however, this storyline is not contrasted contrapuntally with a story of "authentic" love, since Agnes admits that she has never experienced it. In *The Unbearable Lightness of Being*, the Brentano story of false, sentimental love would have created a sharp contrast to the main story of authentic love. Probably to avoid too extreme a contrast leading to an effect of didacticism, Kundera gave up his original plan and opted for a far less sharp contrast by choosing the story of Sabina and Franz for a contrapuntal line. Franz is far from the egocentric narcissism of a Bettina or a Jaromil, yet we can say that he lost Sabina because he was unable to abandon all of his sentimental conceptions. Franz is characterized by the author as a "dreamer" (263) who is seeking a Dionysian intoxication in music (88, 123) and who in lovemaking closes his eyes so that he can experience dissolving in the infinity of darkness (91). Vexed by the "unreality" of his academic life, he longs to merge with people marching for a better future and therefore loves to take part in demonstrations (95–96, 251) and seeks the Platonic idea of womanhood in every woman (86).

Although neither Tomas nor Tereza sentimentalizes love, the endeavor to reconcile love with individuality and meaningfulness creates problems for both of them. They realize that love does not necessarily mean being happy; on the contrary, it may mean suffering as well. Tereza feels miserable because in her eyes Tomas's erotic adventures deprive her of her individuality. In spite of their mutual love, she thinks, they have created hell for each other (71). Tomas asks himself why he considers his love for Tereza to be so weighty. He thinks that whereas sexuality is an inescapable mechanism, love "belongs to us alone and enables us to flee the Creator. Love is our freedom. Love lies beyond *Es muss sein!*" (231). But if love has no connection with our innermost needs and desires, if it arises incidentally like Tomas's love for Tereza, where does its weight come from? Tomas values the freedom offered by love, yet he feels disturbed by the incidentalness of their love. Again and again he recalls the six coincidences which were needed for their love to come into existence, such as the sciatica of the chief physician which forced him to send Tomas on his behalf to the town where he first met Tereza. How can something so weighty ensue from something so incidental?

The most essential element in Tomas's love for Tereza is his compassion for her suffering of jealousy. His love does not entail a merging with the beloved. She remains an independent person, but at the same time she becomes the object of his compassion. He imagines Tereza as a child whom someone has set in a bulrush basket and sent downstream, to land at the riverbank of his bed (6). The metaphor suggests that Tomas looks upon Tereza as someone sent to him without his asking, to be loved by him. It is not a question of what he gets from her, but only of what he can give to her—his love, his compassion. This is Kundera's second attempt to define what nonsentimental love might be. Unlike Tamina's husband, Tomas does not question Tereza, constantly trying to grasp the infinity of her unique personality. Instead, he is sensitive toward her existential problem and her suffering, although he thinks she is wrong when she fears that his erotic affairs are threatening their love. Love as compassion does not ask whether the beloved is right or wrong.

For Kundera, compassion and asking questions are not just the essence of love, but are also essential ingredients of both the parent-child relationship and friendship. In fact, a child's love for his or her parents, friendship, and true, nonideological comradeship are in Kundera's view similar to the love between man and woman. In *The Book of Laughter and Forgetting*, Kundera's alter ego regrets not having searched the depths of his father's soul by asking questions. Yet Kundera seems to believe that this kind of loving relationship with a parent is possible only with the father, while the mother-child relationship is always problematic or even traumatizing. In *Farewell Waltz*, Jakub considers the latter: "There is no stronger bond than the one that shackles mother to child. This bond cripples the child's soul forever and prepares for the mother, when her son has grown up, the most cruel of all the griefs of love" (116).

In a sense, Kundera ascribes to friendship an even greater value than to love. In Dr. Havel's words in *Laughable Loves*, this is the only realm of life which is not impaired by "the idiocy of eroticism" (152). Thus, in Kundera's work, friendship between men occasionally surpasses any other kind of human relationship. This is exemplified in the friendship between Dr. Skreta and Jakub, which elevates them above all other mortals. Friendship is less problematic than love, because it is free of the difficulties created by the antagonism between body and soul. Friendship and comradeship involve absolute and mutual loyalty. The relationship between Jan and Passer in the last part of *The Book of Laughter and Forgetting* is such a friendship, and Kundera considers this friendship to be an important balancing factor in the composition of the novel (Finkielkraut 47). As I understand it, Kundera means that the motif of friendship represents an optimistic and reassuring counterpoint in the somber closing chapter, which deals with eroticism losing significance and the death of erotic culture. Similarly, in *Farewell Waltz,* Jakub leaves his country believing that Skreta has betrayed their friendship, pretending that the harmless pill he had given him was lethal. The reader soon learns that this was actually not the case and we see that Skreta remains loyal to his friend even when Ruzena dies. When asked by Olga, he denies ever having given Jakub any poison (274). This loyal friendship lightens the gloomy story of the murderer and his victim.

According to Kundera, unconditional loyalty toward a friend is "a virtue, perhaps the only virtue, perhaps the only one left" ("Umbrella" 45). This loyalty is praised in Eva, the exemplary friend of the young couple in *The Book of Laughter and Forgetting* and in Tomas, the true comrade of his mistresses. Eva's case shows that for Kundera women, too, are capable of friendship, in contrast to Nietzsche's view (see *Thus Spoke Zarathustra* 83–84). Another example of erotic friendship or comradeship is seen in Tomas's encounter with an anonymous girl with whom he had once spent a pleasant moment of lovemaking, but whom he has forgotten because he did not love her: "By the word 'non-love' I do not wish to imply that he took a cynical attitude to the young woman, that, as present-day parlance has it, he looked upon her as a sex object; on the contrary, he was quite fond of her, valued her character and intelligence, and was willing to come to her aid if ever she needed him" (202). As we can see, Kundera believes in the possibility of true friendship or comradeship, although he does not consider a friendship or comradeship based on shared ideology trustworthy; the latter could be labeled as sentimental friendship or comradeship. True comradeship or friendship, just like a child's love for a parent (the father), can light up moments of life, as exemplified by the middle-aged man's altruism toward the redhead in *Life Is Elsewhere*. Yet friendship alone is not enough to give life its necessary weight and meaningfulness; that remains the task of love between a man and a woman.

However incidental the external conditions of the emergence of love may be, it requires active, creative participation by the individuals involved. In *The Unbearable Lightness of Being*, Tereza and Tomas first meet in the bar of the hotel where Tereza works as a waitress. When she catches sight of the handsome stranger, the radio is playing Beethoven's string quartet, which for her represents a better and more beautiful world, and in the book that the guest is reading she recognizes a sign of his membership in the secret guild of those who know that world. The number of

Tomas's room is six, which is also the street address of her home and the hour when her shift will end, and upon leaving work she discovers the stranger sitting on her favorite park bench where she often spends her spare time reading a book. These coincidences appear to her as signs bearing a secret message for her. Having added up these secret messages, she finds the courage to entrust her whole life to Tomas: "It may well be those few fortuities (quite modest, by the way, even drab, just what one would expect from so lacklustre a town) which set her love in motion and provided her with a source of energy she had not yet exhausted at the end of her days" (48). According to Kundera, it is the human being's sense of beauty that makes us interpret the coincidental as meaningful and use it as a motif in the composition of our lives. Tomas's love for Tereza is kindled when his creative imagination produces the metaphor already referred to: "She was a child whom he had taken from a bulrush basket that had been daubed with pitch and sent to the riverbank of his bed" (6). The author-narrator comments on this that "a single metaphor can give birth to love" (10); in other words, the birth of love is the point where a person "enters her first word in our poetic memory" (203). Kundera does not explain this, but I think that his argument is obvious: metaphors emerge from our creative imagination and are a part of our individual sense-giving activity. Our imagination finds in a metaphor an expression for something exceptional that we have experienced but that cannot—just because it is exceptional, and exceptionally significant—be expressed in normal, everyday language. Thus the emergence of metaphors is a sign of being deeply and personally involved in a matter.

It is Kundera's conviction that an author's imagination is to a great extent metaphorical. As already noted, in the art of the novel, for instance, in Kafka or Broch, metaphors are "phenomenological" or existential, expressing an otherwise ineffable existential situation (*Testaments* 104–05). In *The Unbearable Lightness of Being*, the metaphorical imagination is active in the lives of the characters as well. This is not a question of expressing indirectly, through a simile, something that could just as well be expressed directly, in conceptual language, but of using a metaphor to convey a point as accurately as possible. Kundera contrasts metaphors emerging from the creative imagination of an individual with commonly used symbols. A sentimental person lets familiar symbols—preferably symbols referring to something "great"—determine the meaning of an experience instead of relying upon his or her own creativity. The power of symbols represents for Kundera the power of conventions, since symbols lead our emotions, attitudes, and thoughts to conform to conventional notions. In contrast, the individual striving for autonomy articulates experiences by relying upon his or her own capacity to use analytical concepts and create metaphors. Indeed, one definition of the difference between sentimental persons and those who strive for autonomy and authenticity is precisely the difference between the followers of conventional symbols and creators of metaphors of their own (this interpretation is the opposite of Bertrand Very's, according to whom Kundera sees individual metaphors as unreliable because of their subjectivity [see Very 82]). In *The Art of the Novel,* Kundera defines maturity as "the ability to resist symbols" and he comments on this laconically: "But mankind grows younger all the time" (63). In an interview with Alain Finkielkraut, he commented that it was his political experiences that opened his eyes to the enormous extent to which European humanity of the twentieth century can be led by symbols (Finkielkraut 37). As a novelist, Kundera endeavors to reduce the power of symbols (Donahue 67; Finkielkraut 37).

An example of the individual creation of metaphors is Sabina's bowler hat. The hat means several different things for her. It reminds her of her grandfather and her father and in exile it generally evokes her past, while in an erotic scene between Tomas and the half-naked Sabina with the bowler hat on her head it takes on a connotation of violence against her dignity as a woman which they find erotically arousing. The hat "was a motif in the musical composition that was Sabina's life," which, with each time it returned, gave rise to a new meaning: it was a "semantic river," constantly in change (84). Yet when Sabina wants to find out what new meanings the hat will take on in an erotic scene with Franz, the result is null. When Franz sees the hat on the head of his half-naked mistress, he cannot comprehend its meaning at all. It was "as if someone had spoken to him in a language he did not know. It was neither obscene nor sentimental, merely an incomprehensible gesture. What made him feel uncomfortable was its very lack of meaning" (84). This signifies Franz's incapability of individual sensemaking through creating metaphors.

The bowler hat scene serves as an introduction to the following three chapters, dealing with the different ways in which Sabina and Franz understand important words. For example, Franz understands the word "woman" sentimentally, through the idealized image of his own mother. Although the differences in their understanding are represented as being rooted in their different backgrounds, it is also obvious that Franz understands words more conventionally than Sabina, who often ascribes to them meanings derived from her own individual experience. This accords with the general image of the two characters: she is more an autonomous person, he more a sentimental one. Resorting to conventional symbols enhances identification with others, whereas personal metaphors serve the construction of an individual world of meanings, thus impeding identification with others. This corresponds to the difference between Franz and Sabina. While he desires to belong to a community, she longs for privacy (95–96, 109–10).

No one, not even Sabina, can wholly escape the power of conventional symbols. For Sabina, the image of an idyllic home, with a father and mother, is such a symbol, a home she does not have but sometimes longs for, although she is aware of the kitsch-like character of the image. Similarly, Tereza's mental image of country life stems from children's picture books. An important sentimental symbol for Franz, who is more prone to be led by such symbols than Sabina or Tereza, is the "Grand March." "Grand March" refers to concrete demonstrations, but also to the idea of the historical progress of European peoples toward "brotherhood, equality, justice, happiness," an idea which, according to Kundera, is at the heart of leftist political kitsch (250). Nevertheless, toward the end of the novel Franz seems to break the enchantment of this symbol. He participates in an international rally in Thailand at the Cambodian border, organized by doctors and intellectuals, pleading for permission for medical personnel to enter the country ravaged by war, terror, and occupation and help those in need of medical care. The power exercised by symbols on the minds of individuals is represented pointedly in the scene where, during the march, one of the journalists steps on a roadside mine. The mine explodes, tearing the man's body into thousands of pieces. The demonstrators stand still, dumbfounded by the ghastly sight, until they notice that the flag they are carrying is spattered with blood. A bloody flag is a traditional and powerful symbol and it causes the demonstrators to resume their marching in solemn procession. What this incident shows is that in this action symbols are given more weight than reality. No one is saved by the protest, which remains without any response from the Cambodian side; instead, a life is lost uselessly. Yet the experience opens Franz's eyes; he will no longer prefer symbols over reality. He now decides that once he has returned from this journey—which he has actually undertaken in commemoration of his "unearthly" love Sabina—he will marry his "earthly" love, the bespectacled student. Unfortunately, he does not have a chance to realize his plan because he dies in the hospital from the injuries he received in a street assault. We will never know if Franz would indeed have been capable of abandoning the quest, characteristic of sentimental individuals, for the eternal feminine, choosing instead the love of an actual woman and if by her side he would have learned to create his own individual metaphors.

Authentic sense giving through beauty

In Kundera's novels, complete approval of a present moment is most commonly expressed by saying that a moment is "beautiful." The encounter between the man in his forties and the redhead, for example, is beautiful, and when an erotic scene is experienced as inherently valuable and perfect—including many of Bertlef's, Tomas's, or Sabina's erotic adventures—it is seen as beautiful. Moreover, an erotic fantasy or even an obscene word can be beautiful and calling a girl beautiful means assigning erotic attractiveness to her (e.g., *Immortality* 310, 308, 313–24). But beauty is also closely connected to love. Our sense of beauty plays an important role in the emergence and preservation of love, because it is precisely our sense of beauty that makes us transform particular incidents into important motifs in the composition of our life (like Beethoven's music in Tereza's life). Thus, the relationship between on the one hand beauty, on the other eroticism and love is not accidental or external. On the contrary, it is precisely in the most intense moments of the experience that love and eroticism are perceived as beautiful. For Kundera "beautiful" seems to be the general, all-encompassing attribute conveying that a moment of experience is approvable unconditionally.

That unconditionally approvable moments are experienced as beautiful, meaning that they are recognized as belonging to the realm of the aesthetic and are not valued, for instance, for their moral goodness, I believe goes back to Kundera's conviction that, unlike moral value, aesthetic value is something that is given directly and unmediatedly. For example, Thomas thinks that the boundary between good and evil is "terribly fuzzy" (212). It is difficult or impossible to find reliable criteria for what is good and what is evil. Beauty, on the other hand, is something we cannot doubt when we encounter it. This immediate recognizability is the advantage of beauty compared with moral goodness, which always requires comparisons and the weighing of things against one another. The importance that Kundera assigns to beauty recalls Nietzsche's claim that life can only be justified aesthetically (*The Birth of Tragedy* 52). According to Nietzsche, aesthetic perception halts for a moment the flow of being, letting it appear in a shape that appeals to humans immediately. By showing existence as beauty, the aesthetic shape "justifies" it, or, as Kundera would say, lets existence appear approvable. Kundera would agree with Nietzsche that it is beauty which allows the "dissonance become man" to live and that it is "those countless illusions of the beauty of mere appearance that at every moment make life worth living at all and prompt the desire to live on in order to experience the next moment" (*The Birth of Tragedy* 143). Aestheticism, the appreciation of beauty above all else, was "discovered" in the Romantic era and at the end of the nineteenth century it became a fashionable attitude toward life. Aestheticism can be seen as a solution to the problem of modern existence in a situation where absolute value systems have lost their validity and meaning is to be sought in the immanence of a particular experience.

In Kundera's view, a woman or such things as a park, a building, or a city (in *The Unbearable Lightness of Being* Geneva and in some respects New York) can be beautiful, but they all attain full significance only in moments when one is overwhelmed by the sensation of beauty. The attribute is thus at its weightiest when it describes a scene or a moment, like the amorous night between Bertlef and Ruzena or the sexual episode between Tomas and the anonymous girl on the floor in a friend's apartment. What is essential in a moment of beauty is the spontaneity of the experience and its limited duration. Just like love, a sense of beauty cannot be forced: forcing the experience of beauty can only lead to false beauty, that is, kitsch. The same applies to endeavoring to see the whole world as beautiful or to make it so, as Jaromil does with his communist comrades, as well as aspiring to make one's own life appear beautiful, as Mirek does in *The Book of Laughter and Forgetting*. True beauty can be found only by being attentive to opportunities to experience beauty; in this respect, true beauty resembles true love. In *Farewell Waltz*, Jakub realizes that he has missed opportunities to experience beauty. Although beauty cannot be produced by the human will, it nevertheless presupposes the active and creative participation of the human mind. A particular situation activates one's sense of beauty, whereby the experience of the beautiful arises.

In *The Unbearable Lightness of Being*, beauty and its opposite, ugliness, appear in connection with the most varied things. Something beautiful can be the order to undress in an erotic situation or a feeling of submission (62, 63), as well as the evocation of a sexual episode from the past (202). The melancholy of being left alone may be beautiful (28–29), but so can love in retrospect when looked at as a temporally limited phase of life (28). Sabina is tempted by the beauty of betrayal (87; in the English version, however, "beau" in *L'Insoutenable légèreté de l'être* [136] has been translated as "magnificent"); a world betrayed can also be beautiful, such as a religious service or a church, which were shunned under communist rule (107). Again, beauty and ugliness are not limited to experiences that appertain to private life alone. History may produce common opportunities to experience beauty or ugliness as well (the experiencing subjects being of course individuals). After the Soviet invasion, Prague becomes ugly (227); New York looks ugly, although in some streets its ugliness, when incongruous things suddenly come together, blossoms into an incidental, last bloom of beauty (97–98); and Sabina is repelled by "the mask of beauty" behind which the communist rule hides its true face (242). Some aspects of human life are inherently either beautiful or ugly. Dreams are beautiful (55), the human body, when bereft of its capability to attract erotically or when it displays its functions openly without a sense of shame, is ugly (132), and the feeling of horror "lacks every hint of beauty" (296). The beauty of dreams derives from the fact that for Kundera—and before him for Freud—they are a product of free creative imagination (55). Beauty is also inherent in works of art. In *The Unbearable Lightness of Being*, beauty is mentioned in connection with paintings, buildings, music, and literature. The beauty of a work of art does not just mean that it offers the recipient an experience of the beautiful but that beauty is the mode in which the work of art is related to the world and is the way the truth of the world is revealed. In *The Art of the Novel*, as mentioned above, Kundera declares that whatever aspects of human existence the novel discovers, it discovers them as beauty (122).

Since pure sensual and sexual pleasure turns out to be of little or no significance, hedonism as a possible basis for a meaningful life is questionable, although attempts at a hedonistic attitude to life appear in Kundera's novels from *Laughable Loves* through *Life Is Elsewhere* and *Immortality* to *Slowness*. Nor can love be chosen as a basis for life, because it lies outside the realm of human decisions. The individual either encounters love or not (or one encounters love but fails to recognize it until it is too late, as in Ludvik's case). By desiring love or forcing oneself to feel it, one can only attain a sentimental pseudo-love. Thus we can conclude that of the three alternative sources of authentic sense giving explored by Kundera, aestheticism seems to be the only one which can be chosen as the basis of a meaningful life, in that one can be open to the opportunities offered by life to experience beauty.

In Kundera's thinking, kitsch is related to art—it is a parasite upon it—but it is a general attitude toward life as well. Kundera remarks that in the Central European context kitsch was considered to be the greatest aesthetic evil (*Encounter* 141, *The Curtain* 51). It is a "rosy veil thrown over reality" (*The Curtain* 51), a false beauty, a beauty outworn by being repeated thousands of times and incapable of revealing anything new about reality (Elgrably 6; on kitsch, see, e.g., Kliche; Kulka; Mathias, O'Sullivan, Vorstman; Pross; Schulte-Sasse). Expanded to comprise a general attitude toward existence, Kundera defines kitsch as a "*categorical agreement with being*" (*The Unbearable Lightness* 241) just like the angels' laughter in *The Book of*

Laughter and Forgetting. The difference between the two concepts seems to be that while the angels' laughter signifies the direct emotional expression of the approval of existence, kitsch is an attitude of reflection toward the joy of acceptance. Kitsch is the sentimental pleasure which arises from an awareness of being deeply moved, and the willingness to incite the same state of mind in others (*The Unbearable Lightness* 244). The (US) American senator, an acquaintance of Sabina's, sets an example of this attitude when at the sight of children running and laughing (the laughter of angels) on the grass he exclaims, "Now, that's what I call happiness" (243). Again, the attitude toward kitsch can be recognized both in individuals and in political systems. A totalitarian political system, demanding of its citizens the categorical approval of existence, is a realm of "*totalitarian kitsch*" (245). Totalitarian kitsch banishes every display of individualism, every doubt, all irony (245), the true opponent of totalitarian kitsch being someone who asks questions (247). Kitsch is a recurring theme in Kundera's works and it has even been described as his most important theme (Goetz-Stankiewicz; see also Le Grand, "Kitsch," *Kundera* 3; Wawrzyzka). In my view, however, kitsch is only one form of sentimental sense giving or one name for it, while the nonsentimental possibilities of sense giving are more important to Kundera (thus, the conclusion is likewise false that for Kundera all human creation of values is kitsch, and that when he attempts to escape from it he is condemned to antihumanism [see Thirouin, "La Tentation" 303]).

The practice of kitsch in the sphere of politics is depicted above all through Sabina's experiences. Back in her youth, studying at the Academy of Fine Arts, Sabina was taught that the building of socialism had already progressed so far that "the basic conflict was no longer between good and evil but between good and better" (245–46). Consequently, art—which had to follow the doctrine of socialist realism and in Kundera's view had nothing to do with reality (see Liehm, "Interview" 101)—was expected to depict a beautiful world. The parades in which the students were obliged to participate and the constant background music in the compulsory youth camps encouraged participation in the collective joy of the building of socialism. Everything disagreeable was swept under the carpet. Under these conditions, Sabina's rebellion against kitsch was manifest in her paintings in the form of the recurrent motif of a crack in the screen. From behind the scenery, which is painted so as to conform the decrees of socialist realism, another world is looming. According to her characterization of the paintings, "On the surface, an intelligible lie; underneath, the unintelligible truth" (60). Sabina's private revolt against kitsch is akin to the devil's unmasking laughter. The antagonism between those who cultivate kitsch and those who unveil it thus comes close to the opposition between sentimental individuals and those who strive for autonomy and authenticity.

In *The Unbearable Lightness of Being*, however, the main counter-concept in relation to which Kundera discusses kitsch is not authenticity but "shit." In this pair of concepts, the opposition is not between those who beautify matters and those who unveil the hidden truth, but between the act of veiling and what is being veiled. "Shit" refers to anything which is absolutely worthless or unacceptable in life. Kitsch is "the absolute denial of shit": it "excludes everything from its purview which is essentially unacceptable in human existence" (242). In contrast, a mature, nonideological human being acknowledges the existence of worthless things and is constantly alert so as to distinguish them from valuable things. The playfully narrated macabre story about Stalin's son Yakov, who died during World War II in a prisoner-of-war camp "because of shit" (enraged and humiliated by the order to clean the latrines, he threw himself onto the electrified wire surrounding the camp) is developed into a quasi-philosophical mini-tract on the metaphysics of shit. Shit, Kundera contemplates, is not a moral problem but a metaphysical one: "The responsibility for shit . . . rests entirely with Him, the creator of man" (239). Therefore, a death for the sake of shit is a death with a metaphysical significance (238).

There is yet another opposite or enemy of kitsch which Kundera identifies by calling kitsch "a folding screen set up to curtain off death" (247). This idea was elaborated by Broch in his essays on kitsch, the obvious point of departure for Kundera's reflections on the topic. According to Broch, death is worthlessness, the nonvalue per se, because it denies and annuls everything that is valuable in human life ("Evil" 9). The fundamentally unacceptable aspect of life is that everything in it is subject to death and abolishment. People's prevailing inclination toward kitsch manifests itself in the fact that we are reluctant to face our own mortality and therefore aspire to hide death behind a folding screen. We desire to conceal the fact that our search for the meaningfulness of our existence is conducted in a domain reigned over by death.

In *The Unbearable Lightness of Being* death is not concealed. In the last part of the novel it is one of the main themes, and already before this part not only has Franz died and the reader been informed about the impending death of Tomas and Tereza, but also the author-narrator tells us how they, after their death, before they are forgotten, are turned into kitsch (270). Franz's wife triumphs by letting everyone think that on his deathbed Franz returned to her, which actually was not his intention at all. For his gravestone, she chooses the inscription "A Return after Long Wanderings," which can be read in religious terms but which for everyone familiar with the wife's version of the story now has another meaning as well. Thomas's son, who has converted to Catholicism, has the stone on his father's grave proclaim that "He Wanted the Kingdom of God on Earth" (270) and thus not even Tomas, who in Sabina's words is "the complete opposite of kitsch" (12), can escape kitsch.

Idyll and death

Defining human existence in terms of death links Kundera and Broch to Heidegger and other existentialists. However, unlike Heidegger, who defines being human as an existence oriented toward death, Kundera emphasizes our disposition to ignore our mortality: "'You know, it's really very peculiar,' says Goethe in *Immortality*: 'To be mortal is the most basic human experience and yet man has never been able to accept it, grasp it, and behave accordingly. Man doesn't know how to be mortal'" (240). The difference between the sentimental and those who strive for authenticity is nevertheless once again striking at this point. The sentimental person, following the attitude of kitsch, endeavors to keep the fact of death hidden from his or her sight because anything valuable must be absolute, that is to say, eternal. The nonsentimental person, in contrast, is well aware of the temporal nature of human existence and searches among his or her experiences for moments that can endow life with meaningfulness, without ignoring the truth that life includes innumerable valueless things as well. Is it reasonable even to expect anything more than a moment of happiness, Kundera asks in *Jacques and His Master* (74). Despite all this, in the last part of *The Unbearable Lightness of Being* Kundera explores the possibility of prolonging the pleasant moment so as to cover one's whole life or at least a large section of it. Can one lead a beautiful, happy life through love and by being open to beauty? The form in which Kundera puts the question is whether or not an idyllic existence is possible for a human being.

In *The Art of the Novel,* Kundera notes that owing to the chronological displacement of parts 6 and 7 in *The Unbearable Lightness of Being,* the rustic idyll of the last part, "Karenin's Smile," is subverted by our knowledge of the fact that Tomas and Tereza will lose their lives in a car accident (77). This last part depicts the death of Tereza's dog, but the reader knows that Tomas and Tereza will soon die as well. The couple has moved to the country to escape, as they say to themselves, the ugliness of Prague, but in fact also to escape Tomas's erotic adventures, since in the countryside it is impossible for him to continue pursuing women and Tomas realizes that he can actually do without. Although in the eyes of the locals life in the country is a miserable way of life, to be left behind as quickly as possible, Tomas and Tereza live contentedly in their rural idyll. The idyll, however, is not the paradise Tereza has longed for, something that cannot be attained by human beings (see McEwan 28).

For Kundera the meaning of "idyll" differs somewhat from the usual meaning of the word, and he defines it differently in different contexts. For example, in "Sixty-three Words" in *The Art of the Novel,* he defines the concept as "the condition of the world before the first conflict; or beyond conflicts" (131). The basic conflict between Tomas and Tereza is resolved once Tomas has given up his erotic affairs (at least seemingly: when Tereza observes him trying to hide a letter from her, her jealousy reawakens). In *The Unbearable Lightness of Being,* the possibility of a condition beyond conflict is explored through the life of a dog: Karenin does not know anything about the antagonism between body and soul, but he lives in a paradise that precedes their separation (288), just like the mother and infant in *Life Is Elsewhere*. The idyll in this case means overcoming the conflict between body and soul from which Tereza has suffered her whole life. Yet Kundera also gives the concept of the idyll another definition, likewise illustrated by a dog's existence (290–91). The existence of a dog consists of an endless repetition of events: its happiness is an eternal recurrence of the same. "Pure repetition," repetition of the identical without significant variation, here takes on a new, positive meaning as the mode of idyllic existence. Human happiness is now defined as a longing for repetition (290). Tomas's and Tereza's idyllic life in the country is likewise based on a repetition of the daily routine, thus being in sharp contrast to the modern individual's adventurous exploration of the world. "Karenin's Smile," however, shows that the possibility of an idyll as a pure repetition is not open to us due to our awareness of the temporal limitedness of our existence. Unlike the dog, in human life the boundary beyond which repetition is no longer possible is visible.

In several of Kundera's works, the relationship between humans and animals is taken up as a model for interpersonal human relationships. In *The Unbearable Lightness of Being*, the author-narrator suggests that before people are induced to persecute each other, they are first taught to persecute dogs (280–81). Already in *Farewell Waltz*, the pensioners' chase of dogs is associated by Jakub with hunting human beings (105–09). Similarly, the way cows—who earlier were "persons," with given names—are treated in the collective farms resembles the impersonal treatment of human beings (*The Unbearable Lightness* 281–82). On the other hand, making friends with a dog—or, as in the case of the chairman of the collective farm in Tomas's and Tereza's village, a pig—can serve as a model for mutual love between two creatures. In general, for Kundera "mankind's moral test, its fundamental test . . . consists of its attitude towards those who are at its mercy: animals" (281). He recalls the story of Nietzsche's bursting into tears when he saw a coachman beating his horse: "that is the Nietzsche I love" (282). Kundera thereby joins those readers who, like Mann, see in Nietzsche's preaching of a Dionysian approval of life compensation for his actual suffering from the cruelty of life (see Mann, "Nietzsche"; Schmitt).

Kundera does not hesitate to use the word "love" to describe the tie between a human being and a dog. In fact, he sees in this kind of relationship the prototype of love, in that humans' love for a dog is love for a different creature, one from whom they do not expect identification or mergence with their own selves, or even the reciprocation of their feelings:

> It is a completely selfless love: Tereza did not want anything of Karenin; she did not even ask him to love her back. Nor had she ever asked herself the questions that plague human couples: Does he love me? Does he love anyone more than me? Does he love me more than I love him? Perhaps all the questions we ask of love, to measure, test, probe, and save it, have the additional effect of cutting it short. Perhaps the reason we are unable to love is that we yearn to be loved, that is, we demand something (love) from our partner instead of delivering ourselves up to him demand-free and asking for nothing but his company. And something else: Tereza accepted Karenin for what he was; she did not try to make him over in her image; she agreed from the outset with his dog's life, did not wish to deprive him of it, did not envy him his secret intrigues. The reason she trained him was not to transform him (as a husband tries to reform his wife and a wife her husband), but to provide him with the elementary language that enabled them to communicate and live together. (289)

Love is defined here as an acceptance of the otherness of the other. Whether this is possible between two human beings remains an open question.

One fundamental difference between the existence of a human being and an animal lies in their different relation to time. The dog lives with its master in an idyll. It leads a completely satisfied life in the moment of the present that remains infinitely the same: in this idyll the future exists only as an expectation of the recurrence of a past event. The temporality of animal life thus presents the Nietzschean theme of the eternal recurrence of the same in a new, positive variation. In this experience of time as endless repetition, death does not exist. In the last part of the novel Karenin eventually dies, but since he does not expect death he does not truly encounter it. In contrast, for humans the fact of death is constantly present and the idyll as an infinite repetition of happy moments is thus not possible. The image of a perfect idyll is kitsch, which means that it is thinkable only if one hides death behind a folding screen.

In reading the account of Tomas's and Tereza's idyllic country life, the reader's perspective is determined by our knowledge of their imminent death. The question is how they live immediately before they die. Although the protagonists cannot foresee the tragic accident, the fact of death is already visible in their horizon. Tereza notices that Tomas is grizzled and his physical strength has waned. On the last page of the novel, dancing with Tomas in the bar of a cheap hotel in the nearby country town, the happiness Tereza feels is depicted as follows: "On they danced to the strains of the piano and violin. Tereza leaned her head on Tomas's shoulder. Just as she had when they flew together in the airplane through the storm clouds [in her dream]. She was experiencing the same odd happiness and odd sadness as then. The sadness meant: we are at the last station. The happiness meant: we are together. The sadness was form, the happiness was content. Happiness filled the space of sadness" (305). Death—for it is the expectation of death that is the content of the feeling of having arrived at "the last station"—defines the form of life, which is transience. Death, or rather the awareness of death and thus awareness of the impossibility of an eternal repetition, is the form of life independently of its content. This insight casts a melancholy shadow over the happiest moments of life. The space bounded by death may be filled with different contents, even with happiness, but only transiently. "Karenin's Smile" delineates a human's true possibility for a happy life—a nonkitsch, nonidyllic happiness, which is nonabsolute, transient, and limited by death.

Chapter Nine
Lightness and Death

In *Immortality*, Kundera's alter ego tells his friend Avenarius that he is writing a book that will be given the title *The Unbearable Lightness of Being*, referring to the book the reader is reading. Self-reference and playing with fictionality, often regarded as postmodern traits in literature, fit well to Kundera's novels in which he refrains from creating an illusion of reality. When the friend thinks that a novel bearing this title might already exist, "Kundera" says that he has written it himself, but that the title would be more appropriate for the novel in preparation (267). The remark is pertinent because the themes occurring in *Immortality* are similar to those found in *The Unbearable Lightness of Being* and in Kundera's novels in general: soul and body, sentimental and nonsentimental, weight and weightlessness, contingency and necessity, History, love, eroticism, beauty and ugliness, the "absolutely modern," and death are examined from the perspective of the architheme of sense giving. However, while *The Unbearable Lightness of Being* does not actually end with the unbearableness of the lightness of being, but finds a tolerable and even happy mode of living for the individual who is striving for authenticity, in *Immortality* the outcome is much gloomier: there is no longer any escape in sight from the lightness of being. We might add that the title *Identity,* too, would suit the novel well and even better than it fits the short novel telling the rather simple story of Jean-Marc and Chantal, because it is the question of identity around which the complex thematic texture of the novel is organized. In spite of its playfulness, this grave, even pessimistic work is to be read as in a way Kundera's testament, his conclusive statement about questions of sense giving and the existence of an autonomous human being. The title *Immortality* is typical of Kundera in that it names an important theme, but conceals the fact that its opposites, death and mortality, are even more essential themes in the novel. Indeed, *Immortality* is not merely a novel about the difficulties of determining one's identity and about ending with the lightness of being, but is in particular a novel about being mortal.

The body, self, and being for others

Immortality is a polyphonic thematic composition consisting of seven parts, each named according to a theme word or a metaphor expressing an important theme. In part 1, "The Face," the problem of individual identity is tackled once again, combined with questions of bodily existence and how an individual appears to others. The protagonist in this part is the "heroine" of the novel, Agnes, and the other characters are her sister Laura, her husband Paul, a lawyer, and their teenage daughter Brigitte. Part 2, "Immortality," deals with Goethe's relationship with Bettina Brentano. Part 3, "Fighting," is again about Agnes and Laura. Its main event is Laura's love affair with Paul's colleague Bernard and the breaking up of their relationship, but at a deeper level it deals with Laura's continuous competition with her older sister and her struggle to get the attention of others. Part 4, "*Homo sentimentalis*," again takes up the case of Goethe and Bettina. Part 5, "Chance," brings Agnes's story to an end: she dies in a car accident. This part continues Kundera's exploration of the themes of necessity and coincidence, meaningfulness and its absence, love and beauty, identity, temporality, lightness, and death. Part 6, "The Dial," presents a separate story line about the erotic life of a man called Rubens. The last part, "The Celebration," forms a short and light coda to the novel: the author, sitting beside a swimming pool, celebrates the completion of the novel together with his friend Avenarius and meets Paul and Laura, who now are a married couple. In *Immortality*, Kundera is again more interested in certain themes which appear in his characters' lives than in those lives as a whole and again he feels free to construct the novel as a thematic composition without considering chronology or avoiding repetition if it is useful in his composition.

In symmetry with the ending, the novel begins with a scene at a swimming pool, where the author receives the idea of the heroine of the novel from a gesture by an elderly woman. This gesture, a wave of the hand he sees as extraordinarily attractive and exclusively feminine, is in the author's opinion incompatible with the body that performs it. The gesture is actually only appropriate for a young woman. The author contemplates the fact that we are rarely aware of our age; most of the time we are ageless to ourselves (4). The body ages, but the "I" is ageless—a discrepancy which is a variation on the dualism of soul and body, now viewed from the perspective of temporality.

The woman's gesture induces the author to reflect upon the connection between a gesture and an individual (Kundera does not seem to be aware about recent research on gestures in social psychology and cultural history; see, e.g., Bremmer and Roodenburg; Kendon). Although a gesture is taken to be an expression of a person's individuality, actually the opposite is the case: "Without the slightest doubt, there are far fewer gestures in the world than there are individuals. That finding leads us to a shocking conclusion: a gesture is more individual than an individual. We could put it in the form of an aphorism: many people, few gestures" (7–8). Instead of the gesture having revealed something about this particular woman, for instance, her beauty, the woman has revealed to the spectators the beauty of a gesture: "A gesture cannot be regarded as the expression of an individual, as his creation (because no individual is capable of creating a fully original gesture, belonging to nobody else), nor can it even be regarded as that person's instrument; on the contrary, it is gestures that use us as their instruments, as their bearers and incarnations" (8). Here Kundera considers the language of gestures in a similar way as the structuralists considered spoken and written language. According to the theory of structuralism, language is not the creation of the speaker or an expression of his or her unique thoughts and feelings; rather, the speaker says what it is possible to say in the language. In a sense, the speaker is a means through which the language manifests itself (see, e.g., Benveniste). This mode of thinking was applied to other systems of representation and action as well. Claude Lévi-Strauss applied it, for instance, to mythology, claiming that it is not the individual who is thinking in myths but instead myths which are thinking in the individual (12). In the structuralist mode of thought, the individual is deprived of sovereignty as an acting and speaking agent. The system has primacy over the individual, in that the individual is not able to choose freely what he or she is or says or does, but is merely a temporary occupant of a site in the system. For Kundera, the language of the body is such a system, where gestures are nothing that individuals have themselves invented. They are patterns of action encoded in the body, which the individuals may or may not use. Kundera's thinking, however, differs from that of the structuralists in one important respect: for him the disappearance of individuality and its replacement by a function of the system is a fundamental problem, because for him the uniqueness and autonomy of the individual are inalienable values.

Gestures, seemingly free acts of human individuals and expressions of their subjectivity, are for Kundera products of "the Creator's computer" (12). As such, they are similar to the human body and especially the face, whose identification with the personality was already questioned in Kundera's earlier novels. In *Farewell Waltz*, Olga denies that her face reveals her true identity, in *The Unbearable Lightness of Being* Tereza wonders at what point her face would cease to be hers if her nose was lengthened by a millimeter a day, and in *Identity* Jean-Marc is afraid that a time may come when he will no longer be able to discern in his beloved Chantal the minuscule distinctive features that make her unique (32–34, 81, 96–97, 126). In the part entitled "The Face" in *Immortality,* the question is once again brought up about the possibility for an individual to identify with his or her face. Kundera suggests that each individual human being is a combination of some of those variations on basic patterns that are produced by the "creator's computer." The human face is assembled from different parts which vary within certain ranges. Variation in the length of a nose, for instance, stays within certain limits. The result is not a unique, individual face but a reproduction of the same prototype, the human face, with random variation within certain limits. The face is unique only in the same sense of singularity that every natural being or technically produced item is unique. The face "reflects neither character nor soul, nor what we call the self. The face is only the serial number of a specimen" (13), a token by which a human being is distinguished from all others, like one car among all the others from the same production line.

Kundera's computer metaphor is interesting because it makes clear on the one hand the continuity from the Enlightenment—which modeled nature through the metaphor of the machine (see Wendorff 231–32)—to the present time, on the other hand the difference between the two ages. The clock, with the precision of its mechanism, was the epitome of mechanical causality in nature. It is precisely this aspect that is emphasized in *The Unbearable Lightness of Being,* where Kundera speaks of the "clockwork" of sexual arousal in men (231). Replacing in *Immortality* the metaphor of a clock by that of a computer indicates that nature is still considered to follow laws of necessity, but that this necessity now appears in the form of probability. Kundera puts this as follows:

> In his [God's] place, there is a program which is ceaselessly running in his absence, without anyone being able to change anything whatever. To load a program into the computer: this does not mean that the future has been planned down to the last detail, that everything is written "up above." For example, the program did not specify that in 1815 a battle would be fought near Waterloo and that the French would be defeated, but only that man is aggressive by nature, that he is condemned to wage war and that technical progress would make war more and more terrible. Everything else is without importance from the Creator's point of view and is only a play of permutations and combinations within a general program, which is not a prophetic anticipation of the future but merely sets the limits of possibilities within which all power of decision has been left to chance. (*Immortality* 13)

Our face is given to us accidentally. We enter into the world in a body which is not our choice. But is a human being able to bear this accidentality? What am I, if I refuse to identify with what "the Creator's computer" has happened to assign to me: "Without the faith that our face expresses our self, without that basic illusion, that arch-illusion, we cannot live or at least we cannot take life seriously. And it isn't enough for us to identify with our selves, it is necessary to do so *passionately*, to the point of life and death. Because only in this way can we regard ourselves not merely as a variant of a human prototype but as a being with its own irreplaceable essence" (14). We regard our body, and especially our face, as an expression of our personality, yet our body is an inevitable and at the same time an accidental product of nature: inevitable insofar as it is naturally produced following the genetic code of the species, accidental in that the species is realized in specimens which vary in detail within a narrow range of accidental differences. Kundera thinks that if human beings are equivalent to their bodies, they are deprived of any autonomy of choice. The only alternative is the dissociation of one's identity from the body.

Agnes and Laura take opposite stands on the question of how the self is related to one's face and body. Agnes's attitude is typical of the person who is striving for authenticity, whereas Laura's is typical of the sentimentalist. Agnes wants to escape identification with her face. She imagines another planet, of a higher order, on which one has no face but is totally one's own creation (45–46). For Agnes, the body is not the person himself or herself either; rather, it is a machine which needs constant maintenance. A human being feels ashamed and humiliated by being forced to admit his or her bodily existence, because this means admitting a lack of freedom (275–77, 107–10). In contrast, Laura identifies herself with her body. For her the body is not a machine but has erotic and personal significance: it demands to be accepted and loved, as a manifestation of her self. She feels a constant urge to be bodily present in the lives of those she loves; for example, the white piano she gave Agnes as a present signifies leaving her body in the living room of her admired sister.

Since gestures are not original, a human being who is striving for authenticity cannot identify himself or herself with them. The history of the wave of the hand in Agnes's and Laura's story shows how an authentic and a sentimental individual use gestures differently. Agnes had first encountered the wave of the hand when a female colleague taking leave of Agnes's father turned to him with this gesture. Agnes first uses the gesture to console a young man who, after escorting her home, is too awkward even to ask for a kiss. She abandons it, however, when she notices that Laura, imitating her, uses it in parting from a playmate. Agnes becomes aware of the fact that this gesture is no more a manifestation of herself than any other. She therefore gives up all gestures which might be interpreted as expressions of her individuality, keeping only the most general ones, those which are unambiguously nonindividual, such as nodding and shaking one's head. Laura takes the opposite course of action: she appropriates a number of gestures as attributes of her self and demands that others recognize her in them.

What are, then, the possibilities for human beings to be an autonomous, authentic individuals, if they cannot be such through their body and its gestures? Where can the true self be found? In *The Art of the Novel*, Kundera says that throughout its history the novel has been in search of the self, without ever finding it: "The quest for the self has always ended, and always will end, in a paradoxical dissatisfaction" (25). In Kundera's view this is so because the solution also cannot be simply to separate the soul from the body and let the soul alone determine an individual's identity. In *Immortality*, he writes that in Romanticism after Beethoven, "man, betrayed by the world, escapes into his self, into his nostalgia, his dreams, his revolt, and lets himself be deafened by the voices inside him so that he no longer hears the voices outside" (85). Goethe, in contrast, dissociated himself from this tendency, because for him "the cry from inside sounded . . . like an unbearable noise" (85). Listening only to the cry from our inner self does not mean merely an escape from reality: the cry from inside also means presenting ourselves to others. It does not mean retiring into solitude, which for Kundera would signify authenticity, but is a craving for attention: with his cry from the inner self, the sentimentalist bears his soul in front of him like a flag (158, 236).

But what is a "soul" in solitude? Kundera suggests that, like gestures, thoughts are far fewer in number than human beings: "Many people, few ideas: we all think more or less the same, and we exchange, borrow, steal thoughts from one another. However, when someone steps on my foot, only I feel the pain. The basis of the self is not thought but suffering, which is the most fundamental of all feelings. While it suffers, not even a cat can doubt its unique and uninterchangeable self" (225). Kundera ends up with the paradox of the self. The only thing that is authentic, truly our own, is suffering, because everyone has to endure it themselves (225). This is further evidence that for Kundera the criterion for autonomy is sensing or experiencing something ourselves. But suffering does not distinguish human beings from other creatures. Following this principle, even a cat has a "self." What, then, remains of the object of the individual's pride, his or her autonomous, unique self?

In his earlier novels, Kundera sought the real self in the individual's existential experience and in the freedom to choose his or her own actions. These are allowed to the individual even in the tiny space left in the trap of History. But where in the earlier novels the possibilities left for humankind were sought in the private sphere outside of History, in *Immortality* he seems to be denying the individual any possibility of an authentic, autonomous mode of existence, even in privacy. This is because he now stresses that human beings are bound by biological necessities and natural contingencies, which do not recognize any uniqueness in an individual and which lie beyond our control. Where Tomas and Tereza, even under the harshest circumstances of a totalitarian regime, preserved a modicum of freedom to make choices in their lives, in *Immortality,* human life is trapped not only by history but also by biology, which deprives the individual of the last trace of freedom. However, individual identity is not threatened or even denied in *Immortality* by biology alone, but also by the constraints of society, which now appear as interconnected. Kundera still regards the (negative) freedom of not being determined by others to be the goal of a modern individual, but he seems to be more pessimistic than before about our chance to escape it. In his view, the contemporary West resembles recent Central and East European totalitarianism in that it does not allow the individual to determine himself or herself in the freedom of privacy.

In Kundera's novels, the mere fact of a human being's bodily existence makes him or her dependent on others. Since an individual exists for others only through being perceived by them—as a body, through gestures or words—he or she cannot escape bodily existence. Tomas speculates that if the male sexual apparatus reacted to the flight of a swallow instead of the female body, everyone would realize the separation of soul and body. But, in fact, this separation does not exist; on the contrary, everyone in Kundera's novels encounters others through their physical appearance and the messages sent by their bodies and is similarly perceived by others. The basis for social encounters is shaped by biological necessity and natural randomness, which are responsible for the attractiveness or otherwise of the body and face and their changes through aging. In the social machinery, an individual is what he or she is for others. A sentimental person like Laura reacts to this by identifying herself passionately with what she is for others, whereas a person striving for autonomy and authenticity, like Agnes, is aware of the discrepancy between external determination and striving for authenticity, and feels disturbed when she recognizes the difficulty or even impossibility of escaping the former.

Just as Agnes abandons the special wave of the hand when her sister appropriates the gesture, she also gives up wearing dark sunglasses when Laura adopts them as well. When she was young, Agnes wore dark sunglasses because she thought they were elegant and made her look mysterious. Here, we have to take precise notice of the purpose for which Kundera makes her to wear the dark sunglasses. They are part of her self-fashioning, but in a manner which leaves the precise meaning of the gesture or accessory undetermined. We could also say that their meaning is negative because she uses them to emphasize her withdrawal from the gaze of others. Laura takes the dark sunglasses from Agnes when she is in mourning and in her case the meaning of the glasses is clear: they manifest her commitment to a world that causes her pain. By foregrounding her tears, she manifests her sentimental appreciation of feelings and displays her own emotions.

Both Agnes and Laura construct their own identity, which they think is unique, but this occurs in opposite ways. Agnes attempts to get rid of all external determinants, in order in the end to find out what she is in herself, while Laura constructs her identity out of the attributes bestowed upon her: "There are two methods for cultivating the uniqueness of the self: the method of *addition* and the method of *subtraction*. Agnes subtracts from her self everything that is exterior and borrowed, in order to come closer to her sheer essence (even with the risk that zero lurks at the bottom of the subtraction). Laura's method is precisely the opposite: in order to make her self ever more visible, perceivable, seizable, sizeable, she keeps adding to it more and more attributes and she attempts to identify herself with them (with the risk that the essence of the self may be buried by the additional attributes)" (111). Agnes's strategy of removing from herself everything she recognizes as inauthentic resembles Tomas's endeavor in *The Unbearable Lightness of Being* to disown even inner imperatives in order to ultimately gain his inner freedom. In turn, Laura's strategy is equivalent to that of Helena's in *The Joke*. Ludvik remarks that the special taste for food Helena claims possessing is a means of self-fashioning (180). Agnes feels the glances of others as burdensome and dreams of solitude, with no one looking at her, while Laura who exhibits herself willingly to those around her wants to do everything, loving, mourning, committing suicide as if on stage looked at by her loved ones.

The figure parallel to Laura in the second story line of the polyphonic novel is Bettina Brentano, a variation on the person with a lyrical or kitsch attitude to life from almost two hundred years earlier. Like Laura, Bettina too puts up a performance of herself, but her stage is greater than that Laura's. She wants to make an appearance in History, whereas Laura is content with having those closest to her as her audience. Bettina and Laura represent the first and the third type, respectively, in the classification of people in *The Unbearable Lightness of Being* according to whose gaze they crave: "We can be divided into four categories according to the kind of look we wish to live under. The first category longs for the look of an infinite number of anonymous eyes, in other words, for the look of the public. . . . The second category is made up of people who have a vital need to be looked at by many known eyes. They are the tireless hosts of cocktail parties and dinners. . . . Then there is the third category, the category of people who need to be constantly before the eyes of the person they love. . . . And finally there is the fourth category, the rarest, the category of people who live in the imaginary eyes of those who are not present" (262–63). As a means of gaining access to History, Bettina uses her love for Goethe. Kundera analyzes the content of Bettina's romantic "true love" (*wahre Liebe*): this is not the love for a particular person but a love of love—the feeling of love is elevated to an absolute value, whereas the object of love is incidental (214–15). Here we recognize the idea of sentimental love as depicted earlier for instance in Jaromil in *Life Is Elsewhere*. Laura's conception of love is, likewise, sentimental. She is not in the least interested in the person she is in love with—she actually does not know him at all—but is only interested in his love for her and in love as her own feeling (148). Love for her means "wings beating in her breast," a feeling which makes her do senseless things (203–04). Actually, "absolute love" or romantic "true love" is false love, in that, as we already know, it is an act of sentimental self-embellishment and not at all an encounter with another human being.

Laura represents the private, Bettina the public construction of one's identity by being for others. Bettina lives in the era of Romanticism, the time when absolute feeling was discovered, a feeling which promises an escape from the world, but which can equally be used, as Bettina's ingenious invention shows as a means of ensuring herself a permanent presence in the world. Bettina's maneuver of making herself visible to everyone resembles present-day "imagology" as discussed in *Immortality*, but the rules of the game have changed considerably during the past two centuries. The present-day rules of publicity are discussed, except by the author himself, by Paul, the third sentimental person in the novel. It is fitting for Laura to be Paul's spouse in that Paul wants to be the object of "true" love that makes the lover behave in a senseless manner. Paul constructs his identity on the idea of being "absolutely modern." However, because what is absolutely modern is constantly changing, he seeks help in recognizing it from his young daughter, whom he believes to feel intuitively, as youth does, what is truly new and essential in our time. Following the advice of image consultants, nevertheless, the radio station on which he has broadcasted his brief Sunday morning feature, "Rights and the Law," decides to cancel the program as hopelessly out of date. Yet he speaks in favor of the imagologists because he sees in them representatives of what at the moment is absolutely modern and therefore he actually is, as his boss remarks, "a brilliant ally of his gravediggers" (159). It is Paul who introduces the concept of imagology and ponders how it subjugates the individuals in our contemporary world. The conditions under which the public construction of the self takes place have changed definitively in the course of the last two centuries. Where Bettina managed to gain a position in History, Paul realizes that he is a helpless victim of the imagological machinery.

Imagology against privacy and history

At the beginning of the novel, Agnes says that discovering our individual identity by identifying ourselves with our face has become impossible in our times, because we are confronted every day with hundreds of faces in newspapers, television, and advertisements. Paul would like to see the constant display of faces as a sign of the individualism of our times, but Agnes is of the opposite opinion, finding that the exposure of masses of faces proves that there has never been any individuality at all: "You suddenly realize that it's all just one face in many variations and that no such thing as an individual ever existed" (35). Nature repeats the very same, with insignificant variations. Where, then, is individuality to be found?

The contrast between a sentimental construction of the self and the search for an authentic mode of being is maintained in *Immortality*, but here both are challenged by the new social situation, the reign of imagology. Kundera's concept of imagology means the hegemony of the image as the main form of cultural consciousness; thus a more suitable name for the phenomenon might perhaps be "imagocracy." "Image" refers here concretely to a picture or photograph, but also more abstractly to the public image of a person. The supremacy of the image implies that cultural reality has gone through a process of visualization; events and persons are presented to the public through visual images. In an image, a piece of reality is apparently captured in its immediacy, but the revealed "truth" is superficial and even misleading. There is no effort to explore the issue in its complexity, but on the contrary it is seized with the haste that is characteristic of our time. In visual communication anything that is considered worthy of our attention must be transformed into images. Agnes remarks that in the contemporary world, God's eye that sees everything has been replaced by the camera; consequently, "the eye of one has been replaced by the eyes of all" (33). This does not just concern public figures whose privacy is exposed in photographs on the pages of newspapers. Agnes ponders the fact that no one is safe from the eye of publicity. If we just happen to get involved in a dramatic accident, our face, distorted by pain, might appear in the spotlight of publicity. The right of the photographer to intrude into our suffering means that we are constantly watched by others. No one can escape the gazes of others (Kundera does not relate his notion of imagology to the field of scholarship termed imagology with regard to national stereotypes [see, e.g., Beller and Leerssen; Leerssen]; in some aspects, his concept is parallel to what is called the "iconic turn" and "visual turn," respectively, including the impact of the image and the visual in contemporary culture [see, e.g., Dikovitskaya; Dorfman; Mirzoeff; Mitchell; Moxey; Sachs-Hombach; Viehoff]).

Kundera's imagology means the reign of visual images, but also an imposition on our identity, and this results in the ways our public image is constructed and perceived. The communist ideal of living in a glass house, that is to say, transforming the private into the public, has in a sense become the reality in a West ruled by imagology. Kundera observes that for a long time in our history only in a few special cases was a person granted the right to interrogate another person publicly, for instance, a judge investigating a criminal case. In the twentieth century the fascists and the communists appropriated this right and people became aware that anyone could any time be required to answer questions such as "what they did yesterday; what they think deep in their hearts; what they talk about when they get together with A and if they have an intimate relationship with B"—an awareness which turned them into "infantilized wretches" (122). Now, in the era of imagology, morality is founded upon the imperative of answering—which Kundera calls the "Eleventh Commandment"—with journalists in the role of interrogators. Kundera's example is the "interrogation" of president Nixon by the media during the Watergate scandal. Kundera remarks that truth elicited by the Eleventh Commandment is not connected with religion or free thought: "it is truth of the lowest ontological storey, a purely positivist factual truth," which nevertheless "contains the same explosive force as did the truth of Hus or Giordano Bruno," who because of their heretical views were condemned to be burnt at the stake (124). That journalistic truth concerns "pure facts" means that the evaluation of the actions of the person being interrogated is left to public opinion.

Imagology means the rule of public opinion. Everyone's ubiquitous exposure to the gazes of the public signifies an unprecedented demand for uniformity. Walking in the street, Agnes covers her ears with her hands to protect herself from the predatory noise and a passer-by slaps his forehead as a sign that he thinks she is insane. Everyone has to adhere to a certain behavioral pattern, in this case to acquiesce to the noise; no deviation from the norm is allowed.

The power of imagology in determining our identity is explored in detail in the cases of two persons whose work takes place in public, namely Paul and his friend Bernard, Laura's lover. When Paul is compelled to give up his Saturday morning radio program (one is tempted to ask what this says about our time, which wants entertainment only and is no longer interested in "rights and the law"), he is astonished: "Without his realizing it in the slightest, something must have happened to his image. Something must have happened and he didn't know what it was, and he'd never know" (139–40). Changes in our public image affect our lives, but we are powerless to regulate these changes or even to identify them. Bernard is a young, successful radio reporter whose face is infinitely multiplied on roadside billboards promoting a radio broadcast channel. But when someone unknown to him—who later turns out to be professor Avenarius—knocks on his door and gives him a diploma awarding him the title of "compleat ass," his image in his own eyes collapses (140). Since he cannot resist telling his colleagues about the incident, in their minds the attribute "compleat ass" is from now on definitely associated with him. He no longer feels sure that his nomination as a "compleat ass" will not some day be published in a newspaper as a social announcement. The accidentality of the event is underlined by the fact that Avenarius had mistaken the radio reporter for his father, the politician, to whom he had actually intended to address the diploma of outstanding stupidity. Despite this, the deed and its effects are irremediable.

Since Paul always wants to comply with what is absolutely modern and that is now the supremacy of the imagologists, he yields to their power, although with regret: "Our self is a mere illusion, ungraspable, indescribable, misty, while the only reality, all too easily graspable and describable, is our image in the eyes of others. And the worst thing about it is that you are not its master. First you try to paint it yourself, then you want at least to influence and control it, but in vain: a single malicious phrase is enough to change you for ever into a depressingly simple caricature" (143). Kundera's view is that it is difficult for us to find our true selves through introspection, but if our only graspable self is what we are for others and if these "others" are the omnipresent and yet indefinable public sphere which we cannot manipulate or influence, we are at the mercy of chance. Nothing remains of autonomy in the sense of self-determination, which for Kundera is the core of the modern individual and the source of his or her dignity. But the sentimental strategy of constructing the ego by leaning on emotions and ideas greater than ourselves no longer works either, because we have no say in the process of assigning our own attributes. This was the case in a totalitarian system as well, especially if one opposed it. We might be labeled an enemy of the working class without any chance to counter this attribution. Thus, imagology is not a completely new phenomenon. According to Kundera, history does not in general give rise to anything absolutely new. What is new is that a certain possibility of human existence, which occurred earlier sporadically, is now supreme in the society as a whole. A reporter intruding into the life of the person whom they are interviewing displays the same indiscretion and arrogance as Bettina intruding into the life of Goethe. When Bettina asks Goethe impertinently why he drinks secretly, and later publishes this in her correspondence, she strips him of some of his privacy (77).

Ideology favored the lyrical or sentimental attitude in which we identify ourselves with a great idea or with the course of History. Imagology brings an end both to great ideas and to History. Ideology provided us with a system of doctrines, which was a logically constructed whole. Ideology turns into imagology when a system of ideas is reduced to, or replaced by, a few slogans and affecting pictures, such as a smiling worker waving a hammer in his hand. In the end, when ideologies have lost their credibility, no system of doctrines exists behind the images any longer. While the totalitarian system exerted control through ideology, imagology works through opinion polls: a system of official truths is replaced by the measurement of public opinion. Questions such as "is racism good or bad" or "who is the greatest author of all time" have become issues for which answers are sought in opinion polls: "Public opinion polls are a parliament in permanent session, whose function it is to create truth, the most democratic truth that has ever existed" (128–29).

The rule of public opinion means the totalitarianism of banality. When public opinion is equated with truth, the individual is deprived of the task of searching for truth, which according to Kundera was the task assigned to the modern individual and in particular the core of the ethos of the novelist. Through the figure of Hemingway, Kundera inquires how humankind (i.e., the novelist) has lost his right to explore the phenomena of existence. The public is excited by the latest Hemingway biography, which shows that his work, as Paul puts it, is nothing but a coded form of his life, "and that this life was just as poor and meaningless as all our lives" (377). Thus biographies and studies of writers are not there to elucidate the important things they have discovered or rescued from the "oblivion of being." On the contrary, they are written with the intention of reducing the writer's work to the trivialities of his private life. Paul praises imagology because it means an end to the tyranny of the "immortals," that is, those few culturally creative spirits who were admired for their ability to interpret human existence in their works. Everyone sinks democratically into the same meaninglessness, the surface of which is decorated according to ephemeral fashion dictated by the imagologists.

Although the ideologists' dream of steering the course of History was futile, according to Kundera they actually influenced history by prompting revolts, revolutions, wars, and reforms. Imagology, in contrast, has no effect whatsoever on history, but in a sense means an end to history. Under the rule of imagology, the word "change" has taken on a new meaning. It no longer refers to a historical change, a new phase in historical development, as in modernity, but only to a constant shift, with no direction or goal (129). Images follow each other in constant alternation like trends in fashion: "Imagologues create systems of ideals and anti-ideals, systems of short duration which are quickly replaced by other systems but which influence our behaviour, our political opinions and aesthetic tastes, the colour of carpets and the selection of books just as in the past we have been ruled by the systems of ideologues" (129–30). Broch's destruction of the system of values is accomplished here by replacing values with weightless fashion trends, which dictate how we conceive of ourselves and how we relate to our surroundings. Kundera's thinking can be compared with Jean Baudrillard's notions as to how the reality in which we live has been transformed into a sphere of signs without reference or with the views of Pierre Bourdieu, whose exploration of social behavior and image building shows how people are influenced by current trends and fashions. With regard to the individual's possibilities of choice, however, Bourdieu is less pessimistic than Kundera, in believing that the individual is capable of fashioning his or her own public image.

A parallel can be drawn between the transition from ideology to imagology and what Kundera says about the rejuvenation of humankind and its transition to "infantocracy," although he does not explicitly connect the two. While ideology means an attempt to understand the world in terms of one single idea by young people who lack experience of the world, imagology means remaining in the mode of existence that precedes any attempt at understanding, in the perpetual present of the moment, as on the children's island in *The Book of Laughter and Forgetting*. Discursive statements and concepts require analysis, whereas images are a passive and nonreflective, nonanalytical mode of appropriating the world. Returning to that which is unmediatedly given, prior to any questioning or analysis, is contrary to what for Kundera is valuable in the tradition of European modernity.

Meaninglessness and death

Part 2 of *Immortality* has the same title as the novel itself, but here again the unmentioned member of the pair of opposites, namely, death or mortality, is the more important one. Just as in *The Unbearable Lightness of Being*, Kundera is not interested in death as an event, but in mortality as an inescapable dimension of human existence, one which we prefer to ignore as long as possible. Again, mortality is examined as an attribute of the individual and of society, history, and culture. The question of death is intertwined with that of sense giving, since death means the annulment of anything valuable in life and is therefore, as Broch wrote, the nonvalue per se ("Evil" 9). A thing which loses its previously given significance undergoes a kind of death. While in *The Unbearable Lightness of Being,* a human being could under certain conditions be saved from the weightlessness of the absence of meaning, in *Immortality* this is no longer the case. The novel shows that in our contemporary world, autonomy and authenticity are no longer possible modes of being. Love, eroticism, and beauty are not enough to give weight to the existence of an individual and history has ceased to exist. Although play and laughter—an exposing, scornful laughter—are as strongly present in this novel as in Kundera's earlier works, *Immortality* is the most pessimistic of Kundera's novels. It about the loss of meaningfulness and about death.

The part, "Immortality" deals with Bettina's efforts to slip into History through Goethe. Actually, such attempts may not have been all that infrequent around Goethe—as Hans Blumenberg contends, "people in his [Goethe's] vicinity were in a peculiar way disposed to step with him into immortality" (*Goethe* 147)—but the picture Kundera draws of Bettina and her motives is rather caustic. My interest here is not in comparing Kundera's picture of Bettina Brentano with the conclusions of recent historical research on her (see Bäumer; Frederiksen and Goodman; Messner); in fact, Kundera seems not to be interested in Bettina Brentano as a historical figure, but as the bearer of certain general, transhistorical themes. However, Kundera's tendency to ignore historical specificity has significant implications for his views of people and their existential problems and his depiction of Bettina Brentano serves as an example of this. Studies of Bettina Brentano have connected her adoration of Goethe and her self-fashioning not only to the Romantic idea of love as an educating force (*bildende Kraft*), but also to the subordinate position of literarily or artistically gifted women at that time. We can with good reason call this position a trap: women were excluded from higher education and as writers were not taken seriously. What remained for a woman as a means for self-development was to love a man, since binding oneself with feelings of adoration to a person on a higher spiritual level was seen as a means whereby the lover approached the level of the beloved. Moreover, when Bettina chooses to behave in a calculatedly childlike manner—which Kundera regards as a means of gaining permission to behave badly—she is seizing the only option available to women to be acknowledged as creative individuals, since the Romantics praised in the child what they saw as its originality, authenticity, and creativity (see Bäumer 122). Consequently, what Kundera regards as Bettina's trick to gain attention and possibly even achieve immortality in Goethe's wake could equally be interpreted as an effort at self-assertion by a literarily gifted woman.

According to Kundera, Bettina used the state of mind the Romantics called "true love" as an entrance ticket into History. What interests Kundera in this maneuver—which includes her publication of her correspondence with Goethe, appropriately stylized under the title *Goethe's Correspondence with a Child* (see Arnim)—is her longing for immortality, which Kundera sees as characteristic of the sentimental attitude. This is because a longing for immortality is a form of longing to exist for others, to remain in their memory, an objective Bettina sought on the grand scale of History. Laura, for her part, pursues the same goal on the smaller scale of her personal milieu: "for me that's the only real life: to live in the thoughts of another. Otherwise I am the living dead" (176).

As in Kundera's other novels, in *Immortality* the majority of people are at least to some extent inclined toward sentimentality. This also applies to the "immortals," represented here by Goethe and Hemingway. In two scenes, these two writers meet in the other world and engage in conversation with each other. In the first meeting, Goethe shows up as a toothless, shabby old man. His appearance is meant to humiliate Bettina, whose love for him now seems ridiculous. Hemingway expresses his frustration with the public, which prefers digging into his life to reading his books. The "Judgement of History" is ridiculous, if it is based on trivialities which are found in everybody's life. Goethe affirms that this is in fact the case: the "eternal judgement" of History, which dictates how one is remembered, is "a rod in the hand of a narrow-minded teacher" (91). At the second meeting, Goethe makes his appearance in the full blossom of youth. In the meantime, however, he has gained "adulthood," which is to say, he has freed himself of his interest in his own immortality. He remarks to Hemingway that worrying about one's immortality is immature. In his opinion this is a characteristic of humans, who are unable to face mortality (240). He himself, Goethe, has at last learnt to accept it: he now intends to retire "to enjoy the delights of total non-existence, which [his] great enemy Novalis used to say has a bluish colour" (241). Being able to dispense with the image one has left behind in the minds of others, and to "die" in this ultimate sense, is the final wisdom that a human being learns.

Already before Agnes dies in a traffic accident she has, like Tomas and Tereza in *The Unbearable Lightness of Being*, encountered the fact of being mortal. Actually, she considers death a noteworthy, even desirable alternative to a life without meaning. In *Immortality,* being with others does not mean an encounter between subjects in a world of shared meanings, but being the object of the gaze of others. By removing from her physical appearance any visual signs and gestures that others might interpret as expressions of her personality, Agnes escapes from being determined by the gazes of others. She seeks silence and invisibility, just as—she now realizes—her father did shortly before his death. Following the death of his wife, the father tore up all photographs from the past, revealing his antisentimental attitude. In the light of the reflections in *Testaments Betrayed* on a writer's right to destroy his or her personal papers and belongings before death, the father's act appears induced by "the shame of being turned into an object" which outlives the self and lies open to everyone's eyes (*Testaments* 262). This is in accordance with the father's desire to preserve his privacy and with his feeling of distance from others. Agnes makes a thought experiment. In a sinking ship, where everyone has to fight for a place in the lifeboats, her father would abhor the ensuing physical intimacy with others to the extent that he would prefer dying (*Immortality* 25–26).

Agnes herself feels utterly estranged from humanity: "She once again had the strong, peculiar feeling that was coming over her more and more often: the feeling that she had nothing in common with those two-legged creatures with a head on their shoulders and a mouth in their face. There was a time when she was interested in their politics, their science, their inventions, when she considered herself a small part of their great adventure, until one day the feeling was born in her that she did not belong among them" (43). Agnes has crossed the line beyond which the adventure of humankind—all that has been significant and important either in human history or in the life of an individual—is no longer of any interest to her. She no longer identifies with the ways of the world or with the human condition. This extreme sense of estrangement manifests itself as an estrangement from the physical shape of the human being. It is also mentioned that she gives money to beggars, not because she feels that they too belong to humankind, but because she feels that they are as detached from humankind as she herself is (44).

What causes this extreme alienation from human existence? Kundera does not pose the question in this form, because the question as such already implies that a human being is expected to consent to his or her humanity and to identify with it. From his first novel onward, Kundera scorns those for whom life as such, without any further qualification, is valuable. This mockery continues in *Immortality*, where Bernard's father, the politician Bertrand Bertrand, exhibits his love for life by fighting against abortion and euthanasia (116). In Kundera's view, the fact that Agnes does not identify herself with mankind or with the human condition is not a flaw or a sign of pathological alienation requiring a psychological explanation, but a possibility of human existence realized in the contemporary world. The lack of identification with mankind reappears in *Identity* in Chantal, when she feels that her little son's death sets her free from all bonds with mankind; she is now free to dislike the world (55).

Agnes feels that she has ceased to love the world because it has become ugly (*Immortality* 22–23). Existence thus lacks an aesthetic justification, which, according to Nietzsche, is the only possible justification for it. People no longer even strive for beauty, as evinced for example by the intolerable noise and the acoustic ugliness reigning in the streets. For Agnes, a metaphor for the deliberate ugliness and senselessness of our present world is a motorcycle with its muffler removed (23). She feels that a world in which people no longer even strive for beauty has lost its sense and measure and that the world has reached a border beyond which everything threatens to turn into madness. From Kundera's point of view, Agnes is right in refusing to be part of the world. Unconditional approval of life means accepting the lack of freedom in the Creator's machinery, giving up our right to judge and "voluntarily fall[ing] back into the Creator's web" (286). Human beings can maintain their dignity only by clinging to their right to accept or reject. Is there, then, in a world which has turned ugly, still something that can save humanity from the meaninglessness of existence?

Agnes thinks that "only one thing could wrench her out of it: concrete love towards a concrete person. If she truly loved someone, she could not be indifferent to the fate of other people because her beloved would be dependent on that fate, he would be part of it, and she could no longer feel that mankind's torments, its wars and holidays, were none of her concern" (44). Agnes could embrace love if she encountered it and thereby come to approve of existence or of some essential part of it, or at least to have an interest in it. But if she never meets love, this chance is nonexistent: "How to live in a world with which you disagree? How to live with people, when you share neither their suffering nor their joys? When you know that you don't belong among them? Agnes is driving low a quiet road in her car and she answers herself: love or the cloister" (286). The "cloister" refers to renunciation of the world. Agnes has already internally renounced humanity; the cloister means taking the final steps needed to leave the world overtly as well. Agnes says to herself that she has arrived at the same point as Stendhal's hero Fabrice, at the end of *The Charterhouse of Parma*, who sees the alternatives left to him as either the realization of love or retiring from the world into a monastery. These alternatives may sound romantic, and indeed they are, but not in the sentimental sense that Kundera associates with Romanticism. The love that Fabrice or Agnes are talking about is not the sentimental being in love with love, which is what romantic love means in Kundera's understanding.

It is evident that Kundera agrees with his heroine that most people never encounter love, since most of those who think that they love someone do not really do so. The test question which Agnes comes up with is whether a person would choose to live his or her next life with or without the beloved one. The question is a modification of Nietzsche's idea of the eternal return of the same. Now we are not asked whether we would be willing to live our life over again innumerable times, but whether we would be willing to live with our love repeatedly, over and over again. Agnes realizes that she would answer the question in the negative, which implies that her love for Paul is rather the wish to love than love itself. Thus, she is denied the possibility of oneness with humanity through love. The only alternative left to her is retirement from the world, that is, the cloister. Indeed, she decides to leave her husband and daughter and to move to Switzerland, which for her means nature, mountains, and an absence of people.

Shortly before the fatal car crash, caused by a girl who has likewise "lost the world" (282) and who intended to commit suicide by sitting down on a highway lane in the dark, Agnes travels around in Switzerland, her native country, where she particularly feels the presence of her father. Here she finds a silence that reaches beyond herself: "She lay there [in the grass] for a long time and had the feeling that the stream was flowing into her, washing away all her pain and dirt: washing away her self. A special, unforgettable moment: she was forgetting her self, losing her self, she was without a self; and that was happiness" (287). The experience is evidence, Agnes believes, that "what is unbearable in life is not *being* but *being one's self* . . . Living, there is no happiness in that. Living: carrying one's painful self through the world.

But being, being is happiness. Being: becoming a fountain, a fountain on which the universe falls like warm rain" (288). In her search for an authentic self and an authentic mode of existence, Agnes ends up paradoxically with an existence without a self, dissolving into the universe and leaving the ego behind. Disavowing the "painful self" as described here is a process of de-individuation, which in this case means merging not with the human community but, more radically, with nature, with the universe (289). The experience is evoked in different versions by the Romantics, for whom de-individuation may be reached in Dionysian ecstasy, in dissolving in the infinity of existence in a mystical experience, or in death (see Frank, *Der kommende Gott* 275).

Agnes rediscovers the vanished beauty of the world when she discards her self in the silence of death. She has a presentiment of the beauty of nonbeing, which she has discovered in Goethe's poem "Über allen Gipfeln." It is a poem she had recited as a child with her father, even trying to march to its rhythm. Only at her father's deathbed does she understand that it is death that is described in the poem with such captivating beauty. Already in *The Book of Laughter and Forgetting*, Kundera speaks of the beauty of nonbeing, which Novalis claims to be sweetly bluish in color (236); in other connections, too, super-terrestrial beauty is described by Kundera as bluish in color, as, for instance, the happiness Ludvik feels in his love for Lucie (*The Joke* [1969] 75), or, according to Bertlef, the celestial light that a saint radiates in meditating (*Farewell Waltz* 113). However, since for Kundera, unlike the Romantics, human life is without transcendence, "blue" and "beauty" are not attributes of death itself, but merely attributes of the idea of death in a living person's mind. The presentiment of the beauty of death arises only in contrast with the experience of life, which appears as gray, meaningless, and ugly. Imagining death as a wonderful, blue peace represents most profoundly, but at the same time with playful irony, the worthlessness of life.

The possibilities of a meaningful life which Kundera examined earlier, for instance, in *The Unbearable Lightness of Being*, namely hedonism, aestheticism, and love, are taken up again in *Immortality*, but now each one yields a negative result. Hedonism does not sustain, the pursuit of beauty is no longer possible in a world that has grown ugly, and unless one happens to encounter authentic love, love cannot give one's life meaning either. This loss of all possibilities of meaningful existence for an individual is paralleled by the social or collective loss of meaningfulness, through the disappearance of History.

Hedonism is re-examined in *Immortality* in the case of the man called Rubens. The theme of eroticism is combined in his story with the theme of the temporality of human existence. For the first time, eroticism is not described as a relatively immutable state of affairs, as in the case of the man in his forties in *Life is Elsewhere*, Bertlef in *Farewell Waltz*, Tomas in *The Unbearable Lightness of Being*, or any of the other womanizers in Kundera's novels and short stories. Now eroticism is methodically scrutinized as a life-long project, one which may include quite dramatic changes. Rubens wanted to be a painter, but he failed the entrance examination for the Academy of Fine Arts. Whether he was insufficiently talented or failed because the world we live in is no longer favorable to the fine arts is a question that the author-narrator raises but leaves unanswered. Rubens himself concludes from his failure that "fate was trying to show him where his life's centre of gravity really lay: not in public life but in private, not in the pursuit of professional success but in success with women" (313); in other words, he chooses "life" instead of painting. As a consequence of this choice, he is connected by a single thread with the main storyline, since one of his lovers is Agnes (the structure resembles the manner in which the man in his forties is joined with the main story in *Life Is Elsewhere*). Rubens, however, seems not to have been especially important to her, since he is not even mentioned in the parts concerning Agnes. In the few scenes in Rubens's story where Agnes makes an appearance, the idea crops up again that the core of eroticism is the erotic excitement that is connected to the sense of shame. Agnes is old-fashioned in the sense that in an erotic situation she is ashamed of her bodily existence. Eventually, what remains alive in Rubens's memory as beautiful images are precisely a few moments spent with her.

Having gathered ample experience in multitudinous erotic relationships, in his marriage Rubens wants to live through the sentimental idea of love. Yet the attempt fails, and after his divorce Rubens decides that he has to lead his erotic life "beyond the border of love" (33). This decision turns him into a "pure" hedonist: he is now searching for meaningfulness in his erotic relationships, which are "beyond love." Unlike Tomas, however, he is not interested in the individual differences between women in the act of love, but in different forms of eroticism at a much more general level. This appears in his division of his erotic experiences into five different phases according to the different modes of lovemaking. The period of "athletic muteness" in making physical love is followed by a "period of metaphors," in which the sexual act and the sexual organs are spoken of in "a gentle diminutive or a poetic paraphrase" (307) and by a "period of obscene truth," in which direct language is used, as well as a "period of Chinese Whispers," in which phrases heard from a partner in lovemaking are passed on in the next relationship. This phase leads to the fifth and final period, the "mystical period" of his erotic life, in which Rubens loses the illusion of lovemaking as a moment of absolute intimacy between two individuals and becomes aware of the fact that every one of us actually takes part in the great common stream of erotic images: "An individual does not receive a share of indecent fantasy from a lover by means of Chinese Whispers, but by means of this impersonal (or super-personal or sub-personal) stream. To say that this river that runs through us is impersonal means that it does not belong to us but to him who created us and made it flow within us; in other words, that it belongs to God or even that it is God or one of his incarnations" (310–11). The erotic experience is now characterized as mystical, since it is a kind of merging with God, with something given in the world order independent of the individual (311). But when not only the body but also erotic imagery—which supplies the erotic experience with meaning—is not the creation of an individual, this implies that eroticism as a whole is unable to offer an escape from the Creator's machinery. Eroticism annihilates the individual, instead of providing life with authentic, individual meanings.

One day Rubens has to face the fact that he no longer knows why he is performing the same movements of lovemaking again and again. What Jan in *The Book of Laughter and Forgetting* feared has now taken place: the movements have lost their meaning. Repetition has become pure reiteration without the variations that would make it meaningful. Kundera expresses this through the metaphor of Rubens having landed in his erotic life in a terrain "outside the dial's time," where nothing remarkable ever happens any more (358). This leads Rubens to look back and ask what was meaningful in all his past erotic experiences and he has to realize that there are only a few beautiful moments he can vividly recall. Memory has sorted the incidents, picking out only some of them as meaningful, and has done so following criteria of which he was unaware at the moment of the experience: "seven, eight fragments of less than a second each, that's what remained in his memory of his entire erotic life to which he had once decided to devote all his strength and talent" (350). But even these images, two of which involve Agnes, become mutilated when Rubens hears about Agnes's death. The image of her lying in a coffin or of her corpse being burnt is mingled with the erotic images and conceals them. Rubens, who had thought that in choosing eroticism he had chosen "life," ends up with the image of death and with the vanishing of the memory of the few meaningful moments which had remained from that life.

While part 6 focuses on the "anthropological" difficulties of hedonism as a way of life, other parts of the novel deal with the difficulties of hedonism arising from conditions in the contemporary world. As mentioned above, in *Slowness,* a reason for the difficulty of hedonism is found in the haste that is characteristic of the contemporary lifestyle; on the nudist beach in *The Book of Laughter and Forgetting* the disappearance of the feeling of shame was pointed out as the reason for the vanishing of eroticism and this reason is mentioned in *Immortality* as well (331–32). In addition, imagology appears as an enemy of hedonism. Avenarius says to the author's alter ego that in our contemporary world appearance takes priority over actual erotic pleasure. Let us assume that men were asked whether they would prefer spending a secret night of lovemaking with Rita Hayworth or alternatively walking arm-in-arm with her publicly. Although most men would say that they prefer the first alternative, the opposite is in fact true: "Because all of them are eager for admiration and not for pleasure. For appearance and not for reality. Reality no longer means anything to anyone" (385). Here, "reality" refers to private experience, which remains hidden from others; however, under the rule of imagology, this has become less important—less "real"—than appearance in the eyes of others.

The aesthetic attitude toward life similarly proves to be a difficult option in our contemporary world. Singling out beautiful things and moments still takes place in *Immortality*. Instances of the beautiful include, for example, the calm in Agnes's soul after her father's death (29) and the gesture of the wave of the hand by the elderly woman (40). The author-narrator writes that death and immortality make a beautiful pair (the word "beautiful" [*beau*], however, appears only in the French original *L'Immortalité* [85]), names of trees—"chestnut," "poplar," "maple"—are beautiful (80), Bertrand Bertrand's name is beautiful as a lullaby (99), erotic orgies, the female body, and Beethoven's music are beautiful, and the cat is given attributes of beauty and "constancy of charm" (111). Collecting beautiful moments, however, is made difficult by the fact that beauty and the aspiration to it are losing ground in the contemporary world. Visual and acoustic ugliness have accumulated to a degree never seen or heard before, and changing attitudes have robbed beauty of its previous position. At the beginning of the novel, Agnes walks in the street and becomes aware of how the sound landscape is ravaged by the noise of cars, motorcycles, and drills workers use repairing the street. Suddenly from somewhere above, "like from the sky," a Bach piano fugue is heard: "Someone on a top floor had evidently opened a window and turned up the volume all the way, so that Bach's severe beauty sounded a warning to a world that had gone awry. However, Bach's fugue was no match for the pneumatic drills and cars" (24–25).

Visual ugliness has become as acceptable, and as ubiquitously present, as acoustic ugliness. Agnes looks at the passers-by and sees "in front of her a woman dressed in baggy trousers barely reaching the knees, as was the fashion that year. The outfit seemed to make her behind even heavier and closer the ground. Her bare, pale calves resembled a pair of rustic pitchers decorated by varicose veins entwined like a ball of tiny blue snakes. Agnes said to herself: that woman could have found a dozen outfits that would have covered her bluish veins and made her behind less monstrous. Why hadn't she done so? Not only have people stopped trying to be attractive when they are out among other people, but they are not longer even trying not to look ugly!" (22). In Kundera's aestheticist thinking it is justified to expect people—despite the opposition between body and soul he suggests—to make an effort at a pleasant appearance. The same holds for the concealment of bodily functions. Looking through the window of a fast-food place, Agnes shudders:

> Through the window she saw people sitting at tables, hunched over greasy paper plates. Her eye came to rest on a girl with a very pale complexion and bright red lips. She had just finished her lunch, pushed aside her empty cup of Coca-Cola, leaned her head back, and stuck her index finger deep into her mouth; she kept twisting it inside for a long time, staring at the ceiling. The man at the next table slouched in his chair, his glance fixed on the street and his mouth wide open. It was a yawn without beginning or end, a yawn as endless as a Wagner melody: at times his mouth began to close but never entirely; it just kept opening wide again and again, while his eyes, fixed on the street, kept opening and closing counter to the rhythm of his mouth. Actually, several other people were also yawning, showing teeth, fillings, crowns, dentures, and not one of them covered his mouth with his hand. (21)

Here we see once again Kundera's detestation of bodily functions. Whenever the body is not "fleetingly redeemed" in the moment of erotic excitement (109), modesty requires to hide bodily functions. Peculiar to Kundera is his disgust at the digestive system and especially at its initial opening, the mouth (about this, see also ch. 8), but the eye too—traditionally considered the window of the soul—is depicted as mechanically staring. In *Identity* it is described as a mechanical apparatus that opens and shuts and is supplied with a cleansing system (10–11, 90, 98).

Agnes thinks that the past world was more beautiful, quieter, and more modest than the present one. This view is supported by Avenarius's claim that in the cities beautiful buildings from the past are no longer properly visible because of the congestion of people and cars on the streets. One cannot stop on the crowded sidewalk to look closely at a church. The only thing one can do is to glance at it while passing by, but even in these glances cars are constantly present: "The church of Saint-Germain-des-Prés has disappeared and all the churches in towns have disappeared in the same way, like the moon when it enters an eclipse. The cars that fill the streets have narrowed the pavements, which are crowded with pedestrians. If they want to look at each other, they see cars in the background, if they want to look at the buildings across the street they see cars in the foreground; there isn't a single angle of view from which cars will not be visible, from the back, in front, on both sides. Their omnipresent noise corrodes every moment of contemplation like an acid. Cars have made the former beauty of cities invisible" (271).

Rubens endorses the idea of the growing ugliness of the present world as well, pondering why in classic art the human face was never depicted laughing. Apollo or Aphrodite never laughed, but in the contemporary media politicians and public figures are constantly smiling or laughing, showing their teeth. This does not promote beauty, since "undoubtedly, a face is beautiful because it reveals the presence of thought, whereas at the moment of laughter man does not think" (361). Although laughter is preceded by a thought that identifies something as comical, it comes after it as a bodily reaction, no longer involving any thought at all. Rubens concludes that "the convulsion of laughter (a state beyond reason and will) has been raised by contemporary people into an ideal image behind which they have decided to conceal themselves" (362). It is noteworthy how Kundera, who praises jeering laughter, at this point goes so far in his dualistic thinking as to accept even comicality only as a thought, not as its bodily counterpart, laughter. Rubens sees Agnes as belonging to the past world, in which beauty did not laugh (361) and Agnes herself thinks that when the world has rejected beauty, the only option left will be to buy a single tiny forget-me-not as a memento of that lost beauty and to stare at its light blue corolla in walking in the streets (23). With the forget-me-not, a variation on the Romantics' blue flower of longing (see Boden, *Irritation* 125), Kundera is again alluding to Novalis and the otherworldliness of beauty in the present world.

In a world hostile to hedonism and beauty, the individual who is not saved by love is threatened by the loss of meaningfulness. The ensuing weightlessness resembles death in that nothing meaningful ever happens. The same occurs under the reign of imagology on the level of society: humankind has left History (of world, nations) behind and nothing new ever happens. The only changes that take place are vacillations to and fro; thus, the modern adventure of humanity has come to an end. We have reached a state beyond History, described in *The Art of the Novel* as follows: "The planet is moving through the void without any master. There it is, the unbearable lightness of being" (41).

Kundera's thoughts about the end of History remain sketchy. He is of course not the only one to declare the end of History; the idea is common in postmodern thinking (see, e.g., Calinescu; Foucault, "Archeology"; Harvey; Jameson; Saariluoma [Steinby], *Der postindividualistische*). It is a matter of rejecting the concept of history that arose at the end of the eighteenth century, the optimistic faith in historical progress and in a future that would bring a better world. Kundera's faith in History, however, collapsed through a process dissimilar to that faced by the theoreticians of postmodernism, since he himself participated in a political movement that endeavored to create a better world but failed. It is of course possible to speculate that poststructuralist and postmodern thought derives from a similar political frustration in the aftermath of the revolutionary movements of 1968 in West Europe as that Kundera witnessed in Czechoslovakia after the 1948 revolution; as we have seen, Kundera himself draws a parallel between these two "revolutions." It goes without saying, moreover, that Francis Fukuyama's optimistic interpretation of the "end of history"—History has become futile because the present liberalistic-democratic society satisfies all essential human needs (see, however, Fukuyama's revision of his argumentation in *The End of History* in his 2012 article "The Future of History")—is far from Kundera's, whose view of contemporary Western society is gloomy. Rather than a paradise, the contemporary world appears to him as a trap which allows individuals little space to shape their existence according to their own will. Ultimately, in the age of imagology, the last shadow of hope of change has vanished and the trap in which the individual is caught closes so tightly that no freedom, and therefore no meaningfulness, is left to him or her at all.

In *Testaments Betrayed* Kundera writes that "the words 'the end of history' have never stirred me to anguish or displeasure" (16). This is to be read as a comment on the horrors following from the efforts to steer the process of History. Yet Kundera adds that "applied to art, that same phrase, 'the end of history,' strikes me with terror" (17); however, this is exactly what he thinks has happened in the last few decades. As noted above, already in *The Art of the Novel* Kundera conceives of the history of the world as having become hostile to the arts. At the end of the essay on Broch, he observes that "in Broch, there is the melancholy awareness of a history drawing to a close in circumstances that are profoundly hostile to the evolution of art and of the novel in particular" (67). Kundera does not comment on this in any way, but in standing at the end of the essay the observation is given special weight and one cannot avoid thinking that the view attributed to Broch concurs with Kundera's own. In another essay in *The Art of the Novel* he claims that the history of the novel ended in "Communist Russia," where novels no longer made any new discoveries (14–15), and in the concluding essay of *The Art of the Novel*, "Jerusalem Address: The Novel and Europe," he seems to be talking about the novel and its history in the past tense only. In *The Book of Laughter and Forgetting*, the novel was predicted to disappear in an era of general graphomania, where meaningless chatter has superseded the exploration of existence. Imagology—with its focus on influencing public opinion—is likewise in opposition to the novel, which resists all forms of simplification. In *The Book of Laughter and Forgetting*, the ending of the history of music is depicted as a return to the starting point of banal melody and the simplest rhythm. In part 6 of *Immortality*, Kundera reflects with Rubens upon a situation in which painting has reached a point beyond its history. Just as Rubens's erotic experiences first reveal to him interesting and important insights into the phenomenon of eroticism, similarly the history of painting consists of a splendid series of new discoveries. However, where the painters of the nineteenth and the first half of the twentieth century "all knew that they were blazing a trail into the unknown" (320), this, according to Kundera, is not the case with contemporary painting, where no new discoveries are made, but "already discovered discoveries" are rediscovered time and again (321). Kundera concludes by saying that "midnight had struck on the dial of European art" (321) in which nothing new and significant ever happens any longer—just as in Rubens's erotic life. The end of the history of painting means a shift from repetition in significant variations to repetition without any significant difference. There are still masses of painters, but nothing new and significant is produced any longer (358).

Kundera's idea of the continued existence of the novel or painting beyond their histories resembles Hegel's idea of the death of the arts. According to Hegel, art in the contemporary world—that is to say, the world at the beginning of the nineteenth century—is no longer important, since it has lost its former position as the most complete expression of the Absolute, or the totality of existence, which has now been taken over by religion and philosophy. Things being thus, one can now speak of the arts in the proper sense of the word in the past tense only. It is true that new works of art are continuously being produced in abundance, yet they no longer capture the totality but only some separate element (see, e.g.; Hegel I: 10,11, 103). Unlike Hegel and Broch, Kundera has never considered the novel as something striving for totality, but he always emphasizes that the novel is in search of particular truths and even these are conceived of as only provisionally, hypothetically valid; however, he agrees with Hegel and Broch that the novel uncovers things of which we were not aware of. What makes Kundera's view the death of art more pessimistic than Hegel is that while for Hegel philosophy in modern times assumes a function previously belonging to the arts, Kundera thinks that abstract thinking cannot supplant art, in particular the novel, as a form of exploration of human existence. In accordance with the line of aesthetic thinking from the early Romantics to Heidegger, Gadamer, Adorno, and Broch, Kundera thinks that the arts can reveal something about humankind's being in the world that no other form of knowledge, such as the philosophical or the scientific, can uncover. If art has abandoned its task of saving human existence from the "oblivion of being," as according to Kundera has happened in our contemporary world, there is thus no other institution or human activity to take its place.

Does Kundera, then, not see in our contemporary world any gleam of hope? The last part of *Immortality* deals with hope and hopelessness in a light tone. The topic announced in the title of the final part, "The Celebration," may conceal from the reader the novel's ultimate tone of resignation or at least soften it. In this part, as already noted, Kundera's alter ego is sitting by the swimming pool with his friend professor Avenarius celebrating the completion of his novel *Immortality*. Here he also meets Paul and Laura, and the reader has a chance to get a glimpse into their married life. The reader has already encountered Avenarius's hobby of pricking holes in the tires of cars, which is his way of "fighting Diabolum" (255), that is, anything that is ultimately worthless or unacceptable in human life—even if he knows that this fight is useless. "Kundera" agrees with him: as one can no longer take the world seriously, the only reasonable way to act is to start jesting about the world in its entirety. We might say that Avenarius represents the existential possibility of distancing ourselves from all possibilities available to humanity by refusing to take the world, including ourselves, seriously, seeing it from the point of view of ridicule and play. Instead of talking about Avenarius's "existential situation," Kundera argues that the individual's deepest foundation, as expressed by the German word *Grund* ("ground," "base") which determines his or her deeds and actions, can be expressed only metaphorically. Avenarius's metaphor is a melancholy child, who for lack of a younger brother plays with the whole of the world (387). Playing with and ridiculing the world in its entirety, however, is difficult because "humour can only exist when people are still capable of recognizing some border between the important and the unimportant. And nowadays this border has become unrecognizable" (372). This is why jesting about the world in its entirety is deeply melancholic: it does not connect the jester with the world but rather separates him from it. Avenarius answers to his friend's reflections by calling him his younger brother. This is appropriate, since in his jokes Kundera—both the author "Kundera" in *Immortality* and the real author behind the novels I have been discussing—has the same tone of ultimate desperation. Kundera already commented on this attitude with regard to Eduard in "Eduard and God," saying that not being able to take the world seriously is an abyss (see Biron 11).

Paul tells his friends about his marriage to Laura. She constantly quarrels with her stepdaughter, and Paul is caught in between the two women, both of whom he loves. Kundera's alter ego in the novel observes that to alleviate his distress, Paul has started drinking. Laura makes an appearance at the swimming pool and when she, in leaving, uses the attractive gesture described at the beginning of the novel, Paul's countenance brightens up. He philosophizes about women as the last hope of man: "Either woman will become man's future or mankind will perish, because only woman is capable of nourishing within her an unsubstantiated hope and inviting us to a doubtful future, which we would have long ceased to believe in were it not for women" (383). He ends with a quotation, both grandiloquent and playful, from Goethe: "Das Ewigweibliche zieht uns hinan! The eternal feminine draws us on!" (384). The quotation is from the concluding scene in *Faust*, which Nietzsche travesties in a well-known mock version. It may be that Kundera does not count on his readers' knowledge of this poem, but I do not doubt that for himself as an admirer of Nietzsche, not only the original work by Goethe but also Nietzsche's travesty of it are implicit in the end of the novel. In the travestied poem the Chorus mysticus greets Faust's entrance into heaven after his rescue from the clutches of the devil: "All things corruptible / Are but a parable; / Earth's insufficiency / Here finds fulfilment; / Here the ineffable / Wins life through love; / Eternal womanhood / Leads us above" (Goethe, *Faust II* 288). Nietzsche's poem is the first one in the appendix to *The Gay Science* called "Songs of Prince Vogelfrei," and it is entitled "To Goethe": "The ever-enduring / is merely your parable! / God the all-blurring / your fiction unbearable . . . // World-wheel, the turning one / spawns goals each day: / Fate—sighs the yearning one, / the fool calls it—play. // World-play, the ruling one, / blends truth and tricks:— / The eternally fooling one / blends *us*—in the mix!" (249). The quotation from Goethe is also carnivalized by Kundera not only because seeking salvation in woman must appear to him—as to the reader familiar with his criticism of the Romantic search for the eternal feminine in every woman—as an extreme form of sentimental attitude, but also because the reader notices that Laura has actually addressed her attractive feminine greeting not to her husband but to Avenarius, who is her secret lover. Thus both hope, represented by Paul, and desperation and melancholy, represented by Avenarius, are ridiculed. This lightens the impression the ending of the novel makes, but it does not really take away anything of the novel's ultimate pessimism.

Chapter Ten
The End of Modernity, the End of the Novel?

In 1989, communist rule ceased to exist in Poland, the German Democratic Republic, Czechoslovakia, Hungary, Romania, and Bulgaria. The Berlin Wall was torn down and the following year the two German states were reunited. In 1991, the Soviet Union fell apart and what remained reassumed its old name of Russia. At the beginning of 1993 Czechoslovakia split into two independent states, the Czech Republic and Slovakia. The Cold War ended along with the end of Soviet rule in Central and East Europe, itself a consequence of World War II. Kundera's career as a novelist had started just when the Soviet empire came over Prague, foreshadowing, as he thought, the death of Europe. How did he react to this unexpected turn of events? Did the Czech Velvet Revolution of 1989 and other developments in Central and East European countries indicate for him the beginning of a new European adventure? I think not. His views, as expressed in his works after 1989, remain essentially the same. The idea of the trap of History, a vein that runs through all of his novelistic work ever since *The Joke*, was supplemented in *Immortality* by the anthropological trap, in which humankind finds itself caught from the very beginning and which thwarts an autonomous and authentic mode of existence. Tantamount to a declaration that the adventures of modern humanity have ended, this is Kundera's final message, his testament. The events which reshaped the political map of Europe have not moved him to reconsider his views of History and the possibilities available to the individual. I argue that already prior to these developments Kundera came to hold the conviction that humankind's existence has to be examined outside of History and thus his thinking was not affected by these most recent historical upheavals.

Since *Immortality*, Kundera has written three short novels: *Slowness* (1994), *Identity* (1998), and *Ignorance* (2000). In these novels themes familiar from his previous works are resumed and developed in new variations. Among the most important insights presented in these novels, I would say, are new perspectives upon the temporality of human existence. As a whole, Kundera's outlook has become even gloomier, more resigned, and more cynical than in his previous works, betraying a tedium of life and an aversion toward his fellow humans. Decay and mortality, as essential aspects of human existence along with death, are all pervasive, particularly in

Identity and *Ignorance*. In this chapter, I discuss these novels and I then return, as a form of conclusion, to Kundera's understanding of the existence of modern humanity and of the novel. Finally, I offer a tentative answer to the question of how Kundera might be viewed as a European novelist and thinker, as indeed he himself wishes to be viewed and understood.

The temporality of human existence and death

Compared to Kundera's previous novels, *Slowness*, *Identity,* and *Ignorance* are simple in their structure and their succinctness is paralleled by a new brevity of sentence structure (see Scarpetta xi; Woods, *Translating* 121). The title word in each novel is an abstract noun, which again might be expected to identify the main theme of the novel or at least one of them. However, "slowness," "identity," and "ignorance"—unlike, for example, "lightness" or "forgetting"—are not names for the existential problem of a character. Slowness, according to Kundera, is a prerequisite of hedonism, one possible way of being in the world, but whether it exists or not is more a matter of an era than something characterizing an individual's life. In Kundera's view, identity is not a possibility of human existence either, but rather the main issue with which the novel has been preoccupied throughout its history. In *Identity*, the fragility of the individual's identity is explored once again, with a new emphasis on the temporal dimension of life. In *Ignorance*, the title refers to two different things, both of which are considered necessary components of human life. On the one hand, "ignorance" refers to people's reluctance to know about one another, for instance, what an emigrant has experienced during the decades he has lived outside his home country (e.g., 109–10). In general, people do not bother listening to their partner in a conversation, but prefer talking themselves. On the other hand, "ignorance" refers to the fact that the individual is forced to make the most important decisions of his or her life in youth, when still ignorant as to their possible repercussions, in fact before even knowing anything about life in general (163–64). Thus, ignorance pertains to two themes with which we are familiar from Kundera's previous novels, namely, graphomania or the demanding of the "ear" of others, discussed especially in *The Book of Laughter and Forgetting*, and inexperience as an unavoidable dimension of human existence, one of the themes in *The Unbearable Lightness of Being*. In *Ignorance*, the theme of ignorance is developed especially in connection with émigré(e)s who are weighing the possibility of return, and more generally in the context of the temporal dimension of an individual's life.

The emphasis on the temporal dimension of life in Kundera's late novels does not mean that he now returns to the biographical mode of narration; his manner of writing is as elliptical and thematic as in his previous works. What it does mean is that things are now different according to their position in the total time span of human life. It also means that his characters themselves become aware of the temporal dimension of their experiences, as was already the case in the Rubens part in *Immortality*. Moreover, the individuals in his novels come increasingly to represent the common human destiny. Aging, forgetting and the selectivity of memory, being trapped in a body, and mortality are no longer examined as the existential problems of particular individuals, but appear more directly as inescapable aspects of human existence.

As I discuss in chapter 5, in *Slowness,* three stories are intermingled. The first deals with a visit by the author and his wife to a French château converted into a hotel, the second comprises certain incidents in the entomologists' conference in the author's story, which he is just conceiving and which he places at the same hotel, and the third is the eighteenth-century novella by Vivant Denon about a chevalier's night of love, which the author also imagines as having taken place at the same château. The novella, entitled *No Tomorrow*, tells of a young chevalier who, guided by the more experienced lady of the house, undergoes a one-night amorous adventure of extraordinary beauty. Looking back at the events of the night the following morning, the young chevalier is convinced that the most important thing is to retain the beauty of the encounter in his recollection, paying no heed to how he appears in the eyes of those few who know about the rendezvous and its embarrassing aspects—that the chevalier was used to cover up the actual lover of the lady. In contrast, the modern counterpart of the chevalier, the young entomologist Vincent, is unable to fully devote himself to an amorous adventure, because for him what is more important is how he appears in the eyes of others. In the end, Vincent's wish for an erotic adventure—or possibly even a relationship—does not come true: he only makes it as far as the pretended movements of sexual intercourse with the girl at the swimming pool under the eyes of a Czech entomologist, who is astonished by the habits of Westerners. At dawn Vincent flees on his motorcycle trying to forget what has happened. The motorcycle here represents noise and haste, which remove everything from sight but the empty present moment.

In *Slowness*, the seeking of pleasure as a way of life, that is, hedonism, appears as a possibility no longer available to contemporary individuals. This is so because today we prefer appearance to reality: as already stated by professor Avenarius in *Immortality*, everyone would prefer boasting publicly about a relationship with a beautiful woman to actually possessing her in secrecy. In *Slowness*, another cause of the impossibility of hedonism is given in the hurried tempo of the contemporary world. This haste means that we are interested only in "orgasms," moments of ecstasy without duration; we have lost our sense of the beautiful form of an experience, such as a beautiful night of love as a whole. Conceiving the beautiful form of an experience takes time, but only an experience which has a form can be recollected: "Imposing form on a period of time is what beauty demands, but so does memory. For what is formless cannot be grasped, or committed to memory" (34). Thus, giving beautiful form to an amorous night is precious, because it preserves for us a delightful recollection.

The main tone in *Slowness* is regret for the vanishing of the possibility of hedonism, as expressed in the author's anticlimactic series of questions: "Can the ideal of hedonism be realized? Does that hope exist? Or at least some feeble gleam of that hope?" (121). Apart from hedonism, laughter in its most extreme form, where it turns to desperation—that is, ridicule of the world in its entirety—is also resumed as a theme in *Slowness*. The author's wife warns him not to write a novel "with not a single serious word in it," because "seriousness kept you safe. The lack of seriousness will leave you naked to the wolves" (78). We know from Avenarius in *Immortality* that when one cannot take anything in the world seriously, this means the most profound melancholy or an "abyss" (see Biron 11). Now a new aspect is added to the issue by the warning concerning readers' reactions: they would attack "like wolves" an author representing the world as a whole as something that cannot be taken seriously. The change in Kundera's relationship with his readers is striking. Instead of inviting readers to join him in his adventures in discovering new truths, his "final truth" not only makes any further search futile for himself, but is even expected to render his readers hostile to him.

In *Identity* another matter of fundamental significance for Kundera's modern humankind, namely our individual identity, is questioned once again. Jean-Marc feels that his beloved is in danger of losing her identity in his eyes; this would mean the end of their love, which alone makes his existence meaningful. Chantal is compelled to take on a false identity in her work at an advertising agency, because she cannot identify with her employer's goals and worldview. At work she is another person, someone different from the one whom he loves, and Jean-Marc notices that "between the moment he meets her again [in her office] and the moment he recognizes her for the woman he loves, he has some distance to go" (34). Moreover, Jean-Marc is shocked when he realizes that at a distance he has confused an old woman with his beloved. He asks what would happen if one day he were incapable of distinguishing Chantal from others: then the only bond connecting him with humankind would be severed, and things would completely lose their meaning for him (81). Jean-Marc's fear of not recognizing his beloved indicates that in *Identity* love is no longer conceived of as an exploration of the infinity of the thoughts and experiences of the beloved, which would prevent the beloved from disappearing among others. When identity is sought on the basis of a momentary perception, it becomes frail.

Chantal is passionately attached to the present, where her love resides, and does not want to think about the past—including a previous marriage—or the future. She is upset by her dreams, which annihilate the difference between her past and the valuable, cherished present (6). Here "present" does not of course refer to a passing moment, but to a relatively stable state of affairs from which the past is excluded. As in the case of Tomas and Tereza, love is here set within the temporal frame of an individual's life, and is valued as the most important part of it. Previous experiences, however, form part of the setting for the present state of affairs. Chantal feels that the death of her son has on the one hand made her free not to care about the world, which she dislikes (55); on the other hand, her love for Jean-Marc can be absolute only in the absence of her son (38–39). Thus, the preconditions for her present love lie in the past. At the end of the novel, Chantal experiences a kind of loss of her past, and with it her personal identity. She remembers her youthful dream of sharing herself with men like the fragrance of a rose. She muses about love being like a prison or a cloister, which isolates the individual from others by prohibiting him or her from yielding sexually to whomever she or he wants to (130). She travels to London accompanied by her coworkers, with Jan-Marc following her in the same train. Soon she finds herself in a house where she is stripped of her clothes and deprived of her name and her past. As a substitute, "life" is offered, understood (as in Rubens's case in *Immortality*) as the mere present moment, a moment of sexual excitement. She reacts with a cry of horror that awakens her from a nightmare in her own bed. The author ends the novel with a question: from what point onward were the events of the narrative merely part of a dream, and whose dream was it? The dream, which Chantal has already accused of annihilating the difference between past and present, now no longer means a free display of her identity, but on the contrary may turn into a nightmare of losing her identity.

Consequently, neither love nor dream functions any longer as a guarantee of identity. The fundamental necessity of personal identity is indicated by the fact that Chantal reacts to the idea of a mere present, cut off from her identity and from all her past experience, with a scream of horror. But identity is not threatened only by the loss of the past; it is threatened by the future as well. Already in Kundera's earlier works, especially in *Immortality*, the fact of corporeality constitutes a threat to human identity. In *Identity*, the aging of the body is for the first time presented as both an experience and a devastating fact; in the earlier novels, elderly women (as well as fat ones) appeared as grotesque, while for men aging (or corpulence, as in professor Avenarius) was no issue at all. Even before Chantal's identity is threatened by aging—the novel starts with the menopausal symptoms from which she suffers—Jean-Marc had dropped his medical studies because "he was incapable of looking squarely at death; shortly thereafter he acknowledged that the truth was even worse: he was incapable of looking squarely at a body: its inescapable, un-responding imperfection; the decomposition clock that governs its functioning; its blood, its guts, its pain" (62–63). In a body, there is very little space for the soul (98); after all, does a human being have any alternative other than living the basic life which is tied to the body? We are condemned to the functions of digestion and procreation, doomed to eat, defecate and copulate, as long as our machinery allows it. Where, then, is the freedom of an individual? Chantal's boss at the advertising agency declares that it is the advertiser's task to beautify the inescapable life functions deriving from our corporeality: toilet paper, diapers, detergents, food have to appear inviting (132–33). Our freedom comprises only the choice between feeling happy or feeling desolate in submitting to what is unavoidable (134). The boss's words mean that in the contemporary world real beauty has been replaced by a fake beauty, produced by profit-seeking marketing experts. The Nietzschean idea of an aesthetic justification of life is here resumed, in grotesque, commercialized, and—through Kundera's irony—carnivalized form.

A life consisting of mere bodily functions—eating, drinking, copulating, defecating—generates boredom as its general feeling. If life is nothing but the repetition of meaningless functions of an organism, it is natural to think that humans are bored.

Jean-Marc's ponderings bring a historical dimension to the matter. He thinks that life in the modern world has become a "great common struggle against boredom" (16), because "the old occupations, at least most of them, where unthinkable without a passionate involvement: the peasants in love with their land; my grandfather, the magician of beautiful tables" (75), whereas nowadays people work for the money alone (Chantal being an example of this). Thus the common lot of human beings is now that life appears to them, as to Ludvik in the penal battalion, as a mere passing of time. For Jean-Marc, this boredom of life is expressed in the unarticulated, endlessly prolonged "ahhh" sound coming from the mouth of a dying person (74–75, 152).

Life without meaningfulness comes close to death, or even makes death appear more attractive than life. Jean-Marc realizes that he has always been fascinated by poems dealing with death; he recites Baudelaire's verses, in which the Earth is judged to be tedious and death, as the ship's captain, is asked to set off (28). For Chantal, in our modern world, "life" appears as the suspicious "king of words," surrounded by other great words such as "adventure," "future," and "hope" (28–29). For Chantal herself "future" is not a great word because she wants to live in the present and not think about the future in which she discerns only aging and death. She also acknowledges that she no longer cares about adventures: an adventure is a means of "embracing the world" and she "no longer wanted to embrace the world" (39).

In a scene at the beginning of the novel, where Jean-Marc visits a fatally ill former friend of his, the author remarks that the thought of death has made all other subjects of conversation meaningless (9). This can be extended to the whole of the novel. Where for Tomas and Tereza in *The Unbearable Lightness of Being,* man's mortality became visible as an inescapable aspect of human existence only through aging, for Jean-Marc the thought of death has been part of his love to Chantal from the very beginning (18)—probably simply because she is four years his senior. For Chantal, her blushing—originally a sign of erotic embarrassment, but now one of the menopausal symptoms—brings to mind a burning corpse (52). Before her own death comes to end everything, the death of her son has already put an end to her interest in the world. The last pages of the novel, where Chantal awakens from her nightmare in the arms of her beloved, only partly hide the fact that the possibilities of a meaningful life have one after the other been questioned and that the horizon of death has grown greater than that of life.

While love, the only thing that can still give life beauty and meaning, is presented as frail and constantly threatened by biological necessities and by the social constraints of life, friendship—which is highly valued both by Kundera himself and by many of his male characters—is in his three late novels set up as an illusion only. In *Slowness*, the possibilities of friendship in the contemporary world appear meager. Vincent and his friend Pontevin, like Jakub and Dr. Skreta in *Farewell Waltz*, view friendship as the only sacred value. Despite this, Pontevin does not hesitate to ridicule his friend in order to impress a beautiful woman (22–23). This is consistent with a world ruled by imagology. In *Identity*, this pessimism is carried to its cynical end. Jean-Marc dreams of a friendship which is placed above everything else, greater than truth, ideology, religion or nation—a friendship which Kundera elsewhere proclaims to be "perhaps the only virtue, perhaps the only one left" ("Umbrella" 45)—but he is afraid that this may have disappeared from the contemporary world. Chantal comments on this that the idea of such a friendship has never been anything but men's romanticism; women have never acknowledged it (44). Jean-Marc proposes a more "realistic" idea of friendship in the contemporary world: a friend functions as a witness of our past, whom we need to preserve our identity (11, 43). Chantal's suggestion is even more modest: a friend is not someone who dares to defend you when everyone else is accusing you; a friend is one who does not join the accusers but remains silent (46–47). In *Ignorance*, friendship is no longer an issue. No interest in one's life is expected even from those called friends: "people aren't interested in one another, it's normal" (168).

While *Slowness* and *Identity* are set in France, in *Ignorance* the main characters are Czechs who after the upheavals of 1989 are considering returning to their native country. At the beginning of the novel, the author-narrator expresses his surprise that the "Russian night," which was supposed to last forever, actually lasted only about twenty years. He contents himself with saying that back then—since about 1969—the occupation was thought of by everyone as the final destiny of the Czech nation and he does not go into whether this conception of the history and fate of the nation underwent any considerable changes during the following two decades (in an interview from the mid-1980s, Havel declares that the situation is now clearly different from that of the early 1970s: people are socially and culturally more active, creativity is more visible, freedom is greater [see Havel, *Disturbing* 181–86]). Although the assumption about the death of Europe in Czechoslovakia in 1968 turned out to be false, Kundera did not start reinterpreting historical events, because he had already lost interest in history. The assertion by the cynical Leroy in *Identity* is not refuted by Kundera: "Man is not capable of changing the world and will never change it. That is the fundamental conclusion of my experience as a revolutionary. A conclusion that is, incidentally, tacitly accepted by everybody" (127). Following the tendency already present in *Immortality*, in the three short novels, particularly in *Ignorance*, Kundera continues to explore the biological and social constraints which make human existence desolate. We can even say that rather than the death of Europe, which is a historical event, Kundera is now interested in the death of individuals and in death as the inescapable truth about human life in general.

The polar counter theme expressed in the title, namely, knowledge, is never mentioned in *Ignorance*, although this is the "theme word" of novelistic literature as a whole, since for Kundera the ethos of the novel lies precisely in the enrichment of knowledge. *Ignorance* no longer examines the infinity of human existence, but sets out from the fact of death, which invalidates all existence and all questioning. Around the central theme of death other themes familiar from Kundera's previous novels are assembled, such as the dream, remembering and forgetting, love, the body, and the temporality of existence. What is left of History is seen from the perspective of individual experience and dissolves in the general, suprahistorical conditions of life. Kundera poses the question of what it is that unites the experiences of the émigré(e)s, and replies that émigré(e)s share similar dreams (15–16). We can compare this to people who have lived through certain dramatic historical events, and who identify various phases of their lives in terms of these events. From Kundera's point of view, the fact that the collective memory has come to determine even the contents of dreams means that a domain of individual freedom that still existed even in Kafka's world is now lost.

Memory and the temporality of human existence are explored in *Ignorance* in close connection to aging and death. Kundera previously considered that the soul, in contrast to the body, does not have an age; now he thinks of age as part of one's existence (120–21). Life is short: human life would be something different if the individual could live, let us say, 160 years instead of the average 80. Kundera also explores the different time perspectives of youth and advanced age. He gives an example to illustrate how a young person discovers temporality as a dimension of existence. A young girl notices similarities between the first kiss with her present boyfriend and her previous one, and feels that the recollection of the past moment gives the present one an additional beauty (80). Time is for her no longer "the present moving forward and devouring the future . . . it is the present conquered and captured and carried off by the past . . . In the house of her life there are windows . . . opening to the rear, onto what she has experienced; from now on her existence will be inconceivable without these windows" (77–78). And Kundera adds that when she is older, she will see in repetition only the tedious monotony of events: with age, the "epic" or "musical" repetition in variations gives way to the mute repetition of the same (80–81).

In Kundera's first two novels, time and temporality are explored above all from the point of view of the "lyrical" experience of time typical of youth and sentimental persons, and in his middle novels, from *Farewell Waltz* to *Immortality*, as part of the existence of an "ageless" adult. Now, in *Ignorance*, he has proceeded to scrutinize the experience of time in old age or at its threshold, where it may be difficult to find anything, even in the past, that can support life and endow it with meaningfulness. For Irena, the years after the death of her husband, when she managed on her own with her two small daughters, were significant; for Josef it was his marriage. Both of them, however, feel that their relatives and former friends in their native country are not interested in hearing what they have experienced during the twenty years of their absence. The émigré(e)s are welcomed back home—on condition that they leave behind what they have experienced in exile, and take up again where they left off twenty years ago.

In addition to the frustration arising from others' denial of a person's past, the individual cannot even trust his or her own memory to retain the past. This is because the human memory is unreliable and the bond it creates with the past fragile. Memory generally retains no more than a millionth or possibly a hundred-millionth part of one's experience (123). In addition, memory arbitrarily selects things to be recollected; thus the past can never be reconstructed as it really was (124). What is more, Josef realizes that all he remembers from his youth are situations that make him displeased with himself (74); his memory "did nothing but slander him" (75). It is thus no wonder that two individuals never have the same recollections of a shared experience (126). We even forget the reasons for the most important decisions of our life. Josef thought that he had once chosen to become a veterinarian, instead of a medical doctor like his father, out of rebellion: he had provocatively told his relatives that he liked cows better than humans (65). Now an old friend of his recollects that he had said that his choice was based on his love for animals. Josef is amazed: he cannot himself say whether he acted out of love or of rebellion (152). Moreover, reading his diary from his school years, he is astonished by the discontinuity between his past and his present self. He wonders where the common essence lies between his self of the past—whom he now dislikes—and that of the present (83).

Love—for Kundera probably the most important of the possibilities of an authentic, meaningful life—is in *Ignorance* reflected on through the temporality of human existence and takes the form of either a past love or lost possibilities of love. Irena, who after twenty years in France is considering the possibility of return, in Prague meets Josef, who had emigrated to Denmark, and hopes that he will be a new love for her. From the beginning the encounter is asymmetrical in that Irena has preserved in her memory their previous meeting, decades ago, as a lost chance for love, whereas Josef has no recollection of this event at all. Josef does not want to start a new relationship, although he sees this as his last opportunity, because he wants to go on living with his deceased wife. He feels compassion for the dead one who is so weak: a dead person cannot defend herself, she cannot remind anybody of her likes and dislikes or demand attention from anyone. Josef feels that he has to protect his late wife by cherishing his reminiscences of her, and this is possible only by continuing to live in what had been their shared home. Were he now to move to Prague, where nothing sustains the memory of his wife, he would lose her entirely. He has struggled to have her buried nearby, and he now feels satisfaction when he thinks of their common future in the grave they will share (117). The love for a deceased person thus surpasses that for living ones. Death has occupied the place of life, remembrance of the past has become more vital than anything that happens in the present, and the corpse of the beloved more important than any living body. Here love exists, but it no longer reconciles one with life. The longing for an idyll makes its last, both morbid and kitschy appearance in Kundera's novelistic work with Josef dreaming of his life in their idyllic home, where he will devote the rest of his life to cherishing the memory of his wife, preserving everything in the house exactly as it was during her lifetime.

For Irena, who seeks Josef's love, and for Milada, who had sought it decades earlier, love does not offer an opportunity for a meaningful life. Irena feels that from now on she will remain forever outside the realm of love, which means that she will forever remain non-existent and without significance for anyone. This exclusion from the realm of love became Milada's destiny already when she was a schoolgirl. When Josef threatened to leave her, she wanted to show him the infinity of her love by letting herself freeze to death; instead, one of her earlobes merely froze and had to be amputated. This bodily defect was enough to cut her off from love for good (Milada is one of those who wish we could exist without a body). In *Ignorance*, happy love no longer occurs toward anyone except the dead.

Death, aging, the decay of the body, and living in a body in general, the unreliability of recollection and the frailty of the bond that connects us with our own past through memory, and the lack of interest individuals show toward each other are depicted in Kundera's last novels as experiences undergone by the characters, but not as existential themes characterizing individuals. On the contrary, several of his figures bear the same or similar themes or experience the human condition similarly. This arises from the general determinants of human existence, which nobody can escape. Instead of discovering new possibilities of being in a new historical situation, the author now looks at the possibilities of human existence from a perspective that narrows them down and eventually leads man into a cul-de-sac. In his last novels Kundera has himself given up his love for adventure, which earlier had derived from the infinite plurality of life and ends up with a pessimistic or even misanthropic view of life.

How Kundera's modernity narrows

Kundera requires of the modern individual an experimental mode of being in the world and he constructs his novels correspondingly on a constant variation of themes. The question is, then, whether sufficient weight for living can be found outside any metaphysical systems and outside History. Kundera unmasks sentimental, basically false solutions in ever new variations and searches for authentic ones. For him, authentic possibilities are found merely within the realm of privacy: in erotic pleasure, beauty, and (nonsentimental) love; yet these prove to be unreliable or poorly functioning options. Starting with *Immortality*, Kundera's works emphasize the inescapable biological constraints of human life, such as corporeality and death, which restrict the individual's possibilities even more than History. Kundera's pessimism has eventually expanded to comprehend the anthropological possibilities of humankind outside of History as well.

The "Project of Modernity" that began during the Enlightenment and Romanticism regarded History as an opportunity for man to build for himself a better future. The communist movement, in which Kundera participated before his career as a novelist, was one phase or part of this project, a phase ending in failure. According to Kundera, the "lyrical attitude" as a whole, that is, the desire to change the world so as to correspond to our ideas, is false because it does not take into account the complexity of reality. The failure of the communist experiment in Czechoslovakia, however, is also regarded as resulting from the powerlessness of a small nation to affect the course of History, or even its own history. In an interview, Kundera says that "this feeling of the frailty of existence—this sense of mortality—is linked with a vision of history. Large nations think they are making history. And if you make history you take yourself seriously . . . If you are a small nation, though, you do not make history. You are always the object of history. History is something hostile, something you must defend yourself against. You feel, spontaneously, that history is unjust, often stupid, and you can't take it seriously. Hence our special humour: a humour capable of seeing history as grotesque" (McEwan 27). Here Kundera gives the impression that his pessimistic view of history derives from his experience as a member of a small nation, nevertheless, he does not come to different, less pessimistic conclusions concerning history after living in France. In his interview with Kundera, Fritz Raddatz says of Kundera's view of history that he seems to agree with Gombrowicz: the only means to resist the history of "our time"—referring to the period of the Cold War—is to reject history in its entirety (99).

This rejection of History, however, does not make Kundera a postmodern thinker. Like the postmodernists, Kundera discards all "Grand Narratives" which represent the course of History as a comprehensive, rational whole. From this starting point, however, he proceeds in the opposite direction. He believes that it is necessary to keep the individual human being apart from History, whereas for the postmodernists the individual human being typically "dissolves" into the multiplicity of historical events, in which he cannot perceive any inner logic (see, e.g., Saariluoma [Steinby], *Der postindividualistische*). Contrary to the postmodernists for whom talking about the essence of humanity or about humankind's existential problems no longer makes any sense, Kundera retreats, work by work, further back to anthropology as the basic discipline dealing with human beings. In a way, he is returning to the eighteenth century of Sterne or Diderot, when the human mode of existence was not yet considered to be unavoidably historical. Kundera's view of the anthropological possibilities of man, however, eventually turns out to be the diametrical opposite of the optimistic view of the Enlightenment.

Despite his emphasis on anthropology, Kundera remains caught up in History—although *per negationem*, in the sense of deploring the unavailability of History as an organizing principle for one's actions. In *The Book of Laughter and Forgetting*, Kundera writes that since leaving the ring dance of the builders of a paradise, he has fallen like a stone and has never stopped falling (92, 95). The state of an individual who along with History has lost a solid basis of action has a parallel in the state of a community which is suddenly bereft of its capacity to determine the course of its own history. In *Ignorance*, Kundera comments on the desolate situation in Czechoslovakia after the 1968 occupation: "it was not the pain of their current life but the vacuity of the future that sucked dry their energies, stifled their courage, and made [the period] so craven, so wretched" (13). Indeed, the absence of a History which promises a better future, to be achieved by the efforts of individuals and communities, is constantly felt in his books. Even his mature skeptics, such as the man in his forties in *Life Is Elsewhere* or Tomas in *The Unbearable Lightness of Being*, who are adjusted to life outside History, define themselves in terms of what they lack, a faith in History or in any general, ideological truths. The possibilities of existence left to be examined are those that remain when the steering of History has proved to be an unrealizable alternative.

Kundera's view that one can step into a private life outside History appears problematic from the point of view of contemporary ideas about history and the human being's relation to it. Keeping the collective, the historical, and the public strictly apart from the private, as Kundera desires, is not tenable from the point of view of the humanities and social sciences of our time, since for these fields of scholarship humankind is historically and socially determined in every aspect, including experiences of pleasure, beauty, and love. Kundera does not support his view of the private life with any outline of the history of privacy, except for suggesting that privacy was better protected before the times of totalitarianism and imagology. We know, however, that the distinction between the private and public spheres is a fairly recent phenomenon; the middle ages did not recognize the privacy of bodily functions, sleep, or sexuality (see Elias). The separation of the private from the public sphere in the modern sense was actually achieved only at the end of the eighteenth century, and the process leading up to this is connected with the development of the modern individual identity. The sphere of privacy was then conceived as the realm of the realization of the authentic, innermost self, whereas in the public sphere action is functional and follows social roles (see Luhmann, *Gesellschaftsstruktur*; Schmidt). Kundera is therefore right in connecting the modern individual with an emphasis on privacy, but he overlooks the social process whereby this sphere came into being; in other words, in stressing the autonomy of the Cartesian individual he ignores the fact that privacy, too, is a social phenomenon.

Kundera sees it as a lack of autonomy if the individual is dependent in their identity and activity on others or on being tied to a body. Here he is more Cartesian than Herder, Goethe, Husserl, or Heidegger in thinking that humankind cannot be a social or a biological being without losing its autonomy. For Herder, Goethe, or Wilhelm von Humboldt the identity of an individual has its natural basis, but its development takes place in coexistence with other people, in a common world mediated through common action and communication in speech (see, e.g., Jannidis; Nisbet). In the twentieth and twenty-first centuries a variety of approaches—including psychoanalytical and feminist theories, poststructuralist theories such as those of Foucault and his followers, and theories foregrounding the linguistic and social construction of reality (see Berger and Luckmann; Frank, Raulet, Van Reijen; Kienzle and Pape; Žima)—consider the formation of the individual to be a social process. Intersubjectivity is considered to precede individual subjectivity; the individual self becomes possible only through participation in culturally determined action and in cultural systems of meaning. Thomas Luckmann puts this succinctly: "The personal identity of an individual does not develop from 'inside out' but from 'outside in'" (Luckmann 299; see also Frank, "Einleitung"). A human being does not experience his or her self immediately; she or he is capable of directly experiencing only the surrounding world. We learn to understand ourselves only when we grasp others as expressing their inner experiences in their words and acts and take notice of how others experience us (Luckmann 299).

While one side of the coin is our fundamental dependence on others in determining what we are, the other side is that communication and participation in common action presupposes that we all as participants make our own decisions and are responsible for our words and actions, and in that sense are autonomous subjects. The various "liberation movements" that aim at equality, regardless, for instance, of race, sex or nationality, do not deny the fundamentally social nature of human beings, but merely strive to do away with impediments to the equal realization of our subjectivity. This concept of liberation, in which the liberated subject remains dependent on his or her community, contradicts Kundera's negative concept of freedom. If, as Kundera believes, we really have to be free of any determining whatsoever, even of our own inner imperatives, it indeed becomes inconceivable from where life might gain the necessary weight. In fact, freedom from any determination and dependence equals total indifference and incidentality.

The isolation of a human being from others is manifested by the manner in which Kundera's characters encounter one another. Encounters do not take place in the context of a common action in a shared universe of meanings—this for Kundera would mean being sentimentally imbued with the mass spirit; rather, the individual weighs and classifies the other according to what she or he sees in the other person. The other belongs to the "outer" world in relation to oneself: the other appears as an object of our perception, and can be used to sustain ourselves and to give pleasure. Thus, it is evident that in his understanding of an encounter between two human beings, that is, something that should constitute a subject-subject encounter, Kundera clings to the Cartesian model of subject-object opposition, which Heidegger in *Being and Time* takes as the starting point of his criticism of Western metaphysics. Heidegger argues that man actually does not encounter the world—things and other human beings—by perceiving them as objects, but that man's being in the world means being involved in a common world of utensils and activities and sharing a common understanding of the world (see *Being and Time*). For Kundera, in contrast, the boundary between ourselves and others is seen in strictly Cartesian terms. The world of authentic meanings is for him a private universe of meanings, given to the individual in the living present of experience or created by himself or herself in dreams and private metaphors, a universe from which any collective symbols or collective models of interpretation are excluded. The boundary between two such private worlds of meanings can be crossed in a positive sense, that is to say without threatening our autonomy, only in love which entails a willingness to become familiar with another person's private universe of meanings and to feel with him or her (compassion).

Kundera endeavors to examine the unique identity of an individual by analytical methods, but actually his method undermines the supposition of any such identity. He divides an individual into separate parts, for example face and gestures, and then claims that no individuality can be found in any of these parts. This method indeed very closely resembles the analytic, or resolution-composition, method of Galilean natural science, redefined in Descartes's thinking as the method of philosophy, in which a complex matter is analyzed by dividing it into its elementary components (see *Discourse on Method*). The individuality of a person, however, is not an analytic concept but a synthetic one. It does not imply that the components of a person, or at least some of them, are unique only to him or her: on the contrary, individuality is something that is perceived in the whole of the person and simultaneously in everything he or she is and does. Kundera ignores this insight into the nature of individuality, which stems from the end of the eighteenth century, the period of the "discovery" of human individuality in the modern sense of the word. Goethe's novels, for example, show that he had reflected profoundly on the nature of individuality and on the question of how it can be recognized. The actions of a person are seen as parts of complex situations, they are compared with the actions of other persons and with other actions by the same person, and out of this information a complex, dynamic picture of the person is built up—dynamic because it changes constantly with each new piece of information (see Saariluoma [Steinby], *Erzählstruktur*). For example, an attractive wave of the hand, when seen as a part of a complex situation and compared with the actions of the same person in other situations and the actions of other persons in similar situations, might very well express much more than the same gesture considered purely in the abstract, isolated from any context. Only through grasping the whole, paying attention to all its aspects and to their overall combined effect, can the individuality of a deed or a person be recognized. It is clear why Kundera's thinking, which is oriented toward dissection and analysis rather than synthesis, cannot grasp individuality. We can say that here Kundera's method, derived from the Enlightenment tradition, comes into conflict with his commitment to the Romantic idea of individuality as the supreme value. In *Immortality,* Kundera finally recognizes that the individual essence or *Grund*, "ground," of a person can only be expressed by a metaphor (373); he has discarded the analytical method and taken recourse to a truly Romantic means of grasping the individuality of a person.

For Kundera, however, the most important thing to discover in a person is not his or her individuality but the general possibility of human existence that he or she embodies or represents. Rather than out of interest in the characters' unique personalities, individuality is important for Kundera as a principle and as the basis of autonomous action. This individuality and this autonomy are in Kundera's view more than ever threatened in the contemporary world. Even if one might think—as I do myself—that the cul-de-sac into which Kundera leads the modern individual derives in part from untenable notions of the individual's relationship with his or her own body and with other individuals, what remains relevant is Kundera's acute analysis of the contemporary world and its impact on our self-understanding. Imagology the way Kundera uses it and commercialization are in fact trends in the contemporary world which profoundly affect our identity, our actions, and our relationships with others. It is here, along with his perception of the consequences of "falling out of History" characteristic of the experience of contemporary Europeans—in less sharp terms, the lack of a guiding historical perspective—rather than in his highly sinister view of the fate of human beings bound to a body that I consider Kundera's analysis of the possibilities left for humankind in the contemporary world to be of great value.

"The End of the Novel"

Kundera originally placed the history of the novel in opposition to the history of political systems and nation states, the latter being hostile to humankind, a trap in which his liberty is restricted. The history of the novel is for Kundera a revenge on history itself, it "is neither predetermined nor identical with the idea of progress; it is entirely human, made by men, by *some* men" (*Testaments* 15). The constraints of History are challenged by the history of the arts as a realm of freedom of exploration and experimentation. We can even say that once it has turned out to be impossible to realize a meaningful life through pleasure, beauty, and love, the only domain in which the authentic existence of man is still possible is the novel, or more generally the arts. Paradoxically, Kundera seems to suggest that freedom, authenticity, and beauty are now possible only in the arts (in novels) that examine the lack of freedom, authenticity, and beauty in our contemporary world. But even this realm of freedom, according to Kundera, is vanishing: it too is being suffocated by the contemporary world.

For Kundera, at the heart of modern European culture, literature, and the other arts is the sense of complexity, a willingness to see things in all their multidimensionality, in their infinite plurality and depth. In his opinion, however, our time is hostile to this sense of complexity. In *The Book of Laughter and Forgetting*, Kundera discusses music as an example. The history of music consists of the discovery of the immense possibilities concealed in the apparently simplest sounds. It is a transformation of the trivial into an intellectual adventure. In our world, however, music, according to Kundera, has regressed to its "primeval state" of "music without thought" (*The Book of Laughter* 248). Agitprop music which was offered all the time to arouse the enthusiasm of the masses for the effort of building socialism and Western muzak played as background music everywhere have replaced creative music, in which new things are discovered and felt. In a world that ceaselessly proffers the simplest and most trivial kind of music, serious music is drowned out by totally insignificant "sewage-water music" (*Ignorance* 146, 148–49).

The novel has undergone a similar development. In *The Art of the Novel* Kundera writes that the totalitarian political system has killed the novel, whose ethos is the free exploration of the possibilities of human existence; but the West, dominated by mass media, does not allow the novel to thrive either. The search for a complex truth is displaced by a general writing and exposing mania, a "graphomania," under whose reign nothing important is said any more; the sense of the complexity of matters has been supplanted by the inability to distinguish between important and unimportant experience. Kundera's era of graphomania comes close to Adorno's notion from half a century earlier, of the era of "biographical trash literature": "For telling a story means having something special to say, and that is precisely what is prevented by the administered world, by standardization and eternal sameness. . . . the cheap biographical literature ["biographische Schundliteratur"] one finds everywhere is a byproduct of the disintegration of the novel form itself" ("The Position" 31, "Standort" 42). This world of uniformity excludes the novel, about which, according to Kundera, we now ought to speak in the past tense only. The history of the novel has turned into an archive, a set of documents, in which the past of the European spirit is preserved as an object of admiration for future generations (*The Art* 165).

Kundera is of course not alone complaining: it is a common concern of novelists and other actors in the literary field of our time that the novel, and literature in general, has lost its previous cultural significance. Kundera's view, that one essential factor causing this is mass media entertainment that has replaced the reading of novels as a leisure activity, is also commonly shared. However, when Kundera seems to suggest that at some time in the past the conditions—both in the art of the novel and in life itself—were more favorable for human freedom than in our own time, we are entitled to ask for further details. Kundera gives no clear answer in his writings to the question of what these conditions, favorable to individuality and to a sense of difference and complexity, actually were, nor does he say precisely where and when the arts were allowed to flourish and the European spirit could freely develop. His description of how Cervantes discovered the individual and the complexity of the world, thus initiating the tradition of the novel, is very sketchy, and the only explanation given for Cervantes's initiation of the European adventure is the (alleged) disappearance of God from the world. It seems as though Kundera thinks that at first the void created by the disappearance of God left room for human freedom, but that later it was filled with History and other constraints limiting freedom. Moreover, Kundera does not give any hint as to whether he believes that in the "Cervantean" period, which was so favorable to the novel, individuality, autonomy, and a sense of difference flourished not only in the novel but in real life as well.

Although Kundera is skeptical as to our possibility of detecting any internal logic in History, he claims to discern a descending line in the course of History with regard to the realization of human freedom—that is, a line that is exactly the opposite of the view of history propounded by Hegel and Marx, as a process of increasing human freedom. Thus he does not avoid offering a "Grand Narrative" of History any more than Jean-François Lyotard, the great demolisher of the Grand Narratives of History. In Kundera's vision of the grand course of history, the beginning was a kind of "childhood" of humankind, in which the problematic nature of human existence had not yet become conspicuous. This is the (obviously very long) premodern era, preceding the birth of the novel. Kundera is in fact only interested in the modern era, a time when, unlike the middle ages, religion no longer determines our worldview. In the modern age, "religion yielded its position to culture (to cultural creation), which came to embody the supreme values by which Europeans recognized themselves, defined and identified themselves" (*The Art* 128). His dating of this "sudden" change remains, as noted previously, inaccurate: in some contexts, the modern age begins for Kundera with Boccaccio in the fourteenth century and in others with Rabelais in the sixteenth or Cervantes in the seventeenth century. In any case, in his picture the modern age is now declining toward its end. The modern age cherished the dream of an autonomous, authentic individual and in our time this dream has faded away.

Europe is undergoing the end of the modern age. Individualism and art, constituting the realm of the free development of the European spirit, have reached their end first in totalitarian Central Europe, later also in the West (124, 151). The European spirit no longer exists, except as a longing for its lost core (128–29).

Kundera began his career as a novelist insisting that what is essential in European history is not politics but culture; however, especially in his later novels he is convinced that the contemporary world is bringing European culture, as he understands it, to an end. Kundera disowns "collaboration with our times": "All those who extol the mass media din, advertising's imbecilic smile, the neglect of the natural world, indiscretion raised to the status of a virtue—they deserve to be called *collaborators with the modern*" (*The Art* 125). While "modern" originally connoted a critical attitude, a "non-conformist revolt against received ideas and kitsch," now to be modern means "a strenuous effort to be up-to-date, to conform, to conform even more thoroughly than the most conformist of all" (164; see also Raddatz 107). Kundera refuses to participate in this conformist race and insists on adhering to the original, critical ethos of modernity, emphasizing the individual's ability and duty to judge independently everything that he or she comes across. In contrast to fashionable modernism, Kundera represents what he calls "antimodern modernism" (*The Curtain* 56). Obviously, this is equivalent to being attached to nothing but to the "depreciated legacy of Cervantes" (*The Art* 20).

Kundera set out to follow some of the "unheard appeals" of this legacy (*The Art* 15). Dream or dreamlike narration became an important part of almost all of his novel compositions. He also listened to the "appeal of thought" established by the novels of Musil and Broch, in which the author comments on events in his novel in his own voice and includes essayistic digressions. Furthermore, Kundera aims in his novels at the greatest possible playfulness and lightness, while at the same time maintaining that the novel is a serious examination of human existence. Time or temporality, as the mode of human existence, plays a crucial role in his examination of man's existence as well. He explores the themes of remembering and forgetting, youth and maturity, history, the present, aging and death. Already before *Immortality*, in which the perspective of death for the first time predominates and obstructs the search for meaningfulness in human existence, it is evident that resuming the devalued possibilities of the novel does not necessarily lead to an infinity of new paths. Dream, thought, play and time are taken up in Kundera's works as insufficiently exploited opportunities of the novel, but they turn out to be quite problematic. Dream, which fascinates the author as a domain of free creativity, is no longer that in *Ignorance*, as collectivity and History intrude even into our dreams. Kundera follows the "appeal of thought" to the point where the thematic level dominates the novel so strongly that a considerable number of readers feel uncomfortable, complaining about the thinness of the characters and the absence of the concrete fictional world. Playfulness and laughter, so characteristic of Kundera's novels, do not compensate for the increasing gloominess of his vision. Questions of time remain central to Kundera's novels until the very end, but in his later works death overwhelms the multifaceted experience of the temporal dimension of human existence. Thus, we can say that Kundera not only makes use of the possibilities of dream, thought, play and time in the novel, but also in a way pursues these possibilities to a point beyond which no continuation is possible.

The very "legacy of Cervantes," conceived as the adventure of encountering the world, to which Kundera acknowledges his commitment despite being skeptical toward everything else, proves problematic. Skepticism and adventure as such are compatible for Kundera; they are both characteristic of the individual searching for autonomy and authenticity. An example is Tomas in *The Unbearable Lightness of Being*, who is an adventurer of eroticism. In Kundera's later works, however, a love for adventure either does not lead to any positive result or disappears entirely. Rubens in *Immortality* chooses the adventures of eroticism, but ends up in an emptiness of being. Agnes finds that she no longer wishes to participate in humankind's great adventure; similarly, Chantal in *Identity* lacks any interest in adventure, because searching for them is "a means of embracing the world," which she no longer wants to embrace (39). The last short novels indicate that Kundera himself has lost his love for adventure. Human existence no longer appears as an infinite field of exploration; in fact, when life is seen from the harsh perspective of death, there is little really important left to say. Chantal speaks with irony of the "king of words"—"life"—regarded as the greatest, unquestionable value; when "life" loses this position, so do the great words surrounding it, such as "adventure," "future," and "hope" (28–29). Hope and the future were treated with irony already at the end of *Immortality*, when Paul speaks of woman as the only hope left for man, while the reader can see that his wife betrays him. The scene is comparable to the ending of *Ignorance*, where Josef cherishes the hope of a "happy future" by the side of his deceased wife. Hope and future no longer belong to life but to death.

In his earlier novels and essays, Kundera explains that the novel will die when the world becomes unfavorable to it, but his own novelistic production is a testimony to how the adventure launched by Cervantes fades away once an author loses love for adventure. Human existence is no longer seen as a set of alternative, meaningful ways of being. For Kundera, life and human beings appear boring and uninteresting. In fact, the aging author is interested in scarcely anything but aging and death. Compared to these, the adventure of humankind in History and the adventure of the individual are meaningless. This change in Kundera's views is expressed in his new, gloomier interpretation of what the Cervantean tradition was all about. In *The Curtain* from 2007 he writes: "Don Quixote is conquered. And with no grandeur whatever. For it is clear immediately: human life as such is a defeat. All we can do in the face of that ineluctable defeat called life is to try to understand it. That—that is the raison d'être of the art of the novel" (*The Curtain* 10): Not an infinite space to be explored in ever new adventures, no inexhaustible plurality of possibilities of human existence to be discovered; what remains for the novelist to enquire into is merely the failure of human existence. Kundera does not mention that the shadow of death makes even this enquiry futile.

Summing up, for Kundera, the contemporary world is a place which has annihilated the modern ideal of an autonomous, authentic individual, an irretrievable loss which he mourns. With his love for the autonomous individual and the "legacy of Cervantes," the literary expression of this individuality, he cannot as a novelist be regarded as a postmodernist, although some of his stylistic features, resembling postmodernism, have often led to such a label. Traits considered as postmodern include, for instance, the relinquishing of the illusion of reality, his free combination of various fictional and nonfictional lines, and his play between different "ontological levels," for instance, appearing as himself in a novel which he is just writing. To say, however, that such features indicate Kundera's postmodernity is a misconception. His play with the conventions of the novel is directed first and foremost against realism, his predecessors in this being the modernist European novelists of the first half of the twentieth century. The basic ideas of postmodernist writing are not compatible with his conception of the novel. For the postmodernists, the meaning of a text cannot be defined with any certainty and the author has no special authority to interpret it; the unity of the work is denied, and the text is conceived of as being compounded of different materials borrowed from various discourses. Rather than conveying originality, a text is regarded as the product of recycling—in other words, repetition has replaced novelty. Furthermore, individual human beings are no longer seen as the subjects behind the action, History no longer exists, nor does the reality that is depicted in a text; in the typical postmodern text, different more or less imagined realities overlap and are transformed into each other without any clear-cut boundaries (see, e.g., Hutcheon; McHale; Saariluoma [Steinby], *Der postindividualistische*). Kundera is clearly in opposition to each and every one of these tenets of postmodernism. He insists on the idea of a work of art which is a meaningful, carefully composed whole and an original creation by its author (e.g., *Testaments* 170). The characters in his novels are regarded as acting subjects, and the task of the novel is to explore human existence in its different variations, with special attention to the possibilities of autonomous, authentic modes of existence. Distinguishing between different imagined worlds—for instance, the world of dreams or of ideological truths—and the real world is for Kundera not only possible but of vital importance. His conception of the novel is on all these points in accordance with the modernist novel and in discord with the principles of postmodernism. Nowhere, to my knowledge, does he take an explicit stand on postmodernism either as a literary movement or in the more general sense of a current of contemporary thought—although in one sentence in *Encounter* he does say that the intellectuals of the Prague Spring were proponents of modern art: "I stress 'modern', not 'postmodern'" (117). Yet one can say without any hesitation that Kundera considers postmodern novelists, as well as all those who take an affirmative stance toward our contemporary world, as collaborators with a world gone mad and as gravediggers of the novel. He himself, unlike Paul in *Immortality*, does not want to be an ally of his own gravediggers. Kundera considers himself the heir of Kafka, Hašek, Gombrowicz, Musil, and Broch, and he mourns the end of their and his kind of modernism.

Kundera's claim that the "Russian night" and Western "imagology" have killed the novel certainly appears to many of us as an overstatement and most of us find even less convincing the idea that the novel has now come to an end as a consequence of Kundera's "discovery" of the total corporeal determination of human action. We may think that these facts and "discoveries" shed light on Kundera's novels and on his conception of the state of the novel, rather than actually describing the novel of our time and the history of the novel as a whole. However, Kundera's analysis of the incompatibility with contemporary society and lifestyle of what for him is the essence of the tradition of the modern novel, European culture and modernity is thought provoking and deserves to be taken seriously. And if we want to argue with him about these matters, I am convinced that it would not disturb him. His idea of the novelist, as a thought experimentalist rather than as a presenter of absolute truths, can of course be applied to himself as well. We may doubt whether he has told the whole story as to how the genre of the novel was conceived, how it developed, and eventually perished, or even the truth about his own novels, and we have even better reason to suspect that he has not succeeded in presenting exhaustively the possibilities of human existence in the contemporary world, but we cannot blame him for this. It is enough that in his novels Kundera has kindled lamps which highlight some of the possibilities and some of the problems of the modern individual, as well as certain aspects of the European art of the novel, and in doing so he has both delighted readers and provided them with matter for thought.

Works Cited

Abrams, Bradley. "From Revisionism to Dissent: The Creation of Post-Marxism in Central Europe after 1968." *Promises of 1968: Crisis, Illusion, and Utopia*. Ed. Vladimir Tismaneanu. Budapest: Central European UP, 2011. 179–96.

Adams, Vicki. "Milan Kundera: The Search for Self in a Post-Modern World." *Imagination, Emblems and Expressions: Essays on Latin American, Caribbean, and Continental Culture and Identity.* Ed. Helen Ryan-Ransom. Bowling Green: Bowling Green State U Popular P, 1993. 233–46.

Adorno, Theodor W. *Aesthetic Theory*. 1970. Trans. Robert Hullot-Kentor. Minneapolis: U of Minnesota P, 2002.

Adorno, Theodor W. "Standort des Erzählers im zeitgenossischen Roman." *Noten zur Literatur*. By Theodor W. Adorno. Ed. Rolf Tiedemann. Darmstadt: Wissenschaftliche Buchgesellschaft, 1998. 41–48.

Adorno, Theodor W. "The Position of the Narrator in the Contemporary Novel." *Notes to Literature*. By Theodor W. Adorno. Trans. Shierry Weber Nicholsen. Ed. Rolf Tiedemann. New York: Columbia UP, 1991. 30–36.

Anonymous. "The History of *Ferdydurke*." *Ferdydurke*. By Witold Gombrowicz. 1961. Trans. Eric Mosbacher. Harmondsworth: Penguin, 1986. 7–9.

Aristotle. *Poetics*. Trans. D. W. Lucas. Oxford: Clarendon P, 1968.

von Arnim, Bettina. *Goethe's Correspondence with a Child*. 1835. Boston: Ticknor and Fields, 1861.

Ash, Timothy Garton. "Does Central Europe Exist?" 1986. *The Uses of Adversity: Essays on the Fate of Central Europe*. By Timothy Garton Ash. Cambridge: Granta, 1991. 161–91.

Atkinson, Paul, and David Silverman. "Kundera's *Immortality*: The Interview Society and the Invention of the Self." *Qualitative Inquiry* 3.3 (1997): 304–25: <http://dx.doi.org/10.1177/107780049700300304>.

Auerbach, Erich. "Philologie der Weltliteratur." *Gesammelte Aufsätze zur romanischen Philologie*. By Erich Auerbach. Bern: Francke, 1967. 301–10.

Bakhtin, Mikhail. "Forms of Time and of the Chronotope in the Novel." *The Dialogic Imagination*. By Mikhail Bakhtin. Trans. Caryl Emerson and Michael Holquist. Austin: U of Texas P, 2008. 84–258.

Bakhtin, Mikhail. *Problems of Dostoyevsky's Poetics*. 1929. Trans. Caryl Emerson. Manchester: Manchester UP, 1984.

Baranczak, Stanislaw. "Tongue-tied Eloquence: Notes on Language, Exile and Writing." *Altogether Elsewhere: Writers on Exile*. Ed. Marc Robinson. San Diego: Harcourt Brace, 1994. 242–51.

Barthes, Roland. "The Reality Effect." *The Rustle of Language*. By Roland Barthes. Trans. Richard Howard. Oxford: Blackwell, 1986. 141–48.

Baty-Delalande, Héléne. "Kundera et l'engagement sartrien. Princips du reniement d'une 'idiotie' incontournable." *Désaccords parfaits. La Réception paradoxale de l'oeuvre de Milan Kundera*. Ed. Marie-Odile Thirouin and Martine Boyer-Weinmann. Grenoble: ELLUG, 2009. 231–46.

Baudrillard, Jean. *For a Critique of the Political Economy of the Sign*. 1972. Trans. Charles Levin. St. Louis: Telos, 1981: <http://dx.doi.org/10.2307/3684064>.

Bauer, Michal. "L'Ironie comme mode de polémique et défi au vide dans les écrits de jeunesse de Kundera (1945-1970)." *Désaccords parfaits. La Réception paradoxale de l'oeuvre de Milan Kundera*. Ed. Marie-Odile Thirouin and Martine Boyer-Weinmann. Grenoble: ELLUG, 2009. 101–30.

Bauman, Zygmunt. *Intimations of Postmodernity*. London: Routledge, 1992.

Bäumer, Konstanze. *Bettine, Psyche, Mignon. Bettina von Arnim und Goethe*. Stuttgart: Hans Dietrich Heinz, 1986.

Beall, Joshua Patrick. *The Poetics of Subversion: Irony and the Central European Novel*. Ann Arbor: ProQuest, 2011.

Bedient, Calvin. "On Milan Kundera." *Salmagundi* 73 (1987): 93–108.

Beller, Manfred, and Joep Leerssen, eds. *Imagology: The Cultural Construction and Literary Representation of National Characters*. Amsterdam: Rodopi, 2007.

Benson, Stephen. "For Want of a Better Term? Polyphony and the Value of Music in Bakhtin and Kundera." *Narrative* 11.3 (2003): 292–311: <http://dx.doi.org/10.1353/nar.2003.0013>.

Benveniste, Emile. *Problems in General Linguistics*. 1966. Trans. Mary Elisabeth Meek. Miami: Cord Gables, 1971.

Berger, Peter L., and Thomas Luckmann. *The Social Construction of Reality: A Treatise in the Sociology of Knowledge*. Harmondsworth: Penguin, 1966.

Berlatsky, Eric. "Memory as Forgetting: The Problem of the Postmodern in Kundera's *The Book of Laughter and Forgetting* and Spiegelman's *Maus*." *Cultural Critique* 55.1 (2003): 101–51: <http://dx.doi.org/10.1353/cul.2003.0044>.

Bilek, Petr A. "A Journey of a Name from the Realm of Reference to the Realm of Meaning: The Reception of Milan Kundera within the Czech Cultural Context." *Kosmas: Czechoslovak and Central European Journal* 16.2 (2003): 15–27.

Bílek, Petr A. "Constructing the Paradoxical Middle: Conceptualizations of Central Europe Explored in the 1980s Essayistic Debates." *Models of Representations in Czech Literary History*. Ed. Petr A. Bílek and Vladimír Papoušek. Boulder: East European Monographs, 2010. 131–43.

Bílek, Petr A. "The East, West, and the Center of Europe as Cultural Concepts, Emblems, and Vehicles of Creative Misunderstanding." Petr A. Bílek and Vladimír Papoušek. *Models of Representations in Czech Literary History*. Boulder, CO: East European Monographs, 2010. 89–115.

Biron, Norman. "Gespräche mit Milan Kundera." *Europäische Ideen* 20 (1976): 3–13.

Birus, Hendrik. "The Goethean Concept of World Literature and Comparative Literature." *Comparative Literature and Comparative Cultural Studies*. Ed. Steven Tötösy de Zepetnek. West Lafayette: Purdue UP, 2003. 11–22.

Blanke, Horst Walter, and Jörn Rüsen, eds. *Von der Aufklärung zum Historismus. Zum Strukturwandel des historischen Denkens*. Paderborn: Schöningh, 1984.

Blumenberg, Hans. *Goethe zum Beispiel*. Frankfurt: Suhrkamp, 1999.

Blumenberg, Hans. "Wirklichkeitsbegriff und Möglichkeit des Romans." *Nachahmung und Illusion*. Ed. Hans Robert Jauss. München: Eidos, 1964. 9–27.

Boden, Doris. *Irritation als narratives Prinzip. Untersuchungen zur Rezeptionssteuerung in den Romanen Milan Kunderas*. Hildesheim: Olms, 2006.

Boden, Doris. "Kein Nobelpreis für Milan Kundera. Über einige Irrtümer." *Literatur und Kritik* 429–30 (2008): 16–8.

Boisen, Jørn. "Le Malentendu. Kundera et ses paratextes." *neohelicon: acta comparationis litteraruum universarum* 37.1 (2010): 287–304.

Boisen, Jørn. *Une fois ne compte pas. Nihilisme et sens dans L'Insoutenable légèreté de l'être de Milan Kundera*. Copenhagen: Museum Tusculanum, 2005.

Borges, Jorge Luis. "Kafka and His Precursors." *Selected Non-Fictions*. Vol. 3. By Jorge Luis Borges. Ed. Eliot Weinberger. Trans. Esther Allen, Suzanne Jill Levine, and Eliot Weinberger. Harmondsworth: Penguin, 1999. 363–65.

Bourdieu, Pierre. *Distinction: A Social Critique of the Judgement of Taste*. Trans. Richard Nice. London: Routledge, 1984.

Bremmer, Jan, and Herman Roodenberg, eds. *A Cultural History of Gesture: From Antiquity to the Present Day*. Ithaca: Cornell UP, 1992.

Breton, André. *Manifestoes of Surrealism*. 1924. Trans. Richard Seaver and Helen R. Lane. Ann Arbor: U of Michigan P, 1972.

Broch, Hermann. "Das Weltbild des Romans." 1933. *Kommentierte Werkausgabe*. Vol. 9.2. By Hermann Broch. Ed. Paul Michael Lützeler. Frankfurt: Suhrkamp, 1981. 89–118.

Broch, Hermann. "Denkerische und dichterische Erkenntnis." 1933. *Kommentierte Werkausgabe*. Vol. 9.2. By Hermann Broch. Ed. Paul Michael Lützeler. Frankfurt: Suhrkamp, 1981. 43–49.

Broch, Hermann. "Einige Bemerkungen zum Problem des Kitsches. Ein Vortrag." 1946. *Kommentierte Werkausgabe*. Vol. 9.2. By Hermann Broch. Ed. Paul Michael Lützeler. Frankfurt: Suhrkamp, 1981. 158–73.

Broch, Hermann. "Evil in the Value-System of Art." 1933. *Geist and Zeitgeist: The Spirit in an Unspiritual Age. By Hermann Broch*. Ed. and trans. John Hargraves. New York: Counterpoint, 2002. 3–39.

Broch, Hermann. *The Sleepwalkers: A Trilogy*. 1931–1932. Trans. Willa Muir and Edwin Muir. New York: Random House, 1964.

Brodsky, Joseph. "Why Milan Kundera is Wrong about Dostoevsky." *New York Times* (17 February 1985): 33.

Bürger, Christa, Peter Bürger, and Jochen Schulte-Sasse, eds. *Aufklärung und literarische Öffentlichkeit*. Frankfurt: Suhrkamp, 1980.

Bürger, Peter. *Zur Kritik der idealistischen Ästhetik*. Frankfurt: Suhrkamp, 1983.

Calinescu, Matei. *Faces of Modernity: Modernism, Avant-garde, Decadence, Kitsch, Postmodernism*. Durham: Duke UP, 1987.

Carroll, Michael. "The Cyclic Form of *Laughable Loves*." *Milan Kundera: Bloom's Modern Critical Views*. Ed. Harold Bloom. Philadelphia: Chelsea House, 2003. 93–112.

Cassirer, Ernst. *Die Philosophie der Aufklärung*. 1932. Tübingen: Niemeyer, 1973.

Ceska, Jakub. "Le Roman comme deploiement symbolique de rève. La thematique du rève dans l'oeuvre Milan Kundera." Trans. Marie-Odile Thirouin. *Revue des Etudes Slaves* 83.3 (2011): 457–78.

Christoffel, David. "*Mélos*, roman et re*mélos*." *Désaccords parfaits. La Réception paradoxale de l'oeuvre de Milan Kundera*. Ed. Marie-Odile Thirouin and Martine Boyer-Weinmann. Grenoble: ELLUG, 2009. 279–89.

Chvatik, Kvetoslav. *Die Fallen der Welt. Der Romancier Milan Kundera*. Trans. Susanna Roth. München: Carl Hanser, 1994.

Chvatík, Květoslav. "Milan Kundera als Übersetzer und zweisprachiger Autor." *Literarische Polyphonie. Übersetzung und Mehrsprachigkeit in der Literatur*. Ed. Johann Strutz and Peter V. Žima. Tübingen: Narr, 1996. 149–55.

Chvatík, Květoslav. "Milan Kundera and the Crisis of Language." *Review of Contemporary Fiction* 9.2 (1989): 27–36.

Cicora, Mary A. *Modern Myths and Wagnerian Deconstructions: Hermeneutic Approaches to Wagner's Music-dramas*. Westport: Greenwood P, 2000.

Close, Anthony. *The Romantic Approach to Don Quixote: A Critical History of the Romantic Tradition in Quixote Criticism*. Cambridge: Cambridge UP, 1978.

Cohn, Dorrit. *The Sleepwalkers: Elucidations of Hermann Broch's Trilogy*. The Hague: Mouton, 1966.

Cooke, Michael. "Milan Kundera, Cultural Arrogance and Sexual Tyranny." *Critical Survey* 4.1 (1992): 79–84.

Corngold, Stanley. *Lambent Traces: Kafka*. Princeton: Princeton UP, 2004.

Corngold, Stanley, and Ruth V. Gross, eds. *Kafka for the Twenty-First Century*. Rochester: Camden House, 2011.

Cordle, Daniel. "States of Being not Being in States: Metaphysical Border Crossings in the Work of Milan Kundera." *Displaced Persons: Conditions of Exile in European Culture*. Ed. Sharon Ouditt. Aldershot: Ashgate, 2002. 128–37.

Corino, Karl. *Robert Musil. Eine Biographie*. Berlin: Rowohlt, 2003.

Cornis-Pope, Marcel, and John Neubauer, eds. *History of the Literary Cultures of East-Central Europe*. Amsterdam: John Benjamins, 2007.

Crain, Caleb. "Milan Kundera Is on the Outs with His Translators: But Who's Betraying Whom?" *Elity: Lingua franca* 39 (1999): 40–50.

Cravens, Craig. "Faulty Consciousness: Milan Kundera's *The Joke*." *Slavic and East European Journal* 44.1 (2000): 92–108: <http://dx.doi.org/10.2307/309630>.

Čulík, Jan. "Milan Kundera." *Twentieth-Century Eastern European Writers*. Ed. Steven Serafin. Detroit: Gale, 2001. 208–26.

Degner, Horst G. *Polarität, Steigerung und Metamorphose in Goethes Naturanschauung*. Mannheim: Sokrates, 1984.

Denon, Vivant. *No Tomorrow*. Trans. Lydia Davis. New York: New York Review of Books Classics, 2009.

Derrida, Jacques. "I Have a Taste for the Secret." Trans. Giacomo Donis. *A Taste for the Secret*. By Jacques Derrida and Maurizio Ferraris. Ed. Giacomo Donis and David Webb. Cambridge: Polity, 2001. 1–92.

Derrida, Jacques. *Of Grammatology*. Trans. Gayatri Chakravorty Spivak. Baltimore: Johns Hopkins UP, 1976.

Derrida, Jacques. *Writing and Difference*. Trans. Allan Bass. London: Routledge, 1993.

Descartes, René. *Discourse on the Method of Rightly Conducting the Reason and Seeking for Truth in the Sciences*. 1637. Trans. Norman Kemp Smith. New York: Random House, 1958.

D'haen, Theo, David Damrosch, and Djelal Kadir, eds. *The Routledge Companion to World Literature*. London: Routledge, 2012.

Diderot, Denis. *Jacques le Fataliste et son maître*. 1796. Ed. Jacques Proust. Paris: Livre de poche, 1979.

Dikovitskaya, Margaret. *Visual Culture: The Study of the Visual after the Culture Turn*. Cambridge: MIT P, 2005.

Dilthey, Wilhelm. *Einleitung in die Geisteswissenschaften. Versuch einer Grundlegung für das Studium der Gesellschaft und der Geschichte*. 1883. Göttingen: Vandenhoeck & Ruprecht, 1959.

Doležel, Lubomir. "'Narrative Symposium' in Milan Kundera's *The Joke*." *Critical Essays on Milan Kundera*. Ed. Peter Petro. New York: G. K. Hall, 1999. 125–36.

Donahue, Bruce. "Laughter and Ironic Humor in the Fiction of Milan Kundera." *Critiques: Studies in Contemporary Fiction* 25.2 (1984): 67–76: <http://dx.doi.org/10.1080/00111619.1984.9937788>.

Dorfman, Ariel. "Globalizing Compassion, Photography, and the Challenge of Terror." *CLCWeb: Comparative Literature and Culture* 9.1 (2007): <http://docs.lib.purdue.edu/clcweb/vol9/iss1/3>.

Draper, Marie-Eve. *Libertinage et donjuanisme chez Kundera*. Paris: Balzac, 2002.

du Plessix Gray, Francine. "Journey into the Maze: An Interview with Milan Kundera." *Critical Essays on Milan Kundera*. Ed. Peter Petro. New York: G. K. Hall, 1999. 45–52.

Eagleton, Terry. "Estrangement and Irony." *Salmagundi* 73 (1987): 25–32.

Ehrich-Haefeli, Verena. "Individualität als narrative Leistung? Zum Wandel der Personendarstellung in Romanen um 1770. Sophie von La Roche, Goethe, Lenz." *Geschichte und Vorgeschichte der modernen Subjektivät*. Vol. 2. Ed. Reto Luzius Fest, Roland Hagenbüchle, and Peter Schultz. Berlin: De Gruyter, 1998. 811–43.

Elgrably, Jordan. "Conversations with Milan Kundera." *Critical Essays on Milan Kundera*. Ed. Peter Petro. New York: G. K. Hall, 1999. 53–68.

Elias, Norbert. *Civilizing Process*. 1939. Trans. Edmund Jephcott. Oxford: Blackwell, 2000.

Engel, Manfred. *Der Roman der Goethezeit*. Stuttgart: Metzler, 1993.

Fábry, Andrea. "A Comparative View of Modernism in Central European Literature." *Comparative Central European Culture*. Ed. Steven Tötösy de Zepetnek. West Lafayette: Purdue UP, 2002. 33–49.

Finkielkraut, Alain. "Milan Kundera Interview." *Critical Essays on Milan Kundera*. Ed. Peter Petro. New York: G. K. Hall, 1999. 33–44.

Foucault, Michel. *Power/Knowledge: Selected Interviews and Other Writings 1972–1977*. Trans. Colin Gordon, Leo Marshall, John Mephan, and Kate Soper. Ed. Colin Gordon. New York: Pantheon Books, 1980.

Foucault, Michel. *The Archeology of Knowledge*. Trans. A. M. Sheridan Smith. London: Routledge, 1994.

Foucault, Michel. *The History of Sexuality*. 3 Vols. Trans. Robert Hurley. London: Allen Lane, 1978–1988.

Frank, Manfred. *Das Problem "Zeit" in der deutschen Romantik. Zeitbewußtsein und Bewußtsein von Zeitlichkeit in der Frühromantischen Philosophie und in Tiecks Dichtung*. Paderborn: Schöningh, 1990.

Frank, Manfred. *Der kommende Gott. Vorlesungen über die Neue Mythologie*. Frankfurt: Suhrkamp, 1982.

Frank, Manfred. "Die Philosophie des sogenannten 'magischen Idealismus'." *Euphorion* 63.1 (1969): 88–116.

Frank, Manfred. "Einleitung zur Schlußdiskussion." *Individualität. Poetik und Hermeneutik XIII*. Ed. Manfred Frank and Anselm Haverkamp. München: Fink, 1988. 608–15.

Frank, Manfred, Gérard Raulet, and Willem van Reijen, eds. *Die Frage nach dem Subjekt*. Frankfurt: Suhrkamp, 1988.

Frederiksen, Elke P., and Katherine R. Goodman, eds. *Bettina Brentano-von Arnim: Gender and Politics*. Detroit: Wayne State UP, 1995.

Freed, Mark M. *Robert Musil and the NonModern*. New York: Continuum, 2011.

Freud, Sigmund. *The Interpretation of Dreams*. Trans. James Strachey. London: Hogarth, 1953.

Fukuyama, Francis. *The End of History and the Last Man*. London: Hamish Hamilton, 1992.

Fukuyama, Francis. "The Future of History: Can Liberal Democracy Survive the Decline of the Middle Class?" *Foreign Affairs* 91.1 (2012): 53–61.

Gadamer, Hans Georg. *Truth and Method*. Trans. Joel Weinsheimer and Donald G. Marshall. New York: Continuum, 1999.

Galmiche, Xavier. "Le Rire jaune das l'oeuvre de Milan Kundera." *Esprit* 281.1 (2002): 52–61.

Gambarota, Paola. "Notizen zu Kunderas Broch-Lektüre." *Germanoslavica* 1 (1996): 47–59.

Garfinkle, Deborah. "Betraying K: Milan Kundera on Exile and the Translator's Art." *Modern Czech Studies* (1999): 54–64.

Gaughan, Richard T. "Who Are You? Kundera's *Identity*." *Publications of the Arkansas Philological Association* 25.2 (1999): 13–22.

Gautier, Brigitte. "Valses clandestines. Kundera en Pologne." *Désaccords parfaits. La Réception paradoxale de l'oeuvre de Milan Kundera*. Ed. Marie-Odile Thirouin and Martine Boyer-Weinmann. Grenoble: ELLUG, 2009. 49–57.

Giddens, Anthony. *The Consequences of Modernity*. Cambridge: Polity, 1990.

Goddard, Michael. *Gombrowicz, Polish Modernism, and the Subversion of Form*. West Lafayette: Purdue UP, 2010.

Goethe, Johann Wolfgang von. *Faust*. 1832. München: Deutscher Taschenbuch, 1982.

Goethe, Johann Wolfgang von. *Faust. Part Two*. 1833. Trans. Philip Wayne. Harmondsworth: Penguin, 1959.

Goethe, Johann Wolfgang von. *The Sorrows of Young Werther*. 1774. Trans. David Constantine. Oxford: Oxford UP, 2012.

Goethe, Johann Wolfgang von. *Truth and Poetry: From My Own Life*. Trans. John Oxenford. London: H. G. Bohm, 1848.

Goetz-Stankiewicz, Marketa. "Kundera's Sacred Cows and Bêtes Noires." *Critical Essays on Milan Kundera*. Ed. Peter Petro. New York: G. K. Hall, 1999. 242–54.

Goltschnigg, Dietmar. "Zur Poetik des Essays und des Essayismus bei Robert Musil und Hermann Broch." *Poetik und Geschichte*. Ed. Dieter Borchmeyer. Tübingen: Niemeyer, 1989. 412–24.

Gombrowicz, Witold. Afterword. *Ferdydurke*. By Witold Gombrowicz. 1961. Trans. Eric Mosbacher. Harmondsworth: Penguin, 1986. 273–90.

Gombrowicz, Witold. *Ferdydurke*. 1961. Trans. Eric Mosbacher. Harmondsworth: Penguin, 1986.

Habermas, Jürgen. *The Philosophical Discourse of Modernity: Twelve Lectures*. Trans. Frederick Lawrence. Cambridge: Polity, 1990.

Hagen, J. "Redrawing the Imagined Map of Europe: The Rise and Fall of the 'Center.'" *Political Geography* 22.5 (2003): 489–517: <http://dx.doi.org/10.1016/S0962-6298(03)00030-1>.

Haman, Aleš. "Quelques jalons dans la réception tchèque de l'oeuvre de Milan Kundera." *Désaccords parfaits. La Réception paradoxale de l'oeuvre de Milan Kundera*. Ed. Marie-Odile Thirouin and Martine Boyer-Weinmann. Grenoble: ELLUG, 2009. 139–60.

Hamšík, Dušan. *Writers against Rulers*. Trans. D. Orpington. London: Hutchinson, 1971.

Harrington, Austin. "Hermann Broch as a Reader of Max Weber: Protestantism, Rationalization and the 'Disintegration of Values.'" *History of the Human Sciences* 19.4 (2006): 1–18: <http://dx.doi.org/10.1177/0952695106069665>.

Harvey, David. *The Condition of Postmodernity: An Enquiry into the Origins of Cultural Change*. Oxford: Blackwell, 1989.

Hattingh, Herselman. "Being and the Dialectics of Irony: A Reading of Some of Milan Kundera's Novels." *Literator* 16.2 (1995): 95–121.

Haug, Walter. "Francesco Petrarca—Nicolaus Cusanus—Thüring von Ringoltingen. Drei Probestücke zu einer Geschichte der Individualität im 14./15. Jahrhundert." *Individualität. Poetik und Hermeneutik*. Ed. Manfred Frank and Anselm Haverkamp. München: Fink, 1988. 281–324.

Havel, Václav. *Disturbing the Peace: A Conversation with Karel Hvížďala*. Trans. Paul Wilson. London: Faber and Faber, 1990.

Havel, Václav. "Le Destin tchèque." 1968. *Gulliver* 1 (1990): 100–08.

Hegel, Georg Wilhelm Friedrich. *Aesthetics: Lectures on Fine Art*. 2 vols. Trans. T. M. Knox. Oxford: Clarendon, 1988.

Heidegger, Martin. *Being and Time*. 1927. Trans. John Macquarrie and Edward Robinson. Oxford: Blackwell, 1962.

Heidegger, Martin. *Erläuterungen zu Hölderlins Dichtung*. Frankfurt: Vittorio Klostermann, 1981.

Heidegger, Martin. *Nietzsche*. Stuttgart: Neske, 1998.

Heidegger, Martin. *The Origin of the Work of Art*. 1980. Trans. Julian Young and Kenneth Haynes. Cambridge: Cambridge UP, 2002.

Heinrich, Gerda. *Geschichtsphilosophische Positionen der deutschen Frühromantik*. Berlin: Akademie, 1976.

Herder, Johann Gottfried. *Abhandlung über den Ursprung der Sprache. Werke*. Vol. 5. By Johann Gottfried Herder. Ed. Ulrich Gaier. Frankfurt: Deutsche Klassiker, 1985. 695–810.

Herder, Johann Gottfried. *Ideen zur Philosophie der Geschichte der Menschheit*. Ed. Martin Bollacher. Frankfurt: Deutsche Klassiker, 1989.

Herder, Johann Gottfried. *Journal meiner Reise im Jahr 1769. Werke*. Vol. 9.2. By Johann Gottfried Herder. Ed. Rainer Wisbert and Klaus Pradel. Frankfurt: Deutscher Klassiker, 1997. 9–126.

Herder, Johann Gottfried. "Selbstgespräch." *Werke*. Vol. 3. By Johann Gottfried Herder. Ed. Ulrich Gaier. Frankfurt: Deutscher Klassiker, 1997. 778–80.

Herder, Johann Gottfried. "Über Bild, Dichtung und Fabel." *Werke*. Vol 4. By Johann Gottfried Herder. Ed. Martin Bollacher. Frankfurt: Deutsche Klassiker, 1994. 631–77.

Herder, Johann Gottfried. *Vom Geist der Ebräischen Poesie. Werke*. Vol 5. By Johann Gottfried Herder. Ed. Rudolf Smend. Frankfurt: Deutsche Klassiker, 1993. 661–1308.

Hillis Miller, J. *Fiction and Repetition: Seven English Novels*. Cambridge: Harvard UP, 1982.

Hobsbawm, Eric J. *Nations and Nationalism since 1780: Programme, Myth, Reality*. Cambridge: Cambridge UP, 1990.

Horkheimer, Max, and Theodor W. Adorno. *Dialectic of Enlightenment: Philosophical Fragments*. 1944. Trans. John Cumming. London: Verso, 1979.

Howell, Yvonne. "Baring the Brain as Well as the Soul: Milan Kundera's *The Joke*." *Philosophy and Literature* 34.1 (2010): 201–17: <http://dx.doi.org/10.1353/phl.0.0085>.

Hruby, Peter. *The Literary and Political Development of Milan Kundera*. Perth: Western Australian Institute of Technology, 1985.

Husserl, Edmund. *Ideas Pertaining to a Pure Phenomenology and to a Phenomenological Philosophy*. 1913. Trans. F. Karsten. Dordrecht: Kluwer, 1982: <http://dx.doi.org/10.1007/978-94-009-7445-6>.

Husserl, Edmund. *On the Phenomenology of the Consciousness of Internal Time (1893–1917)*. 1928. Trans. John Barnett Brough. Dordrecht: Kluwer, 1991: <http://dx.doi.org/10.1007/978-94-011-3718-8>.

Husserl, Edmund. *The Crisis of European Sciences and Transcendental Phenomenology*. 1936. Trans. David Carr. Evanston: Northwestern UP, 1970: <http://dx.doi.org/10.1002/9780470755501.ch9>.

Hutcheon, Linda. *A Poetics of Postmodernism: History, Theory, Fiction*. London: Routledge, 1988: <http://dx.doi.org/10.4324/9780203358856>.

Hybler, Martin. "L'Oeuvre poétique et théâtrale reniée de Kundera." *Désaccords parfaits. La Réception paradoxale de l'oeuvre de Milan Kundera*. Ed. Marie-Odile Thirouin and Martine Boyer-Weinmann. Grenoble: ELLUG, 2009. 77–99.

Irmscher, Hans Dietrich. *Johann Gottfried Herder*. Stuttgart: Reclam, 2001.

Ivanova, Velichka. *Fiction, utopie, histoire. Essai sur Philip Roth et Milan Kundera.* Paris: L'Harmattan, 2010.

Jäger, Georg. *Empfindsamkeit und Roman. Wortgeschichte, Theorie und Kritik im 18. und frühen 19. Jahrhundert.* Stuttgart: Kohlhammer, 1969.

Jakobson, Roman. "Two Aspects of Language and Two Types of Aphasic Disturbances." 1956. *Language in Literature.* Ed. Krystyna Pomorska. Cambridge: Harvard UP, 1987. 95–114.

Jameson, Fredric. *Postmodernism, or, The Cultural Logic of Late Capitalism.* Durham: Duke UP, 1991.

Jannidis, Fotis. *Das Individuum und sein Jahrhundert. Eine Komponenten—und Funktionsanalyse des Begriffs 'Bildung' am Beispiel von Goethes* Dichtung und Wahrheit. Tübingen: Niemeyer, 1996.

Jefferson, Ann. "Counterpoint and Forked Tongues: Milan Kundera and the Art of Exile." *Renaissance and Modern Studies* 34.1 (1991): 115–36: <http://dx.doi.org/10.1080/14735789109366547>.

Jungmann, Milan. "Kunderian Paradoxes." *Critical Essays on Milan Kundera.* Ed. Peter Petro. New York: G. K. Hall, 1999. 119–24.

Kafka, Franz. "A Little Fable." 1931. *The Complete Stories.* By Franz Kafka. Trans. Willa Muir, Edwin Muir, Tania Stern, and James Stern. Ed. Nahum N. Glatzer. New York: Schocken, 1995. 445.

Kafka, Franz. *The Castle.* Trans. John R. Williams. Hertfordshire: Wordsworth, 2009.

Kant, Immanuel. *Critique of Judgement.* 1790. Trans. James Creed Meredith. Chicago: William Benton, 1952.

Kaufmann, Walter. *Nietzsche: Philosopher, Psychologist, Antichrist.* Princeton: Princeton UP, 1950.

Kendon, Adam. *Gesture: Visible Action as Utterance.* Cambridge: Cambridge UP, 2004.

Kienzle, Bertram, and Helmut Pape, eds. *Dimensionen des Selbst. Selbstreflexion, Reflexivität und die Bedingungen von Kommunikation.* Frankfurt: Suhrkamp, 1991.

Kliche, Dieter. "Kitsch." *Ästhetische Grundbegriffe.* Vol. 3. Ed. Karlheinz Barck, Martin Fontius, Dieter Schlenstedt, Burkhart Steinwachs, and Friedrich Wolfzettel. Stuttgart: Metzler, 2001. 272–88.

Kondylis, Panajotis. *Die Aufklärung im Rahmen des neuzeitlichen Rationalismus.* München: Deutscher Taschenbuch, 1986.

Koselleck, Reinhart. *Futures Past: On the Semantics of Historical Time.* Trans. Keith Tribe. New York: Columbia UP, 2004.

Kramer, Jane. "When There is No Word for 'Home'." *The New York Times Book Review* (29 April 1984): 46.

Kulka, Tomáš. *Kitsch and Art.* University Park: The Pennsylvania State UP, 1996.

Kundera, Milan. "A Kidnapped West or Culture Bows Out." *Granta* 11 (1984): 95–118.

Kundera, Milan. "An Introduction to a Variation." *Cross Currents* 5 (1986): 469–76.

Kundera, Milan. *Avainten haltijat* (*Majitelé klíčů*). 1962. Trans. Kirsti Siraste. Helsinki: Näytelmäkulma, 2011. Unpubl. ms.

Kundera, Milan. *Člověk zahrada širá*. Praha: Československý spisovatel, 1953.

Kundera, Milan. "Comedy is Everywhere." *Index on Censorship* 6.6 (1977): 3–7: <http://dx.doi.org/10.1080/03064227708532708>.

Kundera, Milan. *Encounter*. Trans. Linda Ashker. London: Faber and Faber, 2010.

Kundera, Milan. "Esch Is Luther." *Review of Contemporary Fiction* 8.2 (1988): 266–72.

Kundera, Milan. *Farewell Waltz*. Trans. Aaron Asher. London: Faber and Faber, 1998.

Kundera, Milan. *Identity*. Trans. Linda Asher. London: Faber and Faber, 1999.

Kundera, Milan. *Ignorance*. Trans. Linda Asher. London: Faber and Faber, 2003.

Kundera, Milan. *Immortality*. Trans. Peter Kussi. London: Faber and Faber, 1992.

Kundera, Milan. *Jacques and His Master*. Trans. Simon Callow. London: Faber and Faber, 1986.

Kundera, Milan. *Jacques et son maître. Hommage à Denis Diderot en trois actes*. Paris: Gallimard, 1981.

Kundera, Milan. *Kniha smíchu a zapomnění*. Toronto: Sixty-Eight Publishers, 1981.

Kundera, Milan. *La ignorancia*. Trans. Beatriz de Moura. Barcelona: Tusquets, 2000.

Kundera, Milan. *L'Art du roman. Essai*. Paris: Gallimard, 1986.

Kundera, Milan. *L'Identité*. Paris: Gallimard, 2000.

Kundera, Milan. *L'Ignorance*. Paris: Gallimard, 2005.

Kundera, Milan. *L'Immortalité*. Trans. Eva Bloch. Paris: Gallimard, 1993.

Kundera, Milan. *L'Insoutenable légèreté de l'être*. Trans. François Kérel. Paris: Gallimard, 1989.

Kundera, Milan. *La Lenteur*. Paris: Gallimard, 1994.

Kundera, Milan. *La Plaisanterie*. Trans. Marcel Aymonin, Claude Courtot, and Milan Kundera. Paris: Gallimard, 2003.

Kundera, Milan. "La 'Parole' de Kundera." *Le Monde* (24 September 1993): 24, 44.

Kundera, Milan. *La Valse aux adieux*. Trans. François Kérel. Paris: Gallimard, 1999.

Kundera, Milan. *Laughable Loves*. Trans. Suzanne Rappaport. London: Faber and Faber, 1999.

Kundera, Milan. *La Vie est ailleurs*. Trans. François Kérel. Paris: Gallimard, 1987.

Kundera, Milan. "Le Destin tchèque." 1968. *Gulliver* 1 (1990): 90–98.

Kundera, Milan. *Le Livre du rire et de l'oubli*. Trans. François Kérel. Paris: Gallimard, 1985.

Kundera, Milan. *Le Rideau. Essai en sept parties*. Paris: Gallimard, 2005.

Kundera, Milan. *Les Testaments trahis. Essai*. Paris: Gallimard, 1993.

Kundera, Milan. *Life Is Elsewhere*. Trans. Aaron Asher. London: Faber and Faber, 2000.

Kundera, Milan. *Majitelé klíčů. Hra o jednom dějství se čtyřmi vizemi*. Praha: Orbis, 1962.

Kundera, Milan. *Monology*. Praha: Československý spisovatel, 1957.

Kundera, Milan. *Nesmrtlnost*. Brno: Atlantis, 1993.

Kundera, Milan. *Nesnesitelná lehkost bytí*. Toronto: Sixty-Eight Publishers, 1985.

Kundera, Milan. "On Criticism, Aesthetics, and Europe." *Review of Contemporary Fiction* 9.2 (1989): 13–16.

Kundera, Milan. *Poslední máj*. Praha: Československý spisovatel, 1955.

Kundera, Milan. *Ptákovina. Divadelní hra*. Praha: n.p., 1968.

Kundera, Milan. *Risibles amours*. Trans. François Kérel. Paris: Gallimard, 1994.

Kundera, Milan. *Slowness*. Trans. Linda Asher. London: Faber and Faber, 1996.

Kundera, Milan. *Směšné lásky*. Praha: Československý spisovatel, 1963.

Kundera, Milan. Speech, Fourth Congress of the Czechoslovak Writers' Union, 27 June 1967. *Writers against Rulers*. Ed. Dušan Hamšík. Trans. D. Orpington. London: Hutchinson, 1971. 167–77.

Kundera, Milan. *Testaments Betrayed: An Essay in Nine Parts*. Trans. Linda Asher. London: Faber and Faber, 1996.

Kundera, Milan. *The Art of the Novel*. Trans. Linda Asher. London: Faber and Faber, 2000.

Kundera, Milan. *The Book of Laughter and Forgetting*. Trans. Aaron Asher. London: Faber and Faber, 1996.

Kundera, Milan. *The Curtain: An Essay in Seven Parts*. Trans. Linda Asher. London: Faber and Faber, 2007.

Kundera, Milan. "The Czech Wager." *The New York Review of Books* (22 January 1981): 21–22.

Kundera, Milan. "The Umbrella, the Night World, and the Lonely Moon." *The New York Review of Books* (19 December 1991): 44–48.

Kundera, Milan. *The Joke*. London: Faber and Faber, 1992.

Kundera, Milan. *The Joke*. Trans. David Hamblyn and Oliver Stallybrass. Harmondsworth: Penguin, 1969.

Kundera, Milan. *The Joke*. Trans. Michael Henry Heim. Harmondsworth: Penguin, 1984.

Kundera, Milan. "The Tragedy of Central Europe." *The New York Review of Books* (26 April 1984): 33–38.

Kundera, Milan. *The Unbearable Lightness of Being*. Trans. Michael Henry Heim. London: Faber and Faber, 1995.

Kundera, Milan. *Umění románu. Cesta vladislava Vančury za velkou epikou*. Praha: Československý spisovatel, 1961.

Kundera, Milan. *Une Rencontre*. Paris: Gallimard, 2009.

Kundera, Milan. *Valčík na rozloučenou*. Toronto: Sixty-Eight Publishers, 1979.

Kundera, Milan. *Žert*. Praha: Žatva, 1996.

Lafargue, Bernard. "Fiction, donjuanisme et kitsch dans l'oeuvre de Milan Kundera." *Fiction & Connaissance. Essays sur le savoir à l'oeuvre de fiction*. Ed. Catherine Coquio and Régis Salado. Paris: L'Harmattan, 1998. 251–78.

Lahtinen, Kai. "Milan Kundera i postmodernismen." *Finsk Tidskrift* 7 (1989): 424–31.

Le Grand, Eva. "Kitsch, roman et beauté." *Visions of Beauty*. Ed. Roseann Runte and Hans Runte. Tokyo: Tokyo UP, 1995. 426–36.

Le Grand, Eva. *Kundera or the Memory of Desire*. Trans. Lin Burman. Waterloo: Wilfrid Laurier UP, 1999.

Le Grand, Eva. "L'Esthétique de la variation romanesque chez Kundera." *L'Infini* 5 (1984): 56–64.

Le Grand, Eva. "Voyage dans le temps de l'Europe (ou de l'esthétique romanesque de Milan Kundera)." *L'Infini* 44 (1993): 73–97.

Le Rider, Jacques. "Adieux à l'Europe Centrale." *Désaccords parfaits. La Réception paradoxale de l'oeuvre de Milan Kundera*. Ed. Marie-Odile Thirouin and Martine Boyer-Weinmann. Grenoble: ELLUG, 2009. 19–36.

Leclerc, Annie. *Parole de femme*. Paris: Grasset, 1976.

Leerssen, Joep. "Imagology: History and Method." *imagologica.eu* (2012): <http://www.imagologica.eu/pdf/historymethod.pdf>.

Lévi-Strauss, Claude. *The Raw and the Cooked: Introduction to a Science of Mythology*. Trans. John Weightman and Doreen Weightman. New York: Harper & Row, 1975.

Liehm, Antonin J. Interview with Milan Kundera. *Trois générations. Entretiens sur le phénomène culturel tchécoslovaque (Generace 1968)*. Trans. Marcel Aymonin. Paris: Gallimard, 1970. 91–110.

Liehm, Antonin J. "Milan Kundera: Czech Writer." *Milan Kundera and the Art of Fiction: Critical Essays*. Ed. Aron Aji. New York: Garland, 1992. 27–43.

Liehm, Antonin J. *Trois générations. Entretiens sur le phénomène culturel tchécoslovaque (Generace 1968)*. Trans. Marcel Aymonin. Paris: Gallimard, 1970.

Lodge, David. "Milan Kundera and the Idea of the Author in Modern Criticism." *Critical Quarterly* 26.1–2 (1984): 105–21: <http://dx.doi.org/10.1111/j.1467-8705.1984.tb00705.x>.

Longus. *Daphnis and Chloe*. Trans. Ronald McCail. Oxford: Oxford UP, 2002.

Luckmann, Thomas. "Persönliche Identität, soziale Rollen und Rollendistanz." *Identität. Poetik und Hermeneutik VIII*. Ed. Odo Marquard and Karlheinz Stierle. München: Fink, 1979. 293–314.

Luhmann, Niklas. *Gesellschaftsstruktur und Semantik. Studien zur Wissenssoziologie der modernen Gesellschaft*. Frankfurt: Suhrkamp, 1989.

Luhmann, Niklas. *Love as Passion: The Codification of Intimacy*. Trans. Jeremy Gaines and Doris L. Jones. Cambridge: Polity, 1986.

Lukács, Georg [György]. *The Theory of the Novel: A Historico-philosophical Essay on the Forms of Great Epic Literature*. 1920. Trans. Anna Bostock. London: Merlin, 1971.

Lützeler, Paul Michael. *Die Schriftsteller und Europa*. München: Piper, 1992.

Lützeler, Michael Paul, ed. *Hermann Broch: Visionary in Exile*. Rochester: Camden House, 2003.

Lutzky, Klara. "Kundera's Reception in the West (1980–1990)." *Literature in Exile of East and Central Europe*. Ed. Agnieszka Gutthy. Bern: Peter Lang, 2009. 105–20.

Lyotard, Jean-François. *The Postmodern Condition: A Report on Knowledge*. Trans. Geoff Bennington and Brian Massumi. Manchester: Manchester UP, 1984: <http://dx.doi.org/10.2307/1772278>.

Macura, Vladimir. *The Mystifications of a Nation: "The Potato Bug" and Other Essays on Czech Culture*. Ed. and trans. Hana Píchová and Craig Cravens. Madison: U of Wisconsin P, 2010.

Maixent, Jocelyn. *Le XVIIIe siècle de Milan Kundera ou Diderot investi par le roman contemporain*. Paris: PU de France, 1998.

Makarushka, Irena. "Redemption and Narrative: Refiguration of Time in Postmodern Literature." *European Literature and Theology in the Twentieth Century*. Ed. David Jasper and Colin Crowder. London: Macmillan, 1990. 143–52.

Mann, Thomas. *Doctor Faustus*. Trans. John E. Woods. New York: Vintage, 1999.

Mann, Thomas. *Nietzsche's Philosophy in the Light of Contemporary Events*. Washington: Library of Congress, 1947.

Mann, Thomas. *The Story of a Novel: The Genesis of Doctor Faustus*. 1949. Trans. Richard Winston and Clara Winston. New York: Knopf, 1961.

Marquardt, Odo. "Anthropologie." *Historisches Wörterbuch der Philosophie*. Vol. 1. Ed. J. Ritter. Darmstadt: Wissenschaftliche Buchgesellschaft, 1971. 362–74.

Marx, Karl. *Economic and Philosophical Manuscripts of 1844*. Trans. Martin Milligan. Moskva: Foreign Language Publishing, 1959.

Matejka, Ladislav. "Milan Kundera's Central Europe." *Critical Essays on Milan Kundera*. Ed. Peter Petro. New York: G. K. Hall, 1999. 210–16.

Mathias, Manon, Maria O'Sullivan, and Ruth Vorstman, eds. *Dangerous Disguise: An Approach to the Relation between Kitsch and Arts*. Bern: Peter Lang, 2011.

McBride, Patrizia C. *The Void of Ethics: Robert Musil and the Experience of Modernity*. Evanston: Northwestern UP, 2006.

McEwan, Ian. "An Interview with Milan Kundera." *Granta* 11 (1984): 21–37.

McHale, Brian. *Postmodernist Fiction*. London: Routledge, 1987: <http://dx.doi.org/10.4324/9780203393321>.

Messner, Elena. "Rezeptionsmodelle in Milan Kunderas Roman *L'Immortalité*." *Arcadia: International Journal for Literary Studies* 45.1 (2010): 177–90: <http://dx.doi.org/10.1515/arca.2010.010>.

Miletric, Tijana. *European Literary Immigration into the French Language: Readings of Gary, Kristof, Kundera and Semprun*. Amsterdam: Rodopi, 2008.

Miłosz, Czesław. "Who Is Gombrowicz?" *Ferdydurke*. 1961. By Witold Gobrowicz. Trans. Eric Mosbacher. Harmondsworth: Penguin, 1986. vii–xxvii.

Mirzoeff, Nicholas. *The Visual Culture Reader*. London: Routledge, 1998.

Misurella, Fred. *Understanding Milan Kundera: Public Events, Private Affairs*. Columbia: U of South Carolina P, 1993.

Mitchell, W. J. T. *Picture Theory: Essays on Verbal and Visual Representation*. Chicago: U of Chicago P, 1994.

Morello, André-Alain. "L'Eclair divin de Kundera." *dix-neuf vingt* 1 (1996): 141–42.

Morello, André-Alain, and Milan Kundera. "Questions et réponses échangeés par écrit entrée André-Alain Morello et Milan Kundera." *dix-neuf vingt* 1 (1996): 145–49.

Moxey, Keith. "Visual Studies and the Iconic Turn." *Journal of Visual Culture* 7.2 (2008): 131–46: <http://dx.doi.org/10.1177/1470412908091934>.

Müller, Klaus-Detlef. "Die Autobiographie der Goethezeit. Historischer Sinn und gattungsgeschichtliche Perspektiven." *Die Autobiographie. Zu Form und Geschichte einer literarischen Gattung*. Ed. Günter Niggl. Darmstadt: Wissenschaftliche Buchgesellschaft, 1989. 459–81.

Musil, Robert. *The Man Without Qualities*. 1930–1952. Trans. Eithne Wilkins and Ernst Kaiser. Bungay: Picador, 1979.

Mytze, Andreas W. "Milan Kundera oder über das Scheitern." *Europäische Ideen* 20 (1976): 37–50.

Němcová Banerjee, Maria. "Czech Laughter between Hašek and Kafka." *World Literature Today* 59.1 (1985): 14–17: <http://dx.doi.org/10.2307/40140524>.

Němcová Banerjee, Maria. *Terminal Paradoxes: The Novels of Milan Kundera*. New York: Grove Weidenfeld, 1990.

Nietzsche, Friedrich. *Also Sprach Zarathustra. Ein Buch für Alle und Keinen*. 1883–1885. Ed. Giorgio Colli and Mazino Montinari. München: Deutscher Taschenbuch, 1999.

Nietzsche, Friedrich. *Beyond Good and Evil: Prelude to a Philosophy of the Future*. 1886. Trans. Judith Norman. Cambridge: Cambridge UP, 2002.

Nietzsche, Friedrich. *Daybreak: Thoughts on the Prejudices of Morality*. 1881. Trans. R. J. Hollingdale. Cambridge: Cambridge UP, 1982: <http://dx.doi.org/10.1017/CBO9780511812040.005>.

Nietzsche, Friedrich. *Nachgelassene Fragmente 1887–1889*. Ed. Giorgio Colli and Mazzino Montinari. Berlin: De Gruyter, 1999.

Nietzsche, Friedrich. *The Birth of Tragedy*. 1872. Trans. Walter Kaufmann. New York: Vintage, 1967.

Nietzsche, Friedrich. *The Gay Science*. 1882. Trans. Josefine Nauckhoff. Cambridge: Cambridge UP, 2001.

Nietzsche, Friedrich. *Thus Spoke Zarathustra: A Book for Everyone and No One*. 1883–1885. Trans. R. J. Hollingdale. Harmondsworth: Penguin, 1985.

Nisbet, Hugh Barr. "Goethes und Herders Geschichtsdenken." *Goethe-Jahrbuch* 110 (1993): 115–33.

Novalis [Friedrich von Hardenberg]. *Heinrich von Ofterdingen*. 1802. *Schriften*. By Novalis. Ed. Paul Kluckhohn and Richard Samuel. Darmstadt: Wissenschaftliche Buchgesellschaft 1977.

O'Brien, John. "Falling into Fiction: Kundera & the 18th Century English Novel." *Milan Kundera and the Art of Fiction: Critical Essays*. Ed. Aron Aji. New York: Garland, 1992. 88–101.

O'Brien, John. "Milan Kundera: Meaning, Play, and the Role of the Author." *Critiques: Studies in Contemporary Fiction* 34.1 (1992): 3–18: <http://dx.doi.org/10.1080/00111619.1992.9935229>.

O'Brien, John. *Milan Kundera & Feminism: Dangerous Intersections*. New York: St. Martin's, 1995.

Oppenheim, Lois. "Clarifications, Elucidations: An Interview with Milan Kundera." *Review of Contemporary Fiction* 9.2 (1989): 7–12.

Palouš, Martin. "Revolutions and Revolutionaries: Lessons of the Years of Crises (Three Czech Encounters with Freedom)." *Promises of 1968: Crisis, Illusion, and Utopia*. Ed. Vladimir Tismaneanu. Budapest: Central European UP, 2011. 21–42.

Papoušek, Vladimir. "Ne vous comportez pas dans mes livres comme chez vous. Le droit de l'auteur chez Milan Kundera." *Désaccords parfaits. La Réception paradoxale de l'oeuvre de Milan Kundera*. Ed. Marie-Odile Thirouin and Martine Boyer-Weinmann. Grenoble: ELLUG, 2009. 19–36. 205–14.

Papoušek, Vladimír. "Strategy of Representations in Literary Texts." *Models of Representations in Czech Literary History*. Ed. Petr A. Bílek and Vladimír Papoušek. Boulder: East European Monographs, 2010. 3–27.

Parnell, Tim. "Sterne and Kundera: The Novel of Variations and the 'Noisy Foolishness of Human Certainty." *Laurence Sterne in Modernism and Postmodernism*. Ed. David Pierce and Peter de Voogd. Amsterdam: Rodopi, 1996. 147–55.

Payne, Philip, Graham Bartram, and Galin Tihanov. *A Companion to the Works of Robert Musil*. Rochester: Camden House, 2007.

Pelikan Straus, Nina. "Erasing History and Deconstructing the Text: Milan Kundera's *The Book of Laughter and Forgetting*." *Contemporary Fiction* 28.2 (1987): 69–85: <http://dx.doi.org/10.1080/00111619.1987.9937831>.

Pérez Gay, José María. *The Unfortunate Passion of Hermann Broch*. Trans. Eduardo Jiménez Mayo. Northridge: Floricanto, 2008.

Petras, Martin. "L'Homme qui interroge et l'homme interrogé. À propos de la réception de *L'Insoutenable légèreté de l'être* en France et en Bohême." *Désaccords parfaits. La Réception paradoxale de l'oeuvre de Milan Kundera*. Ed. Marie-Odile Thirouin and Martine Boyer-Weinmann. Grenoble: ELLUG, 2009. 19–36, 59–74.

Petro, Peter. "Apropos Dostoevsky: Brodsky, Kundera and the Definition of Europe." *Literature and Politics in Central Europe*. Ed. Leslie Miller, Klaus Petersen, Peter Stenberg, et al. Rochester: Camden House, 1994. 76–90.

Petro, Peter. "Milan Kundera's Search for Authenticity." *Canadian Slavonic Papers / Revue Canadienne des Slavistes* 24.1 (1982): 44–49.

Petrović, Nikola. "Kafka, Švejk, and the Butcher's Wife, or Postcommunism/ Postcolonialism and Central Europe." *History of the Literary Cultures of East-Central Europe: Junctures and Disjunctures in the 19th and 20th Centuries*. Ed. Marcel Cornis-Pope and John Neubauer. Amsterdam: Benjamins, 2006. 376–90.

Phillips, John. "L'Insoutenable lègèreté du rire: Laughter and Power in Milan Kundera's *La Lenteur* and Vivant Denon's *Point de Lendemain*." *Laughter and Power*. Ed. John Parkin and John Phillips. Bern: Peter Lang, 2006. 145–58.

Pichova, Hana. "Milan Kundera and the Identity of Central Europe." *Comparative Central European Culture*. Ed. Steven Tötösy de Zepetnek. West Lafayette: Purdue UP, 2001. 103–14.

Píchová, Hana. *The Art of Memory in Exile: Vladimir Nabokov & Milan Kundera*. Carbondale: Southern Illinois UP, 2002.

Pierce, Gillian B. "Theme and Variation: Milan Kundera, Denis Diderot, and the Art of the Novel." *Comparatist* 33.1 (2009): 132–55: <http://dx.doi.org/10.1353/com.0.0044>.

Pike, Burton. *Robert Musil: An Introduction to His Work*. 1961. Washington: Kennikat, 1972.

Porter, Robert C. *Milan Kundera: A Voice from Central Europe*. Aarhus: Arkona, 1981.

Pross, Harry, ed. *Kitsch. Soziale und politische Aspekte einer Geschmacksfrage*. München: Paul List, 1985.

Raddatz, Fritz. "'Ich bin zu skeptisch, um Pessimist zu sein.' Gespräch mit Milan Kundera." *Zeitgespräche 3*. By Fritz Raddatz. Frankfurt: Suhrkamp, 1986. 95–109.

Ricard, François. *Agnès' Final Afternoon: An Essay on the Work of Milan Kundera*. Trans. Aaron Asher. London: Faber & Faber, 2003.

Richter, David H. "Chicago School." *Routledge Encyclopedia of Narrative Theory*. Ed. David Herman, Manfred Jahn, and Marie-Laure Ryan. London: Routledge, 2005. 57–59.

Richterova, Sylvie. "Les Romans de Kundera et les problèmes de la communication." *L'Infini* 5 (1984): 32–55.

Rizza, Michael James. "Continuity and Complexity in Milan Kundera's *Immortality*." *Critique: Studies in Contemporary Fiction* 50.4 (2009): 350–64: <http://dx.doi.org/10.3200/CRIT.50.4.350-364>.

Ross, Stephen. "The Abdication of Culture: The Ideology of Imagology in Milan Kundera's *Immortality*." *Modern Fiction Studies* 46.2 (2000): 331–54: <http://dx.doi.org/10.1353/mfs.2000.0041>.

Rostinsky, Joseph N. "Moravian Triptych: An Iconoclastic Attempt at Depoetization in the Work of Kundera, Trefulka and Vaculík." *Ein Leben für Dichtung und Freiheit*. Ed. Rudnik Hans-H. and Klaus Wissenberger. Tübingen: Stauffenburg, 1997. 227–32.

Roth, Philip. "In Defence of Intimacy." *London Times Magazine* (20 May 1984): 49–51.

Roth, Philip. "The Most Original Book of the Season." *The New York Times Book Review* (10 November 1980): 7, 78.

Saariluoma [Steinby], Liisa. Der postindividualistische Roman. Würzburg: Königshausen & Neumann, 1994.

Saariluoma [Steinby], Liisa. *Erzählstruktur und Bildungsroman. Wielands* Geschichte des Agathon, *Goethes* Wilhelm Meisters Lehrjahre. Würzburg: Königshausen & Neumann, 2004.

Saariluoma [Steinby], Liisa. "Kundera, Broch und die Tradition des modernen Romans." *Poetica* 30.1–2 (1998): 179–99.

Saariluoma [Steinby], Liisa. *Milan Kundera, viimeinen modernisti*. Turku: Faros, 2005.

Saariluoma [Steinby], Liisa. "Narrativisation of Identity in the Novels of the 18th Century." *Interlitteraria* 12 (2007): 111–24.

Saariluoma [Steinby], Liisa. *Nietzsche als Roman. Über die Sinnkonstituierung in Thomas Manns* Doktor Faustus. Tübingen: Niemeyer, 1996.

Sachs-Hombach, Klaus, ed. *Bildtheorien. Anthropologische und kulturelle Grundlagen des Visualistic Turn*. Frankfurt: Suhrkamp, 2009.

Sauder, Gerhard. *Empfindsamkeit*. Stuttgart: Metzler, 1980.

Sauzon, Virginie, and Stéphane Chaudier. "L'Anti-lyrisme et ses enjeux." *Désaccords parfaits. La Réception paradoxale de l'oeuvre de Milan Kundera*. Ed. Marie-Odile Thirouin and Martine Boyer-Weinmann. Grenoble: ELLUG, 2009. 247–64.

Scarpetta, Guy. "Foreword: A Collaborative Reading." *Kundera or the Memory of Desire*. By Eva Le Grand. Trans. Lin Burman. Waterloo: Wilfrid Laurier UP, 1999. xi–xviii.

Schelling, F. W. J. *Philosophie der Kunst*. 1859. Darmstadt: Wissenschaftliche Buchgesellschaft, 1990.

Schiller, Friedrich. *On the Aesthetic Education of Man, in a Series of Letters. 1795*. Ed. and trans. Elisabeth M. Wilkinson and L. A. Willoughby. Oxford: Clarendon, 1967.

Schlegel, August Wilhelm. Review of Soltau's *Don Quixote* translation. *Athenäum* 3.2 (1800): 295–327.

Schlegel, August Wilhelm. Review of Tieck's *Don Quixote* translation. *Allgemeine Litteraturzeitung* 3 (1798): 295–327.

Schlegel, Friedrich. "Athenäums-Fragmente." *Kritische Schriften und Fragmente*. Vol. 2. By Friedrich Schlegel. Ed. Ernst Behler and Hans Eichner. Paderborn: Schöningh, 1988. 105–56.

Schlegel, Friedrich. Review of Tieck's *Don Quixote* translation. *Athenäum* 2.2 (1799): 324–27.

Schlegel, Friedrich. "Über Goethes Meister." 1798. *Kritische Schriften und Fragmente*. Vol. 2. By Friedrich Schlegel. Ed. Ernst Behler and Hans Eichner. Paderborn: Schöningh, 1988. 157–69.

Schmidt, Siegfried J. *Die Selbstorganisation des Sozialsystems Literatur im 18. Jahrhundert*. Frankfurt: Suhrkamp, 1989.

Schmitt, Gerhard. *Zyklus und Kompensation. Zur Denkfigur bei Nietzsche und Jung*. Bern: Peter Lang, 1998.

Schulte-Sasse, Jochen. *Literarischer Kitsch. Texte zu seiner Theorie, Geschichte und Einzelinterpretation*. Tübingen: Niemeyer, 1979.

Schulze Wessel, Martin. "Die Mitte liegt westwärts. Mitteleuropa in tschechischer Diskussion." *Bohemia: Zeitschrift für Geschichte und Kultur der böhmischen Länder* 3 (1988): 325–44.

Sera, Manfred. *Utopie und Parodie bei Musil, Broch und Thomas Mann*. Bonn: H. Bouvier, 1969.

Škvorecký, Josef. "Milan Kundera's Contribution to the Art of the Novel." *Milan Kundera and the Art of Fiction: Critical Essays*. Ed. Aron Aji. New York: Garland, 1992. 4–8.

Slater, Michelle B. "Shifting Literary Tectonic Plates: Kundera's Call for Supranational Literature and the World Literature in French Manifesto." *Modern Language Notes* 125.4 (2010): 913–26.

Solger, K. W. F. *Vorlesungen über die Ästhetik*. 1829. Ed. K. W. L. Heyse. Darmstadt: Wissenschaftliche Buchgesellschaft, 1962.

Spaemann, R. "Freiheit." *Historisches Wörterbuch der Philosophie*. Vol 2. Ed. Joachim Ritter. Darmstadt: Wissenschaftliche Buchgesellschaft, 1972. 1064–98.

Stach, Reiner. *Kafka: The Decisive Years*. Trans. Shelley Frisch. New York: Harcourt, 2005.

Stanger, Allison. "In Search of *The Joke*: An Open Letter to Milan Kundera." *New England Review* 18.1 (1997): 93–100.

Steinby, Liisa. "Ein mitteleuropäischer Zusammenhang: Die Bedeutung von Kafka, Musil und Broch für Milan Kunderas Kunst des Romans." *Deutsch im interkulturellen Begegnungsraum Ostmitteleuropa*. Ed. Ernest W. B. Hess-Lüttich. Bern: Peter Lang, 2010. 103–19.

Steinby, Liisa. "The Rehabilitation of Myth: Enlightenment and Romanticism in Johann Gottfried Herder's *Vom Geist der Ebräischen Poesie*." *Sjuttonhundratal* 1 (2009): 51–76.

Steinecke, Hartmut. "Das Schlafwandeln. Zur Deutung des Motivs in Hermann Brochs Trilogie." *Hermann Broch. Perspektiven der Forschung*. Ed. Manfred Durzak. München: Fink, 1972. 69–88.

Steiner, Peter. "Cynic Hero: Jaroslav Hašek's *The Good Soldier Švejk*." *Litteraria Pragensia: Studies in Literature and Culture* 4.8 (1994): 48–91.

Steiner, Peter. "Ironies of History: *The Joke* of Milan Kundera." *Fiction Updated: Theories of Fictionality, Narratology, and Poetics*. Ed. Calin Andrei Mihalescu and Walid Hamarneh. Toronto: U of Toronto P, 1996. 197–212.

Steiner, Peter. "Justice in Prague, Poetical and Poetic: Some Reflections of the Slánský Trial (with Constant Reference to Franz Kafka and Milan Kundera)." *Poetics Today* 21.4 (2000): 653–79: <http://dx.doi.org/10.1215/03335372-21-4-653>.

Steiner, Peter. *The Deserts of Bohemia: Czech Fiction and Its Social Context*. Ithaca: Cornell UP, 2000.

Strelka, Joseph. *Kafka, Musil, Broch und die Entwicklung des modernen Romans*. Wien: Forum, 1959.

Tachtiris, Corine. "Relation and Identity: Milan Kundera and Dany Laferrière Redefine the World." *Comparatist* 36.1 (2012): 178–95: <http://dx.doi.org/10.1353/com.2012.0011>.

Tägil, Sven, ed. *Regions in Central Europe: The Legacy of History*. West Lafayette: Purdue UP, 1999.

Tautz, Mirjam. "La Migration comme critère dans la réception de Milan Kundera et d'Andreï Makine par la presse française." *La Littérature "française" contemporaine. Contact de cultures et créativité*. Ed. Ursula Mathi-Moser and Birgit Mertz-Baumtgartner. Tübingen: Narr, 2007. 73–87.

Taylor, Charles. *Sources of the Self: The Making of the Modern Identity*. Cambridge: Cambridge UP, 1989.

Thiher, Allen. *Understanding Musil*. Los Angeles: U of South Carolina P, 2009.

Thirouin, Marie-Odile. "La Lentation de l'anti-humanisme dans l'oeuvre de Kundera." *Désaccords parfaits. La Réception paradoxale de l'oeuvre de Milan Kundera*. Ed. Marie-Odile Thirouin and Martine Boyer-Weinmann. Grenoble: ELLUG, 2009. 291–304.

Thirouin, Marie-Odile. "Le Mystère Kundera." *Désaccords parfaits. La Réception paradoxale de l'oeuvre de Milan Kundera*. Ed. Marie-Odile Thirouin and Martine Boyer-Weinmann. Grenoble: ELLUG, 2009. 5–15.

Thirouin, Marie-Odile, ed. *De Hašek à Brecht. Fortune de la figure de Chvéïk en Europe*. Grenoble: U Stendhal-Grenoble 3, 2006.

Thirouin, Marie-Odile, and Martine Boyer-Weinmann, eds. *Désaccords parfaits. La Réception paradoxale de l'oeuvre de Milan Kundera*. Grenoble: ELLUG, 2009.

Thomas, Alfred. *Prague Palimpsest: Writing, Memory and the City*. Chicago: U of Chicago P, 2010.

Tötösy de Zepetnek, Steven. "Comparative Cultural Studies and the Study of Central European Culture." *Comparative Central European Culture*. Ed. Steven Tötösy de Zepetnek. West Lafayette: Purdue UP, 2002. 1–32.

Tötösy de Zepetnek, Steven. "From Comparative Literature Today toward Comparative Cultural Studies." *Comparative Literature and Comparative*

Cultural Studies. Ed. Steven Tötösy de Zepetnek. West Lafayette: Purdue UP, 2003. 235–67.

Tötösy de Zepetnek, Steven. "The New Humanities: The Intercultural, the Comparative, and the Interdisciplinary." *Globalization and the Futures of Comparative Literature*. Ed. Jan M. Ziolkowski and Alfred J. López. Thematic Section *Global Society* 1.2 (2007): 45–68.

Tötösy de Zepetnek, Steven, and Louise O. Vasvári. "The Comparative and Contextual Study of Literature and Culture and Globalization." *Companion to Comparative Literature and Comparative Cultural Studies*. Ed. Steven Tötösy de Zepetnek and Tutun Mukherjee. New Delhi: Cambridge UP India, 2012.

Uerlings, Herbert. *Friedrich von Hardenberg, genannt Novalis. Werk und Forschung*. Stuttgart: Metzler, 1991.

Varsava, Jerry A. "Under Construction: 'World Literature' in the Twenty-first Century." *symplokē: a journal for the intermingling of literary, cultural and theoretical scholarship* 19.1–2 (2011): 329–38.

Very, Bertrand. "Milan Kundera or the Hazards of Subjectivity." *Review of Contemporary Fiction* 9.2 (1989): 79–106.

Vibert, Bertrand. "En finir avec le narrateur? Sur la pratique romanesque de Milan Kundera." *La Voix narrative*. Vol. 2. Ed. Jean-Louis Brau. Nice: U Nice-Hopia Antipolis, 2003. 3–18.

Vibert, Bertrand. "Milan Kundera. La fiction pensive." *Temps Modernes* 629 (2004–2005): 109–33.

Viehoff, Reinhold. "Media Icons of War and the Instrumentalisation of Images in US-American Media Today." *CLCWeb: Comparative Literature and Culture* 7.4 (2005): <http://docs.lib.purdue.edu/clcweb/vol7/iss4/10>.

Waever, Ole. "Europe since 1945: Crisis to Renewal." *The History of the Idea of Europe*. Ed. Pim den Boer, Peter Bugge, and Ole Waever. London: Routledge, 1993. 151–216.

Wawrzyzka, Jolanta W. "Betrayal as a Flight from Kitsch in *The Unbearable Lightness of Being*." *Milan Kundera and the Art of Fiction: Critical Essays*. Ed. Aron Aji. New York: Garland, 1992. 267–80.

Webb, Igor. "Milan Kundera and the Limits of Scepticism." *Massachusetts Review* 31.3 (1990): 357–68.

Weber, Max. *Wirtschaft und Gesellschaft*. 1921. Tübingen: Mohr-Siebeck, 1976.

Weeks, Mark. "A Modern History of Humor amid the Comedy of History." *Journal of Modern Literature* 28.3 (2005): 130–48.

Weiss, Jason. "An Interview with Milan Kundera." *New England Review and Bread Loaf Quarterly* 8.3 (1986): 405–10.

Welfing, Johannes F. "Friedrich Nietzsche and Milan Kundera: A Polyphonous Voice." *A World of Slavic Literatures*. Ed. Paul D. Morris. Bloomington: Slavica, 2002. 107–22.

Wellek, René. "The Two Traditions of Czech Literature." *Essays on Czech Literature*. By René Wellek. The Hague: Mouton, 1963. 17–31.

Wendorff, Rudolf. *Zeit und Kultur. Geschichte des Zeitbewusstseins in Europa*. Wiesbaden: Westdeutscher, 1980.

West, Tim. "Destiny as Alibi: Milan Kundera, Václav Havel and the 'Czech Question' after 1968." *Slavonic and East European Review* 87.3 (2009): 401–28.

Williams, Simon. *Wagner and the Romantic Hero*. Cambridge: Cambridge UP, 2004: <http://dx.doi.org/10.1017/CBO9780511481741>

Winner, Thomas G. "Literature as a Source for Anthropological Research: The Case of Jaroslav Hašek's *Good Soldier Švejk*." *Literary Anthropology: A New Interdisciplinary Approach to People, Signs and Literature*. Ed. Fernando Poyatos. Amsterdam: Benjamins, 1988. 51–62.

Woods, Michelle. "Traduction et réécriture chez Milan Kundera." *Désaccords parfaits. La Réception paradoxale de l'oeuvre de Milan Kundera*. Ed. Marie-Odile Thirouin and Martine Boyer-Weinmann. Grenoble: ELLUG, 2009. 193–204.

Woods, Michelle. *Translating Milan Kundera*. Clevedon: Multilingual Matters, 2006.

Ziarek Płonowska, Ewa, ed. *Gombrovicz's Grimaces: Modernism, Gender, Nationality*. Albany: State U of New York P, 1998.

Žima, Peter V. *Theorie des Subjekts*. Tübingen: Francke, 2000.

Index